THE FAMILY—
CAN IT BE SAVED?

THIS BOOK IS BASED ON A CONFERENCE SPONSORED BY
ST. CHRISTOPHER'S HOSPITAL FOR CHILDREN, PHILADELPHIA,
CHILDREN'S HOSPITAL MEDICAL CENTER, BOSTON
AND
THE JOHNSON & JOHNSON INSTITUTE FOR PEDIATRIC SERVICE
HELD AT PHILADELPHIA, PENNSYLVANIA

The Family— Can It Be Saved?

Edited by

VICTOR C. VAUGHAN, III, M.D.

*Professor and Chairman, Department of Pediatrics,
Temple University School of Medicine, Philadelphia,
Pennsylvania*

and

T. BERRY BRAZELTON, M.D.

*Associate Professor of Pediatrics, Harvard Medical
School, Boston, Massachusetts*

YEAR BOOK MEDICAL PUBLISHERS, INC.
35 EAST WACKER DRIVE • CHICAGO

Library of Congress Catalog Card Number: 75-27701

International Standard Book Number: 0-8151-9025-5

Contributors

ROBERT A. ALDRICH, M.D., *Vice President, Health Affairs and Professor of Pediatrics and Preventive Medicine, University of Colorado Medical Center, Denver, Colorado*

ALBERT BANDURA, PH.D., *Professor of Psychology, Stanford University, Palo Alto, California*

HENRY BILLER, PH.D., *Professor of Psychology, University of Rhode Island, Kingston, Rhode Island*

SARANE SPENCE BOOCOCK, PH.D., *Sociologist, Russell Sage Foundation, New York City, and Visiting Associate Professor, Department of Sociology, Yale University, New Haven, Connecticut*

T. BERRY BRAZELTON, M.D., *Associate Professor of Pediatrics, Harvard Medical School, Boston, Massachusetts and Chief, Child Development Unit, Children's Hospital Medical Center, Boston, Massachusetts*

URIE BRONFENBRENNER, PH.D., *Professor of Human Development and Family Studies and Psychology, Cornell University, Ithaca, New York*

BETTYE M. CALDWELL, PH.D., *Director, Center for Early Development and Education and Professor of Education, University of Arkansas at Little Rock, Little Rock, Arkansas*

J. CRAVIOTO, M.D., *Chairman, Scientific Research Division of the Mexican Institute of Child Welfare and Professor of Pediatrics, University of Mexico, Mexico City, Mexico*

ERIC DENHOFF, M.D., *Clinical Professor of Pediatrics, Section of Human Growth and Development, Brown University Program in Medicine and Medical Director, The Governor Medical Center, Providence, Rhode Island*

LEON EISENBERG, M.D., *Professor and Chairman, Psychiatry, Harvard Medical School and Senior Associate in Psychiatry, Boston Children's Hospital Medical Center, Boston, Massachusetts*

DAVID ELKIND, PH.D., *Professor of Psychology, University of Rochester, Rochester, New York*

STEVEN A. FELDMAN, M.D., *The Governor Medical Center, Providence, Rhode Island*

v

JOHN B. FRANKLIN, M.D., *Associate Professor of Obstetrics and Gynecology, Jefferson Medical College, Philadelphia and Medical Director of Booth Maternity Center, Philadelphia, Pennsylvania*

MS. MARION HOWARD, *Former Director of Consortium on Early Childbearing and Childrearing*

MARY HOWELL, M.D., PH.D., *Assistant Professor of Pediatrics, Harvard Medical School, Boston, Massachusetts*

JEROME KAGAN, PH.D., *Professor of Psychology and Social Relations, Harvard University, Cambridge, Massachusetts*

JOHN H. KENNELL, M.D., *Professor of Pediatrics, Case Western Reserve University Medical School, Cleveland, Ohio*

MARSHALL H. KLAUS, M.D., *Professor of Pediatrics and Director of Neonatology, Case Western Reserve University Medical School, Cleveland, Ohio*

BARBARA KORSCH, M.D., *Professor of Pediatrics, University of Southern California School of Medicine, Los Angeles, California*

MARCIENE S. MATTLEMAN, ED.D., *Professor of Curriculum and Instruction, Temple University, Philadelphia, Pennsylvania*

J. LAWRENCE NAIMAN, M.D., *Professor of Pediatrics, Temple University School of Medicine and Chief of Hematology, St. Christopher's Hospital for Children, Philadelphia, Pennsylvania*

OSCAR NEWMAN, *President of the Institute for Community Design Analysis, New York City, New York*

MICHAEL NEWTON, M.D., *Professor of Obstetrics and Gynecology, Pritzker School of Medicine, The University of Chicago, Chicago, Illinois*

NILES NEWTON, PH.D., *Professor of Psychology, Department of Psychiatry, Northwestern University School of Medicine, Chicago, Illinois*

HON. LISA A. RICHETTE, *Judge of Court of Common Pleas and Adjunct Professor of Law, Temple University Law School, Philadelphia, Pennsylvania*

FRED M. ROGERS, *Creator and Performer in Mister Rogers' Neighborhood, Pittsburgh, Pennsylvania*

JOAN TAKSA ROLSKY, M.S.W., *St. Christopher's Hospital for Children, Philadelphia, Pennsylvania*

SUSAN B. SHERMAN, M.S.S., *St. Christopher's Hospital for Children, Philadelphia, Pennsylvania*

ALBERT J. SOLNIT, M.D., *Professor of Pediatrics and Psychiatry and Director of Child Study Center, Yale University, New Haven, Connecticut*

FRANCES VANDIVIER, M.S., *Assistant Professor of Social Administration and Director of Child Care Training, School of Social Administration, Temple University, Philadelphia, Pennsylvania*

VICTOR C. VAUGHAN, III, M.D., *Professor and Chairman, Department of Pediatrics, Temple University School of Medicine and Medical Director, St. Christopher's Hospital for Children, Philadelphia, Pennsylvania*

Preface

This volume is based on papers presented at a Symposium held in Philadelphia, April 25 through 29, 1975, under sponsorship of St. Christopher's Hospital for Children and the Department of Pediatrics of Temple University School of Medicine, Children's Medical Center of Boston, and the Department of Pediatrics, Harvard Medical School, with support of a grant from Johnson & Johnson Institute for Pediatric Service, New Brunswick, New Jersey.

The planning of the Conference was a joint effort of Victor C. Vaughan, III, M.D., T. Berry Brazelton, M.D., and Steven Sawchuk, M.D., of J & J, who are all pediatricians. The title, "The Family—Can It Be Saved?" was chosen because it was felt to address an area of major concern in today's world and possibly to be attractive to pediatricians, our original, rather parochial goal being to expose pediatricians to as broad a perspective on problems of today's families as could be arranged through the participation of pediatricians, obstetricians, psychiatrists, developmental psychologists, educators, sociologists, anthropologists, and representatives of such other areas as the media, city planning, and law.

The appeal of the theme and of the charismatic group who responded so generously to invitations to participate was beyond our expectations. We were pleased to have several times the number of registrants originally anticipated, and to find that the majority came not from medicine but from those other fields which have a deep concern for the status of the family at this historical moment. The responsiveness of all those who shared this occasion with us was an essential element in the success of the venture. We are grateful to all who attended for their commitment, their candor and their suggestions in both formal and informal discussions. They helped us both to enjoy the success and to identify the shortcomings of what, on the whole, we feel was an exciting and consciousness raising experience.

Special thanks are due those who contributed to the program, and to Steven Sawchuk, M.D., of Johnson & Johnson, for his tireless effort to have the Symposium move smoothly and to have this report reach you as soon as possible.

V.C.V., III

T.B.B.

Contents

Introduction

1

Who Cares for America's Children?

Urie Bronfenbrenner, Ph.D.

*Professor of Human Development, Family
Studies and Psychology, Cornell University,
Ithaca, New York*

It is perhaps characteristic of our culture that discussions about the quality of life in the future are based almost entirely on technologic considerations. How the next generation of Americans will live, we are told, will be determined by the changes in our physical and natural environment. Whatever the predictions, they refer to the altered circumstances under which people will be living, not the changes in people themselves. For the most part, our futurologists, scientific or otherwise, do not suggest that the new environment might produce a different kind of person. Our abilities, our character, apparently are expected to remain much the same.

I do not share this expectation. As I look at the evidence, I see possibilities for significant change in the abilities and character of the next generation of Americans. The most important changes I foresee will not be in the realm of technologic discoveries. Nobel Prize winner Professor Joshua Lederberg to the contrary, I do not think we shall easily produce another Einstein by genetic duplication through cloning[1] or by putting sperm into deep freeze (a proposal, incidentally, that appears to assume that the only talented persons are males). I view the process of making human beings human as somewhat more complex. Nor is my vision of the future quite as sanguine. As I see it, the competence and character of the next generation of Americans will depend less on deliberate genetic selection or modifications of the physical or natural environment than on changes in the human condition, specifically the circumstances in which the next generation of Americans is being raised and developed. I refer to the changes that have been taking place in the structure of the family and its position in society.

---

[1]Lederberg predicts the applicability of this technique within a matter of years rather than decades. As a result, "biologists would at least enjoy being able to observe...whether a second Einstein would outdo the first one." This statement, quoted from an interview published in the *London Observer*, November 6, 1966, rests on some tacit assumptions that are highly questionable for reasons that shortly will become apparent.

THE CHANGING AMERICAN FAMILY

The American family has been undergoing rapid and radical change. Today, in 1975, it is significantly different from what it was only a quarter of a century ago. In documenting the evidence, I shall begin with aspects that are already familiar and then proceed to other developments that are less well known. I then will show how these various trends combine and converge in an over-all pattern that is far more consequential than any of its components.

Since my aim is to identify trends for American society as a whole, the primary sources of almost all the data I shall be presenting are government statistics, principally the *Current Population Reports* published by the Bureau of the Census, the *Special Labor Force Reports* issued by the Department of Labor and the *Vital and Health Statistics Reports* prepared by the National Center of Health Statistics. These data are typically provided on an annual basis. What I have done is to collate and graph them in order to illuminate the secular trends.

More Working Mothers

Our first and most familiar trend is the increase in working mothers (Fig. 1–1). There are several points to be made about these data:

1. Once their children are old enough to go to school, the majority of American mothers now enter the labor force. As of March, 1974, 51% of married women with children from 6 to 17 were engaged in or seeking work; in 1948, the rate was about half as high, 26%.

2. Since the early 1950s mothers of school-age children have been more likely to work than married women without children.

3. The most recent and most rapid increase has been occurring for mothers of young children. One-third of all married women with children under 6 were in

Fig. 1–1. – Labor force participation rates for married women by presence and age of children, 1948–1973. (Data through 1955 from *Current Population Reports* 1955, P-50, No. 62, Table A; from 1956, *Special Labor Force Reports* 1959, No. 7, Table 1; and 1974, No. 164, Table 3.)

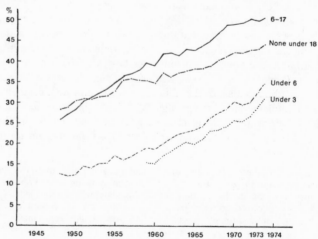

the labor force in 1974, three times as high as in 1948. Mothers of infants were not far behind; 3 of 10 married women with children under 3 were in the work force last year.

4. Whether their children were infants or teen-agers, the great majority (two-thirds) of the mothers who had jobs were 'working full time.

5. These figures apply only to families in which the husband was present. As we shall see, for the rapidly growing numbers of single-parent families, the proportions in the labor force are much higher.

Fewer Adults in the Home

As more mothers have gone to work, the number of adults in the home who could care for the child has decreased. Whereas the number of children per family now is about the same as it was 20–30 years ago, the number of adults in the household has dropped steadily to a 1974 average of 2. This figure, of course, includes some households without children. Unfortunately, the Bureau of Census does not publish a breakdown of the number of adults present in households conta ning children. A conservative approximation is obtainable, however, from the proportion of parents living with a relative as family head, usually a grandparent.[2]

Fig. 1–2.—Percentage of families living with a relative as family head as a percentage of all families with children under 18, under 6 and 6 through 17 years of age.

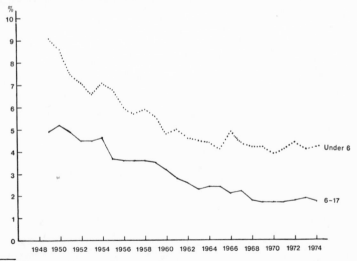

---

[2]This proportion represents a minimum estimate, since it does not include adult relatives present besides parents, when the parent rather than the relative is the family head. For example, a family with a mother-in-law living in would not be counted unless she was regarded as the family head, paid the rent, etc. The percentage was calculated from two sets of figures reported annually in the *Current Population Reports* (Series P-20) of the U. S. Census: (a) the number of families (defined as two or more related persons, including children, living together) and (b) the number of subfamilies (a married couple or single parent with one or more children living with a relative who is the head of the family). Since 1968, information has been provided as to whether or not the relative was a grandparent.This was the case in a little over 80% of all instances.

As shown in Figure 1 – 2, over the past quarter century the percentage of such "extended" families has decreased appreciably. Although parents with children under 6 are more likely to be living with a relative than parents with older children (6 – 17), the decline over the years has been greatest for families with young children.

More Single-Parent Families

The adult relatives who have been disappearing from families include the parents themselves. As shown in Figure 1 – 3, over a 25-year period there has been a marked rise in the proportion of families with only 1 parent present, with the sharpest increase occurring during the past decade. According to the latest figures available, in 1974, *1 of every 6 children under 18 years of age was living in a single-parent family.*[3] This rate is almost double that for a quarter of a century ago.

With respect to change over time, the increase has been most rapid among families with children under 6 years of age. This percentage has doubled from 7% in 1948 to 15% in 1974. The proportions are almost as high for very young children; in 1974, 1 of every 8 infants under 3 (13%) was living in a single-parent family.

Further evidence of the progressive fragmentation of the American family appears when we apply our index of "extended families" to single-parent homes. The index shows a marked decline from 1948 to 1974, with the sharpest drop

Fig. 1–3. — Percentage of single-parent families as a percentage of all families with children under 18, under 6, and 6 through 17 years of age. (From *Current Population Reports, Series P-20, 1948 – 1973.*)

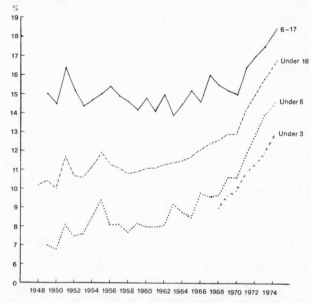

[3]This figure includes a small proportion of single-parent families headed by fathers. This figure has remained relatively constant, around 1%, since 1960.

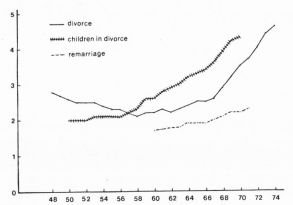

Fig. 1-4.—Rates (per 1000 population) of divorce, number of children in divorce and remarriage.

occurring for families with preschoolers. Today, almost 90% of all children with only 1 parent are living in independent families in which the single mother or father is also the family head.

The majority of such parents are also working, 67% of mothers with school-age children, 54% of those with youngsters under 6. And, across the board, over 80% of those employed are working full time. Even among single-parent mothers with children under 3, 45% are in the labor force, of whom 86% are working full time.

The comment frequently is made that such figures about 1-parent families are misleading, since single parenthood usually is a transitional state soon terminated through remarriage. Although this may be true for some selected populations, it does not appear to obtain for the nation as a whole. Figure 1-4 depicts the relevant data. The solid line in the middle shows the divorce rate for all marriages, the cross-hatched curve indexes divorces involving children and the broken line describes the remarriage rate. To permit comparability, all three rates were computed wih the total population for the given year as a base. It is clear that the remarriage rate, although rising, lags far behind the divorce rate, especially where children are involved.

Moreover, there is good reason to believe that the remarriage rate shown on the graph is substantially higher than that which applies for divorced, widowed or other persons who are single parents. The overwhelming majority of single parents, about 95% of them, are women. In 1971, the latest year for which the data are available, the female remarriage rate per 1000 divorced or widowed wives was 37.3; the corresponding figure for men was 130.6, almost four times as high. Given this fact, it becomes obvious that the rate of remarriage for single-parent families involving children is considerably lower than the remarriage rate for both sexes, which is the statistic shown in the graph.

More Children of Unwed Mothers

After divorce, the most rapidly growing category of single parenthood, especially since 1970, involves unmarried mothers. In the vital statistics of the

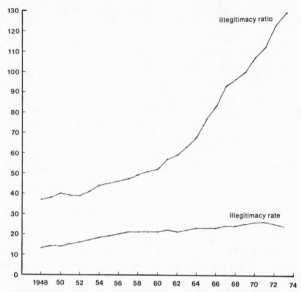

Fig. 1–5.—Illegitimate births per 1000 live births (ratio) and per 1000 unmarried women (rate), 1948–1972.

United States, illegitimate births are indexed by two measures: the *illegitimacy ratio,* computed as the ratio of illegitimate births per 1000 live babies born, and the *illegitimacy rate,* which is the number of illegitimate births per 1000 unmarried women aged 15–44 years. As revealed in Figure 1–5, the ratio has consistently been higher and risen far more rapidly than the rate. This pattern indicates not only that a growing proportion of unmarried women are having children but that the percentage of single women among those of childbearing age is becoming ever larger. Consistent with this conclusion, recent U.S. census figures reveal an increasing trend for women to postpone the age of marriage. The rise in per cent single is particularly strong for the age group under 25, and over 80% of all illegitimate children are being born to women in this age bracket.

Such findings suggest that the trends we have been documenting for the nation as a whole may be occurring at a faster rate in some segments of American society, and more slowly, or perhaps not at all, in others. We turn next to an examination of this issue.

WHICH FAMILIES ARE CHANGING?

Which Mothers Work?

On analyzing available data for an answer to this question, we discover the following:

1. With age of child constant, it is the younger mother, particularly one under 25 years of age, who is most likely to enter the labor force. This trend has been

increasing in recent years, particularly for families with very young children (i.e., infants under 3).

2. One reason why younger mothers are more likely to enter the labor force is to supplement the relatively low earnings of a husband just beginning his career. In general, it is in families in which the husbands have incomes below $5000 (which now is close to the poverty line for a family of 4) that the wives are most likely to be working. And for families in this bottom income bracket, almost half the mothers are under 25. All of these mothers, including the youngest ones with the youngest children, are working because they have to.

3. But not all the mothers whose families need the added income are working. The limiting factor is amount of schooling. It is only mothers with at least a high school education who are more likely to work when the husband has a low income. Since, below the poverty line, the overwhelming majority (68%) of family heads have not completed high school, this means that the families who need it most are least able to obtain the added income that a working mother can contribute.

4. In terms of change over time, the most rapid increase in labor force participation has occurred for mothers in middle and high income families. To state the trend in somewhat provocative terms, mothers from middle income families now are entering the work force at a higher rate than married women from low income families did in the early 1960s.

But the highest labor force participation rates of all are to be found not among mothers from intact families, on whom we have concentrated so far, but, as we have already noted, among mothers who are single parents. Who are these single-parent families, and where are they most likely to be found?

Who and Where are Single-Parent Families?

As in the case of working mothers, single parenthood is most common and is growing most rapidly among the younger generation. Figure 1–6 shows the increase, over the past 6 years, in the proportion of 1-parent families with children under 6 classified by age of head. By last year, almost 1 of 4 parents under 25 heading a family was without a spouse.

The association with income is even more marked. Figure 1–7 shows the rise, between 1968 and 1974, in female-headed families for seven successive income brackets ranging from under $4000 per year to $15,000 or over. As we can see from the diagram, single-parent families are much more likely to occur and increase over time in the lower income brackets. Among families with incomes under $4000, the overwhelming majority, 67%, now contain only 1 parent. This figure represents a marked increase from 42% only 6 years before. In sharp contrast, among families with incomes over $15,000, the proportion has remained consistently below 2%. Further analysis reveals that single-parenthood is especially common for young families in the low income brackets. For example, among family heads under 25 with earnings under $4000, the proportion of single parents was 71% for those with all children under 6 and 86% with all children of school age. The more rapid increases over the past few years, however, tended to occur among older low income families, who are beginning to catch up. It would appear that the disruptive processes first struck the younger families among the poor, and now are affecting the older generation as well.

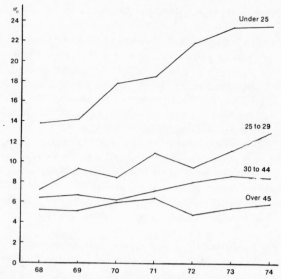

Fig. 1−6.− Percentage of single-parent family heads with children under 6 by age of head.

But a word of caution is in order. It is important to recognize what might be called a pseudo-artifact, pseudo because there is nothing spurious in what appears in the diagram, but the pattern is susceptible to more than one possible interpretation. For example, although the percentage for the highest income group is very low, it would be a mistake to conclude that a well-to-do intact fam-

Fig. 1−7.− Female-headed families as a percentage of all family heads under 65 with children under 18 by income in preceding year, 1968−1974.

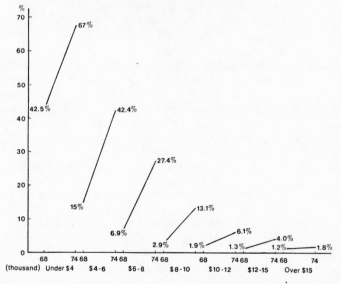

ily is at low risk of disruption, for there is more than one explanation for the falling fence post we see in the figure. The interpretation that most readily comes to mind is that families with children are more likely to split up when they are under financial strain. But the causal chain could also run the other way. The breakup of the family could result in a lower income for the new, single-parent head, who, in the overwhelming majority of cases, is, of course, the mother.

Evidence on this issue is provided by the average income for separated and nonseparated family heads. For example, in 1973, the median income for all families headed by a male with wife present and at least one child under 6 was $12,000. The corresponding figure for a single-parent female-headed family was $3600, less than 30% of the income for an intact family and far below the poverty line. It is important to bear in mind that these are nationwide statistics.

The nature and extent of this inequity is further underscored when we take note that the average income for the small proportion of father-headed single-parent families with preschool children was $9500. In other words, it is only the *single-parent mother* who finds herself in severely strained financial circumstances. Economic deprivation is even more extreme for single-parent mothers under the age of 25. Such a mother, when all her children are small (i.e., under 6), must make do with a median income of only $2800. Yet there are more than a million and a half mothers in this age group, and they constitute one-third of all female-headed families with children under 6.

Does this mean that the low income is primarily a consequence rather than a cause of single-parent status? To answer this question directly we would need to know the income of the family before the split. Unfortunately, this information was not obtained in the census interview. We do have data, however, that are highly correlated with the family's socioeconomic status and generally precede the event of separation; namely, the mother's level of schooling. Is it the well-educated or poorly educated woman who is most likely to become a single parent?

The answer to this question appears in Figure 1–8. In general, the less schooling she has experienced the more likely is the mother to be left without a husband. There is only one exception to the general trend. The proportion tends to be highest, and has risen most rapidly, not for mothers receiving only an elementary education but for those who attended high school but failed to graduate. It seems likely that many of these are unwed mothers who left school because of this circumstance. Consistent with this interpretation, further analysis reveals that the foregoing pattern occurs only for women in the younger age groups, and is most marked for mothers of children from 0 to 3 years of age. In 1974, among mothers of infants in this age group, 14%, or 1 of every 7, were high school dropouts.

This diagram is misleading in one respect. It leaves the impression that there has been little increase recently in the percentage of single-parent families among college graduates. A somewhat different picture emerges, however, when the data are broken down simultaneously by age of mother or child. When this is done, it becomes apparent that college graduates are more likely to defer family breakup until children are older. Once they can be entered into school, or even preschool, the rates of parental separation go up from year to year, especially among the younger generation of college-educated parents.

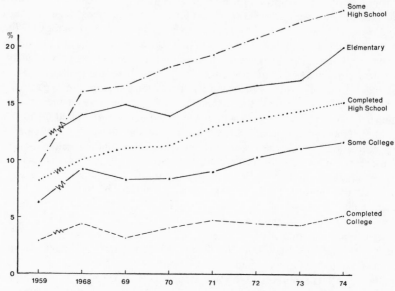

Fig. 1–8.—Percentage of families headed by single spouse by education of head.

In the case of split families, we are in a position to examine not only who is likely to become an only parent but also where, in terms of place of residence. Figure 1–9 shows the rise over the past 6 years in the percentage of single-parent families with children under 6 living in nonurban and suburban areas, and in

Fig. 1–9.—Percentage of female-headed families with children under 6, 1968–1974, by place of residence and age of family head.

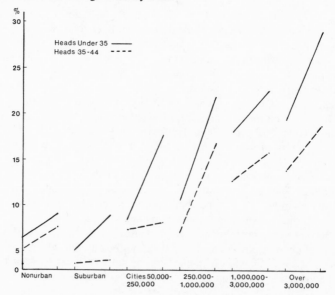

American cities increasing in size from 50,000 to over 3,000,000. The graph illustrates at least three important trends. First, the percentage of single-parent families increases markedly with city size, reaching a maximum in American metropolises with a population of over 3,000,000. Second, the growing tendency for younger families to break up more frequently than older ones is greatest in the large urban centers and lowest in nonurban and suburban areas. Thus, the proportion of single parents reaches its maximum among families with heads under 35 and living in cities with more than 3,000,000 persons. Here, 1 of 3-4 households has a single parent as the head. Finally, the most rapid change over time is occurring not in the larger cities but in those of medium size. This pattern suggests that the high levels of family fragmentation that, 6 years ago, were found only in major metropolitan centers now are occurring in smaller urban areas as well.

The Ecology of a Race Difference

The question may well arise why, with all the breakdowns we have made – by age, income, education and place of residence – we have not presented any data separately by race. We have deferred this separation for a reason that is apparent in Figure 1-10. It shows the rise, between 1960 and 1970, in the percentage of single-parent families by income of head within three types of residence areas: urban, suburban and nonurban, separately for black and white families. Unfortunately, no breakdown was available within the urban category by city size, so that, as a result, the effects of this variable are considerably attenuated. Nevertheless, it is clear that both income and place of residence make an independent contribution to the level and size of broken families.

Fig. 1–10.—Percentage of children in single-parent families by race, family income in preceding year and residence. (Each line segment shows change from 1960 to 1970.)

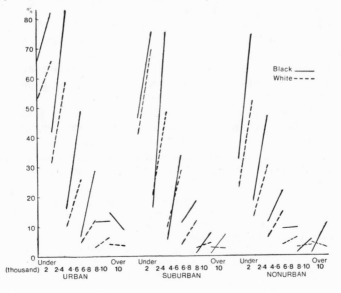

Turning to the issue of race, note that in the graph the rising lines for blacks and whites are almost parallel. In other words, within each setting and income level, the percentage of single parents is increasing about as fast for whites as it is for blacks. To put it in more general terms, *families that live in similar circumstances, whatever their color, are affected in much the same ways.* To be sure, at the end of the decade, the blacks within each setting and income bracket experience a higher percentage of single-parent families than do the whites. But they entered the decade in the same relative positions. This suggests that some different experiences prior to 1960 must have contributed to the disparity we now observe between black and white families living in similar conditions. One does not have to seek long in the historical records, especially those written by blacks, to discover what some of these experiences may have been.

But, of course, in reality, the overwhelming majority of blacks and whites do not live in similar circumstances. It is only in our artificially selected comparison groups, especially in the context that is most homogeneous, namely suburbia, that data for the two races begin to look alike. Without statistical control for income and urbanization, the curves for the two races are rather different; they are much farther apart, and the curve for blacks rises at a substantially faster rate. Specifically, between 1960 and 1970, the percentage of single-parent families among blacks increased at a rate five times that for whites, and at the end of that period the percentage was over four times as high, 35% versus 8%. In the past 4 years, both figures have risen and the gap has widened. In 1974, the percentage of single-parent families with children under 18 was 13% for whites and 44% for blacks.

This dramatic disparity becomes more comprehensible, however, when we apply what we have learned about the relation of urbanization and income to family disruption. On inquiry, we discover that in 1974 about 6% of all white families with children under 18 were living in cities with a population of 3,000,000 or more, compared to 21% for blacks, over three and one-half times as high; this ratio has been rising steadily in recent years.

Turning to family income, in 1973, the latest year for which the data are available, the median income for an intact family with children under 6 was $12,300 if the family was white, $6700 if it was black. Ironically, single-parenthood reduced the race difference by forcing both averages down below the poverty level – $3700 for whites, $3400 for blacks. Consistent with these facts, the percentage of black families that fall below the poverty line is much higher than that of whites. In 1973, 33%, or one-third, of all black families with children under 18 were classified in the low-income bracket, compared to 8% for whites, a ratio of over 4 – 1. Moreover, the advantage of whites over blacks in family income, which decreased during the 1960s, reversed itself at the turn of the decade and has been increasing since 1969. In the language of the latest census report:

The 1973 median income for black families was 58 percent of the white median income and this continued a downward trend in this ratio from 61 percent, which occurred in both 1960 and 1970. In contrast to the 1970s, the ratio of black to white median family income had increased during the 1960s[3a] (p. 5).

[3a]U.S. Bureau of the Census, *Current Population Reports,* Series P-60, No. 97, Money Income in 1973 of Families and Persons in the United States, U.S. Government Printing Office, Washington, D.C., 1975.

We now can understand why non-white mothers have gone to work in increasing numbers and at rates substantially higher than their white counterparts. In 1974, almost one-third of white married women with husbands present and children under 6 were in the labor force; the corresponding fraction for non-white families was over half (52%). Fifteen years ago, the gap between the racial groups was much smaller, 18% versus 28%, and it is of course the non-whites who have increased at the faster rate.

But the more vulnerable position of black families in American society becomes clearest when we examine the comparative exposure of both ethnic groups to the combined effects of low income and urbanization. Unfortunately, once again the data are not broken down by city size, but we can compare the distribution of black and white families with children under 18 living in so-called "poverty areas" in urban, suburban and rural settings, further subclassified by family income. A poverty area is a census tract in which 20% or more of the population was below the low-income level in 1969. As might be expected, more white families with children (44% of them) reside in suburbia than in central cities or rural areas, and the overwhelming majority (70%) live outside poverty areas and have incomes above the poverty line. In contrast, the corresponding percentages for black families are much smaller, 17% and 32% respectively; well over half of black families (58%) are concentrated in central cities, more than half of these live in poverty areas within those cities and half of these, in turn, have incomes below the poverty line. Seventeen per cent, or 1 of every 6 black families with children under 18, are found in the most vulnerable ecologic niche (low income in a poverty area of a central city), compared to less than 1% of all whites. Even though only 14% of all American families with children are

Fig. 1–11. – Percentage of white and non-white families with children under 18 living with a relative as family head. (The base for the percentage is the total number of families for each race with children under 18.)

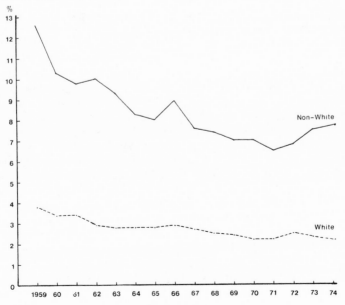

black, among those living in poverty areas of central cities and having incomes below the poverty level they constitute the large majority (66%).

The grossly differential distribution of blacks and whites in American society by income, place of residence and other ecologic dimensions that we have not been able to examine for lack of adequate data makes even more comprehensible the difference in degree of family disruption experienced by these two major classes of American citizens. Indeed, given the extent of the disparity in conditions of life, one wonders what keeps the figures for black families from running even higher than they do.

A possible answer is suggested by the data provided in Figure 1–11, which shows our measure of "extended families" separately for white and nonwhite families. It will be observed that this index is consistently and markedly higher for non-whites. In other words, non-whites are much more likely to be living in a household that includes more than two generations, with another relative besides the child's parent acting as the family head. To be sure, the decline since 1959 has been greater for non-whites than for whites, but the former curve has shown an upswing in the past 4 years.

But there are other less favorable developments as well. If we examine, separately by race, the extent to which single parents head their own families, we observe the same trend toward greater isolation for both whites and non-whites. As we see in Figure 1–12, these two curves are almost indistinguishable. Again, regardless of color, families in similar circumstances are affected in the same way for better or for worse.

What this means is that the disparity in the fate of white and black families in American society is a reflection of the way in which our society now functions and, hence, is subject to change if and when we decide to alter our policies and practices.

We now have completed our analysis of changes in the American family over

Fig. 1–12.—Percentage of white and non-white single-parent families with children under 18 living with a relative as family head. (The base for the percentage is the total number of single-parent families for each race with children under 18.)

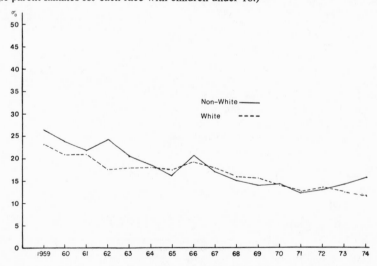

the past quarter century. For the nation as a whole, the analysis reveals progressive fragmentation and isolation of the family in its child-rearing role. With respect to different segments of American society, the changes have been most rapid among younger families with younger children, and increase with the degree of economic deprivation and industrialization, reaching their maximum among low income families living in the central core of our largest cities. But the general trend applies to all strata of the society. Middle class families in cities, suburbia and nonurban areas are changing in similar ways. Specifically, in terms of such characteristics as the proportion of working mothers, number of adults in the home, single-parent families or children born out of wedlock, the middle class family of today increasingly resembles the low income family of the early 1960s.

THE CHANGING AMERICAN CHILD

Having described the changes in the structure and status of the American family, we now are ready to address our next question: So what? Or to be more formal and explicit, what do these changes mean for the well-being and growth of children? What does it mean for the young that more and more mothers, especially mothers of preschoolers and infants, are going to work, the majority of them full time? What does it mean that, as these mothers leave for work, there are also fewer adults in the family who might look after the child, and that, among adults who are leaving the home, the principal deserter is one or the other parent, usually the father?

Paradoxically, the most telling answer to the foregoing questions is yet another question, which is even more difficult to answer: *Who cares for America's children? Who cares?*

At present, substitute care for children of whatever form—nursery schools, group day care, family day care or just a body to baby-sit—falls so far short of the need that it can be measured in millions of children under the age of 6, not to mention the millions more of school-age youngsters, so-called "latch-key" children, who come home to empty houses and who contribute far out of proportion to the ranks of pupils with academic and behavior problems, have difficulties in learning to read, who are dropouts, drug users and juvenile delinquents.

But we are getting ahead of our story. We have seen what has been happening to America's families. Let us try to examine systematically what has been happening to the American child. Unfortunately, statistics at a national level on the state of the child are neither as comprehensive nor as complete as those on the state of the family, but the available data do suggest a pattern consistent with the evidence from our prior analysis.

We begin at the level at which all the trends of disorganization converge. For this purpose, there is an even better index than low income level—one that combines economic deprivation with every kind—health, housing, education and welfare. Let us look first at children who are born to American citizens whose skin color is other than white.

Death in the First Year of Life

The first consequence we meet is that of survival itself.

In recent years, many persons have become aware of the existence of the problem to which I refer, but perhaps not of the evidence for its practical solution. America, the richest and most powerful country in the world, stands fourteenth among the nations in combating infant mortality; even East Germany does better. Moreover, our ranking has dropped steadily in recent decades. A similar situation obtains with respect to maternal and child health, day care, children's allowances and other basic services to children and families.

But the figures for the nation as a whole, dismaying as they are, mask even greater inequities. For example, infant mortality for non-whites in the United States is almost twice that for whites, the maternal death rate is four times as high and there are a number of Southern states, and Northern metropolitan areas, in which the ratios are considerably higher. Among New York City health districts, for example, the infant mortality rate in 1966–67 varied from 13 per 1000 in Haspeth, Forest Hills, to 41.5 per 1000 in central Harlem.[4] One illuminating way of describing the differences in infant mortality by race is from a time perspective. Babies born of non-white mothers are today dying at a rate that white babies have not experienced for almost a quarter of a century. The current non-white rate of 28.1 was last reported for American whites in the late 1940s. The rate for whites in 1950, 26.8%, was not yet achieved by non-whites in 1974. In fact, in recent years, the gap between the races, instead of narrowing, has been getting wider.

The way to the solution is suggested by the results of the two-stage analysis carried out by Dr. Harold Watts for the Advisory Committee on Child Development of the National Academy of Sciences. First, Watts demonstrated that 92% of the variation in infant death among the 30 New York City health districts is explainable by low birth weight. Second, he showed that 97% of the variation in low birth weight can be attributed to the fraction of mothers who received no prenatal care or received care only late in their pregnancy and the fraction unwed at the time of delivery.

Confirmatory evidence is available from an important and elegant study, published in 1973, on the relations between infant mortality, social and medical risk and health care.[5] From an analysis of data in 140,000 births in New York City, the investigators found the following:

1. The highest rate of infant mortality was for children of black native-born women at social and medical risk and with inadequate health care. This rate was 45 times as high as that for a group of white mothers at no risk with adequate care. Next in line were Puerto Rican infants, with a rate 22 times as high.

2. Among mothers receiving adequate medical care there was essentially no difference in mortality among white, black and Puerto Rican groups, even for mothers at high medical risk.

3. For mothers at socioeconomic risk, however, adequate medical care substantially reduced infant mortality rates for all races, but the figures for black and Puerto Rican families still were substantially greater than those for whites. In other words, other factors besides inadequate medical care contribute to producing the higher infant mortality for these non-white groups. Again, these fac-

---

[4]Kessner, D. S., *et al.: Infant Death: An Analysis by Maternal Risk and Health Care* (Washington, D. C.: Institute of Medicine, National Academy of Sciences, 1973).

[5]Kessner, *et al., op cit.*

tors have to do with the social and economic conditions in which these families have to live. Thus, the results of the New York City study and other investigations point to the following characteristics as predictive of higher infant mortality: employment status of the breadwinner, mother unwed at infant's birth, married but no father in the home, number of children per room, mother under 20 or over 35 and parents' educational level.

4. Approximately 95% of those mothers at risk had medical or social conditions that could have been identified at the time of the first prenatal visit; infants born to this group of women accounted for 70% of the deaths.

What would have happened had these conditions been identified and adequate medical care provided? The answer to this question recently has become available from an analysis of data from the Maternal and Infant Care Projects of HEW, which, in the middle 1960s, were established in slum areas of 14 cities across the nation and in Puerto Rico. In Denver, a dramatic fall in infant mortality from 34.2 per 1000 live births in 1964 to 21.5 per 1000 in 1969 was observed for the 25 census tracts that made up the target area for such a program. In Birmingham, Alabama, the rate decreased from 25.4 in 1965 to 14.3 in 1969 and in Omaha from 33.4 in 1964 to 13.4 in 1969. Significant reductions in prematurity, repeated teen-age pregnancy, women who conceive over 35 years of age and families with more than 4 children have also occurred over the populations served by these programs.

It is a reflection of our distorted priorities that these programs currently are in jeopardy, even though their proposed replacement through revenue sharing is not yet on the horizon. The phasing out of these projects will result in a return of mortality to earlier levels; more infants will die.

The Interplay of Biologic and Environmental Factors

The decisive role that environmental factors can play in influencing the biologic growth of the organism and, thereby, its psychologic development is illustrated by a series of recent follow-up studies of babies experiencing prenatal complications at birth, but surviving and growing up in families at different socioeconomic levels. As an example, we may take an excellently designed and analyzed study by Richardson.[6] It is a well-established finding that mothers from low income families bear a higher proportion of premature babies, as measured either by weight at birth or gestational age, and that prematures generally tend to be somewhat retarded in mental growth. Richardson studied a group of such children in Aberdeen, Scotland, from birth through 7 years, with special focus on intellectual development. He found, as expected, that children born prematurely to mothers in low income families showed significantly poorer performance on measures of mental growth, especially when the babies were both born before term and weighed less than 5 pounds. The average IQ for these children at 7 years of age was 80. But the higher the family's socioeconomic level the weaker the tendency for birth weight to be associated with impaired intellectual func-

---

[6]Richardson, S. A.: Ecology of Malnutrition: Non-nutritional Factors Influencing Intellectual and Behavioral Development, in *Nutrition, the Nervous System, and Behavior,* Scientific Publication #251, Pan American Health Organization, Washington, D. C., 1972, pp. 101–110.

tion. For example, in the higher social class group, infants born before term and weighing under 5 pounds had a mean IQ of 105, higher than the average for the general population, and only 5 points below the mean for full-term babies of normal weight born to mothers in the same socioeconomic group. In other words, children starting off with similar biologic deficits ended up with widely differing risks of mental retardation as a function of the conditions of life for the family in which they were born.

But low income does not require a biologic base to affect profoundly the welfare and development of the child. To cite but two examples: Child abuse is far more common in poor than in middle income families,[7] and the socioeconomic status of the family has emerged as the most powerful predictor of school success in studies conducted at both the national and the state level.[8]

Nor does income tell the whole story. In the first place, other social conditions, such as the absence of the parent, have been shown to exacerbate the impact of poverty. For example, in low income homes, child abuse is more likely to occur in single-parent than in intact families, especially when the mother is under 25 years of age.[9] It is also the young mother who is most likely to have a premature baby.

In terms of subsequent development, a statewide study in New York of factors affecting school performance at all grade levels[10] revealed that 58% of the variation in student achievement could be predicted by three factors: broken homes, overcrowded housing and the educational level of the head of the household; when racial and ethnic variables were introduced into the analysis, they accounted for less than an additional 2% of the variation.

Finally, and perhaps most important, low income may not be the critical factor affecting the development and needs of children and families. The most powerful evidence for this conclusion comes from census data on trends in family income over the past quarter century. Even after adjustment for inflation, the level has been rising steadily at least through 1974, and for black families as well as white. A reflection of this fact is a drop over the years in the percentage of children in families below the poverty line, 27% in 1959, 15% in 1968 and 14% in 1973.[11]

Changes Over Time

And yet, as we have seen, the percentage of single-parent families has been growing, especially in recent years. And there are analogous trends for indices bearing on the state and development of the child. Although lack of comparability between samples and measures precludes a valid assessment of change in child abuse rates, an index is available for this phenomenon in its most extreme

---

[7]Gil, D. G.: *Violence Against Children: Physical Child Abuse in the United States* (Cambridge, Mass.: Harvard University Press, 1970).

[8]Coleman, J. S.: *Equality of Educational Opportunity* (Washington, D. C.: U. S. Office of Education, 1966); Jencks, C.: *Inequality* (New York: Basic Books, 1972); *Report of the New York State Commission on the Quality, Cost, and Financing of Elementary and Secondary Education*, Vol. 1. (Albany: New York State Commission).

[9]Gil, *ibid.*

[10]*Report of the New York State Commission, ibid.*

[11]Unfortunately, the curve leveled off in 1969 and has shown no decline in the 1970s.

form—homicide, or the deliberate killing of a child. As shown in Figure 1–13, the rate has been increasing over time for children of all ages. Adolescents are more likely to be the victims of homicide than younger children except in the first year of life, in which the rates again jump upward.

Children who survive face other risks. For example, the New York study cited earlier[12] reports a secular trend in the proportion of children failing to perform at minimal levels in reading and arithmetic: each year "more and more children are below minimum competence."

One might conclude that such a decrease in competence is occurring primarily, if not exclusively, among families of lower socioeconomic status, with limited income, education and cultural background. The data of Figure 1–14 suggest that the trend may be far more democratic. The graph shows the average score achieved each year in the verbal and mathematical sections of the Scholastic Aptitude Test (SAT), taken by virtually all high school juniors and seniors who plan to go to college. The test scores are used widely as the basis for determining admission. As is apparent from the figures, there has been a steady and substantial decrease over the past decade—35 points in the verbal section, 24 in the mathematical section. In interpreting the significance of this decline, Dr. T. Anne Clarey, Chief of the Program Services Division of the College Board, warned that it is incorrect to conclude from a score decline that schools have not been preparing students in verbal and mathematical skills as well as they did in former years. "The SAT measures skills developed over a youngster's lifetime—both in and out of the school setting. . . . It is evident that many factors, including family

Fig. 1–13.—Death rates from homicide by age of child victim, 1951–1973.

12New York State Commission, *op cit.*

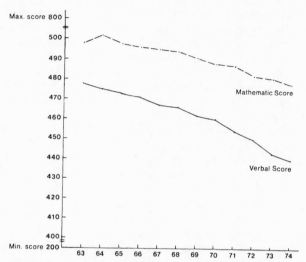

Fig. 1–14.–Average scores for senior high school students taking the scholastic aptitude examinations, 1963–1974. (Data courtesy of Educational Testing Service.)

and home life, exposure to mass media, and other cultural and environmental factors, are associated with students' performance."[13]

Finally, the remaining sets of data shift attention from the cognitive to the emotional and social areas. Figures 1–15 and 1–16 document the increase in suicide rates in recent years for children as young as 10. Figure 1–17 shows an even more precipitous climb in the rate of juvenile delinquency. Since 1963, crimes by children have been increasing at a higher rate than the juvenile population. In 1973, among children under 15,[14] almost half (47%) of all arrests involved theft, breaking and entry and vandalism, and, with an important exception to be noted below, these categories were also the ones showing the greatest increase over the past decade. The second largest grouping, also growing rapid-

[13]Press release, College Entrance Examination Board, New York, New York, December 20, 1973. A recent report in *Time* (March 31, 1975) quotes Sam McCandless, director of admissions testing for the College Entrance Examination Board, as refuting arguments that the decrease in SAT scores is not "real" but a reflection of changes in the tests or in the social composition of students taking them. According to McCandless, the reason for the drop is a decline in students "developed reasoning ability."

The same article reports two other developments that corroborate the downward trend in learning:

The National Assessment of Educational Progress—a federally funded testing organization—reported last week that students knew less about science in 1973 than they did three years earlier. The test, which covered 90,000 students in elementary and junior and senior high schools in all parts of the nation, showed the sharpest decline among 17-year-olds in large cities, although suburban students' test scores fell too.

The results of the third study, sponsored by the U. S. Department of Health, Education and Welfare and announced last week, showed that public school students' reading levels have been falling since the mid-1960s.

[14]The figures that follow are based on the *Uniform Crime Reports for the United States* published annually by the Federal Bureau of Investigation.

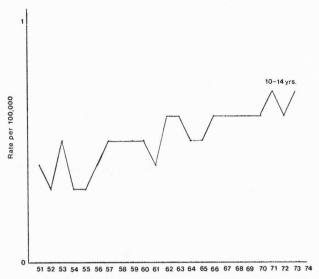

Fig. 1–15.–Death rates from suicide by age of child, 1951–1973.

Fig. 1–16.–Death rates from suicide by age of child, 1951–1973.

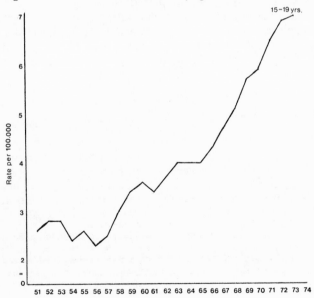

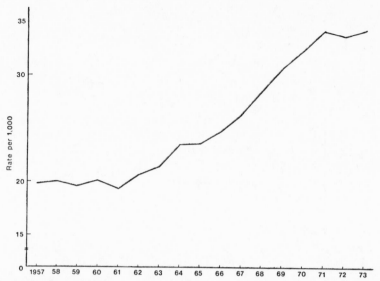

Fig. 1–17.–Rate of delinquency cases disposed of by juvenile courts involving children 10 through 17 years of age.

ly, constituted almost a quarter of all offenses[15] and included loitering, disorderly conduct and runaway. The most rapid rises, however, occurred in two other categories–drug use and violent crimes. In 1973, drug arrests accounted for 2.6% of all offenses by children under 15. The precise rate of increase over time is difficult to estimate because of inconsistent enforcement and reporting. In the same year, the next most rapid rise was for violent crimes (aggravated assault, armed robbery, forcible rape and murder). These accounted for 3.3% of all arrests. Although the proportion of children involved is of course very small, this figure represents at least a 200% increase over the 1964 level.[16] And the total number of children with a criminal record is substantial. "If the present trends continue, one out of every nine youngsters will appear before a juvenile court before age 18."[17] The figures, of course, index only offenses that are detected and prosecuted. One wonders how high the numbers must climb before we acknowledge that they reflect deep and pervasive problems in the treatment of children and youth in our society.

---

[15]It is noteworthy that the highest level and most rapid rise within this grouping occurred for runaways, an increase of more than 240% since 1964 (the rate has decreased somewhat since 1970). It would appear that the trend we have observed in the progressive break-up of the family includes the departure not only of its adult members but its children as well.

[16]We may take what comfort we can from the fact that the reported rates of drug arrests and of juvenile violence have dropped somewhat since 1970.

[17]*Profiles of Children.* White House Conference on Children, Washington, D. C., 1970, p. 79.

THE ROOTS OF ALIENATION

What is the ultimate source of these problems? The data we have examined point the accusing finger most directly at the cumulatively destructive effect of a combination of factors, such as low income, large cities, dense neighborhoods. These are the contexts and forces that appear to produce social and personal disorganization.

But a little more than a year ago, I was in a culture that had all these characteristics to the nth degree, a country that was much poorer than our own, much more crowded, not only in its cities but even in its small towns and villages, and has a far higher proportion of working mothers. My scientific colleagues and I were there to look precisely at those segments of the society in which the forces of destruction we have been examining would be most likely to show their effect. We were observing children and families, and the contexts in which they live out their lives—in the home, the school, the neighborhood and the work place. But though we were experienced child watchers, we saw few broken families and even fewer broken children.

We were in the People's Republic of China. We looked for, but we did not find, sickly babies, youngsters who were apathetic or hyperactive, who couldn't learn, who read poorly, dropped out of school or became juvenile delinquents. Instead, we saw healthy, beautiful, expressive children and competent, self-assured and committed young people. To be sure, China has its problems, but they are not those of ineffectiveness, alienation or violence toward others or self.

How are we to resolve the paradox? If poverty and population are not the sufficient conditions of social and personal disarray, what is? I suggest an answer to this question that I cannot corroborate with the kind of systematic data I have been presenting to you up till now. But I can call your attention to some facts, features of social and human organization that are present in Chinese society, and some others I have come to know, such as in Israel or Switzerland, but are being eroded in our own. And I shall begin on reasonably solid ground.

Studies of human behavior have yielded few generalizations that are firmly grounded in research and broadly accepted by specialists, but there are two answers to the foregoing questions that do meet these exacting criteria.

1. Over the past three decades, literally hundreds of investigations have been conducted to identify the developmental antecedents of behavior disorders and social pathology. The results point to an almost omnipresent overriding factor: family disorganization.

2. Much of the same research also shows that the forces of disorganization arise primarily not from within the family but from the circumstances in which the family finds itself, and from the way of life that is imposed on it by those circumstances.

Specifically, when those circumstances and the way of life they generate undermine relationships of trust and emotional security between family members, when they make it difficult for parents to care for, educate and enjoy their children, when there is no support or recognition from the outside world for one's role as a parent, and when time spent with one's family means frustration of career, personal fulfillment and peace of mind, the development of the child is adversely affected. The first symptoms are emotional and motivational: disaffection, indifference, irresponsibility and inability to follow through in activities requiring application and persistence. In less-favorable family circumstances, the reaction takes the form of antisocial acts injurious to the child and to society. Finally, for children who come from environments in which the capacity of the family to function has been most severely traumatized by such destructive forces as poverty, ill health and discrimination, the consequences for the child are seen not only in the spheres of emotional and social maladjustment but also in the impairment of the most distinctive of human capacities: the ability to think, to deal with concepts and numbers at even the most elementary level.

The extent of this impairment in contemporary American society and its roots in social disorganization are reflected in the data and analyses I have presented to you. But to understand the nature of the process and the methods by which it may be counteracted, we must examine it more carefully. Again, a way to this understanding is provided by studies of how children are raised in other countries. These investigations call attention to a distinctive feature of American child-rearing: segregation not by race or social class but by age. For example, a survey of changes in child-rearing practices in the United States over a 25-year period reveals a decrease in all spheres of interaction between parent and child.[18] A similar trend is indicated by data from cross-cultural studies comparing American families with their European counterparts.[19] Thus, in a comparative study of socialization practices among German and American parents, the former emerged as significantly more involved in activities with their children, including both affection and discipline. A second study, conducted several years later, showed changes over time in both cultures reflecting "a trend toward the dissolution of the family as a social system," with Germany moving closer to the American pattern of "centrifugal forces pulling the members into relationships outside the family."[20]

Although the nature and operation of these centrifugal forces have not been studied systematically, they are readily apparent to observers of the American scene. The following excerpt from the report of the President's White House Conference on Children summarizes the situation as seen by a group of experts, including both scientists and practitioners.

In today's world parents find themselves at the mercy of a society which imposes pressures and priorities that allow neither time nor place for meaningful activities and relations between children and adults, which downgrade the role of parents and the functions of parenthood, and which prevent the parent from doing things he wants to do as a guide, friend, and companion to his children. . . .

The frustrations are greatest for the family of poverty where the capacity for human response is crippled by hunger, cold, filth, sickness, and despair. For families who can get along, the rats are gone, but the rat-race remains. The demands of a job, or often two jobs,

[18]Bronfenbrenner, U.: Socialization and Social Class through Time and Space, in Maccoby, E. E., Newcomb, T. M., and Hartley, E. (eds.), *Readings in Social Psychology* (3d ed.; New York: Holt, Rinehart & Winston, 1958), pp. 400–425.

[19]Bronfenbrenner, U.: *Two Worlds of Childhood: U. S. and U.S.S.R.* (New York: Russell Sage Foundation, 1970); Devereux, E. C., Jr., *et al.*: Child rearing in England and the United States: A cross-national comparison, J. Marriage and the Family 31:257, 1969.

[20]Rodgers, R. R.: Changes in parental behavior reported by children in West Germany and the United States, Hum. Dev. 14:208, 1971.

that claim mealtimes, evenings, and weekends as well as days; the trips and moves necessary to get ahead or simply hold one's own; the ever increasing time spent in commuting, parties, evenings out, social and community obligations—all the things one has to do to meet so-called primary responsibilities—produce a situation in which a child often spends more time with a passive babysitter than a participating parent.[21]

The forces undermining the parental role are particularly strong in the case of fathers. For example, although in one interview study of middle class families, fathers reported spending an average of 15–20 minutes a day playing with their 1-year-old infants,[22] an observational research revealed a rather different story:

> The data indicate that fathers spend relatively little time interacting with their infants. The mean number of interactions per day was 2.7, and the average number of seconds per day was 37.7.[23]

And even when the parent is at home, a compelling force cuts off communication and response among the family members. Like the sorcerer of old, the television set casts its magic spell, freezing speech and action and turning the living into silent statues so long as the enchantment lasts. For example, one study reports that 78% of viewers indicated no conversation while the set was on (except briefly during commercials).[24]

The primary danger of the television screen lies not so much in the behavior it produces as the behavior it prevents—the talks, the games, the family festivities and arguments through which much of the child's learning takes place and his character is formed. Turning on the television set can turn off the process that transforms children into people.

Another factor reducing interaction between parents and children is the changing physical environment in the home. For example, a brochure recently received in the mail describes a "cognition crib" equipped with a tape recorder that can be activated by the sound of the infant's voice. In addition, frames built into the sides of the crib permit insertion of "programmed play modules for sensory and physical practice." The modules come in sets of 6, which the parent is "encouraged to change" every 3 months so as to keep pace with the child's development. Since "faces are what an infant sees first, six soft plastic faces . . . adhere to the window." Other modules include mobiles, a crib aquarium, a piggy bank and "ego-building mirrors." Parents are hardly mentioned except as potential purchasers.

Although no systematic evidence is available, there are indications that a withdrawal of adults from the lives of children is also occurring outside the home. To quote again from the report of the White House Conference:

> In our modern way of life, it is not only parents of whom children are deprived, it is people in general. A host of factors conspire to isolate children from the rest of society. The fragmentation of the extended family, the separation of residential and business areas,

---

[21]*Report to the President: White House Conference on Children* (Washington, D. C.: U. S. Government Printing Office, 1970), 240–255.

[22]Ban, P., and Lewis, M.: Mothers and Fathers, Girls and Boys: Attachment Behaviors in the Year-Old. Paper presented at the Eastern Psychological Association meeting, New York, April, 1971.

[23]Rebelsky, F., and Hanks, C.: Father's verbal interactions with infants in the first three months of life, Child Dev. 42:63, 1971.

[24]Maccoby, E. E.: Television: Its impact on school children, Pub. Opinion Quart. 15: 423, 1951.

the disappearance of neighborhoods, zoning ordinances, occupational mobility, child labor laws, the abolishment of the apprentice system, consolidated schools, television, separate patterns of social life for different age groups, the working mother, the delegation of child care to specialists—all these manifestations of progress operate to decrease opportunity and incentive for meaningful contact between children and persons older, or younger, than themselves.[25]

This erosion of the social fabric isolates not only the child but also his family. In particular, with the breakdown of community, neighborhood and the extended family, and the rise in the number of father-absent homes, increasingly greater responsibility has fallen on the young mother. In some segments of the society, the resulting pressures appear to be mounting beyond the point of endurance. For example, the growing number of divorces now is accompanied by a new phenomenon: the unwillingness of either parent to take custody of the child. And in more and more families, the woman is fleeing without waiting for the mechanism of a legal or even agreed-on separation. Increasing numbers of married women are being reported to police departments as missing. Although no national statistics are available, news media have reported a "quantum leap" in the number of runaway wives whom private detectives are hired to retrieve by the fathers who are left with the children.

As documented at the outset of this report, even in intact families the centrifugal forces generated within the family by its increasingly isolated position have propelled its members in different directions. As parents, especially mothers, spend more time in work and community activities, children are placed in or gravitate to group settings, both organized and informal. For example, since 1965, the number of children enrolled in day-care centers has more than doubled, and the demand today far exceeds the supply. Outside preschool or school, the child spends increasing amounts of time solely in the company of his age-mates. The vacuum created by the withdrawal of parents and other adults has been filled by the informal peer group. A recent study has revealed that at every age and grade level, children today show a greater dependency on their peers than they did a decade ago.[26] A parallel investigation indicates that such susceptibility to group influence is higher among children from homes in which one or both parents frequently are absent.[27] In addition, "peer oriented" youngsters describe their parents as less affectionate and less firm in discipline. Attachment to age-mates appears to be influenced more by a lack of attention and concern at home than by any positive attraction of the peer group itself. In fact, these children have a rather negative view of their friends and of themselves as well. They are pessimistic about the future, rate lower in responsibility and leadership and are more likely to engage in such antisocial behavior as lying, teasing other children, "playing hooky" or "doing something illegal."[28]

[25]*Report of Forum 15.* White House Conference on Children, Washington, D. C., 1970, p. 2.

[26]Condry, J. C., and Siman, M. A.: Characteristics of peer- and adult-oriented children. J. Marriage and the Family 36:543, 1974.

[27] Condry, J. C., and Siman, M. A.: An experimental study of adult versus peer orientation. Unpublished manuscript, Cornell University, 1968.

[28]Siman, M. A.: Peer Group Influence during Adolescence: A Study of 41 Naturally Existing Friendship Groups. A thesis presented to the Faculty of the Graduate School of Cornell University for the degree of Doctor of Philosophy, January, 1973.

What we are seeing here, of course, are the roots of alienation and its milder consequences. The more serious manifestations are reflected in the rising rates already cited of youthful runaways, drug abuse, suicide, delinquency, vandalism and violence.

FAMILY SUPPORT SYSTEMS

How are we to reverse the trend? The evidence indicates that the most promising solutions do not lie within the child's immediate setting – the classroom and the school. An impressive series of investigations, notably the studies published by James Coleman in 1966[29] and by Christopher Jencks in 1972,[30] demonstrate that the characteristics of schools, of classrooms and even of teachers predict very little of the variation in school achievement. What does predict it is family background, particularly the characteristics that define the family in relation to its social context: the world of work, neighborhood and community.

The critical question thus becomes: Can our social institutions be changed – old ones modified and new ones introduced – so as to rebuild and revitalize the social context that families and children require for their effective function and growth? Let me consider some institutions on the contemporary American scene that are likely to have the greatest impact, for better or for worse, on the welfare of America's children and young people.

Day Care

Day care is coming to America. The question is, what kind? Shall we, in response to external pressures to "put people to work" or for considerations of personal convenience, allow a pattern to develop in which the care of young children is delegated to specialists, further separating the child from his family and reducing the family's and the community's feeling of responsibility for their children? Or will day care be designed, as it can be, to reinvolve and strengthen the family as the primary and proper agent for making human beings human?

As Project Head Start demonstrated, preschool programs can have no lasting constructive impact on the child's development unless they affect not only the child himself but also the people who constitute his enduring day-to-day environment. This means that parents and other people from the child's immediate environment must play a prominent part in the planning and administration of day-care programs and also participate actively as volunteers and aides. It means that the program cannot be confined to the center but must reach out into the home and the community so that the entire neighborhood is caught up in activities in behalf of its children. We need to experiment with putting day-care centers within reach of the significant people in the child's life. For some families this will mean neighborhood centers, for others centers at the place of work. A great deal of variation and innovation will be required to find the appropriate solutions for different groups in different settings.

---

[29]Coleman, J. S.: *Equality of Educational Opportunity* (Washington, D. C.: U. S. Office of Education, 1966).
[30]Jencks, C.: *Inequality* (New York: Basic Books, 1972).

Fair Part-Time Employment Practices Act

Such solutions confront a critical obstacle in contemporary American society. The keystone of an effective day-care program is parent participation, but how can parents participate if they work full time—which is one of the main reasons the family needs day care in the first place? I see only one possible solution: increased opportunities and rewards for part-time employment. It was in the light of this consideration that the report of the White House Conference urged business and industry, and governments as employers, to introduce flexible work schedules (for example, to enable at least one parent to be at home when a child returns from school) and to increase the number and the status of part-time positions. Specifically, the report recommended that state legislatures enact a "Fair Part-Time Employment Practices Act" to prohibit discrimination in job opportunity, rate of pay, fringe benefits and status for parents who sought or engaged in part-time employment.

I should like to report the instructive experience of one state legislator who attempted to put through such a bill, Assemblywoman Constance Cook of New York. Mrs. Cook sent me a copy of her bill as it had been introduced in committee. It began "No employer shall set as a condition of employment, salary, promotion, fringe benefits, seniority" and so on that an employee who is the parent or guardian of a child under 18 years of age shall be required to work more than 40 hours a week. Forty hours a week, of course, is full time; Mrs. Cook informed me that there was no hope of getting a bill through with a lower limit. It turned out that even 40 hours was too low. The bill was not passed even in committee. The pressure from business and industry was too great, and they insisted on the right to require their employees to work overtime.

(There is a ray of hope, however. In the settlement of the United Automobile Workers' 1973 strike against the Chrysler Corporation a limit was placed for the first time on the company policy of mandatory overtime.)

Enhancing the Position of Women

These concerns bring me to what I regard as the most important single factor affecting the welfare of the nation's children. I refer to the place and status of women in American society. Whatever the future trend may be, the fact remains that in our society today the care of children depends overwhelmingly on women, and specifically on mothers. Moreover, with the withdrawal of the social supports for the family to which I alluded above, the position of women and mothers had become more and more isolated. With the breakdown of the community, the neighborhood and the extended family, an increasing responsibility for the care and upbringing of children has fallen on the young mother. Under these circumstances, it is not surprising that many young women in America are in revolt. I understand and share their sense of rage, but I fear the consequences of some of the solutions they advocate, which will have the effect of isolating children still further from the kind of care and attention they need. There is, of course, a constructive implication to this line of thought, in that a major route to the rehabilitation of children and youth in American society lies in the enhancement of the status and power of women in all walks of life – in the home as well as on the job.

Work and Responsibility

One of the most significant effects of age segregation in our society has been the isolation of children from the world of work. Once, children not only saw what their parents did for a living but also shared substantially in the task; now, many children have only a vague notion of the parent's job and have had little or no opportunity to observe the parent (or for that matter any other adult) fully engaged in his or her work. Although there is no systematic research evidence on this subject, it appears likely that the absence of such exposure contributes significantly to the growing alienation among children and young people. Experience in other modern urban societies indicates that the isolation of children from adults in the world of work is not inevitable; it can be countered by creative social innovations. Perhaps the most imaginative and pervasive of these is the common practice in the U.S.S.R., in which a department in a factory, an office, an institute or a business enterprise adopts a group of children as its "wards." The children's group is typically a school classroom, but it may also include a nursery, a hospital ward or any other setting in which children are dealt with collectively. The workers visit the children's group wherever it may be and also invite the youngsters to their place of work in order to familiarize the children with the nature of their activities and with themselves as people. The aim is not vocational education but rather acquaintance with adults as participants in the world of work.

There seems to be nothing in such an approach that would be incompatible with the values and aims of our own society, and this writer has urged its adaptation to the American scene. Acting on this suggestion, David A. Goslin then at the Russell Sage Foundation and now at the National Academy of Sciences, persuaded the *Detroit Free Press* to participate in an unusual experiment as a prelude to the White House Conference on Children. By the time it was over, two groups of 12-year-old children, one from a slum area and the other predominantly middle class, had spent 6–7 hours a day for 3 days in virtually every department of the newspaper, not just observing but participating actively in the department's work. There were boys and girls in the pressroom, the city room, the advertising department and the delivery department. The employees of the *Free Press* entered into the experiment with serious misgivings, but, as a documentary film[31] that was made of the project makes clear, the children were not bored, nor were the adults – and the paper did get out every day.

The Fair Part-Time Employment Practices Act and the *Detroit Free Press* experiment are offered as examples, one in the public, the other in the private sector, of the kinds of innovations in policy and practice that are needed if we are to achieve the objective of rebuilding and revitalizing the social contexts that children and families require for their effective function and growth. But even

---

[31]"A Place to Meet, A Way to Understand," available through the National Audiovisual Center, Washington, D. C., 20409.

more fundamental are three basic family support systems that now are being provided in every modern society except our own:

1. The United States now is the only industrialized nation that does not ensure health care for every family with young children.

2. The United States is the only industrialized nation that does not guarantee a minimum income level for every family with young children.

3. The United States is the only industrialized nation that has not yet established a nationwide program of child-care services for children of working mothers.

Our refusal to meet what other modern nations regard as basic human necessities appears to be grounded in our determined resistance to communism or socialism in any form. Such principled but purblind opposition has driven us to pay an awesome price through our foreign policy in Vietnam. We must not, for similar reasons, perpetuate a domestic policy that debilitates the nation's families and, thereby, endangers the integrity of the next generation of Americans.

The future belongs to those nations that are prepared to make and fulfill a primary commitment to their families and their children. For only in this way will it be possible to counteract the alienation, distress and breakdown of a sense of community that follow in the wake of impersonal technology, materialism, urbanization and their unplanned, dehumanizing consequences. As a nation, we have not yet been willing to make that commitment. We have continued to measure the worth of our society, and of other countries as well, by the faceless criterion of the GNP—the gross national product. Up until now we continue, in the words of the great American psychologist William James, to "worship the bitch goddess Success."

But today we are being confronted with what for us Americans is an unprecedented, unexpected and almost unnatural prospect: nothing less than the failure of success. With all the suffering this failure will bring, it may have some redeeming consequences. For, along with Watergate and Vietnam, it may help bring us to our senses; it may reawaken us to a concern with fundamental values. Among them, none should be more dear than a renewed commitment to the nation's children and their families, a commitment to change the institutions that now determine and delimit how children and parents live, or who can obtain health care for his family, a habitable dwelling, an opportunity to spend time with one's children, or receive help and encouragement from one's community in the demanding and richly gratifying task of enabling the young to develop into competent and compassionate human beings.

Part I

Symptoms of Malaise in Our Society

2

Television and the Family

Fred M. Rogers

Mister Rogers' Neighborhood, Pittsburgh,
Pennsylvania

In a great many American families the television set occupies a place at least as important as that of the kitchen table. We *are* a nation of television viewers, but that in itself need not be a cause for alarm. In fact, if we were to see widespread television viewing as a symptom of malaise there would be little hope in what we could contribute to the family through its great potential.

The very ubiquity itself of television can be helpful to families. Take one simple example: Many families who have moved from one part of the nation to another have reported how delighted they and their young children were to find that a familiar television program was being telecast in their new city and that their new neighbors were discussing it and the children were playing about it. A familiar television program in their new home helped with the transition from the old.

There are similar instances with older children. They might ask:

"Do you dig Elton John?"

"How about Chicago?"

"What did you think of that dude on 'Good Times' last night?"

From the answers to their questions, those older children know who they want to be friends with. They use the mass media as an important gauge of like interests.

Adults use it too. Television in our culture is universal. It affects our relationships with our neighbors, our friends and family. It's so widespread that there are some families in this country who buy a television set long before they install indoor plumbing—and what they see on their sets is what everybody else in the country sees on theirs.

In fact, I believe that those of us on television who are available to families on a regular basis must consider ourselves as part of the extended family of all those who welcome us to their homes. Whether we like it or not, we're being talked about and used in the ways American families communicate. The way we "television relatives" solve our problems on the screen will in some respects

35

influence the ways our viewers approach their problems, especially if our dramas have relevance to the ones they are involved with in their lives. This is particularly true in the case of young children who are sorting out the difference between reality and fantasy. But it is true for older children and adults, too.

A person struggling with real problems like cancer or alcohol addiction or loss of a spouse is going to be naturally attracted to programs that include such themes. In fact, every member of a family will have a particular interest that television might address itself to. We need to recognize that each member of the family might need to have the television all to himself or herself at certain times during the week — just as each person needs to be alone with himself or herself at certain times. Nonetheless, there *are* times when a family can *share* a program together. It's for those times that programs need to be more and more carefully conceived — programs that evoke thoughts and feelings of what it's like to be a little child or a teen-ager or an elderly person — programs that attempt to awaken empathy for different members of the family. Television can illustrate the resourcefulness of the human ego and how wonderful it can be when confronted by conflict, how people grapple with real problems and make real solutions with which they then live.

A good example that comes to mind is Chrissy Thompson, a little girl who was born with spina bifida and who has appeared several times on MISTER ROGERS' NEIGHBORHOOD. In response to those appearances, a mother in Northridge, California, wrote the following letter:

Dear Mr. Rogers:
Thank you . . . especially for the series you did with Chrissy. Our three-year-old daughter was also born with spina bifida as well as other congenital defects. After her fifth operation last spring and some subsequent complications, she developed some large fears about walking with her braces and crutches though she had been able to walk prior to the surgery. Several weeks after watching your Chrissy shows and reruns, she asked for her crutches and said, "Anne walk for Mister Rogers." And she did just that. You were the catalyst we needed. Anne loves to sing, "You are my friend, you are special."

By this, Anne's mother means the song *You Are Special,* which Chrissy and I once sang together on the program. Here are the lyrics:

You are my friend, you are special
You are my friend, you're special to me.
You are the only one like you
Like you, my friend, I like you.

In the daytime, in the nighttime
Any time that you feel's the right time
For a friendship with me
You see F R I E N D
Special, you are my friend, you're special to me.
There's only one in this wonderful world.
You are special.

That letter from California arrived on a day when Chrissy was scheduled to tape with us in the afternoon. Our morning schedule was running late, so some of our staff took Chrissy and her family to lunch — at which time they shared that letter with the Thompsons. Though Chrissy didn't seem to be impressed or even all that interested right then, she used its substance that afternoon in spinning an elaborate and spontaneous fantasy about a girl she knew of who had been helped by seeing her on television. It was clear that knowing she had helped someone had really helped Chrissy feel good about herself. And so, Chrissy's television visits had helped Anne and her family, and their response had helped Chrissy and her family, and I'm sure that Chrissy's subsequent visits continue to help families with other children like Anne.

This may be a rare example, but I think it's a neat one of the mutuality that can exist when television people dare to be real, and when those who respond can respond in a real way. Television can be presented and seen in a truly human context.

I feel that one reason there is such an outcry against violence and sex on the screen is that they are both so often presented *out* of human context. A few weeks ago, a Sunday *New York Times* article by William Gale included interviews with members of some South Bronx street gangs. These young people have some striking opinions about television.

Karate Charlie Suarez believes television glamorizes violence.

People, he says, aren't just naturally disposed toward violence.

They've got to be helped along. And he feels TV violence helps a lot: "Bang, bang, you're dead. That's all. They show just the violence.

"No real pain. No funeral. No plot of earth. No sign of what happens to the wife and kids after that guy gets killed."

I think that's a very sensitive statement by a young man who has already seen many of the consequences of violence.

Shakespeare's kind of violence is understandable because he intuitively knew many of the deeper directives of human life and presented them dramatically. *He* showed the pain, and the funeral, the plot of earth and what happens to the wife and kids after the guy gets killed. I have the feeling that Karate Charlie Suarez would approve of Shakespeare.

As for sex, the way it usually is presented on television seems to be totally out of context, too. It gives no sense of the dignity of people and their feelings or their commitments to one another. Soap operas, for instance, give such a base view of human beings. Sex in those programs is something for the moment and nothing lasting ever comes of it. It's this fragmenting view of human experiences and affiliations that can influence the stability of the human family. One would think that those who write for the majority of television were living in the nineteenth century, when people resisted the idea that love and sexuality are fused together in human nature. What we need much more of in our mass communications is to see people emerging out of adolescence and becoming adults who can make a marriage—not that the marriage will be all smooth sailing—not by any means. We need to see the new growth that comes from the conflict and from the striving, and the capacity for parenthood that evolves out of that human commitment to a new generation!

Television doesn't speak to just the tops of our heads. It can speak to the inner nature of the child and the parent. It can speak to issues in a parent-child relationship: what it means to be a family.

Three years ago, a girl named Cookie was vice president of another South Bronx street gang. Two of her older brothers have been sentenced to Attica for their involvement in a gang murder of a prostitute. Last January, her "man" was fatally shot in a street fight. In *her* interview with the *New York Times* about violence on television, Cookie says that right after a child has seen violence on TV, a parent should sit down and talk to him about it. "Tell the kid that that's not the way life should be—that that's not the right thing to do." This is this young woman's counsel.

Well, we all know that there are millions of children who don't have families to sit down and talk with them about what they've seen on TV or families who help them deal with the feelings that are generated by television programming. And those stressful feelings about unresolved violence can easily be carried over into family life. I know this to be a reality and I have always felt it a duty when any programming I produced was stress-evoking, to at least help children to begin to deal with the stress before that program left the air. It is important to have an adult available on the screen to distinguish between fantasy and reality and to help children begin the process of recognizing what they really feel and what they could do with those real feelings. For example, I sometimes sing this song about anger:

> *What Do You Do with the Mad That You Feel?*
> *What do you do with the mad that you feel*
> *When you feel so mad you could bite?*
> *When the whole wide world seems oh so wrong*
> *And nothing you do seems very right?*
> *What do you do? Do you punch a bag?*
> *Do you pound some clay or some dough?*
> *Do you round up friends for a game of tag?*
> *Or see how fast you go?*
>
> *It's great to be able to stop*
> *When you've planned a thing that's wrong,*
> *And be able to do something else instead*
> *And think this song:*
>
> *I can stop when I want to,*
> *Can stop when I wish,*
> *Can stop, stop, stop any time.*
> *And what a good feeling*
> *To feel like this,*
> *And know that the feeling is really mine.*
> *Know that there's something deep inside*
> *That helps us become what we can,*
> *For a girl can be some day a woman*
> *And a boy can be some day a man.*

Dr. James Hughes, an old seminary friend, and I have helped to establish and furnish an appropriate play area within the visitors' space at the Western State Penitentiary in Pittsburgh. Every day, members of Jim's Child Development class at the prison serve as play monitors for the young visitors. These children come with their families to visit fathers, uncles, cousins. Often the visits last 4 or 5 hours. The inmates who are the play monitors often say that their times with the children are the most humanizing times of their prison life. When they can allow themselves to remember what it was like when someone loved and cared for them, they can care better for themselves even inside a prison. One of the prisoners' favorite television dramas is called "Sunshine." It's about a jazz combo player whose wife has died and he takes care of his little daughter. My teen-age son labels the program "too sugary" for his taste; but those prisoners obviously need an extra measure of sugar in their maximum security cells. They're trying to keep alive the feelings of how an adult man takes care of a child. They're doing what they can about their hunger for family relationships.

Johnson & Johnson Baby Products Company has funded a project in which closed circuit television is being used to show and explain to children and their parents what to expect during different aspects of hospitalization. We're convinced that anybody is more comfortable when he or she knows what's going to happen. Television — even when it shows an operating room — can be used to help families come a little closer just by "talking about it" in a human context.

Already television helps us all better to share the understanding of our environment — the cultural heritage of the arts: music, dance, drama — things that once were available to only the privileged few. Those who comprise the leaders of our country's understanding of the behavioral sciences can collaborate with creative artists who are dedicated to writing and producing television and together add something wonderful and constructive to the inner life of families. Television could become one more force for family stability and integrity.

Love and hate and fear and trust are all persisting aspects of persons. We must not allow a medium as far-reaching as television to insinuate over and over again that each human experience is only a thing of the moment, that human affiliations are only fragmented and shifting. We must rather see to it that *all* institutions — including television — encourage the development of the capacity for a continuity of commitment — a commitment that is so deep that it can incorporate the whole range of human feelings and still endure.

I feel confident that there *are* some things that television can do to help influence the stability of the human family.

3

New Perspectives on Violence*

Albert Bandura, Ph.D.

*Profesor of Psychology, Stanford
University, Palo Alto, California*

Human aggression is a fundamental social problem. At the societal level, the spread of technologic capacity for massive destruction poses serious threats to large groups of people. At the personal level, violence increasingly encroaches on daily human affairs to impair the quality of life. A notable example is the public's growing fear of becoming a victim of violence. Although physical assaults against strangers do not occur often, their unpredictability, gravity and lurid reporting arouse widespread anxiety. As a result of heightened concern over personal safety, people lead more self-protective and confining lives.

Aggression refers to behavior that causes personal injury and destruction. Not all injurious and destructive acts are judged aggressive, however. Aggression means different things to different people. There are few disagreements about direct assaultive behavior. But disputes over the labeling of aggression arise in the case of societal practices causing widespread harm, and over the use of coercive power for social control and social change. The injurious consequences of major concern often are created remotely, circuitously and impersonally by social practices judged aggressive by the victims but not by those who benefit from them. And in conflicts of power, one person's violence is another person's benevolence. Whether a particular form of aggression is regarded as adaptive or destructive depends on who bears the consequences.

SOCIAL LEARNING ANALYSIS

A complete account of aggression must explain how aggressive patterns are developed, what provokes people to behave aggressively and what sustains such actions after they have been elicited. Figure 3–1 summarizes the determinants of these three aspects of aggression from the social learning perspective. This

*Preparation of this chapter was facilitated by Research Grant M-5162 from the National Institutes of Health, United States Public Health Service.

41

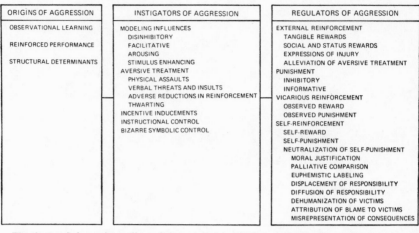

ORIGINS OF AGGRESSION	INSTIGATORS OF AGGRESSION	REGULATORS OF AGGRESSION
OBSERVATIONAL LEARNING	MODELING INFLUENCES	EXTERNAL REINFORCEMENT
	DISINHIBITORY	TANGIBLE REWARDS
REINFORCED PERFORMANCE	FACILITATIVE	SOCIAL AND STATUS REWARDS
	AROUSING	EXPRESSIONS OF INJURY
STRUCTURAL DETERMINANTS	STIMULUS ENHANCING	ALLEVIATION OF AVERSIVE TREATMENT
	AVERSIVE TREATMENT	PUNISHMENT
	PHYSICAL ASSAULTS	INHIBITORY
	VERBAL THREATS AND INSULTS	INFORMATIVE
	ADVERSE REDUCTIONS IN REINFORCEMENT	VICARIOUS REINFORCEMENT
	THWARTING	OBSERVED REWARD
	INCENTIVE INDUCEMENTS	OBSERVED PUNISHMENT
	INSTRUCTIONAL CONTROL	SELF-REINFORCEMENT
	BIZARRE SYMBOLIC CONTROL	SELF-REWARD
		SELF-PUNISHMENT
		NEUTRALIZATION OF SELF-PUNISHMENT
		MORAL JUSTIFICATION
		PALLIATIVE COMPARISON
		EUPHEMISTIC LABELING
		DISPLACEMENT OF RESPONSIBILITY
		DIFFUSION OF RESPONSIBILITY
		DEHUMANIZATION OF VICTIMS
		ATTRIBUTION OF BLAME TO VICTIMS
		MISREPRESENTATION OF CONSEQUENCES

Fig. 3–1.—Schematic outline of the origins, instigators and regulators of aggression in social learning theory.

theory is intended to be sufficiently broad in scope to explain all facets of aggression, whether individual or collective, personally or institutionally sanctioned.

Learning by Example

People do not come equipped with inborn aggressive skills. They must learn them. Most of our behavior is learned observationally through the power of example. This is particularly true of aggression, where the dangers of crippling or fatal consequences limit the value of learning through trial and error. By observing the aggressive conduct of others, one forms an idea of how the behavior is performed and on later occasions the example can serve as a guide for action.

Results of numerous studies reveal that exposure to aggressive models tends to foster similar conduct in children (Bandura, 1973). One illustration of how they pattern their aggressive behavior after the example set by others is presented in Figure 3–2. The influence of aggressive modeling is not confined to children. Adults behave more punitively after they have seen others act aggressively than if they have not been exposed to aggressive models.

Models can teach more general lessons as well. From observing the behavior of others, individuals can learn general tactics for actions that go beyond the specific examples.

FAMILIAL SOURCES

In a modern society, aggressive styles of conduct may be adopted from three principal sources. One prominent origin is the aggression modeled and reinforced by family members. Studies of familial determinants of aggression show that parents who favor aggressive solutions to problems have children who tend to use similar aggressive tactics in dealing with others (Bandura and Walters, 1959). That familial violence breeds violence is further shown in longitudinal investigations of child abuse over several generations. Children who suffer brutal

Fig. 3–2. – Photographs of children imitating the aggressive behavior of an adult model they had observed on film (Bandura, Ross and Ross, 1963).

treatment at the hands of assaultive parents are themselves inclined to use abusive behavior in the future (Silver, Dublin and Lourie, 1969).

SUBCULTURAL SOURCES

Although familial influences play a major role in setting the direction of social development, the family is embedded in a network of other social systems. The subculture in which people reside, and with which they have repeated contact, provides a second important source of aggression. Not surprisingly, the highest incidence of aggression is found in communities in which aggressive models abound and fighting prowess is regarded as a valued attribute (Short, 1968).

MEDIA SOURCES

The third source of aggressive conduct is the abundant symbolic modeling provided by the mass media. The advent of television has greatly expanded the

Fig. 3–3.—Incidence of hijackings of airplanes over a span of 25 years. The rise in foreign hijackings during the 1949 – 50 period occurred in Slavic countries at the time of the Hungarian uprising, and the second flare-up in 1958 – 61 comprised almost entirely Cuban hijackings to Miami. A sudden widespread diffusion of hijackings occurred in 1969 – 71 involving airlines from a total of 55 different countries.

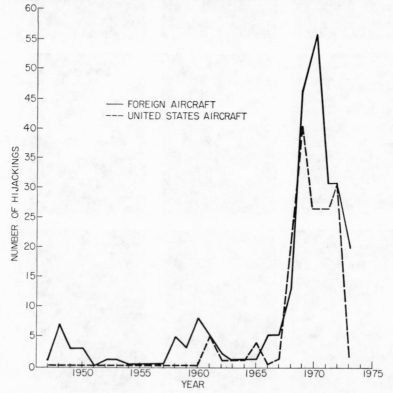

range of models available to a growing child. Whereas their predecessors had limited occasions to observe brutal aggression, both children and adults today have unlimited opportunities to learn the whole gamut of violent conduct from televised modeling within the comfort of their homes. Field studies, in which children and adolescents are repeatedly shown either violent or nonviolent fare, disclose that exposure to filmed violence increases interpersonal aggressiveness (Bandura, 1973; Liebert, Neale and Davidson, 1973).

Being an influential tutor, television can foster humanitarian qualities as well as injurious conduct. Programs that portray positive attitudes and social behavior, as in the *Mister Rogers* series, encourage cooperativeness and sharing, and they reduce aggressiveness in young children (Leifer, Gordon and Graves, 1974). It is regrettable that television does not provide more such experiences to cultivate positive potentialities in the developing child.

Symbolic modeling plays an especially significant role in the shaping and rapid spread of collective aggression. Social diffusion of new styles of aggression conforms to the generalized pattern of most other contagious activities: New aggressive behavior is initiated by salient example. It spreads rapidly in a contagious fashion. After it has been widely adopted, it is discarded, often in favor of a new form that follows a similar course.

Airliner hijacking provides a recent example of the rapid diffusion and decline of aggressive tactics. Air piracy never occurred in the United States until an airliner was hijacked to Havana in 1961. Prior to that incident, Cubans were hijacking planes to Miami. These incidents were followed by a wave of hijackings both in the United States and abroad, eventually involving 70 nations. (Fig. 3–3).

Direct Experience

Patterns of behavior can also be fashioned through a more rudimentary form of learning, relying on rewarding and punishing experiences. Patterson demonstrated how passive children can be shaped into aggressors through a process of victimization and successful counteraggression (Patterson, Littman and Bricker, 1967). Passive children who were maltreated but occasionally were able to halt attacks by defending themselves aggressively not only increased defensive fighting over time but began to initiate attacks on their own. By contrast, passive children who were maltreated and whose counteraggression proved unsuccessful remained submissive.

CROSS-CULTURAL STUDIES

The way in which modeling and reinforcement influences operate jointly in producing aggression is graphically revealed in cross-cultural comparisons of societies that pursue a war-like mode of life with those that follow pacific styles of behavior. In cultures that do not provide aggressive models and devalue injurious conduct, people live peaceably (Alland, 1972; Dentan, 1968). In other societies that provide extensive training in aggression, attach prestige to it and make its use rewarding, people threaten, fight, maim and kill one another (Gardner and Heider, 1969).

INSTIGATORS OF AGGRESSION

A theory must explain not only how aggressive patterns are learned but also how they are activated and channeled. Figure 3–4 depicts three alternative views of aggression instigators. According to the instinct theory, people are innately endowed with an aggressive drive that automatically builds up and must be discharged periodically through some form of aggressive behavior. Researchers have been unable to find any evidence for an inborn mechanism that generates an aggressive drive.

For years, aggression was viewed as a product of frustration. In this conception, frustration arouses an aggressive drive, which, in turn, motivates aggressive behavior. This theory enjoys wide popularity even though it does not fit well with accumulating knowledge. Frustration has varied effects on behavior. And aggression does not require frustration.

What people call frustration includes a wide range of distressing experiences. Aversive experiences produce emotional arousal, rather than an aggressive drive, that activates any number of responses, depending on the types of reactions one has learned for coping with troublesome situations. When distressed, some people seek assistance; others display withdrawal and resignation; some aggress; others respond with psychosomatic disturbances; still others anesthetize themselves with drugs or alcohol against a miserable existence; and most intensify constructive efforts to modify the sources of distress.

Several lines of evidence lend support to the social learning view. Different emotions have a similar physiologic state. The same physiologic state can be experienced phenomenologically at different emotions, depending on what people see as the incitements and how they interpret them. In individuals who are prone to behave aggressively, different sources of emotional arousal can heighten their aggression.

In drive theories, the aroused aggressive drive presumably remains active until discharged by some form of aggression. Actually, anger arousal dissipates rapidly, but it can be easily regenerated on later occasions through rumination on anger-provoking incidents. Many of people's distresses arise because, in their thoughts, they live more in the past and in the future than in the present. By thinking about past insulting treatment, people can work themselves into a rage long after their emotional reactions have subsided. Persistence of elevated anger stems from thought-produced arousal rather than from an undischarged reservoir of aggressive energy. Thus, for example, a person who becomes angered by an apparent exclusion from an important meeting but receives the invitation in the next day's mail will show an immediate drop in anger arousal and aggressiveness without having to assault or denounce someone to drain a roused drive.

Anger arousal decreased through cognitive means will reduce aggression as much, or even more, than will acting aggressively. Indeed, it now has been amply documented that, far from producing cathartic reductions, participation in aggressive activities, either directly or vicariously, tends to maintain such behavior at its original level, or to actually increase it (Bandura, 1973). Aggression-prone individuals, therefore, are helped more by developing constructive ways of coping with conflict than by venting aggression.

Frustration or anger arousal is a facilitative rather than a necessary condition for aggression. Frustration tends to provoke aggression mainly in people who

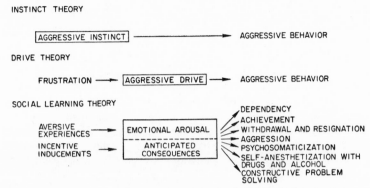

INSTINCT THEORY

AGGRESSIVE INSTINCT ────────────▶ AGGRESSIVE BEHAVIOR

DRIVE THEORY

FRUSTRATION ──▶ AGGRESSIVE DRIVE ──▶ AGGRESSIVE BEHAVIOR

SOCIAL LEARNING THEORY

AVERSIVE EXPERIENCES ──▶ EMOTIONAL AROUSAL / ANTICIPATED CONSEQUENCES

INCENTIVE INDUCEMENTS ──▶

DEPENDENCY
ACHIEVEMENT
WITHDRAWAL AND RESIGNATION
AGGRESSION
PSYCHOSOMATICIZATION
SELF-ANESTHETIZATION WITH DRUGS AND ALCOHOL
CONSTRUCTIVE PROBLEM SOLVING

Fig. 3–4.—Diagrammatic representation of motivational determinants of aggression in instinct, reactive drive and social learning theories.

have learned to respond to aversive experiences with aggressive attitudes and conduct. Thus, after being frustrated, aggressively trained children behave more aggressively whereas cooperatively trained children behave more cooperatively.

Emotional arousal is not the sole determinant of aggressive behavior. A great deal of human aggression is prompted by the benefits anticipated by such actions. Here, the instigator is the pull of expected gains rather than the push of distress.

Aggression elicitors take many forms. Social interchanges often are escalated into physical violence by threats and insults. Humiliating affronts and challenges to reputation emerge as major precipitants of violence in assault-prone individuals (Toch, 1969). Sensitivity to embarrassing treatment usually is combined with deficient verbal skills for resolving disputes and restoring self-esteem without having to dispose of antagonists physically.

In the course of development, people are trained to obey orders. By rewarding compliance and punishing disobedience, directions issued in the form of orders elicit obedient behavior. After this form of social influence is established, authorities can secure obedient aggression from others, especially if the actions are presented as justified and necessary and the issuers possess coercive power. As Snow (1961) has perceptively observed, "When you think of the long and gloomy history of man, you will find more hideous crimes have been committed in the name of obedience than in the name of rebellion" (p. 24).

Studies of obedient aggression corroborate historical evidence that it requires particular social conditions rather than monstrous people to produce injurious deeds (Milgram, 1974).

In addition to the various external instigators, bizarre beliefs can give rise to aggression of appalling proportions. Every so often, tragic episodes occur in which individuals are led by delusional beliefs to commit acts of violence.

MAINTAINING CONDITIONS

Thus far, we have discussed how aggressive behavior is learned and what activates it. The third major feature of the social learning formulation is concerned with the conditions that sustain aggressive tendencies. Behavior is extensively

regulated by its consequences. Injurious conduct, like other forms of social behavior, can be increased, eliminated and reinstated by altering the reinforcing
effects it produces.

People aggress for many different reasons. Some resort to force to appropriate
tangible resources they desire. Some behave aggressively because it wins them
approval or status rewards. Still others may rely on aggressive conquests to
bolster their self-esteem and sense of manliness. Under certain conditions, people may derive satisfaction from seeing the expressions of suffering they inflict on
their victims. Defensive forms of aggression often are reinforced by their capacity, to terminate humiliating and painful treatment. The same aggressive actions
thus may have markedly different functional value for different individuals and
for the same individual on different occasions.

VICARIOUS REINFORCEMENT

People repeatedly observe the actions of others and the occasions on which
they are rewarded, ignored or punished. Observed outcomes influence behavior
in much the same way as directly experienced consequences. People can, therefore, profit from the successes and mistakes of others as well as from their own
experiences. As a general rule, seeing aggression rewarded in others increases,
and seeing it punished decreases, the tendency to behave in similar ways. Observed punishment, however, is informative as well as inhibitory. Given strong
instigation to aggression and limited options, a person witnessing the failures of
others will more likely refine the prohibited behavior to improve its chances of
success than be deterred.

SELF-REINFORCEMENT

People can, and do, regulate their conduct to some extent by the consequences they produce for themselves. They do things that give them self-satis-
faction and a feeling of self-worth, and they refrain from behaving in ways that
result in self-condemnation. Because of self-reactive tendencies, people must
contend with themselves as well as with others when they act in an injurious
manner.

Self-generated consequences, depending on their nature, can either promote or
diminish aggressiveness. Individuals for whom fighting exploits are a source of
personal pride readily engage in aggressive activities. Most individuals acquire,
through example and precept, negative sanctions against cruelty. As a result,
they are restrained from injurious acts by anticipated self-censure. But moral
codes do not function as fixed internal regulators of conduct. Through resort to
self-exonerating devices, people can dissociate their self-evaluative reactions
from ethically questionable conduct. Social justifications and self-exonerations
thus permit variations in conduct in people with the same moral principles.

DISSOCIATIVE PROCESSES

Some of the disinhibiting maneuvers eliminate self-censuring reactions by
construing reprehensible behavior in favorable terms. Activities that ordinarily

are self-disapproved become personally acceptable if structured as serving moral purposes. Over the years, much cruelty has been perpetrated by decent, moral people in the name of religious principles, righteous ideologies and social control.

In everyday transactions, euphemistic labeling is a handy linguistic device for masking reprehensible activities or according them a respectable status. Self-deplored acts can also be made benign by contrasting them with flagrant inhumanities. Moral justifications and palliative comparisons serve as especially effective disinhibitors because they not only eliminate self-generated deterrents but also engage self-reward in the service of inhumane conduct. What was self-condemnable becomes, through cognitive restructuring, a source of self-pride.

Self-evaluative consequences are likely to be activated most strongly when the causal connection between moral behavior and its consequences is apparent. Self-prohibiting consequences, therefore, can be dissociated from conduct by obscuring or distorting the relationship between actions and the effects they cause. People will behave in ways they normally repudiate if a legitimate authority assumes responsibility for what they do.

By displacing responsibility elsewhere, people need not hold themselves accountable for their actions and thus are spared self-prohibiting reactions. Exemption from self-censure is likewise facilitated by diffusing responsibility for culpable behavior. Through division of labor, division of decision making and collective actions, people can behave reproachfully without feeling personally responsible.

Attributing blame to the victim is still another exonerative expedient. Victims are blamed for bringing suffering on themselves, or extraordinary circumstances are invoked as vindications for injurious conduct. One need not engage in self-reproof for committing acts dictated by compelling circumstances. A further means of weakening self-prohibiting reactions is to dehumanize the victims. Maltreatment of people who have been reduced to a subhuman level is less likely to arouse self-reproof than if they are regarded as sensitive individuals.

Many conditions of contemporary life are conducive to dehumanizing behavior. Bureaucratization, technology, automation, urbanization and high social mobility all lead people to relate to one another in anonymous, impersonal ways. In addition, social practices that divide people into in-group and out-group members produce human estrangement conducive to dehumanization. Strangers can be more easily cast as subhuman villains than can personal acquaintances.

Personal deterrents rely on anticipatory self-condemning reactions from the harm caused by blameworthy conduct. Additional ways of weakening self-deterring reactions operate by misrepresenting the results actions produce. As long as detrimental effects are disregarded, misconstrued or minimized, there is little likelihood that self-reprimanding reactions will be activated.

Given the variety of self-exonerating devices, a society cannot rely solely on individuals, however noble their convictions, to protect against brutal deeds. Just as aggression is not rooted in the individual, neither does its control reside only there. Humaneness requires, in addition to benevolent personal codes, safeguards built into social systems that discourage cruelty and uphold compassionate behavior.

REMEDIAL MEASURES

Like so many other problems confronting people, there is no single grand design for lowering the level of destructiveness within a society. It requires both individual corrective effort and group action aimed at changing the practices of social systems.

Space does not permit a detailed discussion of remedial measures. In a recently published book on aggression (Bandura, 1973), I have outlined ways in which social systems that contribute to violence can be changed to function in more constructive ways.

FAMILIAL PRACTICES. — Guidelines are presented for modifying familial practices to reduce dysfunctional aggression in children. In this approach, parents are taught by demonstration and guided practice how to reduce their inadvertent reinforcement of coercive, aggressive conduct and to supplant it by rewarding more constructive forms of behavior.

EDUCATIONAL SYSTEMS. — Given our present knowledge, educational systems should not be turning out large numbers of students so lacking in basic skills that their choices of livelihood are essentially restricted to menial pursuits, dependent subsistence or a life of crime. Methods exist for creating learning environments that can transform academic failure to success.

MASS MEDIA. — Different courses of action are outlined by which the public can reduce the commercial marketing of violence on television and change it into an instrument for human betterment. Public efforts to improve the quality of television programming should not be limited to negative sanctions. Programs relying heavily on dehumanizing ingredients are best supplanted by providing people with interesting alternatives.

CORRECTIONAL SYSTEMS. — Almost everyone acknowledges that present correctional systems are antiquated. High recidivism rates attest to the fact that they do not accomplish the purposes for which they are justified. Although the need for drastic reforms is repeatedly voiced by insiders and outsiders alike, the corrosive practices remain. It is difficult to alter huge malfunctioning agencies by internal modification alone. Agencies can be changed faster by devising successful programs on a limited scale outside the traditional structure, and then using the power of superior alternatives as the instrument of influence. Change through superior alternatives is illustrated in the home-style programs that are being developed for juvenile offenders as a substitute for correctional facilities.

ENFORCEMENT AGENCIES. — Programs are proposed for modifying provocative police practices. Policemen who are prone to provocative aggressive actions are taught how to cope more constructively with potentially dangerous situations. Police misconduct that is organizationally sanctioned requires mechanisms for monitoring enforcement practices.

COMMUNITY SERVICES. — In public agencies that enjoy monopolies over given functions, the practices that evolve are more likely to serve the interests and convenience of those who run the services than to maximize benefits for their clientele. Systems of accountability are described for making public agencies more responsive to the needs of those they serve.

LEGAL SYSTEM. — The law can be used as an instrument of constructive social change as well as to preserve existing practices. People use legal means to secure their rights and to advance their welfare.

POLITICAL SYSTEM. — The political system is a major agency of social change. People improve their society through reform legislation. They rely on the sanctions of agencies to enforce rules that affect their everyday life. The governmental apparatus, however, often is diverted from its public function by the pressure of vested interests. Efforts to improve the functioning of society must also be directed at governmental practices to make them serve the public more equitably.

Since aggression is not an inevitable or unchangeable aspect of people but a product of aggression-promoting conditions operating within a society, social learning theory holds an optimistic view of people's power to reduce their level of aggressiveness. But much greater effort is needed to ensure that this capability is used beneficially rather than detrimentally.

REFERENCES

Alland, A., Jr.: *The Human Imperative* (New York: Columbia University Press, 1972).

Bandura, A.: *Aggression: A Social Learning Analysis* (Englewood Cliffs, N.J.: Prentice-Hali, Inc., 1973).

Bandura, A., and Walters, R. H.: *Adolescent Aggression* (New York: Ronald Press, 1959).

Bandura, A., Ross, D., and Ross, S. A.: Imitation of Film-mediated Aggressive Models, J. Abnorm. Soc. Psychol. 66:3, 1963.

Dentan, R. K.: *The Semai: A Nonviolent People of Malaya* (New York: Holt, Rinehart and Winston, Inc., 1968).

Gardner, R., and Heider, K. G.: *Gardens of War* (New York: Random House, 1969).

Leifer, A. D., Gordon, N. J., and Graves, S. B.: Children's television: More than mere entertainment, Harvard Educational Review 44:213, 1974.

Liebert, R. M., Neale, J. M., and Davidson, E. S.: *The Early Window: Effects of Television on Children and Youth* (New York: Pergamon Press, Inc., 1973).

Milgram, S.: *Obedience to Authority: An Experimental View* (New York: Harper & Row, Publishers, 1974).

Patterson, G. R., Littman, R. A., and Bricker, W.: Assertive behavior in children: A step toward a theory of aggression, Monographs of the Society for Research in Child Development, Vol. 32, No. 5 (Serial No. 113), 1967.

Short, J. F., Jr. (ed.): *Gang Delinquency and Delinquent Subcultures* (New York: Harper & Row, Publishers, 1968).

Silver, L. B., Dublin, C. C., and Lourie, R. S.: Does violence breed violence? Contributions from a study of the child abuse syndrome, Am. J. Psychiatry 126:404, 1969.

Snow, C. P.: Either-or, Progressive 1961, 25:24, 1961.

Toch, H.: *Violent Men* (Chicago: Aldine Publishing Company, 1969).

COMMENTARY

CHAIRMAN DR. T. BERRY BRAZELTON: The first time I met Dr. Bandura was at the FCC hearings about children's television. His powerful presentation to that committee and his ability to stand up to the senators and their incisive questions I think had much to do with changing the whole regulatory power on children's television.

We have time for one or two questions. I have one. What is the relative power of shaping children in a positive way versus in a violent way or an aggressive way? I've always heard that it's much easier to shape them toward aggression than it is in a positive direction.

DR. BANDURA: We do not have any comparative data. Success depends on whether supports for positive behavior are provided in the social system. Given adequate social supports, it would be easier to develop the positive potentialities because aggression carries costs. Aggressors can get beat up and hurt even though they may succeed. So there are some painful effects of aggression. If people are going to resort to aggression it's only because they lack better alternatives or there are substantial benefits for engaging in such behavior. Cooperative behavior does not have the personal injurious consequences.

Given adequate social supports, I would predict that it would be easier to cultivate positive behaviors than it would be to develop aggressive conduct because of the injurious effects that accompany aggression.

CHAIRMAN BRAZELTON: Do you mean by positive supports wanting to have parents there to reinforce the effect of the television show right afterward?

DR. BANDURA: Yes. In the graphs I presented, hyperaggressive children typically responded to conflict by physically aggressive means. An example would be two children wanting the same wagon, so the hyperaggressive child appropriates the toy by wiping out his adversary.

In teaching these children better ways of coping with conflict, you model for them aggressive solutions with the costs to both the victim and the aggressor if the victim has some power to counteraggress, and then you model ways in which they can share playing with the wagon with positive consequences to both.

By modeling alternative ways of responding to conflict, children adopt cooperative modes of dealing with common problem situations. If it turned out that whenever they tried behaving cooperatively it produced no effects, before too long they would discard that style of behavior. But if the environment is so structured that there are more benefits to behave cooperatively than there are to behave aggressively, the social practices will have powerful effects in maintaining cooperativeness. That would be an example of environmental support for a style of conduct.

At the broader cross-cultural level, there are many cultures in which aggression has no functional value and, therefore, it's very difficult to get people to aggress because the culture favors pacific ways of resolving personal problems.

VIRGINIA LOWE (Greenfield, Mass.): This perhaps would be better directed to Mr. Rogers, though I don't know. As long as the networks are dependent on profits and Nielsen ratings rule the choice of programs, how can we promote change based on humanitarian need rather than profits?

52

DR. BANDURA: I would like to respond to that question because it illustrates the extent to which people have been misled into believing why there is such a high prevalence of violent programming. The assumption is that it is due to viewers' preferences. The self-exonerating practices that I discussed earlier are used by the networks to justify the marketing of violence—the same self-exonerating procedures.

If you examine the Nielsen ratings, the violent programs usually do not appear in the top ten; in fact, violence is not that attractive. The reason that it occurs at a high level is because it is an economically attractive proposition. If you are interested in this issue, there is a book written by Les Brown, who analyzes the economics of the business (*Television: The Business Behind the Box,* 1971). The Nielsen ratings show that people are more interested in variety programs.

Moreover, programs that have widespread popularity sometimes are discontinued if they appeal to audiences with the wrong demographics. There have been programs in the top ten that eventually were retired because they were appealing to older audiences. Advertisers are mainly interested in people between the ages of 18 and 49. So if you have the wrong demographics, popular programs, may be terminated.

The reason that the violent formats are used so extensively is that they're relatively inexpensive to produce. If you have 8 or 9 minutes of advertising time in an hour and you multiply the time by whatever the going rates might be, there is a limited amount of income that you can produce in an hour of programming. Programs that have wide appeal may cost a large sum of money, which reduces the profits per hour of programming. Economically, it is cheaper to produce programs that may have a lesser appeal but nevertheless cost less to produce.

The format of the western is well suited for this because all you need is a transient evildoer, a super-hero, a makeshift saloon, a couple of horses and the open range, and you can produce the serials for limited amounts of money. The prevalence of these formats has more to do with the economics of the system than with viewer preferences. But viewers get blamed for what they are shown as due to their attraction to violence.

There often is a misinterpretation of the public's interest in violence, and sports often are cited as an example. If you compare different sports, the ones that have the highest popularity are not necessarily those that involve physical aggression. Most sports would have little interest without built-in elements of conflict and competition. I doubt if many people would attend football games if there were no conferences, rankings and bowl games. Few would spend the time and money simply to see people knocking one another over. So you have to build in artificial elements of interest and excitement that have nothing to do with physical aggression.

Many of the activities are justified as presumably appealing to human aggression, but the answer is more in the economics than in the nature of people.

MR. ROGERS: I'm just curious about the creativity that goes into the writing of television dramas and what it is that helps people create these different violent programs. Why should so many people feel that the sublimation of their drive needs to come out in this way? Are you saying that if the networks and the advertising agencies were to say "We have a great deal of money that we will invest in the kinds of programming that the Waltons present," for instance, that we would find a lot of people sublimating their creative drives into programming like that?

DR. BANDURA: In the Surgeon General's report of the series of studies commissioned to elucidate violence, one of the most revealing papers contains the results of interviews with writers, producers and directors. The effects of television on children have been examined to some extent, but we have not studied the television system. How does the system operate in producing violent programming?

Many of the writers reported that they would prefer more freedom for creative work, that they were bored by these narrow formats and they were concerned by instructions to generate more physical action in order to maintain interest and attention. Most people do not watch television intensively. They tune in and out, so a high activity level is needed to capture and hold their attention.

Another problem with dramatic presentations is that if you have only a half hour it is difficult to present conflict in more subtle ways and to resolve it constructively. So conflict is developed rapidly through physical means and quickly and easily resolved simply by wiping out the protagonist through a physical act.

Problems of time limitations tend to produce heavy reliance on physical forms of conflict resolution.

These are some of the conditions that create an overemphasis on physical dimensions of conflict to the neglect of subtle ways in which conflict occurs in human interactions and constructive ways of conflict resolution.

DR. LEON EISENBERG: I hope that as the audience listened to the very sober and scholarly presentation by Dr. Bandura that you were able to translate some of those terms into what we have had as a national experience. Just as one prototype, what do you think it meant to the adolescents and the elementary school-age children of this country when the ex-President of the United States found reason to extend the Presidential excuse to Lt. Calley after he had been convicted by a jury of other combat officers of having committed heinous crimes in Vietnam?

I am not interested in Lt. Calley's fate. As one person, it really doesn't make any difference. But what about the prototype? What does it mean when there was a TV show that I saw just 2 or 3 weeks ago when ex-General Westmoreland said that if we only went back in with more bombs and a few nukes we would settle things in Vietnam? What does it mean when the present President of the United States in the face of the violence committed against children in Boston defended the right of people to object by such means to so-called forced bussing?

Think of what that means in terms of modeling behavior and the justification of violence, and then you can understand why the Surgeon General in setting up a committee to study television and violence blacklisted my colleague to the right and his colleague to the left from serving on the panel. And then you'll understand that while the report has implicit in it all of the things that Al said, it doesn't come out and say many of the other things that need to be said and ought to be said.

DR. SAWCHUK (Summit, N. J.): I would like to know the panel's opinion of the in-depth news stories that show the effects of violence on the victim's family.

Sometimes they attempt to hook in some empathy. I would like to know what your opinions of these stories are.

MR. ROGERS: I am very concerned about young children watching the news alone anyway. This isn't in answer to your question, but there usually is no show of care. For instance, I remember seeing children in Vietnam hospitals alone in their beds and I am sure it's because they consider the amount of time that you don't see nurses or doctors taking care of them. The view that we might get for a little child is one that the world really is too frightening a place to go outside. And I guess in many instances that is so.

CHAIRMAN BRAZELTON: I am so impressed with what you brought up and how powerful a shaper it can be—about having the family present when children are watching television shows—as Al and Leon bring up the powerful shaping effects of events. It seems easy for parents, for us to control, to blame the television media, blame everybody else. But what do we really do to pick up on what we could do to reshape our children in the face of these influences?

I think this is one of the most interesting things that came up this morning: that we really as parents don't take up our responsibility on some of the very destructive things that are going on in trying to protect our children from them and turning them into a more positively shaped direction.

4

The Search for a New Form of Extended Family

Oscar Newman

President of the Institute for Community
Design Analysis, New York, New York

EDITORS' NOTE

The editors regret that Mr. Oscar Newman's provocative paper will not be published in this volume.

In his presentation Mr. Newman noted that with the progressive shift of the population from agrarian to urban settings and with the increasing mobility of our society geographic distances have developed between the generations of many families which have changed the nature of these families. The nuclear family has emerged as the predominant urban type, with the effect that parents have a less close relationship to their adult children than that which characterized the traditional extended family.

An effect of this has been that upper and middle income families have tended to cluster in areas where they are surrounded by families much like themselves. The poor have not had this option. As an alternative the planners of public housing have attempted to meet the needs of the poor by creating buildings designed to house all kinds of families. For families with children this has often been a dismal failure. Buildings have been constructed in such a way that children at play (especially outside) could not be seen or heard, resulting in less supervision by parents busy in the home. The elderly and families with children have shared such buildings with considerable difficulty and the tensions between generations have been particularly severe where youth and the elderly belong to different ethnic groups.

The design of much public housing has been such that public space—that area to which the public has free access, without the need to account for its presence and without such access being monitored—often extends deep into the housing structures. The result has been a high rate of crime in buildings offering little impediment to access, inasmuch as all that space which lies outside the immediate apartment may be public and therefore dangerous. Crime rates in some studies have been shown to be proportionate to the height of the building and to the amount of interior space open to the public.

Mr. Newman pointed out that crime rates also vary with the socioeconomic status of families and that it is the coupling of sociophysical variables which produces catastrophic situations. He underlined the need to explore architectural planning which will adequately protect the various types of families — such as young families with children, childless couples, working couples and singles, and the elderly — while creating opportunities for them to interact comfortably in space which they can call and manage as their own. Some instances of designs which seemed well calculated to meet these needs were described.

A further discussion of these issues may be found in Mr. Newman's article, "The Effects of the Design of Housing on the Behavior and Attitudes of Residents." which appeared in *Transactions and Studies of the College of Physicians of Philadelphia* in April 1974 (Volume 41, pages 254–261).

5

Youth in a Changing Society

Leon Eisenberg, M.D.

Professor and Chairman of Psychiatry,
Harvard Medical School, Boston,
Massachusetts

Notwithstanding that the topic in this volume was clearly of major import, as the time drew near for preparing a chapter, I became increasingly uncomfortable. Each review of an aspect of the problem seemed to demand that I be, first of all, a moral philosopher familiar, at the same time, with demography, sociology and political science – these, mind you, more insistently than medicine or psychiatry. True enough, clinical experience with the aberrations of adolescent and young adult development was not irrelevant to identifying issues requiring attention, but it had little to offer toward prevention or therapeusis, since the remedies for a social disease on so wide a scale preclude an effective response at an individual or small group level. Accordingly, I have no choice but to be a social and moral philosopher *manqué*, an economist without doctorate, perhaps a prophet without honor.

These prefatory comments herald what I believe to be a major theme running through this symposium. We cannot treat our topic, the family, in a serious and meaningful way except we do it within a framework of human values. Those of us accustomed to view ourselves as scientists or clinicians are likely to feel this necessity as an uncomfortable burden. Values are not quantifiable. They enter into decisions that govern the limits of experimental design. By definition, human values exclude the possibility of attempting deliberately to prove what is expected to be harmful. In such matters, we are restricted to *post hoc* deductions, much like the historiographer. If history is an apt paradigm, the fact that it is constantly being revised warns us in advance of the mutability of our conclusions.

Adding to the complexity is the pervasive influence of belief on behavior. The social prophet affects the events he or she evaluates to the extent that his or her prophesies are believed. The very measure of his or her power may be a reversal in the secular trend of the time series he or she has based his or her conclusions on. Most of us remember the recent predictions of a glut of physicists and engineers, based on a logical extrapolation from rates of graduate school enrollment, changing population ratios and anticipated job opportunities in academia and industry. The figures cannot be faulted; all that was overlooked was that they would be read and, worse than that, believed. Having been put into print, they led to a radical change in student choices; the nation now faces shortages where surpluses had been expected.

Further, we have taken it on ourselves to examine what is closest and dearest to men and women everywhere: the interrelations between them and with their children. Personal intimacies do not lend themselves to exacting scrutiny. Asked to reflect, the doer hesitates and the moment may be lost. All of us have been children; most of us have our own. The vicissitudes of personal experience are not readily put aside for "objective" contemplation. Indeed, objectivity may reflect an inherent disablement when passion alone is an appropriate response to affairs that stand at the center of life. It is the very nature of human consciousness to function as an integrator, seeking and finding interconnections between events, stringing them together in belief systems from which they derive their meaning. True, the family serves biologic purposes in the strictly evolutionary sense. In Darwin's words, "I use the term Struggle for Existence in a large and metaphorical sense, including dependence of one being on another, and including (which is more important) not only the life of the individual but success in leaving progeny."[1] Yet, the limits to variability in family structure set by the demand for "success in leaving progeny" are wide indeed. The fabrication of particular traditions within these broad horizons is determined by patterns of cultural evolution within which the values and meanings given to life and to love are the fulcrums and levers. In a word, it is the essence of the human condition that mankind fashions itself by the choices it makes. Thus, in approaching our topic, I urge that we make no pretense at being value free; rather, we owe it to one another and to our several audiences that we be explicit about the value preferences that govern our judgments.

I should long since have been done with preface. I ask a moment more to set a metaphor before you. The concepts of ecology have become even more widely employed in contemporary political debate as we become aware of the ways in which we have upset the delicate balance of things on this planet.[2] We consume irreplaceable resources; we create more waste than we can dispose of; we multiply without thought of consequence. We have developed technologies of convenience only to discover that we have transmuted gold into dross. When the conveners of this Conference ask "Can the family be saved?", they express concern for a species endangered by the psychosocial fallout from chain reactions within our modes of living that occur at a rate unprecedented in the some 50,000 years of *Homo sapiens* and call into question his designation as "wise."

For almost all of that history, save the last few hundred years, the family served as the principal conservator as well as transmitter of culture.[3] In traditional societies, the young had only to be prepared to emulate their parents' behavior in order to function successfully as adults. Occupational skills were passed on vertically, largely by apprenticeship. Social skills were acquired by imitating the varieties of adult behavior visible to the child and by attending to social sanctions. The family was most often the work unit; parents and children labored as well as lived side by side. Parental norms represented the folk wisdom accumulated over millennia of experience; respect for age was functional as well as demanded; those who had lived longer knew more because they had encountered and overcome more of the expectable vicissitudes of the environment. Note well, however, that this celebration of the virtues of the traditional family refers only to its adaptive function in a static world; in that world, life for the vast majority was marginal and tenuous. Catastrophe, starvation, illness and death were man's constant companions for the greatest part of history.

With the transition from an agrarian to an industrial civilization, the family's role as the economic unit was gradually eroded. Work roles of men and women became more sharply differentiated. The demand for specialized skills led to the introduction of universal schooling as the institutional invention to prepare the young for adult roles, with an inexorable and progressive diminution in the centrality of the family. At the same time, the industrial world required a mobile labor force; in the process of multiple moves, the extended family was lost as a buttress against misfortune and a resource in a time of troubles. Traditional solutions became less effective for the challenges provided by social change; adaptability, the hallmark of youth, had greater immediate salience than the overlearned and more rigid responses of the old. Again, if the price of change was the gradual erosion of traditional values, it also brought with it such benefits as better health, longevity, opportunity and a standard of living that few have hesitated to pay the price. Indeed, the developing nations today, rather than drawing back in dismay at the contradictions glaringly visible in the midst of Western "success," seem hell-bent on following our example.

What we have failed to recognize is that the rate of change is accelerating; the conventional indices of "progress" are insufficient to measure full costs; unevenness in the distribution of benefits belies the appearance of average gains; doubling and redoubling of quantity threatens qualitative deterioration. Changes in our daily lives occur at such a pace that discontinuities rather than mere differences appear between the life experiences of the old and the young. Social pollution undermines the role and function of the family.

The nuclear family has become almost the sole source of affective sustenance. Mobility has attenuated ties to the extended family and to friends. More and more of us live in large metropolitan aggregations, work for ever larger and therefore more bureaucratic organizations and are more remote from and less able to influence governmental agencies. Interpersonal transactions are dominated by ritual and rule that leave little room for affective interchange. With all our emotional eggs in the nuclear family basket, breakage is both more inevitable and more devastating when it does occur. Economic stringency requires both parents to work (when work is available) and thus to be less available to each other and to their children; society has not yet provided social supports in the form of family extenders that could mitigate the impact of work demands.[4] That the family is ill-equipped to withstand these strains is documented by the divorce rate and the growing number of single-parent families, a disproportionate number of which are found below the poverty line, doubly disabled.

That our young are in serious trouble is evident from the merest scanning of such crude social indicators as soaring rates of juvenile delinquency (including a disproportionate increase in crimes against persons), the large numbers who fail to learn to read with proficiency by the time they leave secondary school, and even the decline in Scholastic Achievement Test scores among college applicants, the most privileged of our youth. The over-all figures, appalling as they are, convey only part of the wastage. The situation among minority groups is severalfold worse; it is they who bear the brunt of the social breakdown.

How have we come to be where we are?

As with the family, the circumstances of the young have undergone radical change. To begin with, there has been a cumulative trend toward lowering of the age of puberty such that over the past century in industrial nations the age at onset of menarche has declined by 4 months in each decade because of better nutrition and health. This secular trend has finally reached an asymptote among middle class populations. The lasting result, however, is a significantly younger age of entry into the physiologic state of adolescence.[5] Simultaneously with this biologic transformation, the duration of adolescence as a social stage has been sharply increased at the upper end by the prolongation of the time of schooling as preparation for adult work roles. Whereas at the turn of the century less than 15% of young Americans between 14 and 17 were enrolled in secondary schools, the ratio now stands on its head with well over 90% in school. Colleges and universities, enlisting an elite 4% of the 18–21-year-olds 75 years ago, now incorporate 10 times that many. There have been comparable gains in the proportion attending graduate schools for 4 more years; they comprise about half of those who complete college (that is, 30% of those who enter it). Conversely, there has been a progressive decline, even during the past decade, of adolescents and youth participating in the labor force, even part time.[6]

It is difficult for those of us who grew up considering schooling a privilege (and still regarding it as such) to recognize that schools control a vast legion of draftees, not volunteers. The growth in the population, the lengthening of the school term, the reduction in the frequency of absences and the increasing rates of retention in higher grades combine to produce an aggregate of youth-years in full-time school such as to make schooling a huge growth industry, only now showing the first signs of recession because of a declining birth rate. Emphasis on economies of scale rather than on the quality of the learning environment led to consolidation of schools and school districts. In the 1960s alone, college enrollments doubled; the unprecedented increase in the student population was accommodated by growth rather than multiplication of universities, such that 50 now enroll in excess of 20,000 students (some as many as 50,000!) and 60 enroll more than 10,000. Sheer numbers ineluctably dictate organizational complexity, proliferation of administrative bureaucracy and assignment of priority to managerial goals. However unreal President Eliot's image of the student at one end of a log facing Professor Hopkins at the other, the late twentieth-century counterpart is that of a lecture hall full of students relating to the Professor's image by remote telecast. The potential for diminishing segregation by race and class, which might have offset these diseconomies of size, has notably failed to occur because of housing patterns, the gerrymandering of school districts and selective admission policies.

The environment of the school contrasts sharply with that of the work place. It focuses on learning rather than doing; it provides opportunities for self-development at the expense of contributing to others. Its thrust is competitive rather than cooperative; its graduates filter through an ever-narrowing sieve, safe passage through which is correlated with test and grade performance. Nowhere is the devastating impact of this desperate scramble more evident than in its destructive effect on the college experience of premedical students, only 1 in 3 of whom will gain the coveted laurel of admission. For all of these years, the student remains financially a dependent. In contrast, the young worker is a producer, who not only supports himself or herself but society as well. The nature of the industrial enterprise demands collaborative effort on the production line. Moreover, the worker's limited ability to increase wages can be enhanced only by joining with others in a trade union. The work may be – all too often is – intrinsically unsatisfying, but the only avenue for modifying it lies in common undertakings with fellow workers, both older and younger.

One major effect of the progressive substitution of schooling for working and the gradual constriction of family size and time together has been the age-segregation of youth from adults and children. Commercial enterprises have long since targeted a significant fraction of their promotional efforts on this huge market. In the decade of the 1960s, the population aged 14 – 24 years increased in absolute count by more than it had in all of the 60 preceding years of this century; its ratio to the adult cohort (25 – 64 years of age) grew from 0.32 to 0.45, a 40% change! Coleman[6] has stressed the features that characterize "the youth culture." It looks inward toward its peers who become models for attire, entertainment, politics and "life style." It substitutes age-mates for family members as sources of approval and affection; the isolation and alienation it feels as a group feed its press for autonomy, which often is defined more in the negative than in the positive mode; and its self-perception as underdog generates a receptivity to change, with insufficient attention to social costs. The exuberant and unrealistic slogans of the French "youth revolt" in May of 1968 so threatened the concern for social stability in the rest of the population that the conservative Gaullists received a substantial mandate in the subsequent election.

You will have noticed in this a shift toward a delineation of youth almost as though it were a social class, without differentiation into worker or student, poor or rich, black or white, female or male. Yet, for each of these subcategories, lifetime expectations differ sharply, particularly when disadvantage by income, race and sex is summed. The young in each of these categories share more fully the attributes of their own elders than they do those of youth as a group. We are in danger of perpetuating the very error embodied in the youth slogan popular just a few years ago: "Never trust anyone over 30."

The problems of youth do indeed have special poignancies but they are the problems of society in general and cannot be solved except in that context. When the PSAC Panel on Youth[6] calls, and rightly so, for job opportunities for the young and interleaved work-study programs, with a lower minimum wage to facilitate youth employment, its recommendations are hollow while there are 9,000,000 Americans out of work, with an official over-all unemployment rate of 8.7% but a rate for black teen-agers of 41.6% (*New York Times* 4/6/75). The gradual extension of the school-leaving age and the laws against child labor may have had humanitarian aims; they have also served to restrict the potential labor pool when it threatened to expand beyond national capacity to absorb it. The bitter antagonism among white blue collar workers against affirmative action in behalf of excluded minorities assuredly reflects racism and sexism but it is markedly intensified by the shrinking labor market. We observe precisely the same phenomenon in academe, where the resistance to equity for women and minorities has taken on a new urgency (and more elaborate rationalizations) now that fewer faculty positions are to be had. Unless youth, women and minorities make common cause with white male workers in fighting for full employment, all must suffer.[4]

To state it flatly, the problems of youth in a changing society are the problems of a society in the midst of a crisis of nerve. For the better part of this century, the power of the United States was so awesome that it was—or appeared to be—decisive in events the world over. The fall of the Kuomintang on mainland China was the first major evidence of the era we were entering. It was so out of keeping with America's self-perception that the prevailing theory was that of conspiracy; it wasn't that the outcome was beyond our control; we were betrayed by cryptocommunists in high government positions. The collapse of the regimes in Cambodia and Vietnam is a further blow to belief in American hegemony; it remains to be seen whether this, too, will be explained away or recognized as hard data that must be accommodated within a realistic world view. In the same span of time, the malign neglect of civil rights and the gradual abandonment of even the slogan of a war against poverty force acknowledgment of the necessity for structural change in the distribution of benefits; overflow bounty from an expanding gross national product simply doesn't trickle down equitably.[2] The code word "Watergate" stands for an unwanted view of the extent to which cherished democratic rights have been violated behind a façade of legal government. Inflation and recession bring the mess into every home. We adults have responded by doubting our nation instead of its leaders, by doubting ourselves instead of our misconceptions, by turning against our young because they have insisted on confronting us with our contradictions.[7] Despair substitutes for thought and paralyzes action. The sophisticated professorial stance, 1975 model, is to decry the soft-minded "knee-jerk liberalism" of the preceding decade, to refer learnedly to theologic doctrines of the imperfectability of man and to settle down to an observer's role—on a tenured salary.

Cynicism and pessimism guarantee perpetuation of the status quo. The failure lies not in the grandness of our dream but in our lack of commitment to it. The shattering of illusions opens the way to coping with reality. Let me set forth some of the elements of a social program that can begin to restore ecologic balance in the quality of life.

The essential role of the family and the satisfactions it provides to its members need buttressing. This should include income maintenance, universal health care and a network of child care centers to ensure the healthy development of children. If move we must, we can reinvent the extended family by including friends as kith and kin. Foster grandparents provide gratification for themselves as well as the youngsters they relate to. Our goal must be a culture in which the welfare of children is the concern of every citizen.[4]

A second set of measures would focus on facilitating intergenerational sharing. Day care centers and nurseries can be located adjacent to intermediate and secondary schools. Adolescents not only will provide a source of person power but will learn how to be better parents in the process of contributing to the development of the young. Adolescents can learn to teach as well as be taught by serving as tutors for younger children. In setting classroom goals, emphasis should be placed on group achievement in addition to individual accomplishment; each should feel some responsibility for the success of the other. Work experiences for high school and college students should be facilitated by making time available within the regular program and encouraging experimentation with time out at no cost to subsequent re-enrollment. Social subsidy of both early work and later education should be universal in order that opportunity not be limited by income.

At their best, the adolescent years are characterized by the development of idealism and concern for the general welfare. No educational task is more critical than the cultivation of these most human of all qualities by providing experiences to permit their fullest flowering. However short such programs as the Peace Corps and Vista have fallen from their announced goals, they can serve as prototypes of opportunities for the young to attain full humanity by contributing to others. This is but a special instance of a more general proposition: the need for meaningful work roles throughout the life span. It is obscene that we tolerate unemployment (as a means of slowing inflation by shifting its burden to an underclass) in the midst of work that needs doing for social benefit (housing, urban redesign, recreational facilities, human services). It will be a major challenge to re-examine the nature of work, the ways in which its organization can be modified to enhance the satisfactions it brings and in which a broader range of personal choices can be ensured. Work will remain work, but its significance will differ if it is seen to be contributory, if it is socially valued and if each of us has a felt need to participate in the social enterprise.

In each area, we confront similarities between the problems bedeviling the young and the old and the impossibility of resolving the one without simultaneously attending to the other. The flamboyance of youth enables it to articulate, sometimes in caricature, values implicit in a culture that is excessively individualistic in its orientation. "Doing your own thing," even with the proviso that your own thing not injure others, is grossly insufficient as a precept for the social contract. It gained currency in an era of manifest affluence in which a few could enjoy the luxury of personal indulgence so long as the majority, whether by necessity or by choice, continued to provide essential goods and services. It betokens a serious failure in the process of socialization if our citizens come to maturity without a sense of obligation to others. The lack of a shared moral commitment underlies intergenerational alienation.

Social groups as different in their political structure as the Israeli kibbutz movement[8] and the collectives in the People's Republic of China[9] have succeeded in evoking responsible performance in their youth and, at least to some extent, in internalizing a sense both of social obligation and of personal worth as a consequence of that performance. From our perspective, that spirit of collectivity appears to be exacted at too heavy a price in its loss of individual choice. Let us acknowledge that we have overstressed individuality at a considerable cost to social connectedness. These values should not be antinomies. The social contract exists to foster personal freedom; self-fulfillment enables the individual to contribute most effectively to society. When personal choice is enjoyed by some only at the cost of intolerable restriction to the freedom of others there will be a day of reckoning and an inescapable press for change.

I have done what I said I would do; I have written as a moral philosopher. I hope I have persuaded you that questions of value permeate the issues we are addressing. I have set forth my belief that concern for social justice and equity is the organizing theme for fostering adolescent and young adult development. From that central concept flow parallel proposals for political and educational reform. What youngsters are taught in school and in the home as the good life must bear a recognizable relationship to the world in which they live, as the goal toward which it is striving.[10] The teacher must be a doer as well as a learner. The young question what we have come to accept; if we hear their questions and join them in the search for answers, both will become the wiser.

Let me conclude with words I used in another context[11]: "Our most central task is encouraging the development of humane values based on the recognition that we are a single species. . . . Learning must become a social enterprise informed by concern for others. . . . By acting on behalf of our species we become men and women. . . . The study of man takes its meaning from involvement in the struggle for human betterment. Struggle it is and will be; privilege does not surrender easily; false belief is not readily dispelled. The optimism about man's potential I urge upon you is not the comfort of reading history as a saga of human betterment which will one day be complete. It matters, and matters dearly. . . whether that day comes sooner or later; whether it comes at all is not determined by history but by the men and women who make history. . . ."

REFERENCES

1. Darwin, C.: *On the Origin of Species* (A Facsimile of the First Edition) (Cambridge, Mass.: Harvard University Press, 1964).
2. Eisenberg, L.: Poverty, professionalism and politics, Am. J. Orthopsychiatry 42:748, 1972.
3. Eisenberg, L.: The challenge of change, Child Welfare 39:11, 1960.
4. Eisenberg, L.: Caring for children and working: Dilemmas of contemporary womanhood, Pediatrics 56:24, 1975.
5. Eisenberg, L.: A developmental approach to adolescence, Children 12:131, 1965.
6. Coleman, J. S.: *Youth: Transition to Adulthood* (Chicago: The University of Chicago Press, 1974).
7. Eisenberg, L.: Student unrest: Sources and consequences, Science 167:1688, 1970.
8. Eisenberg, L., and Neubauer, P.: Mental health issues in Israeli collectives, J. Am. Acad. Child Psychiatry 4:426, 1965.
9. Chan, I.: New people in new China: As reflected through education and child rearing. Presented at the Biennial Meeting of the Society for Research in Child Development, Denver, April 11, 1975.
10. Eisenberg, L.: Racism, family and society: A crisis in values, Ment. Hyg. 52:512, 1968.
11. Eisenberg, L.: The *human* nature of human nature, Science 176:123, 1972.

Part II

Preparation for Parenthood and Family Life

6

The Father-Child Relationship:
Some Crucial Issues

Henry Biller, Ph.D.

*Professor of Psychology, University of
Rhode Island, Kingston, R. I., Consultant,
Emma Pendelton Bradley Hospital,
Riverside, R. I., and Consultant, Providence
Veterans Administration Hospital,
Providence, R. I.*

There is little emphasis in our society on fathering behavior. Being a good father often has been equated only with being able to provide an economically sound basis for the child's development. There was a time in our society when a man was regarded as a good father if he had many children, particularly sons. There is more concern now with the population explosion and it is not necessarily looked on favorably to have several children. In any case, there has not been enough acknowledgment of what adult male behavior can have to do with shaping the development of children. There are variations among subcultures, but, in the main, our society is not really reinforcing and acknowledging the kind of impact that men as well as women can have in their relationship with children (Biller, 1971a, 1974b).

Our definitions of masculinity often are related to abilities to control and influence the environment and/or to physical and intellectual prowess, but there is very little emphasis given to the quality of emotional relationships and of interpersonal skills. In terms of definitions of femininity, we have greatly restricted and limited women; the traditional view of femininity has been so overloaded with being a housewife and being a caretaker of children that there was little room for women to develop other talents. Our conceptions of sex roles, and of parental roles, have been very narrow and there has been a severe price paid by many children and adults in terms of their ability to fulfill themselves as individuals (Biller and Meredith, 1975).

Children need both involved fathers and mothers if they are going to be able to realize their talents. There is a need for a cooperative venture, a sharing of commitment by men and women in childrearing. This will help not only men and women to be better parents but to be better people. Adults can grow tremendously from their experiences in being parents. It is a reciprocal process; children influence parents as well as being influenced by them.

PATERNAL DEPRIVATION

An especially dramatic example of the neglect of the father's role can be seen in the literature on the influence of maternal deprivation. The thrust of such literature suggests that the only way a child could suffer from a lack of parenting was to be deprived of a mothering figure. It has just been in recent years that researchers have begun to realize that maternal deprivation is not necessarily equivalent to paternal deprivation and that the potential influence of paternal behavior must also be considered if the effects of parental deprivation are to be understood (Biller, 1971a, 1974b).

Many of the researchers who considered paternal behavior in the early years of family research focused on father-absent families. It seemed difficult to conceptualize specific effects of variations of fathering on children, yet if the father was out of the family there often seemed to be dramatic social and economic consequences and children were more likely to have various types of developmental problems (Biller, 1971a, 1974b; Lynn, 1974).

In most of the initial studies concerning father-absent children, there wasn't any consideration of different types of father-absent families or different types of father-present families. There are tremendous individual differences among both father-absent families and father-present families; yet, some researchers who became concerned with father-absence seemed to be suggesting that it is the only type of paternal deprivation that can exist (Biller, 1971a, 1974b).

It is important to emphasize that father-absence per se does not necessarily lead to developmental deficits and/or render the father-absent child inferior in psychologic functioning relative to the father-present child. Fatherless children are far from a homogeneous group and an almost infinite variety of patterns of father-absence can be specified. Many factors need to be considered in evaluating the father-absent situation: type (constant, intermittent, temporary, etc.), length, cause, the child's age and sex, his constitutional characteristics and developmental status, the mother's reaction to husband-absence, the quality of mother-child interactions, the family's socioeconomic status and the availability of surrogate models. The father-absent child may not be paternally deprived because he has an adequate father-surrogate, or he may be less paternally deprived than many father-present children (Biller, 1970, 1971a, 1974b).

The child who has both mother and father involved and competent is more likely to have generally adequate psychologic functioning and is less likely to suffer from developmental deficits and psychopathology than is the child who is reared in a father-absent family (Biller, 1974b; Biller and Meredith, 1975). This generalization is not the same as assuming that all father-absent children are going to have more difficulties in their development than are all father-present children. For example, there is evidence that indicates that father-absent children with competent mothers are less likely to have certain types of developmental deficits than are children who have a dominating mother and a passive-ineffectual father (Biller, 1968a, 1974b). The father-absent child may develop a more flexible image of adult men, and at least be seeking out some type of father-surrogate, whereas the child with a passive-ineffectual and/or rejecting father may have a negative image of adult males and avoid interacting with them (Biller, 1971a; Reuter and Biller, 1973).

A variety of different types of paternal deprivation in addition to father-absence can be delineated. There is the too frequent occurrence in American society of the father who comes home from work exhausted and all his children ever see is their father lying on the couch or sitting behind a newspaper. A father can be regularly home several hours a day but be giving his children very little (Biller, 1968a; Reuter and Biller, 1973). There are many very dynamic, well liked and professionally successful men who do not constructively relate with their children. Children need to be able to observe and imitate their father's positive characteristics in the context of an ongoing father-child relationship. For example, there is evidence that 4-year-old boys who have fathers who are nurturant with them are likely to be generous with other children (Rutherford and Mussen, 1968).

There needs to be more of a focus on the quality and regularity of the father-child relationship. A strong and positive attachment to a nurturant, competent and available father can much facilitate the child's development, but an attachment to an ineffectual or emotionally disturbed father can be conceived of as a particular form of paternal deprivation. There is evidence that poor personal adjustment is likely to occur among children whose fathers are home a great deal but are very unnurturant or among those whose fathers seldom are home but are highly nurturant. Children need both adequate amounts of paternal availability and paternal nurturance. For example, a child with a highly nurturant but seldom-home father may feel quite frustrated that his father is not home more often and/or may find it difficult to positively imitate such an elusive figure (Biller, 1974b; Reuter and Biller, 1973).

The developmental status of the child when paternal deprivation occurs is another important variable. A meaningful attachment to an involved father can much facilitate the young child's development. For example, there is increasing evidence that paternal nurturance, respect and interest can do much to stimulate the young child's intellectual functioning (Radin, 1972, 1973). On the other hand, the lack of an attachment to a father or father-surrogate during the first few years of life may inhibit some facets of the child's cognitive development (Biller, 1974a, b; Biller and Meredith, 1975; Santrock, 1972).

Paternal deprivation before the age of 4 or 5 appears to have even more of a disruptive effect on the child's personality development than does paternal deprivation beginning at a later age period. For example, boys who become father-absent before the age of 4 or 5 have fewer masculine sex-role orientations (self-concepts) and more sex-role conflicts than either father-present boys or boys who become father-absent at a later time (Biller, 1968b, 1969b; Biller and Bahm, 1971). Other data have indicated that early father-absence often is associated with difficulties in academic functioning (Blanchard and Biller, 1971), a lack of independence and assertiveness in peer relations (Hetherington, 1966), feelings of inferiority and mistrust of others (Santrock, 1970), poor conscience development (Hoffman, 1971), antisocial and delinquent behavior (Siegman, 1966) and various types of psychopathology (Biller, 1974b; Biller and Davids, 1973). There is some evidence that boys are more affected by paternal deprivation than are girls but there is a growing body of research that supports the conclusion that girls are at least as much influenced in their social and heterosexual development by paternal deprivation as are boys (Biller, 1971a, 1971b; Biller and Weiss, 1970; Fish and Biller, 1973; Hetherington, 1972).

THE FATHER-INFANT RELATIONSHIP

The indication that early father-absence can greatly influence the child's personality functioning has led some researchers to take a closer look at the father-infant relationship. Recent studies have revealed that many infants form strong attachments with their fathers even during the first year of life (Kotelchuck, 1973; Pedersen and Robson, 1969; Spelke *et al.*, 1973). These attachments are clearly reflected in the infant's interest in the father's behavior. For example, infants who are attached to their fathers spend much time looking at their fathers, react animatedly when their fathers enter or leave the room and often make movements indicating a desire to be close to their fathers (Biller, 1974b; Pedersen and Robson, 1969). The extent of such father attachment is highly related to the quality of the father's involvement with the infant. Although the formation of the father-infant attachment is generally similar to the mother-infant attachment, many infants tend to differentially express their attachments toward their mothers and fathers. An infant may spend more time looking at his father or may be more interested in playing with his father after he has eaten; he may particularly seek out contact with his mother when he is hungry or tired and prefer cuddling with her. The crucial point, however, is that the infant may, over-all, have as strong or even a stronger attachment to his father (Biller, 1974b; Biller and Meredith, 1975).

Family interaction research has suggested that well-fathered infants are much more curious in exploring their environment than are infants who are paternally deprived. For example, they seem to relate more maturely to strangers and to react more positively to complex and novel stimuli (Biller, 1974b; Spelke *et al.*, 1973). Well-fathered infants seem more secure and trustful in branching out in their explorations and there are also indications that their motor development in terms of crawling, climbing and manipulating objects is advanced. Fathers, when they are involved, tend to be more tolerant than mothers of physical explorations by infants and to actively encourage physical mastery. It is common to observe involved fathers encouraging their infants, vocally and gesturally, to crawl a little farther or climb a little higher. Fathers usually are less concerned if the child gets tired or dirty than are mothers. This generally allows them to tolerate temporary discomforts that the child may experience in his exploration of the environment (Biller, 1974b; Biller and Meredith, 1975).

It should also be added that, unfortunately, fathers are more likely than mothers to institute a clear-cut double standard in terms of the sex of the infant. Some fathers consistently encourage their infant sons' competence in the physical environment but inhibit their infant daughters, fearing for their "fragility." Ironically, there are cases where the daughters were even more robust than the sons were at a similar age (Biller and Meredith, 1975; Biller and Weiss, 1970).

Another factor in the early facilitation of the child's exploration of his environment is that the father provides an additional attachment figure. In many families, the paternally deprived child becomes exclusively attached to the mother, often in a clinging, dependent fashion. Infants who develop an attachment to their fathers as well as to their mothers are likely to have an easier time relating to other relatives and friends. A child who has frequent interactions with both parents has access to a wider variety of experiences and may be more adaptive to changes in his environment. For example, there usually is less separation and stranger anxiety among well-fathered infants. The infant's positive reaction to the returning father may be a prototype to his reaction to the entry of other people into his environment, especially if they are well regarded by those he is already attached to (Biller, 1974b; Biller and Meredith, 1975).

PREPARATION FOR FATHERHOOD

Boys usually do not get many opportunities to interact with young children in a positive, supportive manner. They typically perceive taking care of young children more as a restriction than as a gratifying experience. If older boys can be encouraged to demonstrate their skills, knowledge and experiences to younger children, much can be done to promote a basic foundation for fatherhood. Setting up nursery schools as a part of the family life education curricula of high schools may be one way of giving adolescent males more of an opportunity to interact constructively with young children.

The expectant father should be given more consideration. Often all the attention is focused on the expectant mother and the expectant father is ignored. Many expectant fathers have feelings of alienation and their psychologic and physical health can be adversely affected. Both parents can get involved in childbirth education classes. Husbands can be included in visits to obstetricians and can be with their wives during labor and in the delivery room. The new father should be encouraged to spend considerable time with his wife and infant. The earlier the father can feel involved with the infant the more likely will a strong father-child attachment develop. Whether or not a father changes diapers, dresses or feeds the infant is not the key factor—what is important is that the father and infant find some mutually satisfying activities, and also that the father and mother can develop the view that they both have definite day-to-day responsibilities for the infant's welfare (Biller and Meredith, 1975).

In some cases, the father has to be away from home a great deal. Whether this is a temporary or a relatively permanent situation, adjustments in family schedules can be made to maximize the father's involvement. For example, if the father works until late in the evening, the child can take naps and spend time with him when he comes home, or they can regularly have a special time in the mornings. Also, in many cases children may be able to accompany their fathers to work or the mother and child can go and visit the father during the lunch hour (business and industry should also become more supportive of the father's role). Each family may have a unique situation but there are ways to schedule maximal opportunity for father-child interaction.

CONCLUDING REMARKS

Given the way males and females have been socialized in our society, it is likely that, over and above constitutional predispositions, fathers and mothers will have different ranges of competencies and interests. For example, a father may be more assertive and independent whereas a mother may be more interpersonally sensitive and able to communicate feelings. The optimal situation for the child is to have both an involved mother and an involved father. The child then is exposed to a wider degree of adaptive characteristics. If parents participate in a cooperative way, a better balance for the child can be achieved (Biller and Meredith, 1975).

The opportunities the child has to spend together with both his mother and father are of crucial importance. A child forms much of his attitude toward male-female relationships by watching his mother and father interact. The effective father values his wife's competencies and respects her opinions. The child's self-concept is much influenced by the quality of the father-mother relationship. A father who feels certain about his basic masculinity is more likely to positively accept his wife than one who rejects his masculinity or must constantly prove that he is a man. The effective father encourages his daughter to feel positively about being a female and his son about being a male. He communicates his pride in his children's developing bodies and biologic potentialities. However, this does not mean that he expects his children to rigidly adhere to cultural stereotypes. For example, he fosters the development of assertiveness and independence in his daughters as well as in his sons and the development of nurturance and sensitivity in his sons as well as in his daughters (Biller and Meredith, 1975).

Similarly, school situations that give children the opportunity to interact with competent teachers of both sexes may help facilitate the child's development. Female teachers all too frequently react negatively to assertive behavior in the classroom and seem to feel much more comfortable with girls, who are generally quieter, more obedient and conforming. Boys typically perceive that teachers are much more positive in responding to girls and to feminine behavior and interest patterns (Biller, 1974a). Unfortunately, the type of "feminine" behavior reinforced in the classroom often is of a very negative quality if one is using self-actualization as a criterion. For example, timidity, passivity, dependency, obedience and quietness usually are rewarded. The boy or girl who is independent, assertive, questioning and challenging often is at a great disadvantage in the traditional classroom. Even though girls generally seem to adapt more easily to the early school environment, such an atmosphere is not conducive to their optimal development. Girls as well as boys need to learn how to be independent and assertive.

Of the teachers in the first grade, kindergarten and nursery schools, more than 99% are females (Biller, 1974a). Many of them are very adequate and competent, but if children are going to be more positively socialized and if the massive amount of paternal deprivation in our society is going to be effectively remedied, men are going to have to get involved more in early childhood education, in day care centers and in other child-focused institutions in society (Biller and Meredith, 1975).

REFERENCES

Biller, H. B.: A multiaspect investigation of masculine development in kindergarten-age boys, Genet. Psychol. Monogr. 76:89, 1968a.

Biller, H. B.: A note on father-absence and masculine development in Negro and white boys, Child Dev. 39:1003, 1968b.

Biller, H. B.: Father absence, maternal encouragement, and sex-role development in kindergarten-age boys, Child Dev. 40:539, 1969.

Biller, H. B.: Father absence and the personality development of the male child, Dev. Psychol. 2:181, 1970.

Biller, H. B.: *Father, Child and Sex Role* (Lexington, Mass.: Lexington Books, D. C. Heath, 1971a).

Biller, H. B.: Fathering and female sexual development, Med. Aspects Hum. Sexuality 5: 116, 1971b.

Biller, H. B.: Paternal and Sex-Role Factors in Cognitive and Academic Functioning, in Cole, J. K., and Dienstbier, R. (eds.), *Nebraska Symposium on Motivation, 1973* (Lincoln: University of Nebraska Press, 1974a), pp. 83–123.

Biller, H. B.: *Paternal Deprivation* (Lexington, Mass.: Lexington Books, D. C. Heath, 1974b).

Biller, H. B., and Bahm, R. M.: Father absence, perceived maternal behavior, and masculinity of self-concept among junior high school boys, Dev. Psychol. 4:178, 1971.

Biller, H. B., and Davids, A.: Parent-Child Relations, Personality Development and Psychopathology, in Davids, A. (ed.), *Issues in Abnormal Child Psychology* (Monterey, Calif.: Brooks/Cole, 1973), pp. 48–77.

Biller, H. B., and Meredith, D. L.: *Father Power* (New York: David McKay, 1975).

Biller, H. B., and Weiss, S.: The father-daughter relationship and the personality development of the female, J. Genet. Psychol. 114:79, 1970.

Blanchard, R. W., and Biller, H. B.: Father availability and academic performance among third-grade boys, Dev. Psychol. 4:301, 1971.

Fish, K. D., and Biller, H. B.: Percieved childhood paternal relationships and college females' personal adjustment, Adolescence 8:415, 1973.

Hetherington, E. M.: Effects of paternal absence on sex-typed behaviors in Negro and white preadolescent males, J. Pers. Soc. Psychol. 4:87, 1966.

Hetherington, E. M.: Effects of father-absence on personality development in adolescent daughters, Dev. Psychol. 7:313, 1972.

Hoffman, M. L.: Father absence and conscience development, Dev. Psychol. 4:400, 1971.

Kotelchuck, M.: The nature of the child's tie to his father. Paper presented at the meeting of the Society for Research in Child Development, Philadelphia, April, 1973.

Lynn, D. B.: *The Father: His Role in Child Development* (Monterey, Calif.: Brooks/Cole, 1974).

Pedersen, F. A., and Robson, K. S.: Father participation in infancy, Am. J. Orthopsychiatry 39:466, 1969.

Radin, N.: Father-child interaction and the intellectual functioning of four-year-old boys, Dev. Psychol. 6:353, 1972.

Radin, N.: Observed paternal behaviors as antecedents of intellectual functioning in young boys, Dev. Psychol. 8:369, 1973.

Reuter, M. W., and Biller, H. B.: Perceived paternal nurturance-availability and personality adjustment among college males, J. Consult. Clin. Psychol. 40:339, 1973.

Rutherford, E. E., and Mussen, P. H.: Generosity in nursery school boys, Child Dev. 39: 755, 1968.

Santrock, J. W.: Influence of onset and type of paternal absence on the first four Eriksonian developmental crises, Dev. Psychol. 3:273, 1970.

Santrock, J. W.: Relation of type and onset of father-absence to cognitive development, Child Dev. 43:455, 1972.

Siegman, A. W.: Father-absence during childhood and antisocial behavior, J. Abnorm. Psychol. 71:71, 1966.

Spelke, E., Zelazo, P., Kagan, J., and Kotelchuck, M.: Father interaction and separation protest, Dev. Psychol. 9:83, 1973.

COMMENTARY

DR. MARV MATTHEWS (Honolulu): I am a child psychiatrist and I certainly applaud and agree with everything Dr. Biller said. I see a lot of disturbed families and I am trying to find ways to get fathers more involved. I've tried behavioral prescriptions, lectures, scolding and a good deal of modeling behavior on my part. But so far I really find little that works effectively, so I would like to get you to focus from the global down to the specific. Have you found anything that works clinically?

DR. BILLER: When I am doing family therapy or family diagnosis, I clearly state that the father should be there right from the first. Very often there is all kinds of resistance: The father is working. The father is not really interested. Or the father's responsibility is defended, with the mother saying "It's not really his fault."

What I have found is that if I reach out and am very firm and clear that the father needs to be involved, that I value him, that he is important—not that he has caused the problem, but that he can help—if we can just get him there the first time we're likely to have the beginning of a good therapeutic process.

One of the things that often happens is that we as professionals make it very difficult for the father. We have to be very careful to talk in terms of wanting to learn from him, that we've got to help and share with each other. Therapists and other professionals have to be careful not to give rigid prescriptions or take over family conferences and leave the father feeling left out.

We need to give a tremendous amount of attention to the father's feelings and perspective and also to try to appeal to his strengths and what he can contribute as part of the team, whether it be an educational, medical or psychologic problem.

HENRY MORGANTHAU: I am a public television producer and I produced a program with Dr. Brazelton called *What Makes a Good Father*. Dr. Biller, do you see special and significant differences in the father-son and father-daughter relationships?

DR. BILLER: Yes. Many fathers who on the surface are really involved and care about their daughters have been some of the main perpetuators of our sexist society and our double standards. There are many, many fathers who are very nurturant and very caring but have very low expectations for their daughters in terms of the development of competence in intellectual and physical areas. We have to educate fathers to be more aware of their stereotypes. Fathers are particularly sensitive, seemingly more so than are mothers, to culturally expected differences between boys and girls.

It is very interesting that recent research on adult women who have achieved in science and mathematics and in other areas, including professional athletics and the arts, indicates that they are likely to have had fathers who didn't stereotype them and gave them the strength to be able to deal with authority figures who may have had very low expectations for women. They treated them as individuals and as capable people and then helped them constructively deal with some of the barriers that are so strong in our society against women achieving and contributing outside the home (Biller, 1974b; Biller and Meredith, 1975).

7

Families, and Work, and Jobs

Mary Howell, M.D., Ph.D.

*Assistant Professor of Pediatrics, Harvard
Medical School, Boston, Massachusetts*

I am so glad to have been preceded by Dr. Biller and to hear him argue so strongly that there is no genetic or constitutional reason why men cannot be caretakers. And I presume that to this audience we don't even have to argue that there is no constitutional reason why women cannot be competent workers.

I want to present the thesis that our conventional relationships between work and jobs and families constitute a major stress for families right now, and a major impediment to healthy family life. One of our central assumptions about work and jobs is that while we value work, we despise our jobs. Few of us have jobs that are so comfortable and so substantially rewarded that we find them to be sources of recognizable pleasure.

We are used to thinking that jobs must be draining, aggravating, taking, in return for the income that we have to have. The relatively fortunate few who are professionals, whose jobs have high status and high pay and some autonomy, also complain about their jobs: too demanding of time, too tension-filled and too pressing.

Most jobs in this society are burdensome and they fail to return reward or pleasure in proportion to the time and energy that they take from us. On the other hand, we believe that work is inherently good. We celebrate honest toil and labor in our arts and literature. Our work ethic prescribes a positive attitude toward work, the belief that work should be both necessary and deeply satisfying. We are taught in a thousand ways that the reward of work should be worth the sacrifice of other, perhaps more immediate, gratifications. Freud proposed that a single index of maturity was the ability to love and to work.

In addition, we value effort, mastery and competence. Those values combine with whatever drives are inherent in human beings toward creative completion of tasks. We are thus strongly impelled to believe that we want to work and to do our work well. It seems impossible to discover exactly to what degree those values and drives are wired in as constitutional predispositions of our human existence and to what degree they are learned from our culture. What we extol is

77

work that is done competently and with an invéstment of creativity, involvement, pride, even passion.

Since very few jobs permit that investment, an institution has evolved that justifies, even demands, that it is sufficient to work for income alone. We are carefully instructed from our early years that most people would not work at necessary jobs unless it is arranged that their very livelihood—that is, their ability to feed and clothe and shelter themselves and their families—is at stake. The dreariness and the impossibility of creative investment in most jobs for pay is thereby accepted, for we have been taught that we are basically lazy and that we will do only what needs to be done with that stick of financial fear at our backs.

This schism between valued work and the jobs we are allowed or required to do forces a condition of profound emotional conflict into our everyday lives. Often we turn away from that conflict; we refuse to see it, perhaps because it's too painful to confront. And we argue that the conditions of our jobs have to be unfulfilling, that it would be futile, foolish or idealistic to expect more. Yet, I think we cannot consistently deny the undercurrent of our needs for creativity and mastery and competence in work, and that undercurrent feeds our resentment about our jobs. Jobs don't *have* to be bad, we then think; they just *are* bad.

Our jobs are key factors in our relationships at home, for they are both the means by which we provide money for our families and the major reason, if not excuse, when we fail to provide other kinds of support to family members. As Dr. Biller said in the interchange after he spoke, the father can't come because he has to work. You can't be with your kids because you have to work. There isn't time and there isn't energy because you have to work.

Our jobs, the kinds of work we are allowed to do, dramatically affect the lives of our families. This connection of work, jobs and the earning of family income has a central and pervasive relationship to the quality of life in families. If our investments in our jobs were fully rewarding, if they permitted energetic and creative work in the most positive sense and, most important, if we could moderate our job responsibilities in accord with family needs, we would discover a key element for a society that is truly family supportive.

We exist now amidst conventions that are the polar opposite of family supportive. Most of us labor at jobs that discourage the investment of our individual talents, jobs that are arranged for the profit of others, jobs that are personally demeaning and inadequately paid, jobs that require effort schedules that disregard our membership in families.

Although most of us are not permitted to have creative work to do, we are allowed to work productively. At best, our opportunities for work permit us to know that we have accomplished something worthwhile through a measure of productivity. An exertion of energy and effort that has no recognizable productive outcome does not seem to us to be really worth the label "work." The product that can result from our work may take one or more forms: (1) The product might be a tangible thing, a whole. Crafts work results in objects that are decoratively useful. Farmers and gardeners grow food. Authors write plays or novels or poems. Cobblers make shoes. Relatively few paid jobs now permit a single worker to create a whole product. Some workers, such as artists and crafts workers and many farmers, are self-employed and they create products that they then may sell, but this often is not a source of sufficient income for a family's needs.

(2) The product might be part of a whole instead of a whole. Most factory jobs limit the individual worker's contribution to a relatively small part of the whole item that is produced. This is the principle of assembly line work. Workers have described how they sometimes mark the parts that they produce so that later they can be recognized or identified, even if that mark is defacing. Construction workers also contribute to the making of a whole. Perhaps because their projects take a long time to complete and are one of a kind, construction workers often point out years afterward their contribution to that building or that road "that I have built."

(3)The product can be measured in the aggregate as a lot of little tasks completed. People who do repair work or piecework and most service workers — barbers and nurses and clerks in stores—can identify a product by the number of pieces of work done in a day or a week: TV sets repaired, patients cared for, items sold, customers waited on. The more discrete and individual the tasks, the easier it is to count the aggregate as a product.

(4)The product can be measured by a demarcation of time. Toiling a whole day, with or without punching a time clock, may identify the productivity of one's work as time set off from other time. Work begins and work ends and the time spent in between is a product that can be identified by its duration.

(5)Finally, the product may be a pay check or money earned as fees. Work for pay is in fact the most usual definition of productive work in our society, but it seems restrictive to exclude work that is productive by other criteria even if it is not worth a salary. Still, we do tend to rate effort according to the salary that is paid for it. Salary scales are critical determiners of the flow of money and goods and services between us, even though many of us would agree that the income of some workers does not correspond to the true value of their work.

U.S. Census reports list the earnings of adults employed full time and that list gives a kind of ranking of the worth of various jobs in our society. Workers who provide services to people—that is, caregivers—are among those who earn least. Caring for children, when it earns any salary at all, is so disgracefully ill-paid that it's hard to believe that children have any value, even as objects, in the institution of work and jobs. Taking care of garbage—that is, collecting garbage—is a more valued occupation according to salary paid for it than taking care of children or other dependent folk.

About a third of adults in our society spend most of their time in another kind of effort—the maintenance of their households and the personal sustenance of members of their families. "Are you a housewife or do you work?" accurately reflects the irony of that arrangement. Taking care of family members and their property does not in its essentials meet the criteria for productive work. There are no products, either in whole or in part, that need to be made by the homemaker. Nor is time defined by a limited schedule of hours. Nor is there any pay.

There are, after all, very few products that a contemporary homemaker needs to make. Almost every conceivable kind of household goods can be purchased at a price less than the cost of homemade. Store-bought socks and bread in their inexpensive varieties may not be as well made nor as suited to family tastes as the products that most homemakers could create, but by their very existence they negate the necessity of the homemaker's efforts to make socks and bread. It usually is an extravagance of time and money to create a product for family use.

Can the child that one cares for, or one's spouse, be counted as product? Certainly in many societies children have been looked on as their parents' property, to do with as parents will without outside interference. And wives sometimes do take surrogate pride in their husbands' appearance, behavior and career success. But to count another human being—no matter how much one has worried and fussed and invested in the other's welfare—to count a person as a product, a thing, is really deeply demeaning of that other person. They say that behind every good man there is a good woman, but if he is her product, what credit goes to his own efforts? If my children are my products, then they are only objects kept in good repair without the inner stuff of humanity.

Further, both husband and children then are obligated to act for mother's sake in order to validate her sense of productivity. The husbands of traditional homemakers find ways to defend against their wives' need to regard them as product. Children, however, have fewer defenses and the children of traditional homemakers can be made to feel that they are required to confirm mother's work by their very existence.

Most of the tasks the homemaker accomplishes are continuous and have no end point. In any family with several members, neither the kitchen counters nor the floors stay clean for any perceptible space of time. As soon as the cleaning task is finished, and sometimes before it is even done, crumbs and dirty dishes and bits of paper and toys and coats and mittens are strewn about. One of the sad/funny games of family life is the game of "stay out of the kitchen for an hour, mother has just cleaned it up"—an artificiality of pretense to counter the fact that her efforts are unending.

Many of the traditionally male chores of household maintenance are discontinuous and can more easily be countered as tasks completed. Building shelves, repairing electrical appliances, laying carpets are once-only events, or at least chores to be done on separate and discrete occasions. Unlike the so-called traditionally female chores, the jobs customarily assigned to men and boys can also be postponed to a moment of convenience whereas feeding hungry people, keeping clothing in wearable condition and washing dishes and cookware cannot wait.

Homemakers do not, of course, punch a time clock. "Woman's work is never done" is an apt description of the responsibility of housekeeping and also an acknowledgement that the never-ending chores of homemaking have readily been assigned to (although perhaps not so readily accepted by) women. The responsibility of sustaining the members of a family runs for 24 hours of the day and 7 days of the week. There is no sick leave, often no vacation and almost certainly no sabbatical. Without any demarcation, time loses the landmarks of productive work.

Finally, the homemaker is not paid a salary. Housewives' wages have been proposed. The discussion has arisen more and more frequently in recent years and I think it warrants very careful consideration. For instance, will the hourly wage be at a very low level, thus further reinforcing our regard for the responsibility of other people as of little value? (Does "priceless" sometimes mean of no value?) Is the rationale that assigns this work primarily to women, or to any *one* person in a family, so clear and so desirable that it should be reinforced? What will happen to our already fragile family solidarity if we exchange money for the services that we have been doing for one another in unpaid exchange? If the exchange now is uneven in traditional families, as many believe it is, will the translation of personal caregiving into wage work help resolve those irksome inequities? Could that monetary adjustment really enable men and women, husbands and wives, fathers and mothers, to participate in adult life more even-handedly?

I think that to establish the system of wages for keeping one's own house and family in order could threaten family life as no other recent change has done. To discredit our private systems of exchange of unpaid services and to bring government regulation into our most personal relationships could change families profoundly. To seal any adult, male or female, into full-time involvement in a single one-sided role—sealed either into a role that severely restricts the satisfactions of productive work or into a role that precludes the satisfactions of contributing to the personal maintenance of one's family—could shatter the very bonds that now seem most likely to hold us together as families.

Despite these forebodings about the effects of instituting housewives' wages as a long-term strategy for strengthening our families, such a scheme might be useful or even necessary as a tactic in the short run. There is no question that segregation of the bulk of the responsibility for family and household maintenance into the hands of only one family member now stands as a major impediment to family solidarity and collaboration. The arrangement often is justified because it allows the adults who are taken care of to invest the greatest part of their time and energy in paid jobs. This arrangement suits the needs of employers and thus is a linchpin of our commercial economy.

If all family members shared their mutual responsibility to maintain themselves, their dependents and their property, jobholders would not be able to make the same degree of personal investment in the commercial interest of others, as now is the rule. Every worker then would have to create a balance between work investment and family investment.

It might be that the most direct redress of this economic ill is to be found in an economic solution, that is, the temporary institution of housewives' wages. The effects of paying family members for their family maintenance efforts would include a near-overthrow of our usual and customary conventions of gross national product, unemployment calculations, employment benefits, including vacations and retirement income, and taxation. If we go through and beyond this upheaval, we might then revise policy to promote a livable range of options, permitting each family member to work productively and to take care of family responsibilities, with those family responsibilities again secured in the realm of private and unpaid exchange of service.

It is important to reflect on the distinction between paid work and productive work. Although paid work is always productive in the sense that the pay check or salary is one kind of product, productive work need not be paid work. Many who are not employed for salary, and some who are, find or take the time to work productively at home or at volunteer jobs, making a variety of products (such as paintings and furniture) or parts (collective quilting, fund-raising) or aggregates (like house-to-house canvassing or neighborhood service projects).

Although earning a paycheck is only one of several criteria for a sense of productivity in work, there are significant consequences to an arrangement in which only one adult meets the family's needs for income. When one parent is entirely exempt from the responsibility of earning family income, or even when the income that he or she earns is earmarked for luxuries or supposedly unnecessary expenses, any productive work done by that person is viewed as being of less value and importance to the family's welfare than is the work for essential income.

Do adults need to do productive work? Like most questions about human needs and motives, that question is very difficult to answer as an absolute. We can, however, consider what people tell us about their lives when they don't do productive work, either by choice or by force of circumstance.

Productive work in our society is so highly valued that it serves as a measure of self-esteem. The self-esteem is partly internally imposed. Men and women who have engaged in productive work and then have lost their jobs give eloquent testimony to their ensuing self-disparagement, depression, self-blame and guilt. The reaction is similar whether the employee is male or female, and whether the job was lost because of a layoff or because family needs demanded a presence that was incompatible with job requirements.

In addition, there is self-esteem externally derived from the opinions of respected others. Anyone who is not a productive worker is discouraged, sometimes subtly and sometimes openly, and is assumed to be less than adult in an essential dimension, whether one is an unemployed male, a retired worker, a homemaker or a mother on welfare.

Productive work, if it accrues any income at all, offers a degree of economic independence. The converse, economic dependence, is for an adult a condition that is both demeaned and insecure. Young adults who still are students, not welcome in the job market and therefore engaged in prolonged education or training programs preparing them to find "good" jobs, are belittled for their dependence on parents or on scholarship funds. Their behavior often is closely monitored and strongly censured because they are not economically independent. Homemakers with no personal income are equally subject to stringent control of their behavior, both by their husbands and by others who believe that economic dependence justifies or requires subjection to supervision. The fact that some homemakers do not perceive themselves to be closely supervised is not contradictory. For many of them a serious error of judgment in management of the family budget, in care of the household property or in child rearing would bring criticism from their husbands (who are arbiters of errors of judgment) in a manner more appropriate to a disparaged employee or an immature child than to an equal partner. Single parents using Aid for Families with Dependent Children funds are similarly subject to regulation in return for the receipt of public funds.

Effective protest against such regulation is difficult if there is no foreseeable means of becoming economically independent, as when an unemployed wife has not held a job for many years. If protest involves risk of losing one's means of financial support, there is reason for fear. The precipitous drop in the living standard of most women who are divorced is well documented.

When family responsibilities are entirely segregated, when one adult produces income and the other maintains the household, both parties may feel aggrieved, may argue that their burden is the more onerous, and no reasonable comparison can be made between them. Apples and oranges cannot be precisely valued against each other. We can assume, however, that the marriage partner who is unwilling to share his or her responsibilities and to undertake a share of the other's burdens probably believes, despite any verbal arguments to the contrary, that his or her present status is the more privileged.

Productive work also gives a variety of personal benefits over and above self-esteem and the capability for economic independence. Unless the job is done alone there are likely opportunities to talk with others about a variety of things, to have conversations that might never occur with members of one's own family. There are opportunities also to develop strong and sustaining personal friendships. We know, understand and develop affection for those whom we see repeatedly on a face-to-face basis and with whom we share space and time. If the work is away from home there is refreshment in the daily cycle of leaving home and returning. Some adults who have no reason or obligation to separate from home base virtually imprison themselves at home.

There may also be opportunities in work to learn new skills, which can be valued as opportunities for personal growth and change. Some workers change jobs when new jobs are available as soon as they feel they have learned all they can in their present situation.

Any given work opportunity thus offers a mix of these dividends. Sometimes the dividends are social contact, friendships, bits of gossip and news, a change of scene, the development of a sense of competence in the minutiae of one's work. Sometimes these are the predominant benefits of our jobs. Something like three-quarters of adults holding paid jobs say they would continue at their work even if they did not need the money, which attests to the varied benefits we perceive to come from our jobs over and above the incomes we earn.

Some adults are not permitted to engage in productive work. There may be no jobs available for them. Or they don't have access to education and training in skills that enable them to find work, paid or unpaid. Or they are victimized by discriminatory employment practices. Or members of their family forbid them to take employment. Or they themselves are caught in a net of self-definition that damns them if they do not hold jobs and damns them in a different way if they do; the conventional obligations of full-time housewifery make many employed mothers feel guilty.

All who are excluded from opportunities for work are deprived of formal and informal benefits. As individuals, we need these benefits in different proportions and we give them different priorities, but it seems likely that most adults would profit from the experience of doing productive work.

The nature of the jobs available to us is a grievous problem for families. At present, most jobs in our society are unsuitable for any adult who is deeply engaged in the life of his or her family, especially when the family includes small children or any member with special needs. Most jobs require a time and energy commitment that leaves the worker little to invest in family matters. Many workers hold more than one job to try to meet their family's financial needs. Others, especially in career jobs, find themselves obligated to work many more than 40 hours a week. Responding to an article about flexible training hours for young physicians who are also parents, one man wrote about "the system that trains us to help others solve marital and personal problems and is designed to weaken or destroy our personal and marital lives."

Over and above the formal requirements of time spent at the job or in job-related activities, there is an assumption, sometimes implicit and sometimes made forthrightly to job applicants, that the affairs of one's work will be a consuming interest and will take priority over merely personal matters. Few employees feel comfortable about taking time off from work to nurse a sick child or spouse, to shop for family needs or to attend a child's school play or a spouse's seminar. The activities of caring for one's family are somehow counted as frivolous, in the same category as sunning on the beach or going to a movie. On the contrary, many employers expect that workers are cheerfully willing and able to work overtime on short notice no matter what their families' needs or the expectation for their presence at home. By the time employees rise to executive positions, they often are so well trained in this attitude that they regard a game of golf or a long lunch with business contacts as permissible, but equal amounts of time off on behalf of family needs as out of the question.

This psychic devotion to job, employer and corporation that is expected of the worker is in the long run probably more destructive to family life than the flat fact of hours at work. Up to a point, energy, time and interest invested in our jobs can refuel or refresh our availability to family members. Beyond that point, we are drained, preoccupied and irritable. We may even resent expectations that our relationships within our families involve personal giving as well as taking. The irritability arises not just from fatigue but also from our own repressed desire to give and from internalized guilt about impotence in becoming more available to family.

I just want to mention two other conventions in work arrangements. One is that most of our jobs are so physically distant from our homes that when we leave home to go to work we virtually lose contact with our families. Many employees are forbidden to have phone calls even to keep them in touch with family members. The other is that we have in this society punished small collaborative or family-owned businesses and organizations and have rewarded enormous institutionalized bureaucracies as places for people to work; in the process of doing so, we have also managed to make it difficult, if not impossible, for employees to band together and to take effective action to determine the style in which they work—such things as whether there are day care facilities on-site at the place of work, and the whole question of hours and flexibility with regard to family needs.

I'm going to stop there with an analysis of the problem of work and jobs and families because time is up. I am sorry that there is not enough time for me to drop the other shoe and to discuss solutions. The problem, I think, is very pressing: unless solutions begin to be evolved, I think our families are in real jeopardy.

COMMENTARY

CHAIRMAN DR. WILLIAM CAREY (Media, Pa.): What differences can you point to in the physical health of those who are productively and unproductively occupied? I know they're there. I am wondering what you can tell us about that.

DR. HOWELL: I certainly don't have any data on it, except, of course, that those who are not productively employed tend to be poor and that has all kinds of consequences for physical health in terms of nutrition.

THE CHAIRMAN: But the loss of job has not only psychologic hazards, but physical health may also suffer as well.

DR. HOWELL: I expect that is true. When I was reviewing the literature for this I found it fascinating that the great bulk of studies on the effect of loss of employment or being unemployed are all about men. We have now, increasingly, anecdotes about how women feel when they are unemployed or when they have lost their jobs. There probably are some studies that I am not aware of about consequences for physical health. I would guess, however, that they mostly deal with male subjects.

THE CHAIRMAN: But they surely are there. At least I have the impression that it makes a big difference.

Are there other questions for Dr. Howell?

MARY CHRISTINA DE LA TORRE: I am a resident physician in family medicine at Duke in Durham. I would like to ask you some solutions. What are your thoughts regarding women in medicine, especially during their training years, when apparently the system distorts our values so that the mother who gives the least supervision to her child apparently is seen as the most dedicated physician?

I've been working an average of 100–120 hours a week on 75% of my rotations during the past year. I think that as physicians we are concerned about children's emotional development, but with the present system our own homes are far away from being models.

Do you have any suggestions about what could be done to improve the emotional needs of our own families?

DR. HOWELL: I couldn't agree with you more. I think the problem may be more acutely realized by women in medicine, but it is not a problem of women. It's a problem of parents and family members. Fathers are hurt by that schedule of 100–120 hours a week just as much as mothers are, and their children most of all. It is an insane way to train people to understand what family life is like.

DR. BILLER: I wonder if I could make a few brief comments. I think that that is a major occupational hazard and certainly most particularly and keenly felt in training in medicine. Obviously there needs to be a real concerted effort in making the training demands more realistic. In many fields I think the people who are being trained get treated like slave labor. They get treated in a way that really demeans them, makes them hostile toward the people they're working with as well as possibly toward their families, if they're living with their families.

I think it really has a terrible cost on our society and it needs to be changed. I have one suggestion that is only a very temporary kind of thing and maybe only covers a minute number of cases. Many people who work long hours or have

85

very different kinds of schedules can at least to some extent work with their families so that they can spend time with their children, even if it means that the kids take naps so that they can see their fathers and mothers between 2 and 4 in the morning or if it means that the family is going to eat their dinner at 6 o'clock in the morning.

This may seem radical and impractical, but with the kind of effects on families when the children don't have any kind of continuity and regularity in their relationships with their parents this might make some improvement. I think we can be more flexible in terms of what kinds of schedules our children have. Some of us get locked in—that the kids have to get up at a certain time, go to bed at a certain time, eat at a certain time.

Another suggestion—and maybe people in mental health professions can lead the way in this—is taking children to work with us. For some of us that may be very impractical, but it can be sometimes taking them to class or to conventions or to certain meetings or to the office, or maybe trying to do more of our work at home.

I know, and probably many of you know, in terms of generations of physicians in different families that one reason why many people have kept their commitment to medicine is that they really got involved with their fathers and mothers when they were young children, when there used to be more family medicine and people used to make house calls. In the case of some physicians I've talked to they got intensely involved in medicine when they were watching one of their parents go out and answer emergencies and they weren't left at home. It wasn't something that was separated. Obviously those are relatively rare occurrences, but I think children can learn so much from being with us and I think we've got to break down this terrible segregation between our work days and our time at home.

DR. HOWELL: This is an aside, but I was remembering when one of our children was 4 and used to come with me on house calls. He said one time in the car, "Why do you give shots to people when you go and visit them? That's not polite!"

8

Effect of Modern Obstetric Care on the Family

Michael Newton, M.D.

Professor of Obstetrics and Gynecology,
Pritzker School of Medicine, The University
of Chicago, Chicago, Illinois

The family begins with the relationship between a man and a woman, but it really is not a family until a child is born. Therefore, the events immediately preceding and surrounding the birth of a child have great importance for family development.

These events perhaps are most significant for the first child and for the mother and her child, but they are also vitally important in the patterns of relationship between the father and the child, between the mother and the father in their role as parents and also for the introduction of other siblings into the family.

What do we mean by obstetrics? Traditionally, obstetrics means standing by or standing with a woman who is laboring and delivering. It refers to the presence and assistance that may be given to such a person. More broadly, however, it may be used to cover the whole series of events surrounding the arrival of a child.

It is impossible, of course, to separate obstetrics either in the narrow or the broad sense from cultural, social and economic factors affecting the family. Because obstetrics may be pivotal, even crucial, in the development of family relationships, I think that it is important to examine what we do now and how it may affect the family.

I would like, first, to make a comparison between what I would describe as nonmodern or traditional obstetric care and modern obstetric care; second, to break down the component parts of modern obstetric care and evaluate their effect on the family; and, third, to attempt to analyze some of the trends in current obstetric care and figure out how perhaps these may affect the family.

First of all, what do we mean by nonmodern or traditional obstetric care? It is hard to make a clear distinction in dates between nonmodern and modern obstetrics. I suppose I would really regard the dividing line as about the year 1800. This may surprise you, but in the early 1800s we had the development, first of all, of ergot derivatives to prevent postpartum hemorrhage. We had the acceptance to a greater extent of obstetric forceps. We had the development of anesthetics for delivery. And, finally, we had what people have described as the rise of the male midwife.

I would like to divide obstetric care into five parts. The first part is the diagnosis of pregnancy. If we look at the diagnosis of pregnancy in traditional obstetric care, it really was a haphazard matter. Many preliterate peoples did not really understand physiology, so that pregnancy was diagnosed by suspicion, by movement and even by the appearance of the baby.

Those of you who are familiar with medical history will also recall some of the fascinating tales about uroscopy, which from olden times has been regarded as a method of diagnosing pregnancy by studying, usually with the naked eye, the urine of a woman [1]. These, however, are mostly fantastic tales.

The second area of obstetric care is that of care during pregnancy – antepartal care. When we go back before 1900, when the first prenatal care clinics were developed in Boston, we can discern no regular pattern of obstetric antepartal care. On the other hand, many peoples had patterns of behavior toward the pregnant woman. For example, many cultures felt responsibility for the development of the fetus, with protective feelings toward the mother and the father. Some social groups also felt solicitude for the pregnant woman. Various feelings were associated with pregnancy, such as feelings of sexual adequacy, vulnerability or even shame. Last, most preliterate cultures had elaborate dietary patterns for pregnant women. Often these patterns involved deprivation of important elements in diet, such as protein. Frequently they had taboos. For example, one tribe is reported to have had the taboo that the pregnant woman should not eat howler monkey meat because if she did it might predispose the infant to excessive crying [2].

Third, labor and delivery. Labor and delivery in traditional obstetric care was conducted as a home experience – the laboring woman attended by a specially knowledgeable woman or midwife or often by no attendant at all. Pain relief in the form of analgesics or anesthetics was not known, nor was operative intervention; and for both mother and child, the mortality and morbidity often was very high.

The fourth part of obstetric care is the postpartum period or puerperium. In traditional obstetric care, mother and baby were close, usually in the same room, often in the same bed. Breast-feeding was universally accepted and practiced. Because the laboring woman usually was part of an extended family, they were able to provide her with care in the puerperium. But she was also subject to some dangers, such as puerperal fever.

The last aspect of obstetric care is that of family planning. In traditional obstetric care, there was no consistently effective method of planning families. Individually used methods had varying success among different peoples. For example, such practices as coitus interruptus, various medications and even occlusive devices are widely described [3]. Abortion was a somewhat uncertain affair. For example, in a 1969 article in *Science,* 17 possible methods of causing an abortion were taken from the works of Pliny, a Roman historian. Among these were the use of the raven's egg and of vipers. Exactly how these technics were to be employed was not explained in the translation and I doubt if Pliny knew either [4].

Let us now compare traditional care with modern obstetric care. What is modern obstetric care? It is a little difficult to define. I suppose that most of us think of obstetric care today as doctor, hospital, delivery room, nursery—four characteristic descriptive words.

I am reminded of four films that were produced in the past 12 years, entitled *Modern Obstetrics,* and all made by groups of people intimately involved in the delivery of care. The first one was entitled *Normal Delivery,* and this showed the typical hospital delivery, with one operative delivery (including the use of forceps) and an episiotomy and then, as an afterthought, a spontaneous delivery. The others were entitled *Postpartum Hemorrhage, Pre-eclampsia-Eclampsia* and *Cesarean Section* [5]. This, I think, provides an addition to the words I mentioned earlier, the application of modern technical achievements that go into obstetric care.

Modern obstetric care in the early 1800s wasn't quite always like this. Richard Tuite [6] wrote a book published in New York in 1828 entitled *A Compendium of Operative Midwifery*. He started out with a rather idealistic statement: "If the importance of a science is to be calculated from the practical ability to which it may be applied and the beneficial effects which may result from it, what can be more important than that science whose immediate object is to assist woman laboring with her birth? What charge can be more responsible than the trust of the lives of both mother and offspring, or what idea more impressive than the reflection that their fate not infrequently depends upon our judgment and skill?"

One of our current dilemmas is that these ideals have been overshadowed by our many technical achievements.

Modern obstetric care has had profound effects on maternal mortality. In 1920, we had a maternal death rate of approximately 80 per 10,000 live births in this country. In 1960, the rate was 3.7 per 10,000 live births. In 1972, the last year for which data are available, the rate was 2.4 per 10,000 live births. In 52 years, the maternal death rate has fallen to about 3% of the original rate. As a specific recent example of this, in Mississippi maternal deaths from hemorrhage fell from 29 to 10 between 1957 and 1961 [7].

There has been a similar fall in neonatal and perinatal deaths, and whether we worry about our country's position relative to other nations or not (and I think we should), we still can demonstrate a dramatic fall in perinatal mortality in this country over the past 50 years.

What about the specific effects of modern obstetric care on the five categories of obstetric care that I mentioned earlier in relation to nonmodern or traditional obstetric care?

First of all, diagnosis. We are a lot further ahead in the diagnosis of pregnancy. It now is easily possible to make a diagnosis of pregnancy approximately 40 days after the last normal menstrual period, and it is very likely that within a short period of time the use of the radioimmunoassays of chorionic gonadotropin will permit a diagnosis of pregnancy before the missed menstrual period. This is an enormous development from uroscopy or even waiting until the baby has moved.

Second, antepartal care. Here, we begin to see some of the effects of modern obstetrics on the family. Modern antepartal care, to most people, implies attendance at a physician's office or a clinic, having a detailed history and examination performed, usually including a pelvic examination plus laboratory work, all of which might be described as a variety of invasive and noninvasive technics. Often in the course of antepartal care, the family and the husband are excluded. Advice given by professionals to women often comes in the form of specific instructions, and sometimes these instructions have been misguided, as, for example, the instruction not to gain too much weight during pregnancy and not to eat salt during pregnancy. Both of these should now be fading from the scene. Also, a pregnancy with its antepartal care and the visits to the physician and hospital involves a financial commitment, which places a great burden on the family.

Third, labor and delivery. We are dealing here with an entirely different situation from traditional obstetric care. In the United States, except for a few places, delivery is conducted in the hospital. This is in contrast to Holland and to large portions of the world. The hospital is a strange place to most young women having their first baby. They usually have to drive some distance to get there. They are subjected to all kinds of new procedures. The unfamiliar surroundings and people are naturally conducive to fear, and this leads to tension and then to pain, as Dr. Grantley Dick-Read described many years ago [8].

The fear/tension/pain syndrome has its own medical consequences. It results in the necessity for using pharmacologic methods of relieving pain and this, in turn, results in more operative deliveries, such as the use of forceps and episiotomy. One result of this is illustrated by a study I and my co-workers reported several years ago. When episiotomy is performed, the amount of blood loss by chemical measurement is considerably greater than when neither episiotomy nor laceration of the birth canal occurs—360 ml as opposed to 207 ml. This amount of blood loss may not be immediately serious, but it may produce some debility for the puerperal woman, which may prevent her being able to look after her family adequately [9].

The last consequence of hospital delivery is the immediate separation of the mother and baby, which is practiced in most hospitals in the United States. This means, of course, that the baby may be shown to the mother, but then is promptly whisked off to a nursery to be observed by "qualified nurses and pediatricians."

Fourth, the postpartum period. There are certain consequences of our form of care. First, the puerperal woman is exposed to a conflict in medical care. She has had her obstetrician for a number of months and now she must carry out his instructions while her baby is in charge of a pediatrician, and sometimes the twain never meet.

A second thing that happens is that she usually does not, in this culture, in the United States, breast-feed her baby. This is a consequence of mother/baby separation, but also a part of the emotional factors surrounding the hospital confinement. Even if she tries to breast-feed, she often is disturbed and the amount of milk she gives is sharply reduced because of failure of her ejection reflex. Such disturbance can also affect milk secretion and therefore may be a further important factor in decreasing the incidence of breast-feeding. Attitude toward breast-feeding has many components, but greatly affects milk yield and is also important in the current incidence of breast-feeding [10].

Perhaps the characteristic feeling of a woman in a hospital environment after delivery is that of loneliness. She is lonely for her children (if she has them), for her husband, for her extended family. Too often, visiting hours are limited. Finally, when she goes home, she is lonely again because her husband, having taken a few days off from work, then has to return to work and it often is difficult for her mother to come from, say, Seattle to Philadelphia to take care of her; thus, she is alone with her newborn child.

Last, modern obstetric care and family planning. We now have reasonably reliable methods of family planning that were not available even as little as 15 years ago, and this makes an enormous difference in the ability of a parent or parents to plan their families. We also have in this country, at least at present, reliable methods of terminating pregnancies should contraceptive measures fail.

If I were to summarize the effects of modern obstetrics, I would say that we have reduced remarkably (and we should not forget this) maternal and perinatal mortality. We have taken birth out of the family environment and in so doing we have to a large part excluded the father—in some cases I think we may have substituted the obstetrician for the father. We have made the mother lonely, lonely in the clinic, in the office and in the hospital. And we have separated the mother from the baby. Another consequence is that the incidence of breast-feeding has decreased, and perhaps this is the greatest change in infant nurture that has occurred in the human race. Last, we now have available reasonably reliable methods of family planning.

All of these things have some good and some bad and some incalculable effects. The trouble, it seems to me, is that the good often affects the individual and the bad or incalculable affects the family. For example, it is, I should say, a good thing that perinatal mortality has been reduced, but, on the other hand, this has resulted in the survival of sick, delicate babies who pose an enormous economic and emotional strain on the family.

Births in the hospital perhaps have helped reduce some of the complications of delivery. On the other hand, they have developed an emotional bias that has militated against family closeness, closeness between father and mother, closeness between mother and baby and closeness of the family as a whole.

The decrease in breast-feeding has affected the health of our babies and the closeness between the mother and her baby. We were traveling to San Diego recently and a young lady with a baby sat down beside us in the airplane. The sequence of events that followed is interesting. At first, the baby slept in a little cart in front of the mother. After a while, about an hour and a half into this 4-hour flight, the baby began to stir. The mother woke the baby up, played with him for a while until he was fully awake. The baby then made that characteristic noise that says "I want to feed." Those of you who have breast-fed babies know the curious noise that babies make under these circumstances. The mother immediately fed the baby and he went back to sleep. There was an interaction between two people here. The baby made a little stir, the mother woke him up, the baby made a feeding noise and the mother fed him. Both were satisfied. The baby went back to sleep and the mother went back to reading her book. This kind of intensely close personal relationship is one of the things that perhaps we have lost by the decrease in breast-feeding.

Finally, the effect of contraception. We now have a method of spacing children, but we also have side-effects. The hormonal and emotional effects, particularly of the oral contraceptives, have yet really not been determined. I think we have both good, bad and incalculable effects with that aspect of modern obstetric care.

How does the future look? Are the antifamily effects of modern obstetric care going to get worse? Or are there encouraging signs that something will occur or can be done to ameliorate them?

I think that there are some encouraging findings, some encouraging activities. Let me list a few of the things that I believe are hopeful signs in obstetrics, particularly in this country.

First, in pregnancy, preparation in parenthood classes seems to me to be a substantial advance in knowledge for the pregnant mother and father.

Second, I think that there is more consciousness of dietary advice. Yesterday morning when I was driving down to the Chicago Lying-in Hospital I turned on the radio—and this was prime time, about 9 o'clock—and I heard an advertisement for good nutrition in pregnancy. To me, this was a sign that the public was becoming conscious of the importance of good nutrition in making a pregnancy healthy and in preparing for a healthy baby.

Third, I think that we have increased involvement of fathers before, during and after birth, and this is a valuable step forward.

Fourth, I think that the distinction between normal and abnormal obstetrics is important. We have tended to regard in our modern obstetric care both the abnormal and the normal patient as presenting the same kind of problem, and I don't think that this is really true. Dr. William Smellie, one of the first male midwives, writing in 1752, said the following: "For a further illustration and to inform young practitioners that difficult cases do not frequently occur, suppose of 3,000 women in one town or village 1,000 shall be delivered in the space of one year, and in 990 of these births the child shall be born without other than common assistance..." [11]. What he meant was that there was only about 1% of abnormalities in obstetrics. He may have been underestimating this, but the basic point that he made, and one that we need to recognize and I think are beginning to recognize, is that obstetric care can be divided into that of the normal patient and the abnormal patient.

As a consequence of this, a fifth point. The use of nurse-midwives and nurse-clinicians to provide support and help for the normal patient is extremely important.

Sixth, making the hospital surroundings more home-like. I believe that this is a slow process but one conducive to a better obstetric experience for the family.

Seventh, increased attention to physical and emotional support during labor and delivery. This can increase closeness of a family at a crucial event in their lives, and also enable the mother to better cope with her puerperium.

Eighth, I think that we are tending—at least I hope we are tending—to separate mothers and babies less during hospitalization; and I believe that the encouragement of breast-feeding, such as is being promoted by the La Leche League, is a very important step.

Ninth, some sort of return to the extended family, whether it be by family members themselves or by neighbors, may provide the mother who just comes from having a baby with the support that she needs in the early days and weeks after delivery and so contribute to family closeness.

Finally, the greater availability and effective use of family planning as a family affair will help us produce, I think, more wanted children.

To conclude: The family starts before a child is born. Second, family patterns are, I believe, set long before slow learning, truancy and adolescent rebellion appear. One of the most important areas in which we can concentrate now and in the future is the pregnancy, labor and delivery and immediate postpartum experience of mother, father and child—not only as individuals, as I think we do to some extent now, but, more important, as a unit.

REFERENCES

1. Forbes, T. R.: Pregnancy and Fertility Tests, in *The Midwife and the Witch* (New Haven, Conn.: Yale University Press, 1966), Chap. 3.
2. Mead, M., and Newton, N.: Cultural Patterning of Perinatal Behavior, in Richardson, S. A., and Guttmacher, A. F. (eds.), *Childbearing: Its Social and Psychological Aspects* (Baltimore: The Williams & Wilkins Company, 1967).
3. Newton, N.: Population limitation in cross-cultural perspective. I. Patterns of contraception, J. Reprod. Med. 1:343, 1968.
4. McCully, J.: Pliny's pheromonic abortifacients, Science, p. 165, July 18, 1969.
5. Film Series. Modern Obstetrics (Normal Delivery; Postpartum Hemorrhage; Preeclampsia-Eclampsia; and Cesarean Section): Produced by the American College of Obstetricians and Gynecologists and the American Medical Association in cooperation with Ortho Pharmaceutical Corporation; available from Ortho Pharmaceutical Corporation, Raritan, New Jersey.
6. Tuite, R.: *Compendium of Operative Midwifery* (New York: Charles S. Francis, 1828).
7. Newton, M.: Maternal mortality in Mississippi: The first five year report 1957–1961, J. Miss. State Med. Assoc. 5:453, 1964.
8. Dick-Read, G.: *Childbirth Without Fear* (New York: Harper, 1953).
9. Newton, M., Mosey, L. M., Egli, G. E., Gifford, E. B., and Hull, C. T.: Blood loss during and after delivery, Obstet. Gynecol. 17:9, 1961.
10. Newton, N., and Newton, M.: Psychological aspects of lactation, N. Engl. J. Med. 277:1179, 1967.
11. Smellie, W.: *A Treatise on the Theory and Practice of Midwifery* (London: D. Wilson, 1752).

COMMENTARY

DR. PETER SAWCHUK (Summit, N. J.): Dr. Newton, what are your feelings on Dr. Leboyer's thoughts on childbirth?

DR. NEWTON: My wife sponsored Dr. Leboyer when he was in Chicago and I went to a lecture he gave on the Northwestern campus and had a chance to talk to him. I think the important thing is that he is paying attention to the baby as a person shortly after birth. He describes himself as being a standard routine-type obstetrician, who then became satisfied that mothers were obtaining a good experience because of the use of psychoprophylaxis and similar technics. Thus, he came to worry less about the mother and began to pay attention to the baby.

He is emphasizing the importance of treating the baby gently after birth. It actually is a technic that is worthy of experimental investigation and I think that it would be relatively easy to do such a study.

Dr. Leboyer spoke at Rush-Presbyterian Medical Center in Chicago and the next morning a baby was delivered there using the Leboyer technics. Shortly after the baby reached the nursery, the nursery nurse spoke to the obstetric supervisor and said, "What was wrong with that baby? It acted so differently from the other babies." It was more alert and yet not fussing as much.

I thought this was an interesting confirmation of attention to the baby. But, as I say, I think experimental evidence on the subject would be useful.

DR. RICHARD NUGENT (North Carolina): I would like to address my question to both Dr. Newton and Dr. Biller. Are we gathering some evidence to the effect that the presence of fathers in the delivery room with positive interaction with the infant from the first few minutes after birth is beneficial to the psychosocial development of the infant and the future father-child relationship?

DR. NEWTON: Let me say that I don't know. Actually, of course, fathers who are with their wives in the delivery room are self-selected as a group to a large extent, and it would be hard to conduct long-term studies of this sort. It's possible that Dr. Biller may know of some studies, but I do not. Theoretically, one would like to think that it would make a difference to father-child relationships at a later time.

DR. BILLER: I think the point that Dr. Newton is making is very important in terms of the motivation to get involved to begin with. We might argue that some of these fathers who are participating in natural childbirth classes and are in many cases involved in delivery would still be involved fathers anyway, but my impression clinically is that it does really make a difference.

In fact, we have a graduate student at the University of Rhode Island who is working on a study. It is more of a survey/questionnaire type of study in terms of interviewing and finding out what fathers' reactions are on seeing the infant, comparing those of fathers who were present at delivery with those who weren't, and fathers who have been involved in natural childbirth classes and those who were not. There are the kind of methodologic problems that Dr. Newton alluded to, of course.

I've heard of other studies. I have not seen published clear-cut findings. People have mentioned to me that they have engaged in these kinds of studies and that they have certain kinds of findings that would be consistent with a positive effect of father participation. Aside from observational reports, however, I haven't seen any real hard data on this.

DR. FREEMAN (Seattle, Washington): Dr. Newton, in terms of the future, what do you see as a possibility for home deliveries for what expects to be a normal delivery, with a backup system, that would eliminate some of the antifamily effects of hospitalization? Would that, in fact, deteriorate the health care and the maternal mortality statistics?

DR. NEWTON: I suppose I'm Establishment enough to believe in hospital deliveries. I could conceive, however, that with the circumstances that you suggest—adequate screening and backup services—home delivery could occur perfectly satisfactorily in this country, as it has in other countries.

My own view is that I think we should attempt to make the hospital a better place, a more home-like place, where facilities for emergency care are easily available; and that we should not keep a woman in the hospital very long after delivery. There is no reason, generally speaking, for her to stay for 3, 4 or 5 days, provided that she has care at home, someone to provide for the food, look after the house and support her in looking after the baby.

9

Stability of the Family in a Transient Society

Niles Newton, Ph.D.

Professor, Division of Psychology,
Department of Psychiatry, Northwestern
University Medical School, Chicago, Illinois

We are all concerned about the institution of the family and how we can help it meet modern needs and stresses and strains. With this deep concern, we are going to take a brief look at how the family got to be as it is today—where we came from and what seems to have caused recent changes. Then I will discuss a number of ideas and suggestions for stabilization of the family amid the new challenges it faces. These ideas and suggestions will fall in four main categories:

1. Economic.
2. Psychobiologic.
3. Social Interaction in the Family.
4. Community Influences.

I have had great fun preparing this talk because I have asked many people in the past few weeks for suggestions about family stability. I have gotten a number of ideas from them and hope to get more from you in the discussion after the talk, for there is an enormous amount of wisdom in this audience. After all, a great many of you are actually engaged in building families. In fact, you probably are the keystones of your families. So keep in mind, as I list my proposals, that you have a lot of good ones tucked away in your minds as well, which I hope we will hear about at this conference.

First, let us review briefly what has happened to the family.

Our traditional agricultural economy has gradually, in the past 200 years, been transformed into an industrial, manufacturing economy, based on wages and salaries rather than home industry. Here is a list of changes within the family as our economic system has changed:

The role of men has changed markedly. Many worked at crafts and farming in or near the home. They were around and nearby to eat all meals with the family, to help in case of need, and they worked alongside their sons for a good part of the year, as soon as the boys could help in a simple way. The work load of men in traditional agricultural society was heavy, but it was shared. A whole group of people were working in unison to feed and clothe the family.

In contrast, the work tasks of the modern male are far away from the family in an office or factory, and what he earns there supports not only him but to a large extent the whole family. Most husbands and fathers get far less economic help from women and children and old folks in the home than they did two centuries ago. As a result, family members in the home, instead of being seen as economic help, may be seen as severe economic burdens that must be borne.

The role of women has changed possibly even more than that of men. My grandmother made soups and apple butter, bread and even soap. My great-great-grandmother still used a spinning wheel occasionally, and, awhile before that, housewifely arts included clothing manufacture and hand sewing of all clothes. Hard work, but requiring a very high level of skill, and challenge. This type of creative work is not demanded of women in homemaking today.

While the basic staples of the family, one by one, stopped being made at home, the birth rate dropped as well. American birth rates began dropping about 160 years ago. The changes have actually come gradually over many generations.

Most mothers would agree that the busiest time for mothers is the time when their children are under 5. There has been a tremendous drop of children in this age category since 1810, when U. S. Census reports indicated there were more than 1300 of such children to every 1000 white women aged 20–44. By 1850, this amount dropped to about 900 children, and by 1900 there were fewer than 700 young children for every 1000 comparable childbearing women.

By 1940, after the very low birth rate of the depression years, the number of young children for comparable women was 419. Unfortunately, the U. S. Census Bureau does not appear to be issuing this statistic at the present time, but since our birth rate now has gone down even lower than the 1930 levels, the ratio of childbearing women to young children probably is even lower.

From 1300 to around 400 children under 5 is a major drop. Put in terms of men's activities, the impact would be similar to shortening their work hours from 45 to 15 hours per week.

The role of children has also changed radically. Instead of being baby-sitters, mother's and father's helpers, they now spend long hours, 5 days a week, many months of the year, away from their families, and when they are at home they are not often engaged in much family interaction, but have homework and television to keep them busy.

This contrasts with the fact that going to school was a minor activity of children even a hundred years ago. In 1870, only 57% of the children between 5 and 17 attended public schools, and then attended on the average of only 78 days per year. Instead of school, mothers and fathers worked together to train children in the skills of living.

Other public institutions were equally rudimentary and this, too, increased responsibilities on the family until fairly recently. The care of the vast majority of old and sick people was the cooperative effort of the whole, larger family group.

The family was a much larger family group in those days. In 1790, the time the first U. S. Census was taken, the median size of people living in one household group was about 5.7. In 1972, it had dropped to about 3.1 people, a decrease of nearly half. And now the most recent Census reports convey that the typical American household size is fewer than 3 persons per household—due in part to the increase in people living alone.

The larger households of yesteryear often included grandparents, in-laws, other relatives, hired hands on the farm, apprentices and lodgers and domestic servants. All of these non-nuclear family people have tended to disappear, especially domestic servants and dependent elders.

Basically, what this means is that homes used to have enough hands to help in times of crisis and to prevent young women from carrying the burden of baby and toddler alone day after day, as happens today.

With the lack of helping hands and increased industrialization have come radical changes in infant care, differing both from those of other mammals and from those used in traditional and preliterate societies.

Briefly, let me show you how our ideas have changed by sharing data gathered by Alice Judson Ryerson concerning medical advice on child rearing published between 1550 and 1900. Her sample was based on texts written in English or translated into English. No books by doctors about children for laymen originated in America until nearly 1800, and so Ryerson used only English sources published before that time. After 1800, she recorded only sources published in America, although these, too, sometimes were reprints of books by European authors.

With regard to the recommended age of weaning from the breast, all of three texts published between 1550 and 1650 recommended 2 years. Breast feeding until the age of 4 must have continued until 1725, because some books published that late mentioned it with disapproval. There was a marked drop in the recommended age in books of the mid-eighteenth century.

Up until the nineteenth century, wet nurses and human milk rather than cow's milk or pap were considered desirable when the mother did not lactate.

Over these centuries there have been growing attempts to regulate the baby without regard for its own biologic rhythms. Schedules of feeding appear to have been invented in the early eighteenth century but did not really become popular until after 1825. With this there have come growing numbers of expressions of disapproval of masturbation and sex play. It may be noteworthy that expressed disapproval of masturbation and sex play came to the fore at a period when schedules were becoming popular and the weaning age was getting lower and lower.

Now let's look at the other end of life. The situation of the aged has changed radically within the family. In the years of large families, the so-called crises of middle and old age were muted.

Actually, a study done by Robert Wells of Quaker families in the eighteenth century, who appear to have been demographically similar to the rest of the American population, indicates that for them child rearing was a 40-year project, on the average. It took almost 40 years from the time of the marriage to the time the last child married and left home. Babies kept coming until mother reached her late thirties or forties. The median mother was 60 years of age when the last child left the home.

In fact, when wife or husband died, it was likely that there would be children in the home at the time of widowhood or widowerhood. The Quaker family statistics indicate that the median length of child rearing in the family was longer than the duration of 69% of the marriages, which in those days were almost always terminated by death. In fact, Quaker widows or widowers, if their experience held to the median, could expect to have children to care for 9 years after the death of the first spouse!

In the eighteenth century there was a different type of family instability. It was caused by the death not only of children but of spouses. This type of family instability has been conquered to a large extent by methods largely unknown and unforeseen in the eighteenth century — by the development of modern preventive medicine, and effective drugs.

This gives me hope that our family instability, which comes from such different causes, may also have solutions. The Industrial Revolution saved lives of babies, children, husbands and wives through the technology it developed, but at the same time the changes wrought in family living have accentuated a new kind of family instability.

Small and broken families, dependent on the industrial money economy, force some members to work away from the family for many hours a week and leave lonely and overstrained people at home.

Homo sapiens is not usually a solitary animal. We have evolved in groups and lived in groups as far back as recorded history. In fact, one of the worst punishments we can think of giving a person is to put him in solitary confinement, without human contact with others. We simply need other people to talk to, interact with and, above all, other people who really care about us and whom we care about.

The problem is that although most of the once normal communal economic activities of the family are gone, the psychologic need for family life still remains. Man is a social animal. What can be done now to encourage stronger human ties?

What can we do to stabilize family ties despite modern distractions?

ECONOMIC ISSUES

With the coming of the industrial economy, women and children have become increasing burdens. Insofar as money influences emotions, women and children may not be as beloved as formerly. What can we do about it without turning our backs to the Industrial Revolution?

1. Possibly we should consider elevating the status of part-time work. Currently, when women work outside the home part time, they often get lower pay per hour than if they were working at equally responsible jobs full time. Part-time workers often get no credit for vacations or retirement pay.

Much more of work currently done in the office could be done at home in a family context — typing, accounting, sales work by phone, anything you do alone without too much equipment. My daughter currently is writing her second novel with a friend. They get together three times a week in the afternoon while their four preschool children play together. The work schedule calls for the last chapter being finished the week before the next baby is due. Their arrangement illustrates that where there is concern about keeping mother and children together, a way often can be found to combine work and family care. For another example, La Leche League International's headquarters have hours suited to mothers with school-aged children. They start work very early and close at the time children are let out of the local grade schools.

My dream world is the world where the standard workweek for both men and women would be 25 hours. This amount of working time allows for free time for doing homemaking tasks and for plenty of interaction with the children. Those of us who enjoy work would take on two shifts of work, or 50 hours of working, during the years when home demands are low, if our energies are high. A man could retire to one unit of work from two in his sixties, when he wants to slow down, yet continue to contribute constructive energies to society. An energetic woman in her forties, whose children are gone and whose husband helps with the housework, might take on two units of work a week if she needs an extra challenge or wants money for her children's college or professional education.

Letting children work more might also be considered. Current minimum wage laws and the regulations that prohibit children under 16 working except with complicated permits overlook the fact that, *for children, work is a valuable education;* and part-time work, as long as it does not overfatigue, is highly desirable. It is far better to work as a stock boy or baby-sitter for 2 hours each afternoon than to sit passively in front of the TV for the same amount of time. It is better for self-esteem and self-support, helping the child both to contribute to the economy and to feel needed and wanted.

2. Another way to ease the economic burden brought on by the industrial money economy might be to pay very high child-care allowances to all women with children under 5, thus recognizing the social value of their work. They could, in turn, use the allowance to purchase day care privately, if they preferred not to look after their children themselves during portions of the day.

In our society we tend to distrust mothers. But I personally feel that mothers, as a group, should be less indifferent to the welfare of their children than would be unrelated and more superficially involved professionals. Mothers are in close, immediate contact with their children and see the effect of abuse or unhappy situations the very day they occur to their children at school or in day care.

3. As a third economic suggestion, we might consider income tax deductions for children that reflect realistically their actual cost to us.

I am aware that the last two points involve a great deal of tax money, but if families are strengthened, the cost of other social services is likely to go down as the families handle problems more directly and with fuller knowledge of the individuals involved and, most important, with fuller emotional commitment.

Since most of the other changes in family life appear to have occurred as a consequence of the economic revolution, it would be well to examine further the problem of children being economic punishment, which may have made them less beloved and secure in their parents' love.

PSYCHOBIOLOGIC ISSUES

We often overlook the fact that the only way we human beings have of expressing love is through our bodies. We speak words of love through opening our mouths. We do acts of love by moving our bodies. Our bodies are fundamental to building a family life, and yet we often overlook ways in which bodies can be used to build strong families.

1. In the first place, good physical health leads to better mental attitudes and more energy to solve problems. It is possible to lead a happy family life if the members have too little sleep, have nutritional deficiencies of the type that influence behavior and are tense and tired from too little exercise, but this is very difficult and improbable. I would bet any time on the greater stability of a family that makes it a point to get enough sleep, enough exercise to minimize tension and a well-balanced diet.

2. Sexuality is another psychobiologic item that can be used to really strengthen family life, if it is enjoyed within the family. We hear a lot about open marriages nowadays, but the truth of the matter is that heavy love affairs and sexual friendships outside the home take time and energy away from spouse and children.

As a society, we readily accept the idea that love should lead to sex, but we overlook that the converse is equally true. Sex leads to love. The countries of the world that arrange marriages for their children count heavily on this inverse truth. The pleasure of sex leads to love and commitment. It is love and commitment outside the family rather than transient coitus that may be most disruptive to family life.

Sexuality is two-pronged, then, but a very potent factor. Good sex in a marriage can certainly greatly strengthen it. Good sex outside marriage tends to build auxiliary commitments that may interfere with family life in many instances.

Strangely, at the same time, we overlook an aspect of broader sexuality much enjoyed by our preindustrial ancestors, who experienced a lot more touching and body contact—the friendly, gentle type of love. In fact, they spent many hours each day touching each other in those big beds you see in the museums. The big family bed with mother and father and young children used to be the pattern, the twin bed being a recent invention. Old child-care books warn that when the baby is weaned from the breast at 2 years and no longer sleeps with the parent, it is important to give the child a brother or sister or servant to sleep with so that he is not lonely.

I have devoted a considerable part of my life to research on the psychologic aspects of breast feeding. I do believe that this form of touching between mother and baby is well worthwhile as a foundation for building close family relationships. There is no experimental proof of this in humans, since woman cannot be randomly assigned to breast-feeding and bottle-feeding groups. On the other hand, a number of studies have revealed that mothers who breast feed tend to interact with their babies in ways different from bottle-feeding mothers. Bernal and Richards observed mothers feeding their babies on the second, third, eighth, ninth and tenth days after birth. When the researchers compared the behavior of breast-feeding mothers with that of bottle-feeding mothers, they found that the nursing mothers touched their babies significantly more in ways apart from feeding, and that they also kept nipples in their babies' mouths significantly longer. Feeding observations done at Stanford University by Evelyn B. Thoman and co-workers revealed another surprising difference. The new mothers who talked to their babies the most during nursing on the second day after birth were likely to continue to breast-feed the longest.

In my own work with Carolyn Rawlins and Dudley Peeler, we studied matched pairs of mothers; one member of the pair was giving no breast milk and the other member of the pair was giving no formula, no solid foods, nothing but breast milk 1–2 months post partum. We found that 71% of the mothers who were breast feeding said that they sometimes or often slept in bed with the baby as opposed to only 26% of the bottle feeders.

In a recent, as yet unpublished study, Nancy Paschall, Audrey Melamed, Nell Ryan and I again found similar differences between active breast feeders and bottle feeders. We excluded the token breast feeders so prevalent in our society in the early postpartum period. We defined *active breast feeders* for the purposes of this study as mothers who breast fed five or more times a day, gave formula only occasionally or not at all. Regretfully, we had to include mothers who gave up to two solid feedings a day in order to get a large enough sample of active breast feeders. Some marked, statistically significant differences in reported behavior were found: 63% of the active breast feeders reported that they often rocked the baby, as opposed to 29% of the bottle feeders; 44% of the active breast feeders reported that they never slept with the baby, as compared with 75% of the bottle feeders.

One of the ironies of modern family life behavior is the strange reversal in areas of prudishness. Exotic sexual acts of all sorts now are acceptable, but simple family cuddling throughout the night has gone out of fashion. Even if double beds are used, few men now wear nightshirts, which make their bodies so much more accessible to contact, and even many women now have turned from nightgowns to pajamas, which limit easy skin contact.

ISSUES IN SOCIAL INTERACTION

Before the Industrial Revolution, families used to work together. This still is a good way of building social interaction.

1. Working together can take many forms. A good place to start is family clean-up after supper. In our family, we have a firm rule—everybody but the person who did the cooking helps with the clean-up. It goes quickly and pleasantly that way.

Another good time to have community work is to have the whole family work together on a Saturday morning housecleaning and laundry. If everybody pitches in, with even the 5-year-old emptying wastebaskets, it goes quickly and, again, promotes community spirit.

2. Communication is another very important aspect of family interaction. It may become necessary to set the time and place so that you get the most out of your communication time. Each family is different.

In our family, we have a social time in the early morning reading the papers, drinking tea and coffee and chatting on our big double bed. It's just a natural gathering time ever since the babies got their early morning nursing in bed. They have been coming back for pleasant visits at this time for the many years since then.

We also tend to visit when we come home at night, home after school, home after work. Any homecoming usually is a family visiting time, with even longer visits during the weekend at times that develop at odd moments. Shared breakfasts and dinners help our communication too.

The cooking of breakfast is not a very popular chore in our house. Currently, my 15-year-old son and I take turns. Actually, it is his assigned work load, but he can win an exemption from breakfast cooking by jogging 1 or 2 miles the night before or by playing tennis at the crack of dawn. It works quite well, resulting in a more relaxed and well-exercised teen-ager and family breakfasts with somewhat sleepy conversation.

The art of communication does take time, a willingness to listen, a willingness to care and, above all, a willingness to inhibit destructive criticism. We all can learn from suggestions and reactions from other family members, but telling them that they are foolish or making derogatory remarks stops good communication for a long time.

3. Shared rituals and holidays do much to cement the family together. Special get-togethers for Christmas, trips to visit relatives or sightseeing are long remembered and give a feeling of solidarity.

Shared recreation is especially emphasized in our society and does have a place if the recreation involves interaction or group action. I am rather doubtful whether staring at TV together does much for family solidarity, when compared to recreation with more movement and interaction.

ISSUES INVOLVING THE COMMUNITY

The community can help strengthen family life if it is used constructively. The points that come to mind are:

1. Make friends with other families on a family-to-family basis. Visit back and forth and really get to know one another well. The most solid friendships are born when whole families know one another. Sharing and combining families may be particularly important when families are small, so that diversity of social contact can be fostered by the wider social group.

2. Join groups that are family oriented and give you a chance to be with others who are seeking strong family life. Some church and social action groups are like this.

My daughters have both received and given a great deal of social support by serving as La Leche League leaders. Through the League, they have gotten to know other women who place value in close mothering in the early years and who help one another in other ways, baby-sitting and giving emotional support during a period that tends to be lonely for mothers.

3. When seeking professional help, seek help that is family oriented. There are pediatricians who welcome fathers and like to discuss problems with the whole family. There are obstetricians who welcome fathers in their offices during pregnancy and in the delivery room, and there are psychologists and psychiatrists and social workers who like seeing the whole family together. They are showing you where their values lie.

4. Another point is to consider the source of the advice. Parents and professionals have a right to ask, "Is this person who is giving advice really experienced in the field?"

For instance, when you read a child-care book, ask yourself: "Has this person had any practical experience raising children? How much?" When you read a book on family relationships, ask yourself: "Does this person have a family life of the type I want?" Find out about his demonstrated capability in the field about which he is theorizing.

Finally, I would like to say that if families are to become strong in the United States again, it is not going to be done by professionals but by individuals within the context of their own families, each working to make his or her own family a better and more loving unit.

REFERENCES

Bernal, J., and Richards, P. M.: Effect of bottle and breast feeding on infant development, J. Psychosom. Res. 14:247, 1975.

Newton, N., and Newton, M.: Mothers' reactions to their newborn babies, JAMA 181: 206, 1962.

Newton, N., Peeler, D., and Rawlins, C.: Effect of lactation on maternal behavior in mice with comparative data on humans, Lying-In: J. Reprod. Med. 1:257, 1968.

Ryerson, A. J.: Medical advice on childrearing, 1550–1900, Harvard Ed. Rev. 31:302, 1961.

Thoman, E. B., Leiderman, P. H., and Olson, J. P.: Neonate-mother interaction during breast feedings, Dev. Psychol. 6:110, 1972.

United States Bureau of the Census: *Historical Statistics of the United States, Colonial Times to 1957* (Washington, D. C.: U. S. Department of Commerce, 1960).

United States Bureau of the Census: *Historical Abstracts of the United States* (Washington, D. C.: U. S. Government Printing Office, 1949).

Wells, R. V.: Demographic Change and the Life Cycle of American Families, in *The Family in History: Interdisciplinary Essays* (New York: Harper Torchbooks, Harper & Row, Publishers, 1973).

10

Institutional Barriers to the Family

John B. Franklin, M.D.

*Associate Professor of Obstetrics and
Gynecology, Jefferson Medical College,
Philadelphia, Pennsylvania*

Institutions may have profound impact on family life, and particularly hospitals. Most of us are connected with institutions and here I will discuss change within an institution. I'll give an example of how an institution changed and try ·to identify the factors that made change possible.

The place of the family in pediatric hospitalization now is well established. It was achieved through the analysis of what hospitalization means to a child, particularly one experiencing surgery. I find that childhood hospitalization may be one of the influences on interest in natural childbirth. Some of the pregnant women I have interviewed were prepared for childhood tonsillectomies whereas others found the experience terrifying. When the only hospitalization has been terrifying, it seems to me that part of the motivation to do without drugs stems from a bad childhood experience. But childbirth is far more than simply the threat of surgery; it is the beginning of a family life.

When our program at Booth Maternity Center began, we followed the psychiatric analysis of pregnancy as a task for the mother, a time in which pregnant women work on the answers to these questions: Is it safe to be pregnant? How will I do in my role as a mother? Will I love my child? The word "task" is inadequate; it implies an outcome measured in black and white terms of success or failure. By it is meant rather the continuing process of adjustment to childbearing and child-rearing.

These questions in the task of pregnancy were based in part on the description by the Cantors and Bibring in the 1950s. Their data were the easily confirmed observations that women recall their pregnancies and deliveries in great detail and readily share accounts indicating the importance of childbirth in their experience. The details of childbirth touch all aspects of self—physical, emotional and social; and questions relating to childbirth may be interpreted at all levels. Thus, the question about whether it is safe to be pregnant may find expression in the commonly asked questions about abdominal pain. Instead of "Why do I have pain?" the question is "Will this new discomfort that I am feeling hurt me or my baby?" Similarly, a woman may state that she finds herself profoundly disturbed during pregnancy by an injury to something helpless, such as seeing an animal hit by a car. Gratuitous advice from acquaintances often is taken more seriously than any similar comment to a nonpregnant person. In short, questions asked during pregnancy are rich in meaning. Identifying these underlying meanings saves prenatal care from the monotonous repetition of weights, blood pressures, fundal heights and fetal heart sounds. One can trace the progress of a pregnancy as the dreams go from injury and violence in the first trimester to dreams of a baby after fetal movement has begun.

It is my belief that men have an agenda that is very similar, and I listened with great interest to Henry Biller and Mary Howell. Too often I hear that a father has prepared for the arrival of a child by steps to increase his income, steps that make him less available at home and less able to work through his own feelings about the baby with his wife and child. I often hear reluctance on the part of fathers to commit themselves to support of labor because of expectations of their job and the fear of lost wages. We need paternity leave as a union benefit.

The task of pregnancy is a concept that makes the identification of psychopathology easier but it is not an adequate description of birth. Its utility may be seen in the following example of pathology. In the course of an initial interview with a couple, the mother stated that after an uncomplicated pregnancy she had gone to the hospital in labor. She was given drugs, presumably including scopolamine, and had awakened post partum confused and in a different place. Later she was told that her baby was dead but no reason was given. She had to be transfused. At home, she came down with hepatitis, which was attributed to the transfusions. She was put on steroids for the hepatitis and while on them gained 50–60 pounds. During her second pregnancy, she and her husband split up for a time. The ending, however, was a reasonably happy one, with a safe delivery and a reunion around the delivery. It is hard to imagine a more fear-confirming experience, but it is one that can be easily analyzed by the questions of the task of pregnancy.

But there obviously is more to the early family experience than just the presence or absence of pathology. The cultural evidence of our fascination with birth is immediate. The biggest Christian holiday celebrates birth; the same holiday is assimilated, complete with music, by non-Christian Japan. Sales are virtually guaranteed for nearly any book on birth, and volumes on childbirth can cover several feet of shelf space in a paperback store. Birth is the closest thing to a supernatural event in normal life. Sharing the event becomes at times a secular religion, and descriptions of the joys of childbirth suggest a transcendent experience.

The beginning of the family at the birth of the first child can be more than just making a good adjustment; it is an occasion for true celebration. The delivery of a live, normally developed child whom the parents can see, hear and touch is the beginning of the affiliation of parents with child. I remember vividly two mothers of babies with cleft palates and cleft lips. In one case, the mother herself had had a palate and lip repair. At the birth of her affected child, she turned away and would not look at it; the second mother grasped and cuddled her baby immediately after delivery. The attachments of parents to children, the formation of family ties and emotional bonds that last, is what this conference is about. Too often, though, I believe that we have built into the events surrounding the first contact between parents and children barriers to their attachment. Although we do not have immediate measures for that mother who rejected her child, I believe that it is possible and relatively easy to eliminate these institutional barriers to the attachment process. In obstetrics, obstacles to the growth of family life have sprung up like weeds, at times threatening the value of our services.

For some, the barrier is the hospital itself. Hospitals represent the confirmation that it may not be safe to be pregnant. Often the hospitals are proud of their life-and-death image with all its panoply of technical equipment. Whatever the defects in the design, appearance and atmosphere of our hospitals, they are a symbol for a generation that has avoided most life-threatening disorders. Visible cripplers like polio have seemingly vanished, and death and injury come from automobiles, drugs and wars. The lack of firsthand experience with serious illness has changed the perception of nature as capricious and arbitrary into nature as a benign force that asks only to be accepted and worked with. Home delivery, it is believed, can be accomplished with a little understanding of the old-time ways of having children, and a boiled shoestring for the cord. Numerically, those rejecting hospital delivery are few, but the success of *The Birth Book* and the incredible response to Leboyer indicate that disenchantment with the hospital as a place for childbirth is far greater than measured by the number of home deliveries.

Large institutions generally are most responsive to their employees. When prenatal care comes from such institutions, it is antifamily in its orientation, in order to permit the family life of the employees.

If pregnancy is a task for both husband and wife, either the husband must be released from work to accompany his wife or the prenatal care must be offered after work, with some provision for other children to come along. We have two evening sessions a week, and these sessions tend to have the most crowded waiting rooms. Time is available during the day, but the tolerance for the waiting and the crowding reflect the preference of families for evening visits.

For the mother's questions as to how she will do in her role, she needs answers from authorities and from peers as well. Authorities often give unrealistic answers, such as advising rest for the mother of small children. Childbirth classes such as those provided by the Childbirth Education Association (CEA) and Lamaze groups provide an opportunity for answers from both peers and professionals. Most of our couples seem disappointed to learn that classes do not begin until the 6th or 7th month. In these classes, husbands find themselves in the familiar classroom setting and their enthusiasm for natural childbirth originates here rather than in their contact with cautious and wary physicians. If our area is a true indicator, far more couples receive preparation for childbirth away from their hospital than attend classes within the hospital. An inevitable apprehension develops that the hospital may not share the implied values of the class leader. By·supplying their own programs, hospitals can rationalize their procedures for their patients; at the same time, these hospitals will be forced to examine their procedures.

At the time of delivery, many hospitals pose barriers to the husband in the lack of any provisions for him, such as chairs, food, toilets. He often is excluded from the examinations of his wife, whose fears are confirmed that she is on her own and that worse is in store. Tolerance without encouragement is the rule rather than the exception for fathers, which confirms their fears that they have little to contribute to women in labor. More than once I have given heartfelt thanks to a supportive husband who coaxed an extra effort from his wife or whose calming effect made my intervention bearable. As in other places, sexism is found in delivery rooms. These barriers to attachment exist not out of malice or even insensitivity but out of a reluctance to change procedures—particularly in someone else's territory. Our fear is that if a task is to be done at the patient's convenience, then the task won't get done. Yet we miss the point that routines create indifference and that the need to adapt to each patient is the challenge and interest of the job. Too often, the hospital has its own hidden agenda in its routines. Personnel may need to be moved from one area to another. Procedure books specify the tasks expected of each shift. Human needs are grafted onto the procedures rather than vice versa.

These barriers can be eliminated by restoring a common viewpoint and goal to the entire staff. Where family adaptation is the goal, everyone's contribution has value to the family. Housekeeping and nursing care blend just as they do in the home. Routine medications are secondary to services that let a mother function. A midnight snack may be far more important to the normal patient than a routine dose of Ergotrate. Where adaptation is the goal of the obstetrician and pediatrician, the service is not organized for disease detection; rather, disease detection is grafted onto a program of learning for mother, father and infant.

How do you make the necessary changes in a service to bring this about? Our situation in Philadelphia may be unique. The real impetus to starting our alternative program came from offering childbirth preparation to our service patients and finding that they could not obtain the same deliveries that attracted patients to the private staff of the hospital. That was a parochial issue more than 5 years ago. The context today has changed and I believe that it makes the possibility of change more likely. At present, teaching hospitals, particularly medical school hospitals, are reorganizing to qualify as tertiary hospitals. In obstetrics, the tertiary hospital is supposed to have expertise in the care of those pregnancies representing a threat to the life of the mother and/or the infant, and it is supposed to have a large volume of obstetrics—up to 10,000 deliveries per annum—that will support a large staff of subspecialists. Because attention is focused on the risk in delivery, care will be organized around the technical aids to safe delivery.

Leadership in detecting and treating pathology has been construed as synonymous with leadership in patient care, but I believe that this is not correct in obstetrics. We have accepted the installation of some highly technical facilities in smaller hospitals, and kidney transplants and bypass surgery take place often very successfully in suburban hospitals. My fear is that the smaller secondary and primary hospitals will give only technical care to obstetric patients, in imitation of the teaching hospital. On the other hand, I believe that the concentration of high-risk cases in the tertiary hospital should permit smaller units to be more family-centered than ever before. The model I am advocating is not necessarily our own, for I believe that there is a general lack of innovation in providing care. I can imagine everything from hospital-sponsored home delivery, as in Amsterdam, to extended care facilities for single parents and their children in cases where there is no larger family. My concern is that the impetus for alternative care programs is originating outside medicine. Although physicians are rushing to identify themselves as subspecialists, the numbers favor the primary care facilities. So many deliveries are normal that one may expect primary care in a variety of settings, whereas low morbidity in a climate of institutional barriers and high costs will fail to attract 10,000 deliveries a year unless there is conscription or heavy subsidies.

For the past 4 years I have been associated with a freestanding maternity service that was organized around the adaptational task of pregnancy. In using a freestanding maternity unit, we raised questions about safety and cost that for many critics constituted a medical adventure. To date, our mortality figures are about the same as a large teaching hospital and less than the city reports as a whole, although our clientele parallels the general population of Philadelphia in terms of race and marital status. Since the true costs of obstetric services are obscured by cost averaging, we have been pleased to find ours below that of the community, and our occupancy has reached 75% without inclusion of any gynecology.

Note that I proposed to discuss change within an institution and yet clearly I am describing an alternative. I believe that where change fails, alternatives should be strongly considered. As I look back on our earlier efforts to change a teaching hospital to embrace family-centered care at all levels, I believe that this effort ran counter to the evolution of that hospital into a place for highly specialized care subordinating emotional needs to technical necessity.

The ingredients for changing a small institution came from prolonged planning. The persons who did the planning at our hospital were also planning their own jobs, not those of others, so that self-interest was very high. To reduce competition and to translate our various languages, a psychologist skilled in organizational planning was added to the staff, with the support of a grant from the Merrill Foundation. Strict rules were followed at meetings, including such requirements as paraphrasing and checking any statement of a colleague before agreeing or disagreeing with it. Recipients of hospital care were permanent members of the planning group, along with providers. Each meeting ended in a debriefing that dissipated the tensions that had accumulated.

We were able to combine prenatal care and intrapartum care in one building, with a great increase in physician productivity. The key to our structure was the employment of nurse-midwives for prenatal care, labor support and postpartum supervision. The nurse-midwife, with her traditional commitment to normal obstetrics, was seen as the symbol of continuity rather than the physician. She was to emphasize the universal theme of normality while the physician, who worked side by side with the midwives and *not* independently, was restored to the role for which he or she was trained — to intervene in the abnormal or to employ pain-relieving technics that called for special skills and experience. Registered nurses are still employed, but the leadership is from the midwives.

For prenatal care, we decided to permit visits to last as long as a couple had any questions. This open-ended visit prolonged waiting but maintained satisfaction. Anyone asking to talk with a physician could see one on any visit. All new patients see the physician to establish his availability and to obtain a sense of contract as to appropriate expectations and the services to be offered. At the first visit, a recording of the wishes of the patient for delivery is made. These wishes range from highly specific requests to deliver in a labor bed outside the delivery room to general requests for the maximum available anesthesia. Whatever the initial wishes may be, some discussion is given to the available anesthetic technics—epidural, paracervical, local and use of meperidine (Demerol). Patients are told that they are experts in their own comfort and that any medication will be discussed with them prior to any proposed administration.

Presence of the father during examinations is offered from the start, and the program is described as being dependent on fathers or other support figures. Labor is accompanied by the constant attendance of the midwife except when several persons are in labor or the patient is in a latent phase. Usually midwives obtaining refresher programs fill gaps when more than one person is in labor. Breathing technics are encouraged from the onset of labor, regardless of the patient's experience, until some other need is felt, such as for conduction anesthesia. At delivery, the baby is put on the mother's abdomen, and parents are encouraged to touch the child at once. Following any necessary repair, mother and baby return to the mother's room, where nursing may be started.

Postpartum patients are offered nursery care of their infants any time they choose. If nursery care is desired, babies are brought out for feedings, although the mother may negotiate to skip a feeding in order to sleep. The lack of pressure on the mother after delivery helps identify those mothers who are having problems with their role or with their attachment to the infant and helps ease the otherwise sometimes heavy sense of responsibility for the mother. In offering care of the baby rather than assuming it, our experience has been that mothers seldom relinquish their infants and the result is the same as rooming-in. Fathers are welcome as visitors all day and for a time after evening visiting hours. When labor is prolonged, a folding cot may be placed beside the labor bed so that fathers may nap. Children visit postpartum mothers in first-floor lounges or in the ground-floor cafeteria. We have not followed the British practice of permitting children on the hospital floor.

Decision-making in our hospital follows the hierarchic pattern with the exception that we have continued the Task Force that planned the present program. This meets twice monthly (without a psychologist) and consists of the directors of obstetrics, pediatrics, midwifery and social service, the administrator and the assistant administrator and the controller. The Task Force makes policy and may change existing policy, subject to review by the Salvation Army. There is machinery for firing members of the Task Force.

For those who have not worked with such a system, a common reaction is that patients will dictate care. We have found that just as a mother when given the option of nursery care for her infant will choose herself to keep her baby beside her, so women, including many adolescents, make very conservative choices. We have about a 20% incidence of epidural anesthetic procedures, but nearly all of our patients have tried to cope with labor with the support of the nurse-midwife. Most patients will have some analgesia before labor is over. Because the nurse-midwife is constantly present, the amount of medication does not simply measure the attention from staff.

In summary, then, our program has succeeded through the restructuring of roles in the hospital and through sharing responsibility with patients. All of the hospital employees have discussed the philosophy of the program and support it. A powerful force has been to survive, for prior to the family-centered program, low occupancy and rising costs threatened the future of this hospital. Our seemingly permissive system has attracted a number of minorities. Some were religious: Orthodox Jews came from the neighborhood, Black Muslims came to avoid male physicians and followers of the Divine Light sought joy. Some were intellectuals bringing requests for variations on natural childbirth that we felt we could support. Some came for social reasons, including many single women and couples in relationships enjoying varying degrees of social approval, including polygamy. Dietary minorities appeared, some with their own herbs and honey. Lately, people have come purely for financial reasons, and they may be as surprised by the program as we are by their occasional lack of interest in it.

On more than one occasion, individual members of our team have found themselves unable to cope with a certain patient or couple, but each time another member has always come forward with the missing understanding and patience. We have learned our dependence on one another and have learned much from those who have trusted us with their care. It has been possible to avoid the pretense of being god-like, but instead to develop skills. In the long run, I believe our patients have benefited, and that by stressing the individual we have strengthened family ties.

11

Parent-to-Infant Attachment

Marshall H. Klaus, M.D.

*Professor of Pediatrics and Director of
Neonatology, Case Western Reserve
University Medical School, Cleveland, Ohio*

and

John H. Kennell, M.D.

*Professor of Pediatrics, Case Western
Reserve University Medical School,
Cleveland, Ohio*

Over the past 40 years, investigators from a wide variety of disciplines have elaborated in great detail the process by which the human infant becomes attached to his mother (Bowlby, 1958; Spitz, 1965). They have described the disastrous effects of long-term maternal-infant separation on the infant's motor, mental and affective development.

We will discuss the development of the attachment process in the opposite direction, from the parent to the infant: how it grows and develops and what disturbs, promotes or enhances it. This attachment is crucial to the survival and development of the infant. Its power is so great that it enables the parents to make the unusual sacrifices necessary for the care of the infant day in and day out, night after night, attending to the baby's cries and protecting him, and giving feedings in the middle of the night, when they may desperately need to sleep.

It is the nature of this attachment that we will explore. This original mother-to-infant bond is the wellspring for all of the infant's subsequent attachments and the relationship through which the child develops a sense of himself.

An attachment can be defined as a unique relationship between two people that is specific and enduring. Although it is difficult to define this enduring relationship operationally, we will take as indicators of this attachment behaviors such as fondling, kissing, cuddling and prolonged gazing, which serve to maintain contact and show affection between individuals.

Although this definition is useful in experimental observations, it is important to distinguish between attachment and attachment behaviors. Close attachment can persist during long separations of time and distance, even though at times there may be no visible signs of its existence. A call for help even after 40 years may bring a mother to her child and evoke attachment behaviors as strong as in the first year of his life.

The early studies of mother-to-infant attachment were those by Bibring (1961) and Benedek (1952). A new impetus to study the mother-infant bond began 10 years ago, when the staffs of intensive care nurseries observed that sometimes after heroic measures had been used to save small premature babies they would return to emergency rooms battered and practically destroyed by their parents, even though they had been sent home intact and thriving.

More careful studies of this phenomenon have consistently shown a dispro- portionate amount of battering, failure to thrive without organic cause and acci- dents among infants who were prematures or who were hospitalized for other reasons during the neonatal period (Klein and Stern, 1951; Shaheen *et al.*, 1968). (Failure to thrive is a syndrome in which the infant does not grow, gain or de- velop normally during the first few months of life but shows leaps in develop- ment and weight gain with routine hospital care.)

To learn more about the parental requirements for attachment 12 years ago, mothers were for the first time routinely allowed to come into the premature nursery (Barnett *et al.*, 1970). When we permitted mothers to enter the prema- ture nursery to touch their babies, they would poke at them as women poke at a cake with a straw to test whether it is done, touching the tips of their fingers to the tips of the baby's extremities. We wondered whether this was normal. Our ideas about this behavior have evolved as we have gone back and forth between the intensive care nursery and the normal full-term nursery, studying mothers' inter- actions with their infants (Klaus *et al.*, 1970).

We also became interested in whether human mothers exhibit some form of species-specific behavior at the birth of their children, such as those observed in various animal species.

When we allowed mothers into the premature nursery, they circled the incuba- tor for two or three visits, then began the poking behavior, and finally began to stroke the extremities and then the trunk. On the fourth to eighth visit, a mother often would begin to place her hands on the baby's trunk and then turn her head into the same parallel plane as the infant's for a very short time.

We then attempted to find out what a mother of a full-term baby does at their first meeting if she is left in a private room with her baby. We filmed mothers and their infants and found that all had a specific sequence of behavior. Each mother first touched the tips of her baby's extremities and moved on to the trunk in the next 7 or 8 minutes. She appeared very excited. When we tape-recorded what she was saying, we found that 80% of the verbal content was related to the eyes. "Please open your eyes. If you open your eyes I'll know you're alive." We heard comments we hadn't anticipated. We noticed at this early time that the mother had a high-pitched voice, but we didn't fully appreciate what it meant.

We made many errors in the interpretation of this complex interaction until we looked at both members of the pair. This area has been greatly augmented by the recent explosion of information about the abilities of the newborn. Detailed studies of the amazing behavioral capacities of the normal neonate have shown that he sees and hears, and that he moves in rhythm to his mother's voice in the first hours of life. Wolff (1959), Prechtl (1967) and Brazelton *et al.* (1966) have noted that there are six separate states of consciousness of the infant. States one and two are sleeping states. In state three, the baby is waking up and state four is the quiet alert state, in which the baby's eyes are wide open. State five is moving around and state six is screaming.

Brazelton *et al.* revealed that if you whisper in the baby's ear while he is in state four, the baby turns to the voice and that if you show your face, the baby follows the face. Then we began to understand what the mother was telling us. In the first hour of life, the baby is in state four for prolonged periods. The mother is interested in the baby's eyes and at the same time the baby has an unusual ability to attend and follow words and objects.

Recently, Condon and Sander (1974) have made even more complex observations. They noted that not only does the baby follow but he moves in rhythm and becomes entrained to the spoken word for short periods even in the first day of life. He will move in rhythm to the spoken word, whether English or Chinese, but not to discontinuous symbols.

This ability to move in rhythm to the spoken word is what allows each of us to say to himself when talking to somebody, "He's not listening." Throughout the world, when one individual speaks to another, the listener moves in rhythm to words as long as he is listening. Condon and Sander found that a baby moves in rhythm within 16 hours of birth. This is one of the infant components in mother-infant interaction.

Up until that time, we had not understood the meaning of the discussion about the eyes. What the mother actually was looking for was a response. We believe that a mother cannot easily become bonded to her infant unless the baby himself dances in rhythm to the mother's words or responds to her in some manner—in a sense, making love to her. One of the principles of bonding we believe important is that you cannot make love to anyone who does not make love to you.

To further explore species-specific behavior, we have begun to study home deliveries in California. From these observations, our conceptions of this early period have been radically altered. Preliminary studies of home deliveries have been made from videotapes and 8-mm films as well as from long discussions with Raven Lang, a perceptive midwife who has made valuable naturalistic observations of 52 home deliveries (1974). Lang's work pointed out a very important element that we had neglected. In all the deliveries that we had recorded, the mother was passive. She was on her back being acted on by the nurse and the physician. But in the home deliveries observed by Lang, we saw the mother as an active participant for the first time. She was on her hands and knees, she had decided to deliver at home, whom to invite and had chosen the room, the spot within the room and the position in which she was to deliver.

One of the interesting points Lang (1974) has made, and probably a very important rule of attachment, is that those who watch the delivery become more closely attached to the baby than very close friends who do not watch the delivery. In times past, this was very important; if the mother died, someone else was ready to begin caring for the baby.

We are trying to understand the principles behind attachment because some difficult decisions have to be made: How are we going to weigh each procedure in the hospital? Should a father be present at delivery? Should a mother and father receive their infant immediately after birth? If a mother has a very sick baby, how much should we attend to her attachment? How closely should we monitor the mother's postdelivery condition? How much emphasis should we give to each area?

Once we have laid the foundations of attachment, we can understand how important each move we suggest will be.

Lang observed that a few minutes after the birth of the infant, but before the delivery of the placenta, the mother turns and picks up her infant and often assumes the "en face" position. Other midwives assist mothers deliver in a lateral position, which allows a mother to watch the birth of her own infant. Immediately after the delivery, she appears to be in a state of ecstasy. The observers are also elated during the delivery and offer the mother support and encouragement. In the film, the observers' interest in the infant is striking, especially in the first 15–20 minutes after the birth. This supports the observations of Eibl-Eibesfeldt (1971), who has emphasized the unique qualities of the human infant, such as large forehead and small face, large eyes, chubby cheeks, small mouth and unequal physical proportions. These attractive and compelling properties tend to draw not only the mother and father but all of those present to the infant. Lang has noted that the infant quiets down when given to the mother. Almost always, she rubs her baby's skin with her fingertips in a gentle stroking motion, starting with the face. This occurs before the initial nursing and before the delivery of the placenta. The mother usually offers the breast but the baby often does not suck right away. Most commonly, he licks the nipple over and over (Long, 972).

In the home deliveries, most parents used high-pitched voices when talking to their infant, and there seemed to be a higher level of excitement than in hospital deliveries. We would like to name this the state of ekstasis, using the Greek word for ecstasy. Many mothers who delivered at home have reported sensations similar to orgasm at the time of delivery.

The pattern of behavior that was seen in these home deliveries with a select population is different in some aspects from that observed in hospital deliveries. In a home delivery: (1) The mother is an active participant. (2) She picks up the infant immediately after delivery. (3) She begins to stroke his face with her fingertips and moves to palm contact within a few minutes. (4) A striking elevation of mood is observed in association with great excitement in all participants. (5) Everyone is drawn to look at the infant. (6) The mother is groomed by one of her female friends. (7) Breast-feeding is initiated within 5–6 minutes and begins with licking of the nipple by the infant (Lang, 1972).

At the time of the first mother-infant interaction there is a transfer of endocrinologic, immunologic and bacteriologic factors as well as behavioral components.

The baby licks the nipple and the mother's pituitary secretes prolactin and oxytocin as a result. The oxytocin helps contract her uterus and reduce bleeding. At the same time, her milk gives her baby all sorts of immunologic substances that act like an antiseptic to protect his gut.

One of the most exciting advances of the past years has been the finding that during the nursing on the first day of life, the baby receives a number of specialized cells in breast milk — T and B lymphocytes and macrophages — that give him special protection against infectious agents in the environment. Large and small lymphocytes of the mother may persist in the gastrointestinal tract of the baby for the first week or two of life (Walker, 1973).

Fresh breast milk banks now are being developed for premature nurseries, and we predict that in the next year or two many prematures in the United States will receive fresh, unboiled colostrum. Some of the cells in this colostrum have originated and developed highly specialized qualities in the Peyer's patches of the intestines of the mother; they travel through the lymphatics and bloodstream and become deposited in the breast. These specialized cells with the immunologic intelligence of the mother are either producing specific antibodies in the breast or are being themselves delivered in the colostrum to the baby's gastrointestinal tract.

As an example of the potential of these cells, a baby living in Guatemala in a little village that has endemic shigellosis, salmonellosis and paratyphoid doesn't get sick as long as he is nursing, even though his mother does not clean her breast. The baby takes in milk loaded with pathogenic bacteria; but at the same time he takes in the specialized cells and gamma globulin until he can build his own defenses.

A second principle we have considered is the existence of a sensitive period in the human mother. Is there a period in the first hours of life during which it is essential that the mother and father be with their baby for the optimal development of maternal behavior in the years to come?

We know that if baby lambs are taken away from their mothers in the first hour of life and then returned, about 40% of the mothers will not accept their own lambs. On the other hand, if the mother and baby are left together during this first 60 minutes, the mother will accept only her own lamb, even after a short separation. We ask the question: Do human parents exhibit a sensitive period?

Eight of nine separate studies give evidence of a sensitive period in the human mother and father. This evidence comes from studies of both premature and full-term infants in Sweden, the United States, Guatemala and Brazil (Lind, 1973; Klaus *et al.*, 1970; Sousa *et al.*, 1974).

It has been shown that fathers who were given their nude babies to play with soon after birth spent much more time with them during the first 3 months than if they did not have this opportunity (Lind, 1973). Mothers who have this early period with their nude babies spend more time with the baby during the first month, will stand close and soothe him during an office visit, in stress situations will come to the baby's aid and, 2 years after the early contact, will speak to the baby differently from control mothers, using more questions, fewer demands and more adjectives and adverbs (Ringer *et al.*, 1975).

One of the studies of premature infants has shown a significant difference at 4 years of age between the developmental quotients of babies who were given to their mothers in the first day and those of babies given to their mothers on the twentieth day (Klaus and Kennell, 1975).

We believe that the following seven principles probably are crucial components of the process of attachment.

1. There is a sensitive period in the first minutes and hours of life during which it is necessary for optimal later maternal behavior that the mother and father have close contact with their neonate in a private situation. We have called this the period of parental neonatropy.

2. There appears to be species-specific behavior in the human mother and father when they are first given their baby.

3. The process of attachment is structured so that the father and mother will optimally become attached to only one infant at a time. Bowlby (1958) earlier stated this principle for the attachment process in the other direction and termed it monotropy.

4. During the process of the mother's attachment to her infant, it is necessary that the infant respond to the mother by some signal such as body or eye movement. We have sometimes termed this "You can't love a dishrag."

5. People who witness the birth process become strongly attached to the infant.

6. The processes of attachment and detachment probably are mutually incompatible. It is difficult to go through the process of attachment to one person while mourning the loss or threatened loss of the same or another person. For example, if a mother loses a baby, she should get over the process of the loss, which might take 7 or 8 months, before she becomes pregnant with her next infant.

7. Early events have long-lasting effects. Anxieties in the first day about the well-being of a baby with a temporary disorder may result in long-lasting concerns, which may cast long shadows or adversely shape the development of the child (Kennell and Rolnick, 1960).

In the past 60 years, the hospital culture has taken birth and death away from the home and placed them in the hospital, to the exclusion of the traditions of the past that were established over centuries. It is time to bring back the family and some of the family customs into the hospital. This will not be easy.

Twenty-five years ago, in our early days in pediatrics, parents were allowed to visit small children only twice a week for a half hour. We know that this was disastrous. Yet, when it was first suggested that a mother might visit every day for an hour, some physicians and nurses said that they wouldn't be able to get their work done.

Now, the practices in children's hospitals are very different from those of years ago and children do cry more; but they are more like normal children following discharge.

We are on the verge of making major changes in our delivery units. In indicating that home delivery may foster attachment, we do not mean to imply that we believe delivery should be at home. We think that our hospitals should provide a wider range of services, so that some mothers can deliver in a hospital bed, or in a traditional setup, whereas others can deliver with a midwife in a room with rugs on the floor and pictures on the wall, and can invite their friends, and possibly even their other children, to be present, but with a blood bank, an infant resuscitator and other emergency resources available. Modern hospital obstetrics and pediatrics have significantly lowered maternal and infant mortality. These major gains must not be lost in the changes we propose.

REFERENCES

Barnett, C. R., Leiderman, H. R., Grobstein, R., and Klaus, M.: Neonatal separation: the maternal side of interaction. Pediatrics 45:197, 1970.

Benedek, T.: *Studies in Psychosomatic Medicine: The Psycho-Sexual Function in Women* (New York: Ronald Press, 1952).

Bibring, G., Dwyer, I., Huntington, D., and Valenstein, A.: A study of the psychological processes in pregnancy and of the earliest mother-child relationship, Psychoanalysis of the Child 16:9, 1961.

Bowlby, J.: The nature of a child's tie to his mother, Int. J. Psychoanal. 39:350, 1958.

Brazelton, T. B., Scholl, M. L., and Robey, J. S.: Visual responses in the newborn, Pediatrics 37:284, 1966.

Condon, W. S., and Sander, L. W.: Neonate movement is synchronized with adult speech: Interactional participation and language acquisition, Science 183:99, 1974.

Eibl-Eibesfeldt, I.: *Love and Hate* (New York: Holt, Rinehart & Winston, 1971).

Kennell, J. H., and Rolnick, A. R.: Discussing problems in newborn babies with their parents, Pediatrics 26:832, 1960.

Klaus, M. H., and Kennell, J. H.: Parent-to-infant attachment, Recent Adv. Pediatr. (in press).

Klaus, M. H., Kennell, J. H., Plumb, N., and Zuelkhe, S.: Human maternal behavior at first contact with her young, Pediatrics 46:187, 1970.

Klein, M., and Stern, L.: Low birth weight and the battered child syndrome, Am. J. Dis. Child. 122:15, 1971.

Lang, R.: *Birth Book* (Cupertino, California: Genesis Press, 1972).

Lang, R.: Personal communication, 1974.

Lind, J.: Personal communication, 1973.

Prechtl, H. F. P.: Neurological findings in newborn infants after pre- and peri-natal complications, Nutr. Symp., May, 1967.

Ringler, N. M., Kennell, J. H., Jarvella, R., Navojosky, B. J., and Klaus, M. H.: Mother-to-child speech at 2 years—effects of early post-natal contact, Behav. Pediatr. 86:141, 1975.

Shaheen, E., Alexander, D., Truskowsky, M., and Barbero, J.: Failure to thrive—a retrospective profile, Clin. Pediatr. 7:225, 1968.

Sousa, P. L. R., Baros, F. C., Gazalle, R. V., Bigeresi, R. M., Pinherro, G. N., Menezes, S. T., and Arruda, L. A.: Attachment and lactation. Presented at Pediatria XIV: Nutrition, Toxicology and Pharmacology, Buenos Aires, Argentina, 1974.

Spitz, R.: *The First Year of Life* (New York: International Universities Press, 1965).

Walker, A.: Immunology of the gastrointestinal tract, J. Pediatr. 83:517, 1973.

Wolff, P. H.: Observations on newborn infants, Psychosom. Med. 21:110, 1959.

12

Perspectives from Ethology

Victor C. Vaughan, III, M.D.

*Professor and Chairman, Department of
Pediatrics, Temple University School of
Medicine; Medical Director, St.
Christopher's Hospital for Children,
Philadelphia, Pennsylvania*

In the observations made by Marshall Klaus regarding the immediate postpartum behavior of mothers and infants and its long-range impact on their relationship we have an example of the ethologic method used in the study of human behavior. The concepts of *ethology* and of the *ethologic method* are relatively new, and warrant some definition.

The field of ethology is a product of the past 50 years, and chiefly of the work of Konrad Lorenz and Nikolaas Tinbergen. Briefly put, and perhaps oversimplified, ethology concerns itself with the study and characterization of animal or human behavior in its *natural* setting, particularly in terms of its survival value or of its evolutionary value. Among the kinds of behavior of interest to the ethologists are patterns of recognition, attachment, greeting, courting, aggression, defense of territory, dominance and formation of hierarchies of dominance among members of a species.

Among a variety of species of animals, similar or markedly different patterns may be observed for a given class of behaviors. Moreover, naturalistic patterns of behavior can be shown to be profoundly modified by experience. The defective socialization of monkeys in the laboratory or of infants and children in institutions [6] offers ample evidence of this.

It is noteworthy that the ethologist is likely to have little concern for the inner experience or emotional state implied by observed behavior. These are more likely to be the concern of the comparative psychologist or of the psychiatrist.

The question raised as to whether patterns of behavior in animals have analogues or homologues that can be profitably studied in man by the ethologic method has been answered with a resounding affirmative, and the number of exciting and revealing studies of man that use the ethologic method is increasing rapidly. In this connection, the difference between analogue and homologue deserves definition. Analogous behaviors may be said to include those that have elements of cause and effect in common and seem to serve similar ends; to say that an analogous pattern in two species is additionally homologous would imply that similar or identical physiologic mechanisms, perhaps genetically related, served the designated behavior in each of these species. Truly or completely homologous patterns are more likely to be found between closely related species, say between primates and man, than among more distant cousins, such as man and bird. On the other hand, such essentials for survival as establishment of patterns of social bonds and structure, food gathering, defense of territory, courting, protection and nourishment of the young and defense against predators are all so universal among vertebrates that it would be surprising if there were not many analogues easily to be found, and homologues as well.

Not everyone has accepted enthusiastically the notion that some forms of behavior in the categories of aggression or dominance may have genetic programs in man just as in animals. I will not discuss the controversy surrounding aggression, but I would like to examine with you some of the infant's activity fostering attachment, which I believe offers evidence of the presence and the power of programmed behavior. I should like first to review a kind of attachment behavior well studied in animals and known to most if not all of you. This is *imprinting,* one of the earliest ethologic concepts, which can, in oversimplified terms, be described as a process through which the very young animal identifies the living (or sometimes inanimate) things or kinds of things to which it will be related in later life as refuge, or as social or sexual objects, in nature most often other members of the same species, or in some abnormal situations, *as if* conspecific.

The elements of imprinting in precocial birds and in some mammals appear to have as essentials the opportunity for the young animal to *follow* a nearby moving object during a critical period of development in which the behavior of following is translated into the identification of the moving object as refuge or as appropriate for social interaction. After the critical period, the intrusion of another, different moving object is likely to be anxiety-provoking and to drive the young animal toward the original, followed object, often with evidence of anxiety.

It is not difficult to find an analogue of this process in man, though the time-scale is quite different from what it may be for other animals. It seems likely that the important element analogous to following in the attachment between normal infants and their caretakers will be the visual activity of the infant. The complexity of the infant's visual apparatus and the surprisingly sophisticated way in which very young infants can use this in developing an appreciation of their environment has been shown by recent studies to be far ahead of what we have rather naïvely judged to be the case in times past. It can be shown, for example, that the newborn infant already in the first days of life has a lively interest in geometric figures projected on a translucent screen in front of his face, and that he is selective among these figures for those that particularly hold his attention. He is, for example, more interested in vertical bars of light in the visual field than in horizontal ones, and is able to scan triangular figures in ways that not only reflect the manner in which certain elements in the figure are joined, but which are rather individualistic to the particular child [7]. It has been proposed that the newborn infant is more attracted to a bull's-eye pattern of concentric circles than to either a vertical or a horizontal line or a triangle, and the suggestion has been made that the bull's-eye pattern corresponds to the infant's impression of the maternal breast or possibly of the maternal or paternal eye (Lee Salk).

The studies by Jerome Kagan [4] have indicated that during the first 8–12 weeks of life, the visual attention of the child appears to be most attracted to points of sharp contrast in the visual field, to elements in motion or to places in the visual field where there is a change of intensity of light taking place. After 8–12 weeks, the infants studied by Kagan, presented diagrams or pictures in a relatively motionless visual field, appeared to be most attracted to those patterns that represented the human face. Kagan has also shown that the intensity of this attraction is susceptible to sociocultural factors, in that it varies with the amount of face-to-face or eye-to-eye contact between infant and mother.

By 5–8 weeks of life, most infants have begun to smile, the smile appearing universally to be a very powerful socializing instrument, inasmuch as it is responded to by the healthy mother with a smile of her own and with vocalization and other forms of communication with the infant that often involve face-to-face contact.

By 4 months of age, the earliest evidence may be found that the infant has a way of identifying the face of his mother as distinct from other faces to which he may be exposed, and we are accustomed to thinking of the 6–8-month-old infant as having a very clear preference for the face of his mother, and beginning to look on the intrusion of new or unfamiliar faces with anxiety.

I think that we need have no uneasiness about accepting this course of events as an analogue of imprinting, or primary socialization, and accepting that the process of attachment of the infant to mother or father or other closely related caretakers has elements like those that attach other small animals to their parents or other conspecifics. It seems further acceptable that an early appreciation of the human face and the ultimate differentiation among faces are elements of this process.

How much of this is programmed genetically or is *homologous* in the sense defined above? The answer may not be easy to find, but there are some powerful indicators that some of the needs for social responses in the newborn infant may have been anticipated in the structure of the central nervous system. For example, Carolyn Goren and her co-workers in Los Angeles [2] have shown that if a representation of the human face is presented in motion to a sufficiently alert newborn infant of 2–22 hours of age, the infant will in many instances be shown to fixate such an object and to turn the head to attempt to maintain fixation from a neutral position as far as 90° from that neutral position. When the same representation is presented to the infant with the features disordered but still symmetric, the infant shows a somewhat less intense interest; if the features are scrambled in a disorderly way, still less; and if the vehicle on which the representation of the face is presented is blank, the infant shows still less interest.

These surprising results indicating a visual preference for a representation of a face within the first 2–22 hours of life raised a question as to what experience in the earliest minutes of life might have already identified human features for the infant prior to 2 hours of age. In an attempt to answer this question, Goren and her associates repeated the study as early as possible, and have obtained the same results for alert infants examined between 2 minutes and 9 minutes of age.

The most conservative and economical interpretation of these results suggests to me that the newborn infant is programmed to give visual attention to a symmetric array in the visual field, and to prefer among symmetric arrays those that more closely approximate the normal arrangement of the features of the face. In these terms, the programmed readiness of the infant seems undeniable for the kind of social interaction that, for most infants, is an essential element in the reciprocal attachment of infant and mother.

What use, if any, should we make of these observations? To translate them into some kind of planning or action, we have the choice of teleologic or intuitive standpoints, or we may be more inclined to actions that simply seem right or humane or personally satisfying. Perhaps no action is required other than that these physiologic gifts be enjoyed and shared among infant, mother, father and other caretakers as exquisite evidence of life's potential. On the other hand, these observations clearly ask us to re-examine our institutions and our child-caring practices, as our obstetric colleagues already have suggested. These observations further ask that we open new options for mothers, fathers and infants to know and appreciate one another and that we continue to carry out studies, some of which will be ethologic in nature, that will identify other important elements in human attachment and socialization.

That there are other important elements besides the visual in human socialization is certain, and they may run the gamut of sensory input. It has already been shown[3], for example, that if a mother is encouraged to speak the name of her child as often as she feels she wishes during the first hours or few days of life, between 3 and 8 days of age many infants can be shown reliably to turn their heads to the voice of their mother speaking their own name in preference to another voice speaking that name or their mother's voice speaking something that they have not previously heard. The importance of kinesthetic and somesthetic input to the baby has been less well studied, but studies in primates (Harlow, Mason and others) leave us no doubt that these may also be of major interest.

A lively discussion [1] surrounds the question whether aspects of socialization or other developmental processes in man have critical periods, in the sense that if an essential step is not achieved at a particular time, the capacity for achieving that step may wane with the further passage of time. In this connection, we are reminded of the observation made by Provence and Lipton [6] that deficiencies of language development in a group of institutionalized children were generally not recovered by infants and young children for whom other impairments were restored to normal range following placement in adoptive or foster care homes in the second year of life.

Animal or primate ethologies have a host of other questions for us. These include such concerns as the nature of and need for play involving siblings or peers, the ways in which children and especially adolescents form and defend notions of territory and the relationship between programmed intraspecific aggression and the destructive violence with which an aggressive or assertive motive in human behavior may be identified or confused. All of these need much further study.

A word of caution is in order. With all the opportunities new insights give us to view human institutions and relationships in new perspectives, we must be cautious not to overinterpret or overreact to what we see and learn. On the other hand, there are some teleologic, intuitive, humane or likely satisfying changes in infant or child care or maternal or paternal care that it seems to me we ought to be able to make without demanding that we prove with new double-blind studies the inappropriateness of some procedures regarding which we already have come to feel uncomfortable. I believe that we should already be setting priorities for change as well as for further study.

REFERENCES

1. Connolly, K.: Learning and the concept of critical periods in infancy, Dev. Med. Child Neurol. 14:705, 1972.
2. Goren, C. C., Sarty, M., and Wu, P. Y. K.: Visual following and pattern discrimination of face-like stimuli by newborn infants, Pediatrics 56:544, 1975.
3. Hammond, J.: Hearing and response in the newborn, Dev. Med. Child Neurol. 12:3, 1970.
4. Kagan, J.: Early Influences and Social Class, in Vaughan, V. C., III (ed.), *Issues in Human Development* (Washington, D. C.: U. S. Government Printing Office, 1971).
5. Klaus, M. H., *et al.*: Maternal attachment: Importance of the first postpartum days, N. Engl. J. Med. 286:460, 1972.
6. Provence, S., and Lipton, R. C.: *Infants in Institutions* (New York: International Universities Press, 1962).
7. Salapatek, P. H.: Discussion, in Vaughan, V. C., III (ed.), *Issues in Human Development* (Washington, D. C.: U. S. Government Printing Office, 1971).
8. Vaughan, V. C., III (ed.): *Issues in Human Development* (Washington, D. C.: U. S. Government Printing Office, 1971).

COMMENTARY

SUSAN LUDDINGTON (Chicago): I react very strongly to Frederick Leboyer's inflexible regimen for a method of childbirth in which he doesn't permit his mothers to talk to the newborn infants during the immediate postpartum period, up to 24 hours. I was wondering how you feel about that.

DR. KLAUS: I've had the good fortune to see his movie, and I'm in the midst of reading his book. I think he is a gentle man, but I disagree with him on two or three points. In the film, I saw that Leboyer was doing the touching of the baby, with the baby lying on the mother. This period does not belong to Leboyer. He is a baby lover, but the mother and father should make their own decisions as to what they want to do with the baby, if the baby is well.

The quiet alert state that Berry Brazelton and others have pointed out has obviously excited Leboyer. There is a large amount of state four in the first 30 minutes of life and he is picking this up, but he attributes it to the effects of the water. I don't agree. The large amount of state four would be present anyway, so long as the baby is kept warm.

Six to 8 years ago, Kenneth Cross put 3 perfectly normal infants at 2 hours of age into a water bath at the mother's temperature, except for their faces. He was interested in respiratory control. All 3 babies stopped breathing completely, and after about 45 seconds they turned dusky and he quickly took them out. Leboyer must be putting the babies in water at a temperature that is slightly different from the mother's. Otherwise, I think these babies would stop breathing.

DR. VAUGHAN: May I add that I cannot accept the notion that the mother shouldn't talk to the baby. It has been shown that if mothers are encouraged to say the name of their babies as often as they like in the first day of life, babies as young as three to eight days can be shown to turn their heads reliably to the sound of their mothers speaking their name, in preference to somebody else speaking that name or their mothers saying something else. So the baby has a way of identifying significant sounds. The mother has some way clearly to give them significance. I would hate to find this aborted.

DR. BRAZELTON: All of us who care about small babies feel competitive with everybody else and we all feel we can do all that's necessary for that baby. It interferes with day care when day care operators cannot let parents get to their children. It interferes in the medical emergency wards. It interferes in premie nurseries. It interferes at every stage of caretaking for small children.

This is a very strong unconscious reaction that none of us is really aware of most of the time, but it makes Leboyer want to touch the baby and shove the mother out. It makes us pediatricians treat mothers as if they were completely idiotic with their questions, and it makes nurses say they won't have time for the children if the parents are there.

This is something we must all be aware of and take into account, and get out of the way, if we are really interested in cementing parents to their children.

SUZANNA GILBERT (Raleigh, North Carolina): I have two questions. First, I would like some discussion about the effects of obstetric medication on the attachment process. Also, I would like to discuss the attachment process if the baby is stillborn or grossly deformed.

128

DR. KLAUS: I think there have been a number of observations that if a mother is medicated enough she may have a baby limp as a dishrag, whose eyes are closed and who doesn't respond to her. About 10% of all babies in full-term nurseries who weigh more than 2500 gm are really immature—less than 37 weeks. They also act like medicated babies. Nurses, physicians and mothers are terribly concerned with these babies because they don't respond like normal babies. Their necks are limp. They don't nipple easily. It's therefore important to assess the true age of every infant. If the baby is immature, it must be explained to the mother. That's what a mother discovers when she receives a baby following anesthesia—the baby does not respond as she anticipates. Her own sensations are also dulled.

As to your second question—what do you do following a stillbirth or the birth of a malformed baby? The first is a very important mental health question because very few people lose babies. The mother becomes attached when the fetus moves. She goes through the same mourning and grief response as she would if she had had the baby and he lived for 2 months. She must be helped with this.

I think you can help her in several ways. First, you can help her and her husband to understand the process they're going to go through in the next 6 or 8 months, what their feelings are, and let them know that you're going to stick with them even though they lost the baby.

The question of malformation is a whole separate area. The parents have to mourn the loss of the perfect baby they planned to have before they can become attached to the actual baby. This takes a long time, during which you have to be with them so that they can finally begin to take care of the needs of the baby they did not plan to have.

DR. VAUGHAN: There is a very closely related question: If the baby is deformed or if the baby dies, how soon, if at all, should the mother have an opportunity to handle this child, or to see the baby? I think many of us feel very strongly that a prevalent attitude that the mother shouldn't be allowed to know the deformity or see the baby, since she might become attached, is something we should not just re-examine but reject. It's very important, it seems to me, for the mother to have some experience with this child.

I have carried dead babies a mile or so in hospitals to the bedsides of their mothers, so that each mother could see, feel, hold and find that the reality of her baby's existence and of her baby's death was something that she could fully know and in fact live with, with all the need for working through grief that Marshall has referred to.

DR. BRAZELTON: I guess I can't help but interject again. It seems to me this is one more instance of our putting parents down and neglecting to realize that they have strengths, and that if we combine with them in an effort to overcome their grief reactions and deal with them they have strengths to do it that we have not heretofore been giving them credit for. I think this is what is so exciting about the work of Marshall Klaus and John Kennell. They say that a woman who has a premature baby or an at-risk baby is of course going to grieve and feel guilty and feel like she has done it to the baby, but you can help her with that because she has strengths to deal with it if you take her in and let her participate with you in the process.

DR. KLAUS: The point about touching the sick baby or seeing the malformed baby is important. Throughout much of the country we now have a transportation system for the very sick baby. The baby comes in, but the mother stays back.

I have a videotape that shows a father who supported the mother—visited her and mobilized himself—but during the period without her baby she began to mourn. People came into the hospital room and said, "How is your fine baby?" forgetting that it was sick in the other hospital. In the future, a high-risk mother should be taken to the center where her baby is going to be hospitalized so that the baby isn't in one hospital and the mother 25 or 50 miles away.

DR. MURIEL SUGARMAN (Boston, Massachusetts): There is some work coming out of Lou Sander's group in Boston. His work has to do with the establishment of biorhythms in the neonate, and he has shown that babies who have a single caretaker show less feeding distress and more rapid establishment of visual biorhythms and sleep biorhythms; and that when the caretaker changes or the baby has multiple caretakers, the infant shows distress.

Could you make a comment, Dr. Klaus, about the newborn nursery in light of that material?

DR. KLAUS: I think nurseries are set up to protect the babies from infection. Lou Sander's work has really led the way in showing that if the mother can have her baby as much as physically possible, it's much more likely that the two will exhibit the neat rhythmicity that he and his colleagues have demonstrated, and that the baby will have minimal periods of crying. The matching of rhythms may even start earlier if she receives the baby immediately after delivery while he is in the quiet alert state.

DR. SUGARMAN: Could I also mention that I talk to mothers who have rooming-in. One of the problems is that the setup we have for rooming-in doesn't let the mother get to her baby as easily as she might. If we could somehow arrange it so that the basinette is higher or closer or attached to the bed the way in some countries they hang a cradle from the foot of the bed and the mother can just reach over and get the baby, that's the kind of change that I think we're going to make only when we realize the importance of the mother being able to have this contact with her infant.

DR. KLAUS: There is the only point on which I will differ. Moving the cradle next to the mother would be better than leaving it at the foot of the bed. In the hospitals where it is right next to her, you'll see the mother always looking at the baby.

DR. OLSON HUFF (Charlotte, North Carolina): What effect does silver nitrate, which produces a chemical ophthalmitis, have on the eye contact that is so important to child and mother?

DR. KLAUS: I am glad you raised this point, Dr. Huff. We do not put the silver nitrate in until an hour after birth, after the parents have had their infant to themselves.

Part III

Socialization in Early Infancy

13

Early Parent-Infant Reciprocity

T. Berry Brazelton, M.D.

*Associate Professor of Pediatrics, Harvard
Medical School, Boston, Massachusetts*

The confusing demands of a complex, undirected society, coupled with the
lack of support (often even negative support) that is provided new parents by
our present nuclear family system, leave most parents insecure and at the mercy
of tremendous internal and external pressures. They have been told that their
infant's outcome is to be shaped by them and their parenting; at the same time,
there are few stable cultural values on which they can rely for guidance in setting their course as new parents. Most new parents are separated emotionally
from their own parents' standards by the generation gap and all that that implies.
Our present generation has actively separated itself from the beliefs and mores
of the preceding generation. For example, we can cite the ambivalence with
which the press and other media are treating Ben Spock's previously accepted
ideas. I am not questioning the need for a change in child-rearing practices, for I
certainly endorse many of the revisions (as does Dr. Spock), but I want to show
how one more potential prop has been eliminated from the young parents'
armamentarium for support. Physicians are not readily available to many young
parents and nurse-practitioners are not quite filling the gap yet, although I hope
and believe that they will be doing so before long. Pediatricians and physicians
in family medicine will be pressed toward a primary care paradigm lest they lose
the most rewarding and precious asset a physician has: the feedback from maintaining a supportive, interactive relationship with parents as they foster the development of their children.

Our society's backup for parenting often is a negative one. There is virtually
no opportunity for most children as they grow up in small, lonely nuclear family
settings to experience how their own or other parents go about raising small
brothers and sisters. As a result, they come to parenting with little experience of
their own.

The childbirth education groups have demonstrated the importance of preparation for childbirth itself. This preparation demonstrates another missed but
powerful potential – that of preparing young couples for their roles as parents.

But there are few programs yet at this level. To mention one in passing, we have been preparing a high-school-level curriculum in child development for young teen-agers. The strength of this curriculum is that it is combined with practical experience with young children in a day care setting. In pretesting the audio-visual material, we have shown one film of a newborn's behavior as he enlists his new mother's attention around a first feeding. As he captures her by turning to her voice, following her face in eye-to-eye contact, and by cuddling actively into her the first time she holds him, grasping her gown and looking up into her face, the audience of teen-agers was tested for degree of attention by dropping chains behind them in the classroom. The 14-year-old girls jumped, looked around and laughed when they discovered our device. By contrast, the 14-year-old boys jumped but never turned around, so deep were they immersed in these pictures of baby and his mother. To me it represented the kind of hunger and affect that we could and should be mobilizing in our youth around caring for and understanding others—in this case, small and dependent others.

Margaret Mead commented on the value of such a program in setting the stage for parenting later on by saying, "Sure that's great, but why do you wait to introduce them to babies until they're teen-agers? No developing culture would wait that long—they'd never capture their youth. Most stable cultures indoctrinate children of 5 and 6 into caretaking of the young of their society." We are certainly not giving children or adults enough opportunity to capture the excitement of child development, nor to find early the security they will need when they are faced with their own new babies.

But an infant is not as helpless as he seems, and there are rewards as well as messages from an infant that can guide a new mother and new father as they become faced with their new roles. We have been stuck with one model of child rearing that has long since done its damage and must soon be eradicated. In the 1950s when I began my work, parents were taught that their infants were lumps of clay, to be molded by their environment—for better or worse. Since this idea was exploited by the process of looking at the outcome of children as if the results were due to parent's mistakes, and since that outcome was evaluated by physicians interested in pathology (psychiatrists, neurologists and disease-oriented pediatricians), the literature of that era and the popular literature for mothers and fathers available today still is loaded with a pathologic slant. Most of the books for parents are framed with "How to—," "How to be a good parent," "How to avoid problems." Implicit in this approach is that you *may* luck out and do a few things right, but the chances are far greater that you won't. And unless you do everything exactly right, your child will be scarred by his association with you. Everything that goes wrong will be due to your mistakes, and everything that goes right can be chalked up to luck and/or his own strength in the face of an adverse environment. Since most parents feel insecure in their roles, this thinking reinforces their feelings of inadequacy. The end result has been a generation of tensely anxious, burdened young parents. My own children and the teen-agers among my patients will all tell you, "The worst thing about our parents is not whether they did or didn't discipline me, or whether they did or didn't do things right but that they *never* smiled." I am sure that we have put American families under stress with our medical-pathologic model—looking for mistakes and failure—far too long.

I'd like to begin to point to some of the strengths that are inherent in the parent-infant system, including the guidelines that a reciprocal interactional system between a baby and its parents can produce to guide them and to reward each of them, for the infant comes well equipped to signal his needs and his gratitude to his environment. In fact, he can even make choices about what he wants from his parents, and shut out what he *doesn't* want in such powerful ways that I no longer see him as a passive lump of clay, but as a powerful force for stabilizing and influencing those around him. What I believe we must do is to uncover and expose these infant strengths to parents, to demonstrate the infant's behavior on which they can rely and to support young parents in their own individualized endeavor to reach out for, attach to and *enjoy* their new infants! But this is no mean task.

What is the adaptive purpose of prolonged infancy in the human? No other species has as long a period of relative dependency, and I believe with Dr. Vaughan and many others that it is important to look for the adaptive advantages in rules of nature, selected over many generations for their survival value. Compared to any other species, the human neonate is relatively helpless in the motor sphere and relatively complex, even precocious, in the sensory sphere. This enforces a kind of motoric dependence and a freedom for acquisition of the many patterns of sensory and affective information that are necessary to the child and adult human for mastering and surviving in a complex world. In other words, the prolonged period of infancy allows for early and affective transmission of all the mores and instrumental techniques evolved by society — and a kind of individuality inherent in each culture with this society that fairly blows your mind as soon as you think of it. I am convinced by my own cross-cultural research that each culture's individual values and expectations are passed on and established in the infants in the first few months of life by the patterns of response and the child-rearing practices to which he is exposed by his parents and other caregivers around him. I even believe that each culture's expectations for its adults are based on an interaction in infancy between the endowment of its infants and the capacity of this endowment to respond to the adult and societal expectations.

In a culture of poverty in which intrauterine malnutrition has already depleted at birth the DNA (number of cells) content of brain, adrenals and thyroid, it is no wonder that the parental expectation no longer is that of reinforcing the baby and child for complex learning tasks, which require motivation and excitement and prolonged attention, all of which are dependent on optimally functioning central nervous systems and properly activated adrenals and thyroids, which help to maintain long attentional cycles. Parents of our black poor can hardly be expected to value the motor excitement of their newborns in a world that fosters such statements (completely refuted by our own research) as "If a black baby is precocious at motor tasks, he will be poor at cognitive learning," and which sets up such unyielding, unsympathetic school systems that his motor assets become deficits and his excitement in motoric learning becomes the most dangerous attribute he can have in our first grades. It is no wonder that some black mothers label any autonomy in their babies as "fresh" or "bad." It certainly is counterproductive in an unwelcoming society.

What are some of the built-in strengths of the human neonate? A few examples will demonstrate how powerful these are as economical determinants of how he will conserve himself in a new overwhelming world and how he can quickly acquire the information he needs to choose to make his caregivers familiar with him and responsive to him in a way that will latch them on to him at a critical period for them both. Right out of the uterus (1) he can and does turn his head to the human voice repeatedly, and his face alerts as he searches for its source; (2) he will attend to and choose a female vocal pitch over any other [4]; (3) humanoid sounds are not only preferred to pure tones in an equivalent range of pitch but when he is tested with continuous sucking as a response system, he stops sucking briefly after a pure tone, then goes on sucking steadily, whereas to a human tone he stops sucking and then continues in a burst-pause pattern of sucking (as if he were expecting more important information to follow, and as if the pauses in the sucking were designed to allow for attention to this further information) [5]; (4) he will attend to and follow with eyes and full 90°, head turning a picture of a human face, but will not follow a scrambled face, although he will look at it wide-eyed for a long period (in the delivery room and before any care taking has been instituted) [7]; (5) he will turn to and prefer milk smells above water or sugar water; (6) he can taste and respond to with altered sucking patterns the difference between human milk and a cow's milk formula designed to exactly reproduce the contents of breast milk [8]. There are many more such fascinating behavioral patterns that we have captured in a Neonatal Assessment Scale, which after 20 years of work now is available in manual form and on film [1]. The Scale examines 26 behavioral and 20 reflex activities of the human neonate as he interacts with an examiner. And we hope and trust that it captures the assets and skills he will bring to the early mother-father-infant interaction. We do have evidence to show that if new mothers (and work in process is designed to show the same thing with fathers, Ross Parke [9]) are shown their infants' behavioral responses in the neonatal period, these mothers behave significantly differently from a control group 1 month later in a feeding situation, and on a scored interview feel and say that their attachment and their self-image as parents are significantly enhanced by having been encouraged to see their babies as individuals, as "people," strong enough to withstand any mistakes they may make due to their inexperience as parents.

The payoff to us as physicians in demonstrating neonatal behavior to parents comes as a bonus, as if they included us in the enhancement of their attachment to their babies through seeing them as well-equipped individuals. For they say, "I *knew* he could see and hear me, and that he knew it was me, but I was afraid it was just wishful thinking. But if *you* tell me it's true, I can believe in it and enjoy it." They come in for our weekly research sessions in blinding snowstorms—never missing a visit—and speak gratefully of all we've taught them about their babies. Indeed, it is not we who have taught them, but we have simply provided a supportive framework for the attachment energy available around birth with which they can begin to foster the important reciprocal interaction between their infants and themselves.

In our laboratory at Children's Hospital Medical Center, we have been looking at this early reciprocal interaction between infants and their parents and, more recently, infants and strangers. We start at 2 weeks and continue with them until 24 weeks in a laboratory situation, designed to film and analyze the ingredients of early reciprocity as it develops between infants and familiar adults. We film the infants in a reclining chair (or baby seat) as the adult comes in to lean over him and enlist his attention in "games" or "play." We first found that as early as we could film it, we saw completely different kinds of behavior and attention with a mother and with an attractive object [2].

With an attractive object, as it was brought into "reach" space (about 12 inches out in front of him), his attention and face became "hooked," his extremities and even his fingers and toes pointed out toward it, making brief swipes out toward it, as he attended with a rapt, fixed expression on his face. When he was satiated, his attention broke off abruptly and he averted his eyes or turned his whole head and body away for a brief period before he came back for a further period of "hooked" attention. Thus, he established a jagged homeostatic curve of attention, and his arms and legs displayed jerky components of reach behavior as they attended to the object—all at a time when a reach could not be achieved successfully.

With his mother, his attention and motor behavior were entirely different; his eyes, his face, his mouth, his extremities all became smooth and cyclic. As he attended, he moved out slightly toward the object with his head, his mouth, his eyes and even with his legs, arms, fingers and toes. But, almost immediately, the approach behavior was followed by smooth, cyclic withdrawal behavior, as if he expected his mother (or father) to come out to him. His attention was cyclic also, and he looked intently at her (his) face, lidded his eyes or turned them slightly to one side, or up or down, still keeping the parent in peripheral view, but alternating between attention and reduced attention, in average cycles of 4 per minute over a 3-minute observation period. This attention-withdrawal cycle within a period of reciprocal interaction looked as if it followed a homeostatic curve of involvement and recovery that was smooth and signaled a period of intense involvement between infant and parent. The parent cycled, too—playing a kind of swan's mating dance, as he or she moved in to pass on information or behavior when the infant was looking, and withdrew slightly to let up in intensity when the infant withdrew.

We have been able to characterize the relative reciprocity and amount of affective, and even cognitive, information that a parent can transmit in such a period by the cyclic quality of the interaction. In parents who are too anxious and are insensitive to their infants' homeostatic needs (for this parallels the demands of the physiologic systems of an immature organism such as is the neonate), the infant necessarily turns off his attention and spends most of the period keeping the tense parent in his peripheral field, checking back from time to time. In failing interactions, the jagged attentional system of the infant resembles a very sparse period of object attention. One can see from some of the failing interactions that the sparseness of message transmission is in direct contrast to a smooth homeostatic curve of attention in an optional period of reciprocity. Not only does such a cycle allow for long periods of attention without exhausting the immature physiologic systems of the infant but it provides a rich matrix for choices and change in attention at any moment. These cycles also provide a matrix for adaptability of a very sensitive kind to the few caregivers who must become important to the infants.

We think that we are seeing a reliable difference between mothers and fathers as they perform in this system. Mothers start out and remain smoother, more low-keyed, more cyclic themselves, using other behaviors, such as touching, patting, vocalizing, smiling to "contain" the baby and provide him with a gently containing matrix for early responses, such as smiles, vocalizations, reaches, etc. But they don't seem to be in such a hurry for these to develop, and they are sensitive (often extremely so) to the competing physiologic demands of the infant [2, 3].

On the other hand, most fathers (and there are notable exceptions) seem to present a more playful, jazzing-up approach. Their displays are rhythmic in timing and even in quality, but the behaviors are presented with a more incisive, heightened and heightening quality. As one watches this interaction, it seems that a father is expecting a more heightened, playful response from the baby. And he gets it! Amazingly enough, an infant by 2 or 3 weeks displays an entirely different attitude (more wide-eyed, playful and bright faced) toward his father than to his mother. The cycles might be characterized as higher, deeper and even a bit more jagged. The total period of playful attention may be shorter if the small infant gets overloaded, but, as he gets older, the period of play is maintained for a longer time [14].

With a stranger, the reciprocity is very difficult to achieve. The stranger does not sense quickly or adapt himself to the baby's cyclical rhythms, and, as a result, very early in infancy one can see the jagged kind of attention-nonattention that we first saw with objects, and which does not result in long attention spans. It seems to be a behavioral precursor to the awareness of strangers seen at 5 months and anxiety toward strangers seen at 8 months. For the infant demonstrates clear behavioral differences as early as 4 weeks as he attends to a stranger's overtures and lack of reciprocal "fit" in the interactional situation. Even though the infant may be attentive, and even "hooked" in his attention to the new person, he attends with what appears to be a more expensive, demanding kind of cyclical attention. We now think we can look at any part of a baby's body without actually seeing his face and predict with some degree of certainty whether the infant is interacting with an object, a stranger or a familiar caregiver.

What does this kind of reciprocal "set" mean to the infant? It certainly appears to be basic to the healthy development of infant-parent reciprocity. My own feeling is that we are tuning in on the basic homeostatic systems that govern the physiologic processes as well as the attentional ones in the developing infant. If these are "shaped" by his environment in one way, they may press him toward a psychophysiologic adjustment of one kind or another. And we may even be seeing the potential for understanding the anlage of psychosomatic disease. Certainly when an environment can tune to the baby's needs for such elegant homeostatic controls, the attentional *and* physiologic cycles can be smooth, rich, adjustable. I can easily jump to the kind of tuning up of the CNS cycles that must find regulation as well as input from the environment to proceed toward optional development of motor and cognitive skills. I think we are looking at the precursors of affective development that are so necessary to the child's total development. We have examples from Harlow's [11] monkeys, from René Spitz [12] and from Provence's later studies of institutionalized infants [10], which show that development did not proceed when there was no such nurturing from the environment. I think we are seeing that it is not just stimuli from the environment that are necessary but certain kinds of "appropriate" stimuli embedded in a matrix of reciprocity between the infant and his caregivers. The reciprocity is sensitive to the individual tuning of the infant's particular homeostatic controls and his needs for input and overloading. It is represented by his cyclical curve of attention-nonattention when the environment is not in tune. We may see in such syndromes as failure to thrive that the infant's entire physiologic and psychologic systems have been entrained in a failing downward curve of development.

For the infant, such a reciprocal system, when it is going well, acts as fuel and information for his ongoing development, entraining the fueling from within that he receives as feedback from learning each new developmental task. Robert White called this latter force a "sense of competence." Both an inner sense of competence and feeling from a gratifying reciprocity with his environment are necessary to the infant's optimal development.

For the parents, the feedback from such a reciprocal system is just as rewarding as it is to the infant and fuels their energy for continuing in such a demanding ongoing relationship as "good" parenting requires. Their awareness of when they are successful must be felt unconsciously when things are going well, and we as supportive experts could and should point out such periods so that they can become consciously aware of their successes as guidelines to their parenting efforts.

Their power in shaping their children to their own requirements might be frightening, but it certainly must be pointed out to them as absolutely necessary for the child's ultimate capacity to grow emotionally and fit into a demanding society. Within such a framework, one could build a matrix for informing parents of the importance of each child's individual needs and individual ways of responding within any situation. These reciprocal needs as well as the child's individual needs will change a bit at each stage of development, but basically the reciprocal feedback system can be relied on as a guide for when it's going well, and when it's not, between parents and their small children.

I suppose that this expresses my basic philosophy about the important aspects of parent-child interaction.

With this kind of reciprocity as the basis for his affective, motor and cognitive development, how does this apply to some of our society's new programs? Should we continue to press for early stimulation programs? Yes, *if* these provide a focus around which reciprocal interaction between parents and their babies can form more important affective interaction. *But,* if stimulation with objects or toys intrudes on the interpersonal or is substituted for it, it must be obvious that the infant will lose out on more important learning than he will ever gain by interaction with objects or toys. The possibility for overloading him with too much or inappropriate stimulation can easily be visualized as one thinks about the static, jagged homeostatic curves of his interaction with objects. The possibility that mothers might substitute "learning environments" for themselves makes me shudder.

The day care situation poses potential problems and questions within this kind of understanding of early infant experience. (Let me say quickly that I think day care is important and here to stay.) How early can parents expect an infant to learn the systems of another caregiver? Will he or she miss out on important information gained within the reciprocal systems established by his own parents? I cannot really answer these important questions. We shall be looking for the answers to them. But I do worry about separation from parents before these patterns are well established and are familiar and understood by each member of the dyad or triad.

We think we have seen that infants by 4 or 5 months can maintain a lower order of cycling for interaction for an 8-hour stay in a day-care center, and can save up the important parts of themselves, the disintegration as well as the excited interactional energy, for their parents at the end of the day [14]. Parents who feel guilty about having left their infant all day often take the intense reactions of their infants as they pick them up at the end of the day as a reprimand from the baby or as evidence of how "bad" they are as parents. This may, indeed, be the best testimony to their importance to the infant as anchors and as providers of important affective experience. But I worry more about parents who must give up their infants to other caregivers, for I see far too many who suffer deeply and seriously over the separation and the loss of contact with the infant. Their grief causes them to overreact with guilt, with competitive feelings toward the secondary caregiver and with a constant unconscious or conscious comparison of themselves as parents with the often idealized caregiver, or with ideas of what they might have been as parents had they not left the child for whatever reasons. As a result of some of these too-painful feelings, some parents may pull away from the child and/or dilute their strong feelings of attachment for the infant with such feelings as "He's better off than he would be with me," or with attempts at denying their primary role for him. I worry more about them as people, and I certainly worry about them as a family. I'm sure that day care and all of our programs could act as backups for families caught in the web of our demanding, lonely, nuclear family society—*if* the programs were oriented as supports for the mother-father-infant triad, and with the importance emphasized of maintaining reciprocity in these triads. They could offer an extended family experience within the day-care setting for all young families and become a major source of stabilization for families.

The excitement and feedback rewards of interacting with infants and small children are as great for *all* adults as they are for the parents of the infant or child. Unfortunately, competitive feelings for the child can easily dominate a substitute caregiver, so that the richness and importance of the reciprocity I've been describing *could* become a threat to the families of these babies if we allow such caregivers to see their goals as replacing the parents of the babies in their charge rather than that of fostering and reinforcing the excitement of reciprocity between parents and their offspring in a lonely, demanding world! All of us who are interested in preserving the family as an optimal source of important experience for the vulnerable developing infant must see our goals clearly. We must be careful to provide environmental supports that reinforce the strength and rewards of reciprocal affective ties *within* the family!

REFERENCES

1. Brazelton, T. B.: *Neonatal Behavioral Assessment Scale* (Clinics in Developmental Medicine, No. 50) (London: William Heinemann Medical Books, Ltd.; Philadelphia: J. B. Lippincott Company, 1973).
2. Brazelton, T. B., Koslowski, B., and Main, M.: The Origin of Reciprocity in the Moth-

er-Infant Interaction, in Lewis, M., and Rosenblum, L. (eds.), *The Effect of the Infant on its Care Giver* (New York: John Wiley & Sons, Inc., 1974), Vol. I, pp. 49–76.

3. Brazelton, T. B., Tronick, E., Adamson, L., Als, H., and Wise, S.: Early Mother-Infant Reciprocity. C.I.B.A. Symposium, London, 33:137, 1975.
4. Eisenberg, R.: Auditory behavior in the human neonate–a preliminary report, J. Speech Hear. Res. 7:245, 1964.
5. Eimas, P., Signeland, E., and Lipsitt, L.: Work in progress, Brown University, 1974.
6. Fox, E. M., Rosenn, D., and Harken, L.: Expanding the Role of Pediatricians in Daycare Centers. Paper presented at annual meeting, American Academy of Pediatrics, San Francisco, October, 1974.
7. Goren, C.: Form Perception, Innate Form Preferences, and Visually Mediated Head-Turning in the Human Neonate. Paper presented at S.R.C.D. Conference, Denver, April, 1975.
8. MacFarlane, A.: Personal communication. Oxford University, England, 1975.
9. Parke, R. D.: Family Interaction in the Newborn Period: Some Findings, Some Observations and Some Unresolved Issues, in Riegal, K., and Meacham. U. (eds.): *The Developing Individual in a Changing World*, vol. 2, The Hague, Mouton, 1975.
10. Provence, S., and Lipton, R. C.: *Infants in Institutions* (New York: International Universities Press, 1962).
11. Seay, B., Hansen, E., and Harlow, H. F.: Mother-infant separation in monkeys, J. Child Psychol. Psychiatry 3:123, 1962.
12. Spitz, R.: Hospitalization: An Inquiry into the Genesis of Psychiatric Conditions in Early Childhood, Psychoanalytic Study of the Child, I:53–74, 1945.
13. Tronick, E., Adamson, L., Wise, S., Als, H., and Brazelton, T. B.: Mother-Infant Face-to-Face Interaction, in Gosh, S. (ed.), *Biology and Language* (London: Academic Press), 1975.
14. Yogman, M., Dixon, S., Adamson, L., Als, H., and Tronick, E.: The Development of Infant Interaction with Fathers. Work in progress, Children's Hospital Medical Center, Boston, 1975.

14

Mother-Child Interrelationships and Malnutrition

J. Cravioto, M.D.

Chairman, Scientific Research Division of
the Mexican Institute of Child Welfare;
Professor of Pediatrics, University of
Mexico, Mexico City, Mexico

Man is first of all just another animal species; at the macromolecular and at the atomic level he does not differ from any other species. The way in which he builds energy is exactly the same way in which an ameba or a tubercle bacillus will do it. His cells can synthesize protein like any other cell in any other animal or vegetable. But in trying to conceptualize what man is as a biologic species, we find that man tries to search for a place where his favorite food is abundant, to eat as much as possible and to produce as many offspring as possible, so that they will go and search for their favorite food, eat as much as possible and give as many offspring, and so on in a continuing biologic cycle.

One day, for unknown reasons, man discovered that there were other men present and that the behavior of one was influencing the behavior of the other; and the day one of them questioned authority, both would suffer the consequences.

Man invented culture and man invented technology, but generally this culture and technology have been used for one man to enslave other men, forgetting that in moving from biologic species to a social species, interaction was the main element of difference between his behavior as a biologic animal and his behavior as a social one.

He built beautiful temples for his ego, not for interaction with other settlements. Until recently, he did not consider that his behavior would influence the behavior of his species throughout time; and the historical transcendency of his behavior at present would be his best way of showing that he can be something more than the biologic species to which he belongs.

He is beginning to realize that some children are born in the best of conditions that he can think of, that they grow in environments or cultures full of the technology and information he has been able to store up. Boundaries of such cultures tend to be universal, and as offspring grow, everything in the environment might be favorable for them. But man is also beginning to realize that there are some other members of his species who are born and grow in conditions that hardly would be called human. They start early to play roles that should not be required at their age, which should be the ages of learning and of enjoying life at each stage of development.

Under these latter conditions, nutritional deficiencies are one of the prices paid because of these differences. One finds that mild and moderate malnutrition and severe malnutrition come to affect one-third of the total number of children in these communities.

In our institution, we have been trying for many years now to assess how malnutrition develops and what the influences are beyond the nutrients and beyond the biochemistry of malnutrition, including the social elements, that come into play; and, particularly, why is one-third of the population at risk of severe malnutrition? Less than 10% of children develop this disease; and generally only one within each family develops a severe episode of the disease, and not the others. It is very seldom that in a single family there develop two cases of severe malnutrition. It generally is only one; why is this child singled out in this particular case for a negative outcome?

I will try to show some of the data that we have in studying the total number of children who were born in a calendar year in a community of 7000 people in which malnutrition, particularly severe malnutrition, is highly prevalent.

During the first 53 months, despite the efforts of the team in advising the families in the classic ways on food and disease, 22 cases appeared. Seven of them corresponded to what is called the marasmic type and 15 to the kwashiorkor type. Marasmic here refers to a child who is practically skin and bones, and kwashiorkor to the picture with edema, skin lesions, mucous membrane lesions, etc.

These 22 cases were distributed as 14 females and 8 males. Malnutrition is more prevalent in the female despite requirements that the female of all the species be more resistant to stress than the male. It is discrimination against the female, a higher social value being attached to the male than to the female in the society, that sets a pattern of distribution of food and distribution of care.

Some cases were treated at home because they could not be removed to the hospital, although at that time we thought that the hospital should be the place to treat all cases. The mortality at home was higher because of the conditions under which these children were treated, as you will see later.

We started by examining the biologic characteristics of the parents, trying to see if there was any difference between the group with malnutrition and the group selected from the same community, the same gestational age, same weight, height, chest circumference, girth circumference, arm circumference and psychomotor behavior at birth.

We found that there were no differences in mother's or father's ages, heights of parents, weights of parents, number of pregnancies. The characteristics of families with malnutrition did not differ in respect to size, number of living children, ages of previously born siblings or ratio of nuclear to extended families.

The economic characteristics indicated severe poverty. The annual income per capita was about 41 U. S. cents per day per individual in the group that had severe malnutrition. But this was only about 3¢ less per day per individual than in the control group. So poverty does not explain the occurrence of children with severe malnutrition on the whole.

The percentages of total expenses spent on food did not differ, nor the sanitary facilities available in the home.

When we get to the social and cultural characteristics, the personal cleanliness of the mother was not different, nor the father's personal cleanliness. The number of school years spent and degrees attained was from the grandmother to the mother no different. The proportion of literate to illiterate mothers was no different.

Contact with the outside world through radio listening was twice as much or three times as much in those without malnutrition than in those with malnutrition. At this time, the presence of just one positive correlation could be interpreted either as that one correlation out of twenty that is without significance, or as indicating that we are here in the presence of mothers of a different type in respect to their relationship to the outside world.

The mothers who did not listen to the radio in the village would be those mothers attached to a traditional pattern, and the mothers in contact with the outside world would be mothers of the innovating type.

We turned our attention then to the microenvironment. We selected the inventory of stimulations that has been devised by Bettye Caldwell and tried to quantitate the stimulation available for the child in the following areas proposed by Caldwell: (1) organization of a stable and predictive environment; (2) development of stimulation; (3) quality of language environment; (4) the need for gratification and avoidance of restriction; (5) fostering maturity and independence; (6) emotional climate available in the home for the child; (7) aspects of physical environment; and (8) the presence of play materials.

Let me present an idea of things that go into the inventory. For example, in the area of quality of language environment: whether the family usually converses freely at meals at which the child is present, with the child's participation; whether the parent occasionally sings to the child or sings in the presence of the child; or whether the parent encourages the child to relate experiences or takes time to listen to him relate experiences. With respect to play materials: whether there are toys or games that facilitate learning of numbers, letters, colors, sizes and shapes; whether there is a real or toy musical instrument; or whether a toy or game necessitates free movements and refined movements. These many items were scored by direct observation of whether the mother or father or other members of the family interact with the child or not.

Results of our studies showed at 6 months of age a difference between malnourished children who started to be malnourished after 6 months of age and a control group of children who were exactly the same as the others at birth. The difference indicates the protective value of home stimulation. This was a longitudinal study; we did not know how to predict previously who would most likely be malnourished.

Later, at 48 months of age, after the child had already been cured of malnutrition, the differences persisted. None of the controls scored at less than 90 points in the scale whereas close to two-thirds of the malnourished had scores lower than that.

We turn now to something that is present all through the animal kingdom: the mother-child relationship. We have watched the mother's reaction when the child was being tested by a psychologist, describing her behavior using a scale originally devised by Nancy Bayley. We observed the reaction of the mother while the child was performing easily, comparing control mothers with those of malnourished children during the first 6 months of life of the child. We found the mother of the child destined to be malnourished typically completely passive, with minimal reaction, or with acceptance without expression. None of the mothers of the future malnourished children was proud and admiring of the performance of the child. Four of 10 such mothers scored below a point of the scale below which none of the controls were performing.

These two groups of mothers had different responses to the interview, mothers of the malnourished tending to be defensive whereas other mothers were enthusiastic when talking about their child. The difference between the two was striking. One-half of the mothers of the malnourished did not go beyond slight elaboration in the interview about their children whereas 9 of 10 mothers of the controls talked more freely.

Mothers in the two groups differed in the amount of verbal communication that the mother had with the child, once again slanted to low values in the mothers of the future malnourished children in comparison with those of control children.

We examined the mother's reaction also when the child was performing extremely well. None of the mothers of the future malnourished children encouraged their children to do something, showed admiration or showed real exuberant joy whereas 3 of every 10 in the control group were doing that; and none of the mothers of controls showed apathy whereas some of the mothers of the malnourished were really effectively absent from the room while the child was doing a real good job of showing off all his abilities.

What are some of the repercussions of this? Let us take now a child who was malnourished and a child who was not malnourished as two real-life representatives of the two groups. Now we will make demands on the children. We received 60% satisfactory responses from the child who was malnourished, by this time completely recovered, as against 77% responses from the child never malnourished. What is more important is that the responses of the malnourished child were verbal in 46% of instances whereas the responses of the control child were 66% verbal.

We examined this a little further in respect to whether the child's response to failure was expressed in terms of competence, such as when the child says "I'm too little to do it" or "I never did it before" or "I have no experience" and so on; whether the response was expressed as negation or substitution, such as "I better go to my mother" or "Give me a glass of water" or "I better play with the dolls" or "I'm too tired" or "Better take me to the bathroom" and so on; or as requests for aid: "Do it for me" and so forth.

We found that the malnourished child gave mainly responses of substitution whereas the nonmalnourished child responded mainly in terms of competence, which meant a relationship of their own age in terms of behavior in working out a demand.

What would be the reaction of a schoolteacher to the passive child showing behaviors of substitution? Naturally, for a child who does not like to work, a child who is passive, a child who is rebelling against commands and so forth, the expectation is school failure. Prophecy fulfilled, of course.

Now let me relate one more thing. I indicated at the beginning that one of the important things in interaction is that my behavior will influence your behavior. We test this in this way. We say to the child: "Here is a picture of a schoolteacher. She is very happy. Why do you think she is happy? Because the child is trying hard to do her best or because the teacher likes the story?" Or "Here is a father and son. The father is very happy. Why do you think he is happy? Because the son is trying to do his best or because the father had an easy day at work?" Or "Here is a schoolteacher and she is very sad. Why do you think she is sad? Because she lost her purse or because children have been bad?" Or "Here is a teacher who is very happy. Why? Because the children learn a lot or because it was a very nice day?"

In other words, is my behavior influencing the behavior of other persons or is the behavior of others independent of my behavior?

Data on three groups of children, including malnourished children and a group of controls for IQ and sex, indicate that children who have been malnourished do not believe that their behavior influences the behavior of others.

So you have here then the influence on early socialization—a condition that we call malnutrition. We spent many years studying the biochemical aspects of the disease; now we find these consequences, in terms of the production of individuals who have different behavior. This behavior, then, will be the feedback to their own children, perpetuating a system and indicating the reason why some families continue for generations to be families with severely malnourished children whereas other families, under similar conditions of economics and even of formal education, do not become families of severely malnourished children.

If we want the activity not to be the particular involvement of a very small group, if we want the activity to belong to all the human species through time, then we have to be very specific in not letting us do the same to the children as we can do with a tree that measures normally 10–15 feet high, 4–5 feet in diameter—to become a dwarf.

These are the different levels of conception that we must have in dealing with this kind of problem: The child is malnourished because he has a reduced intake of adequate food. Why? Because the mother has inadequate knowledge of the child's needs, nutritional and non-nutritional. The family has a low purchasing power, so we have to lift the community out of the pre-industrial stage of development with appropriate programs. We should never confuse malnutrition of the individual in need of food with the malnutrition that is a deficiency in socialization for the mother, the family and the community. If we want to break the chain, the vicious cycle of malnutrition, then we have to attend to relevant aspects of socialization from the beginning of life.

COMMENTARY

JONATHAN KATSCH (New York City): I have been an admirer of Dr. Cravioto's work for some years. I would like to ask a question that has recurred in the popular literature recently. What is the physiologic relationship between malnutrition and intellectual retardation? The data that you presented today show how maternal psychologic deprivation is related to malnutrition. Can the physiologic effects on intellectual retardation be separated out from the social and psychologic effects?

DR. CRAVIOTO: I am afraid that for the human it would be impossible really to separate the effects. We must think of food not only as a carrier of nutrients to provide chemicals to the body for growth, maintenance and regulation. Food has color, aroma, consistency, texture, etc., and these are sensory inputs to the child. At the same time, mealtime is the time at which experiences are interchanged.

Who's who in the family and who's who in the community are questions related to the mealtime. Who is served first? Who sits on what side of the table? Who moderates the conversation? Who can get away with everything? When the child is old enough and a visitor comes in to be with the family and he sits at a certain place at the table, the child may ask, "Why is he taking your place?" And then you have perhaps to explain that it may be the boss and that you're due for a promotion, or any of those other things that will tell him the meaning of role and status.

When a child is deprived of food, he is deprived not only of chemicals but of sensory stimulation, and he is automatically deprived of an opportunity for social experience.

These cannot be separated. When we put together the animal world with the human world, then what we can really say is that the data apparently are leading toward the conclusion that nutrient deprivation raises the threshold at which the stimulation is effective for the animal; and you then may have the two effects combined in malnutrition, a result of the physiologic effect of the nutritional deprivation and the raising of the level at which effective stimulation will come into the picture. In real life you have both depressed; when you have both depressed, then there will be an interaction with an effect similar to that on an animal who is malnourished and isolated at the same time.

We have data to show that if you can really mount an effective program of stimulation through, first of all, teaching your staff, nurses, auxiliary social workers, dietitians and pediatricians how to formulate good patterns of motherhood or parenthood and use those patterns in the programs to stimulate the children, then children we thought were having some permanent sort of retardation of optimal function can come very, very close to being within the normal limits of children who have never experienced deficiencies of nutrition or stimulation.

But an effective program has to take into consideration human interaction and not just providing things or objects. It's human stimulation rather than an object-mediated stimulation that has been used in the past as synonymous.

That's where we stand at present in the relation between nutrition and mental development.

DR. CAROL GARVEY (Boston): Marshall Klaus pointed out that premature in-

148

fants have a higher rate of later malnutrition and of battering. I think there is good reason to think that the intensification or improvement of the relationship between infant and mother right after birth may be very helpful. What is not mentioned as often is that when the baby goes home he or she will weigh 2 or 3 pounds less than the usual full-term baby, will require more feedings and will require more sleep, so that such a baby will be at once more demanding and less responsive than babies that we otherwise see. While the baby is in the hospital, the mother can sleep at night; but when the baby comes home, the mother sleeps less than the mother of the usual newborn.

I think that this is therefore a particularly vulnerable period, and it's extended because it may take 18 months for such babies to catch up fully. They may be waking up at night for many more months than the average baby. I wonder how we can alert ourselves to this period of vulnerability and deal with it more adequately.

DR. KLAUS: I think that there are some attempts now being made in this country to arrange for a mother to live in with her baby in the hospital for 3 or 4 days before it goes home, until she can discover the baby's rhythm and they can get locked on together. I think that Catherine Barnard is taking Berry Brazelton's scale and showing mothers what her babies are like. If mothers can have this period caring for the baby and being in control of the baby, having the nurses and other people as consultants, then they can get locked into such a reciprocal relationship.

We really should think about changing our hospitals so that the premature nursery is circled by beds in which mothers can live as they take care of their babies. Many nurseries in the world have an advantage in that they don't have enough money for incubators. Instead, they've made hot rooms, in which the babies are all bundled up, sometimes wearing little hats, and the mother gives the care.

I think we should think now in terms of having mothers live in. And in order to do this in the United States you have to have a cot for the father.

DR. GARVEY: But I think we also have to address ourselves to the problems of the mother after she goes home with the baby. The problems last a lot longer and are more severe than those of the average mother.

DR. VAUGHAN: Isn't there another aspect that we might give attention to here? And that is a preventive aspect that extends back into the period before you knew that this baby was going to be premature—the need to give mothers a different kind of expectation. Some of them will be frustrated by the fact of the premature delivery of the baby; but with adequate preparation and expectation, and then with adequate involvement in the care of the baby during the critical phase, you may find that you can slide through this with much less disability than if the mother had to learn all of these things about her premature baby without any preliminary preventive work.

DR. BRAZELTON: I think there is something that interferes with our helping a mother with this. All the mother really needs is enough information about what to expect with a baby like this to help her through this period. But we have our own ideal version of what the baby ought to be, and we then reinforce the mother's loss of her ideal version. We pediatricians would like to see the baby as perfect; and in the process we often really desert people by withholding the useful information that we have. We know they're going to sleep more and demand more. If we could really convey this in addition to interpreting the behavior that the baby shows—with an expectation for the mother as to how long it's going to last—then I think we could make a big difference.

DR. CRAVIOTO: Another thing very important in this same relation is that if the baby is premature, the mother automatically assumes that she was incapable of having a baby meeting the expectations of the community or of the professional group. We are trying at present in our obstetrics clinic to show each mother the variations in the community in terms of weight, size and behavior of infants, trying to impress her with the fact that it is an individual that is going to be born and not a pattern.

What has to be done is that she identify the individuality of her baby and then treat that baby according to that individuality and form a pattern of behavior for him or for her.

DR. BRAZELTON: We have been looking at 6-pound babies, small for gestational age, that everybody says are normal, spontaneous, full-term deliveries because they weigh 6 pounds. We've been interested in them because their ponderal indices, which compare length and weight, are below the fifth percentile. We now have a group of about 20 of these babies who are either quite irritable or very slow to build up to an alert state. Moreover, when these sluggish babies reach an alert state they look right through you. They never really look into your eyes and lock you into their rhythmic interaction.

These are the kind of babies who are prone to failure to thrive and to abuse later on. Most babies presented to me at Children's Hospital as failure to thrive or an abused child have been small for gestational age.

One may say, "That 6-pound baby should have been easy to attach to. Why did the mother fail?" But these babies are different; their cycling is different, and their capacity to hook you in interaction is just slightly different; but it's enough to distort an idealized image for a mother, and I think at all the levels we've been talking about this morning.

DR. MURIEL SUGARMAN (Boston): Dr. Cravioto, in your study you don't differentiate between breast-feeding and bottle-feeding mothers and babies. I wonder if that may not make a tremendous difference in the mother's response to the baby's needs and in her ability to know what the baby needs at a particular time; the mother who is lactating may respond much more intuitively to the baby's needs to be fed and not to be fed.

DR. CRAVIOTO: Fortunately, from this point of view we are old-fashioned. All our babies are breast-fed for periods of no less than 6–8 months. They were breast-fed from the beginning, and the beginning is within 2–3 hours after delivery.

DR. LEONARD FINN (Worcester, Massachusetts): I would like to ask about mothers and fathers who work outside the home. How long does the attachment process take in terms of weeks, and how much time must they spend with their newborn infants in order for this attachment process to be complete?

DR. BRAZELTON: I really wish we had the answer to that. We are getting at it. It takes weeks, not days. That initial 3 months may be a ghastly period of adjustment—the colicky period, with all the other things that go on in the first 3 months. I really think that to allow a mother or father to go back to work or to part with their baby before the end of that period really sells it down the river. The baby may be able to manage it, but I think the parents may never be able to do it if they have never received the reward that comes at the end of 3 months, when the baby looks back into their faces and says "Gee, aren't we great."

A mother and, I think, a father have got to reach that period before either can feel "This is me that has done that." Without that, I don't see how parent/child interaction will ever have the same energy it might otherwise have. So it has to be at least 3 months, or probably even longer, for the parents' sake.

DR. FINN: How about the amount of time spent each day with the child?

DR. BRAZELTON: I think it's not really the amount of time as much as the kind of time. We have been looking at babies in day care, for instance, and now we are looking at an extended family situation in Africa where the mother leaves her child to go to the field at 6 weeks, with a secondary caretaker for the infant. But the mother never really separates from this child. When the baby cries, though she may be a mile away in the field, we can watch her head pop up to see that somebody is there to take care of the baby.

This is very different from the kind of thing that endangers our mother/father/infant relationships in this country, where separation is implicit, expected, understood. This is different.

We have been watching 4-month-old babies in day care centers. In our day care center, their activity cycle remains at a low-grade level all through the day. They don't go into deep sleep, nor do they go into very active upset states or into active participation during an 8-hour day. But when their mother or father comes at the end of the day, they disintegrate and begin to thrash around. Their mothers and fathers blame themselves for this disintegrated period and may say to themselves something like "I haven't been with that child all day and she's mad at me now." I don't believe that interpretation is correct. Rather, these babies have saved up all the important stuff for this period of disintegration and for the alert period that follows it. I would suggest that those periods at the end of the day can make up for a lot of low-grade cycling during the 8-hour day if their involvement was what was at premium.

PARTICIPANT (Burlington, Vermont): I would like to add that home-health-care programs for high-risk parents and children should be an important component of the system.

DR. BARRY FARBER (Philadelphia): What I am hearing today is talk about change in our political/social system and in our health care delivery system. We're also talking about the importance of early attachment and bonding behavior on development.

The program at Booth Hospital in Philadelphia was mentioned earlier. Dr. Franklin's program offers family-centered care, integrating fathers and families into the predelivery and the newborn periods. Some parents who go through Dr. Franklin's program—and I am one of them—have found that after delivery there was a sort of letdown. Before delivery, the parents had a lot of support, and were integrated into the care. Father and relatives would be there when the baby was born; but afterward, what was left?

A number of parents have asked: Can we do this in the postnatal period? Can we pull together the so-called lonely nuclear family, meet together and keep talking with other parents? These concerned mothers came through the Childbirth Education Association and other organizations that really lend support to young parents.

A program has been developed with planning through a task force and a steering committee. The parents can do this with the help of the medical establishment; where we're flexible, we'll come in the evening, we'll talk and we'll share the parents' concerns.

DR. KLAUS: There is a real success story in Booth Maternity Center here in Philadelphia, but throughout the country it has not been easy to change institutions. We have to find out why it is so difficult — impossible in many hospitals — and we must learn the process by which we change. I think we have to be instrumental in setting this as national policy at the level of our obstetric and pediatric and psychologic societies, as well as with the people who use the hospitals, the consumer.

I think it may end up in this case that the consumer movement is going to have to change many of the hospitals in our country. We have to lay the cards on the table about one issue, and that is the notion that authority and control rest with the physician who is delivering the mother. I think that the obstetrician is in many cases intruding on family affairs, and he sometimes makes very arbitrary decisions that make no sense: fathers in the delivery room/fathers not in; babies to be warm and dry/babies not to be dried. In other words, the decision-making process is such that you get all sorts of alternatives. And that is, I believe, because the physician is in a situtation where he really doesn't belong.

I think the physician should be a consultant for complicated obstetrics in the hospital, and I think delivery should be in the hospital. But I think the physician is probably often making these moves to exert control and to maintain his position. His position is well grounded, and though he can save fantastic numbers of babies, I think he has to give up certain areas to the family. I don't know how this can be done in this country easily at the present time.

DR. VAUGHAN: I agree completely with Marshall. One of the problems that we have to face is that we have been given a medical model. It may be really a disaster that the medical model or, still worse, the surgical model has been adapted to the birth of a baby, which is actually a social event. I think it's about time that we recreated the birth of the infant as a social event, took it out of the medical arena and gave it back to parents and families.

DR. CRAVIOTO: There were measures in the past that were very good for what we called a cultural survival. We didn't let mothers be near babies who were at risk of having infection because we wanted to save the life of the baby. But when we move historically from a culture of survival into a culture of quality, then we have to make a full review of all those practices that enabled lots of children to be saved. But at the expense of what? At the expense of optimal functioning in both mental and physical and social capacity.

We need to have a review of practices no longer applicable that were excellent in other historical times.

DOROTHY GROSS (Banks Street College, New York City): All that we have heard this morning puts emphasis on the roles of the mother and the father in terms of attachment, as the stimulating person and as the person with the contact with the outside world.

It seems that two things may be pointed to. One is that the traditional clinical role of the physician needs to be radically restructured or possibly added to, and/or that there may be a need for new roles or new fields for professionals, which is something we are beginning at Banks Street now—a graduate program to train child development specialists, focusing on the years under 3 and on family dynamics.

Here and there in certain hospitals—heavens knows, not connected with schools or centers—I am finding an interest in having such a person, whose expertise is in development and in working with families, a kind of supportive, quasi-social-work role but focused on the first 3 years of life and on family dynamics.

I wonder if someone would comment on that.

DR. BRAZELTON: At a cocktail party about a year ago, Selma Fraiberg, Anneliese Korner, Leon Yarrow—about 6 of us—decided that what we really needed was an interdisciplinary and interorganizational group that would train all disciplines who were interested in prevention with mothers/fathers/babies, and share across disciplines some expertise that all of us have at our fingertips now and for which the precise discipline is irrevelant as preparation. We have stuff in pediatrics that psychologists studying infancy now feel they've got to go back to medical school to get. What a waste of time! And what a danger to put these people through the brainwashing that medical school offers them!

I think it's time we got on now with a new discipline, which is a preventive, interventive discipline aimed at preserving the attachment of mothers, fathers and infants with a supportive point of view. I couldn't agree with you more.

PARTICIPANT: Coming back to the point of the obstetrician's control of early infancy, I have been distressed by the tendency in the past 50 years toward the separation of pediatrics and obstetrics, the pediatrician caring about the baby and the obstetrician focusing on the mother. I think much of our problem is because of this and also because the mother is attached to the obstetrician, who suddenly disappears, when she doesn't have rapport with the pediatrician yet. It seems to me that a rapprochement of pediatrics and obstetrics would be most constructive.

You want people who follow the biology and the psychology of the mother and the baby. It takes the same sort of personality to be a good obstetrician and a good pediatrician, and that is a different kind of personality from that of the good surgeon.

I wonder what can be done to make pediatrics and obstetrics a real working team.

DR. KLAUS: Wouldn't it, for most mothers, be a little bit easier—as I saw in Denmark and in other places—that the mother see a midwife for a half hour on each of twelve visits and have an obstetric checkup two or three times during pregnancy, and if everything was going well that she be delivered with the aid of another woman unless a complication brought her obstetrician?

I am a little concerned about the attachment a woman makes to her obstetrician. Shouldn't that be to her husband and to the baby?

PARTICIPANT: Isn't it true of the pediatrician, too?

DR. KLAUS: The pediatrician, too! We never see ourselves as others do.

MARVIN MATTHEWS (Honolulu): I am a child psychologist particularly interested in child psychiatry/pediatric liaison. I feel somewhat in the state of ekstasis myself since this morning. However, confronting harsh realities, I want to know about specific strategies that have worked and specific ones that haven't worked with respect to changes that Dr. Klaus has referred to.

DR. BRAZELTON: We have one that we're working on at Boston Children's in terms of changing pediatrics, and maybe child psychiatry too. We're trying to reorient physicians at a postresidency level to a positive model for looking at children and their parents, and it's the hardest thing to do you ever thought of. All of medical school and all of internship and residency training is aimed at looking at people with a pathologic model, probing for their weaknesses and their deficits; and when you begin to try to reorient yourself to look at development as if it were positive and ongoing and as if it were a family affair rather than a pediatric affair, you begin then to realize how really powerful our effect has been on people in terms of their seeing themselves as weak and deficient.

I think one of the things we've got to do is reorganize our own way of looking at ourselves, at people, at development, with a new model; and the second we do that, the strength behind putting over the kind of things that Marshall has been talking about becomes very different.

BARBARA HANLEY (Family Nurse Practitioner, University of Rochester, New York): Dr. Klaus's observations this morning on the attachment behavior of the observer were very meaningful to me. I see this as a strong force for us to capitalize on in trying to change the development of staff perceptions in departments of obstetrics and in perinatal areas. I see it as a really strong force for introducing new roles into the perinatal areas – bringing nurse midwives and clinicians together and trying to focus a whole new interdisciplinary effort. It's a fantastic concept!

BETTY HARRIS (Raleigh, North Carolina): We have heard a lot this morning about the necessity for restructuring the attitudes of the medical profession and changing the institutional setup, but many of us are actually caught in situations where we are preparing people in the best way we can to cope with *traditional* medical setups. I would like some suggestions for things that one could teach to parents during the prenatal period about how they can work with the institutional setup in such a way that they can get something out of it.

DR. VAUGHAN: I think that consumers are simply going to have to make their voices heard. The Childbirth Education Association is having an ever wider impact in its insistence that the system has to change, and it is enlisting the help of numbers of responsive, thoughtful and perceptive obstetricians and pediatricians in rethinking and reworking the system in some areas.

I think this is something for which the time has come. If we as consumers want it, we may have to demand it as nicely as we can, and insist on it.

DR. BRAZELTON: I think there are some specific answers to your questions. One, of course, is educating people to what they are going to face in the way of insults from the medical environment. Even more important is something we have sort of stumbled into – having prenatal interviews with mothers by pediatricians. The most powerful thing that has come out of it is that they turn to anybody who will listen in the prenatal period. They hear you say "I'm here to talk to you about having a baby and about your baby after he comes. I'm a pediatrician." Immediately the mothers launch off into their own concerns about themselves.

It has scared my pediatricians who are in training because the mothers talk about themselves for the next six interviews. The pediatricians come back saying "But they treat me like I'm a psychiatrist and they keep telling me all their dreams and fantasies." I must say to them "Just wait, around the new baby they will reorganize themselves, and they won't mention themselves again." After this kind of contact, they turn to these pediatricians at every opportunity for help in dealing with the medical system, in dealing with their own concerns around the new baby. Although they've been having only four to six prenatal interviews with mothers, I think we can do the same thing in one interview by giving mothers a chance to talk about themselves — in a one-to-one transference interview in which a pediatrician is really aiming at making a transference with the mother — this may make him a supportive figure that really isn't paralleled in our medical system.

DR. VAUGHAN: There is something else that might be added, from the standpoint of education. There is nothing that has been said here in the past couple of days that shouldn't be said to junior high school and high school students. I think that if they can be given a different view of what life is like and where they've come from and where they're going, they will be able to see their lives and their futures in quite different perspectives. They may then come up to the great adventures in life with a wholly different set of expectations, couched in some measure in demands that the system meet them at a different level from the usual one.

DR. CRAVIOTO: One thing we are trying to do is actually force the medical establishment to a definition of the role of the parents within each one of the processes in which the medical profession is involved. The simplest to us is in the way of treatment, restoration of health: first of all, to define and to accept that the father and the mother have a role in the restoration of health of the child and are not just nuisances that one has to deal with.

With defining the parent's role, then, the activities within that role can be at least described, and then a teaching program for future parents and parents can be started. This is working *within* the system to force the medical establishment to accept that there is a role to be played by father and mother in various situations. We have started with that, and then with trying to build into the children's experience at the high school level ideas of the roles that they will play later.

MARILYN HUFF (Charlotte, North Carolina): This morning has been fantastic. I would like to express a frustration however. Several of the speakers have said we would like to hear from the tremendous amount of expertise, the interdisciplinary team if you will, that is here today from so many kinds of child-caring people. Yet, the framework for this meeting is still the medical model, where the professional expert comes and tells all of us poor simple people of these great things, without much opportunity for interaction.

NANCY BRADLEY (Reading, Pennsylvania): The focus this morning has been on the biologic parents and their biologic infant. I am wondering how the speakers see the evidence influencing our roles and expectations for and with adoptive parents. What about current policies in getting infants to such parents as seen in this concept?

DR. BRAZELTON: I think this is the sort of thing that we ought to be prepared for and ought to be able to help people with. Probably in all adoptions there are things that we've got to be ready for and prepare parents for and help them with in the initial period, when they're trying to sense and adapt to the rhythms that will ultimately help them get off the ground.

DR. KLAUS: We should also look at other cultures. In Russia, prospective adoptive mothers pad their abdomens. When they know that they've been checked out by the Social Service and that they will be able to adopt the baby, they come into the hospital, occupy a room, and then leave with their padded belly. Later they come back to receive their babies and stay with their babies like the other mothers.

I am not suggesting that we do this, but I think that the long separation of the adopting mother from the event of the infant's birth is just making things more and more difficult for her.

MARY LISROCK (Family Doctor, Pittsburgh, Pennsylvania): I would like to comment on the concept of the family doctor, meaning that you see people for the premarital exam and you're not just the baby's doctor or just the prenatal doctor. You're the father's doctor and the mother's doctor and maybe the grandmother's doctor, and as a result you're not a stranger. As a result, you participate with everybody who is there. You're not someone who is going to disappear after they go out of the hospital.

You're going to be their continuing physician, not just for the baby but also for family planning post partum. If there is distress in the marriage, you know about it, or if there is distress in the mother/child or mother/father or father/child relationships.

The family practice movement is on. Maybe we should talk more about the family doctors and less about the *baby* doctor or the *prenatal* doctor—but in terms of someone who can participate as part of the family.

JERRY RUFF (Pediatrician, Bloomington, Indiana): Along with many of the other people here, I have agonized on how we can implement these beautiful ideas. As long as we're making unreasonable demands on our panelists' time, I would like to make another unreasonable demand. I guess I could summarize this by paraphrasing our friend W. C. Fields and say that I would rather have Victor Vaughan in Bloomington, Indiana than in Philadelphia.

It's one thing for Jerry Ruff to go back and talk to these bulwarks of conservatism that we have in our hospitals and tell them that we need to do certain things in our nurseries. They'll ask for a serum LSD level and they'll refer me as an urgent psychiatric casualty or turn me over to the John Birch Society. It's another thing when somebody with some clout tells them. The people who need to be told these things are not here. They're back in Bloomington, Indiana and Missoula, Montana and Tijuana, Mexico. But these are the people who need to be talked to. They don't come to meetings, and unless Marshall Klaus comes down to Indianapolis (where he was just this week) and talks to the medical obstetric societies in Bloomington and tells them about these things we're not going to get them done.

We don't have the clout. It takes somebody who is nationally known. By the way, I talked recently to a group of high school juniors and seniors—and this will reinforce this idea that *you* people can get the job done on a local level—and they were just enthralled with the film that they had seen by Berry Brazelton.

DR. BRAZELTON: Listen, Dr. Ruff, I'm not gong to let you off that easily. One of the things you are picking up here is our conviction and our enthusiasm and our determination to change things. If you are that convinced, sooner or later you can't lose. I'm convinced of that. Johnson & Johnson is just about ready to think about doing a national program series for young parents in which we literally can portion out some of these tasks and get them on film for a national audience. I think that will have a very powerful effect.

I am convinced also that people like you at the grass roots can do so much to back up what is obviously a national surge toward a reorganization of the family that you shouldn't put yourself down.

DR. RUFF: Another thought occurred to me. I have noticed that when speakers do come, if they bring along a nurse to convince our sister nurses that these are worthwhile things, that helps tremendously. When I hear a surgeon say something, I can think it's pretty good; but if I hear a pediatrician say it, I believe it! The nurses might say that Berry Brazelton is weird, even as weird as Dr. Ruff, but if a nurse comes along and reinforces it, they'll be more likely to believe it.

Part IV

Preschool Experience and Child-Rearing

15

The Role of Family during the First Half Decade

Jerome Kagan, Ph.D.

*Professor of Psychology and Social
Relations, Harvard University,
Cambridge, Massachusetts*

It is an undeniable fact that experiences in the family have a profound influence on the young child's psychologic development. One of the most persuasive empirical supports for that conclusion is found in the fact that there is typically no relation or a very low relation between the social class of the parents and aspects of infant behavior during the first 6 months of life. But by 1 year, middle class American infants, in contrast to lower middle or lower class children, are more attentive and vocally expressive to interesting visual and auditory events and by 2 years of age speak more complex sentences, have a larger vocabulary, exhibit more sophisticated problem-solving strategies and inhibit impulsive responses in problem situations. However, the social class of the parents usually is unrelated to the child's temperament—factors like irritability, smiling or excitability (Kagan, 1971). When observations in the homes of middle and lower class parents are made, we see that well-educated mothers talk more to their infants than do working class parents and otherwise act in ways that would produce the differences that we see at 24 months.

Psychologists interpret these data to mean that middle class American mothers care about the cognitive development of their very young children and believe in a set of instrumental practices that affect the child's development. Hence, they begin to implement their convictions earlier and with more consistency than do lower class mothers, and by the second year of life the effects of those experiences have become public. Moreover, there is recent evidence indicating that school-age children of mothers whose practices during infancy accelerated cognitive development obtain higher scores on the ITPA index of cognitive development than do children whose mothers were less interactive with them during the first year. Tulkin and Covitz (1975) administered the ITPA, Peabody and the MFF tests for reflection-impulsivity to 25 middle class and 18 working class 6-year-old girls—first-born—who had been observed at home and tested in the laboratory by Tulkin when they were 10 months old (Tulkin, 1970).

At 10 months, the middle class mothers were more likely than the working class parents to engage in reciprocal vocalization with their infant, to entertain their child and to encourage mastery. In the laboratory, the middle class infants were likely to look toward their mother when her prerecorded voice was played and toward a strange woman when an unfamiliar female voice was played. The working class infants did not look differentially following termination of the two voices.

Correlation between the maternal practices and laboratory data gathered at 10 months, on the one hand, and the 6-year-old data on the other revealed that within each class sample, the children with the highest ITPA scores had mothers who had been more interactive with them as infants ($r = .55$ [$p < .01$] for middle class; $r = .33$ for working class children).

Further, within each class, the 10-month-old infants who looked differentially to mother rather than stranger after hearing their mother's voice reading prose through a speaker had higher ITPA scores at 6 years ($r = .37$ [$p < .10$] for middle class; $r = .45$ [$p < .10$] for working class).

These data, which should be viewed with caution because of the small sample size, imply that experience that accelerates aspects of cognitive development during the first year and may facilitate a slight precocity that is moderately stable through the preschool years.

It also appears that the home environment has a primacy that is not easy to understand. We are completing a 5-year longitudinal study of more than 90 children, half of them Caucasian and half of them Chinese. Half of these children attend a day care center in Boston, 5 days a week, 7 hours a day. Each of the children in the group care setting is matched with a control child living at home, of the same ethnicity, sex and social class. All infants are assessed in an extensive battery at $3\frac{1}{2}$, $5\frac{1}{2}$, $7\frac{1}{2}$, $9\frac{1}{2}$, $11\frac{1}{2}$, $13\frac{1}{2}$, 20 and 29 months of age. At this moment there are no dramatic differences between the group care and home care children during the first year of life. However, there are ethnic differences. The Chinese children, who normally experience less reciprocal vocalization from their parents at home – which is in accord with a philosophy of child care held by Chinese mothers – are markedly more quiet than the Caucasian children. This result holds both for the Chinese infants in the day care center and for those residing at home. Since the Chinese infants in group care experience as much vocal interaction as the Caucasians, one might expect them to be similar in the frequency of vocalization. However, the Chinese day care children are just a little more vocal than the Chinese children at home and far less vocal than the Caucasian children in the day care center. This fact suggests the importance of the home environment and perhaps of the role of temperament. A second finding also underlines the importance of the home experience.

At 20 months of age, all the children in the study are exposed to the following episode. They come to a large living room setting in William James Hall (Cambridge) in which there are some toys, their mother and a strange woman, and, for the day care children, their primary caretaker from the Center. For the home child, the third adult is a friend of the family. We observe the child in this setting for 45 minutes. We code the targets of his visual orientation and time spent proximal to each of these adults. All the children, both day care and home reared, walked to their mother when bored or distressed. They never go to the stranger and rarely to the caretaker or friend of the family. The day care children did not approach their primary caretaker more than 1% or 2% of the time. This fact should allay the apprehensions of those who fear that day care may affect the attachment of an infant to his mother. This datum also implies the special influence of the home, for the day care children are in the Center as many hours as they are at home. Yet, the mother remains the primary attachment figure. It is likely that the singularity of the relationship between the mother and infant, and the fact that it is the mother, not the day care surrogate, who tends to the child when he is seriously ill (when he stays at home) makes home experiences primary and leads to the development of a special bond between infant and mother.

These facts, together with similar ones reported by other investigators, have led many parents, pediatricians and psychologists to the belief that most of the problems of the older child and adolescent can be traced to experiences with his family during the opening 3–5 years of life. Therefore, it is held that the best approach to eliminating these problems is to alter the practices of parents of young children in order to prevent the problems from occurring. This conclusion rests on three presuppositions regarding development, and it will be useful to make those presuppositions explicit.

The first premise is that each day the child is being seriously influenced by the actions of others and that the relation between these social experiences (say, spanking the child for dirtying himself) and his future behavioral, motivational and moral development is absolute and knowable. The second notion is that it is difficult, or perhaps impossible, to rehabilitate an older child whose early experiences were so toxic as to produce psychologic dispositions that would be maladaptive in his society. Contrariwise, early attainment of the dispositions that are adaptive would facilitate adaptation throughout childhood and adolescence. The final premise, which is at once the most profound and the most controversial, is that there is an ideal best adult and, correspondingly, a best collection of experiences that maximizes the probability that the ideal adult will emerge from the cacophony of childhood encounters. In simpler terms, most American parents believe in the existence of a small set of psychologic traits that are necessarily correlated with a maximally happy adulthood. If parents and teachers praise, punish and posture at the right time and with the proper enthusiasm—like the conducting of a major symphony—they will create the perfect adult. This last idea troubles me, for there are several reasonable answers to the query, "What are a child's psychologic requirements?" The substance of each of the answers depends, first, on one's views concerning the nature of the human child and the mechanisms that mediate his growth and, second, on the subtle messages the larger society communicates to parents regarding the kinds of adults that are needed for the succeeding generation.

The most popular contemporary American conception of the young child is that he is an inherently helpless, dependent organism prepared by nature to establish a strong emotional bond with the adults who care for him. If these adults attend to his drives and desires with consistency and affection, it is assumed that he will gradually learn to trust them, be motivated to adopt their values and develop such a sturdy concept of self that he will possess a vital capacity for love and will be able to deal with conflict, anxiety and frustration effectively. The traditional Japanese mother, prior to the Western acculturation of her attitudes, viewed her young infant through different lenses. He was neither helpless nor dependent, but a willful, asocial creature destined to move away from people unless she could tame him and deflect his natural instincts. Hence, she usually soothed and quieted her infant, suppressing the excitement that the American mother tried to arouse. The Indian mother in the highlands of Guatemala believes that infants are born with different dispositions depending on the day of their birth. She is convinced that there is little she can do to change these fixed developmental directions, and her fatalism leads her to stand aside so that her child can grow as nature intended. Most children in all three communities grow up equally adapted to their societies. Moreover, there is such a remarkable similarity among the 10-year-olds in each of these settings that one is forced to question the validity of these local theories.

Most parents are absolutist in their view of psychologic growth, assuming that all children should be headed for the same ideal telos and require a best combination of psychologic nourishment to complete the long and difficult journey. Contrast this view of the infant, which is predominant in the United States, with the more relativistic notion that a child's psychologic requirements not only change with his stage of development but also become, with age, increasingly dependent on the local culture. Lest this statement sound too general, consider a concrete illustration. In contemporary America, a willingness to defend intrusions into one's space and property and acceptance of the affect of anger and the motive of hostility are regarded as necessary for facing each day. Hence, it is generally acknowledged that the family should not always punish mild displays of anger or aggression in or out of the home. A parent who never permitted the child any expression of hostility would be called bad names by the majority of American psychologists, psychiatrists, pediatricians and social workers.

Among the Utku of Hudson Bay, who are restricted for 9 months a year to a tight 300 square feet of living space, it is necessary that any sign of anger, hostility and aggression among people be consistently suppressed. A good mother conscientiously starts to train this inhibition as early as 24 months of age by ignoring acts of defiance. By age 9, the behavioral indexes of anger, so common in American children, are not in evidence (Briggs, 1970). An Eskimo mother who allowed her child easy displays of aggression would be called the same bad names we apply to the American mother who did not permit this behavior. And the Eskimo 10-year-old is as well adjusted to his community as his American counterpart. But if the Eskimo and American children exchanged locales, each would quickly develop the symptoms psychiatrists call neurotic. Each would have brought to his new home a set of dispositions inappropriate to the standards of that residential space.

Freda Rebelsky has noted that during the first 10 months of life, infants in the eastern part of Holland are held only when they are being fed. At other times, they lie tightly bound in bassinets that are placed in small rooms isolated from the more dynamic parts of the house. They have no toys, no mobiles, minimal stimulation and the amount and variety of adult contact is far less than that encountered by the average American infant. Yet, by age 5, these Dutch children do not seem to be fundamentally different from 5-year-old Americans. Indian infants living in the isolated highlands of Guatemala are held by adults over 6 hours a day, in contrast to the 60 minutes of maternal carrying characteristic of

American homes. Yet, at age 10, there is no evidence of major differences in fundamental trust of parents or affective vitality between Indian and American children.

Since these are not uniquely exotic examples of relativism in child development, it is reasonable to repeat the question contained in the title of this chapter; namely, "What do children need?", when food and protection from excessive disease and physical discomfort are guaranteed. I suggest that *children do not require any specific actions from adults in order to develop optimally.* There is no good evidence to indicate that children must have a certain amount or schedule of cuddling, kissing, spanking, holding or deprivation of privileges in order to become gratified and productive adults. The child does have psychologic needs, but there is no list of parental behaviors that can be counted on to fill these critical requirements.

Psychologists must develop an appreciation for the message it took biologists so long to learn; namely, that environmental niches are neither good nor bad in any absolute sense. Rather, they are appropriate or inappropriate for a specific species; hence, an organism's requirements can never be separated from the environment in which it grows. Frogs are best actualized in a New England forest, not in the Mojave Desert; lizards have the opposite profile of ecologic requirements. To ask what a child needs is to pose half a question. We must always specify the demands the community will make on the child, adolescent and young adult. Since we are primarily concerned with the problems of psychologic growth in this society, the remainder of the discussion will take America as the context of development, though it is hoped that some of the presumptuous statements to be made have some generality beyond North America.

An American child must believe, first of all, that he is valued by his parents and a few special people in his community (usually a teacher or two, but often older peers, uncles, aunts and coaches). Since our society makes personal competence synonymous with virtue, the sculpting of a particular talent or, better yet, talents, usually is a necessary but not sufficient requirement for the development of a sense of worth. Obviously it is possible to list the appropriate set of competences to be attained only if one knows the domains of mastery that the community values. In the rural Guatemalan village in which we work, the ability to care for young children with efficiency and skill produced this feeling of worth in preadolescent girls. In the United States, it is more closely tied to quality of performance in junior high school. Hence, competence in academic subjects is a sine qua non for the American child. It is difficult, if not impossible, to fail this requirement completely and still retain a sense of dignity and worth in adulthood.

The American child must also develop autonomy, the belief that he or she is able and desires to make decisions regarding his conduct and his future, independent of coercive pressures from parents, teachers and friends. The recent increase in drug use among American youth threatens older Americans not because of an automatic revulsion toward pills or smoking but because it is believed that marijuana and heroin destroy the desire to be independent and autonomous. In a culture in which the majority of 25-year-olds do not live within visiting distance of the family and friends with whom intense childhood intimacies were shared, it can be argued that it is adaptive for autonomy to be promoted so conscientiously. There is another reason why autonomy has become such a precious characteristic. A society's typical mode of livelihood always exerts some influence on the psychologic characteristics it extols. There is greater independence, autonomy and permissiveness toward aggression among African tribes in which pastoralism dominates the economy than among tribal groups in the same country where agriculture is the main source of income (Edgerton, 1971). The reasonableness of this correlation derives from the fact that a 12-year-old boy who is given daily responsibility for 50 head of cattle must make a series of independent decisions that do not arise for a 12-year-old who helps his father plow a field or plant maize. Moreover, personal disputes are less disruptive in a pastoral setting, where the disputants can easily put miles between them, than in a fixed agricultural village where actors are totally captive in a small area, and where feuds, therefore, must be suppressed.

Most Americans earn and increase their livelihood by perfecting talents that an institution wants. We have an economy in which services and skills are offered for payment. Unlike modern Japan, where each worker has a primary lifetime loyalty to the company for which he works (Nakane, 1972), the unwritten understanding in the United States is that primary loyalty is not awarded to the institution (be it company, university or governmental agency) but to the self. (I assume it is understood that the writer is not condoning this arrangement, but merely describing it.) If financial gain is to be maximized, young adults must be socialized to make decisions that are best for them. Hence, most parents unconsciously encourage their children to decide conflicts for themselves. The parental admonition to a 15-year-old, "You will have to decide whether you want to go to the movies or save your allowance," which is rare outside the Western community, is part of the daily preparation for adulthood. Parents probably are unaware of the hidden message in these communications, but their effect is measurable nonetheless.

Finally, and here we are more similar to other cultures, America requires the young adult to be heterosexually successful; to be able to love and be loved and to take pleasure from sexual experience. As a result, we promote a permissive attitude toward sexuality.

These attributes comprise the core of America's current ego ideal. There is much to celebrate in this list, but also much to mourn. There is, in our opinion, insufficient emphasis on intimacy and too much on self-interest; insufficient emphasis on cooperation and too much on competitiveness; insufficient emphasis on altruism and too much on narcissism. But we cannot alter this catechism by shaking our heads and pulling at our chins. These values derive, in part, from the form of our economy, our densely crowded, impersonal cities and the fact that our educational institutions function as 12–16-year selection sites for tomorrow's doctors, teachers, lawyers, administrators, scientists and business executives. These basic structures will have to change a little if we want our values to reflect more humanism. Put succinctly, the fact that Bobby Fischer's flagrant narcissism was excusable because he beat Boris Spassky for the chess championship in 1972, suggests that the only thing more important to Americans than character is individual success.

Since it is not likely that our economy, our cities and our institutions will change dramatically during the next decade—perhaps they will over a longer period – American parents probably will not alter their tendency to encourage the values and associated competences listed above; namely, academic success, autonomy, independence and a permissive emotional attitude toward hostility and sexuality. However, at another time, they might easily be persuaded to promote a different creed.

The ego ideal we have been considering is most appropriate to the adolescent and adult. There is merit in considering the more specific accomplishments appropriate to the first two developmental stages – infancy and the preschool years – and it is to these to which we now turn our attention. Again, these suggestions are to be taken as speculations for discussion and hypotheses for testing in the harsh empirical arena, rather than firm inferences from reliable empirical information.

INFANCY. – During the first 1½ – 2 years, the infant seems to need at least four classes of experience. He must have some *environmental variety* that can be assimilated with moderate effort. An excessively homogeneous environment with little discrepant experience temporarily retards psychologic growth, and turns the child away from the world around him. My observations in a remote Indian village in western Guatemala suggest that infants who received an abundance of physical contact – they were on their mother's body a large part of the day – but insufficient experiential variety were intellectually retarded and affectively depressed in comparison with American children during the first 2 years of life (Kagan and Klein, 1973). These infants, who were nursed on demand and held for hours but rarely spoken to or played with, resembled the marasmic infants Spitz saw in the South American orphanages he visited almost 30 years ago (Spitz and Wolf, 1946). These Indian infants had sufficient physical affection and love but insufficient stimulus variety. The studies by Dennis and others affirm the importance of variety and opportunity to practice maturational competences. Most American homes have enough assimilable variety for proper psychologic growth. For the very few that do not, existing information suggests a mild retardation in cognitive and affective processes.

Experiences that are too discrepant to be understood often frighten the child and provoke withdrawal and inhibition; excessive homogeneity promotes a listless, nonalert attitude. The first task of development is to understand unusual happenings in the outside world.

The infant also needs some *regularity of experience*. Regularity is, of course, a relativistic concept. It does not mean that the mother must put the child on a 2-, 4- or 8-hour schedule, but on a regular one. The child needs some predictability, for by the time he is 6 months old he is making predictions and altering his sleeping, activity and eating cycles as a function of the regularities in his day. When his expectations are not realized, uncertainty grows and can disturb major aspects of functioning. The child needs *caretaking by adults* rather than machines because our culture requires the older child to relate to people rather than to objects. Finally, the infant needs the *opportunity to practice* his emerging motor skills. There is cognitive and affective gain derived from banging mobiles, shaking rattles, knocking down block towers and crawling. If the infant has variety, regularity and care of his physiologic needs, he seems to grow normally.

PRESCHOOL CHILD, AGE 2 – 5 YEARS. – The child continues to need opportunities to master body and object problems. Additionally, when he has begun to master the symbolic language of his community—anywhere from 18 to 30 months of age—he needs exposure to language. If he does not live in a world of speech he will remain mute, even though he possesses the biologic competence for talking and understanding. Existing evidence suggests that all the child needs is exposure—no special tutoring, books, television programs or radios. The simple experience of hearing people talking—especially to him—seems sufficient.

The child of 3 now is symbolic and must encounter actions, gestures and communications that symbolically affirm his virtue, value and worth. Families will communicate this message in different ways. Hence, the concept of parental (later, peer) rejection should not be biased toward an absolute definition. There is no definable set of behaviors that always represents rejection and leads inevitably to a particular form of the child's self-concept. There has been a tendency for American psychologists to assume that there are specific parental actions that signify rejection, for there is an enormous degree of commonality in the definition of this concept among investigators who have studied a mother's behavior with her child (Baldwin, Kalhorn and Breese, 1945; Becker, 1964; Kagan and Moss, 1962; Schaeffer, 1959; Schaeffer and Bayley, 1963; Sears, Maccoby and Levin, 1957). These and others decided that harsh physical punishment and absence of social play and affection are the signs of maternal rejection. It would be impossible for an American psychologist to categorize a mother as high on both aloofness and a loving attitude. But that view may be provincial. Alfred Baldwin reports that in rural areas of northern Norway, where homes are 5–10 miles apart, one sees maternal behavior that an American observer would regard as pathognomonically rejecting in an American mother. The Norwegian mother sees her 4-year-old sitting in a doorway blocking the passage to the next room. She does not ask him to move, but bends down, picks him up and silently moves him away before she passes to the next room. A middle-class observer would be tempted to view this indifference as a sign of dislike. However, most mothers in this Arctic outpost behave this way; and the children do not behave the way rejected children should by our theoretic propositions.

An uneducated black mother from North Carolina slaps her 4-year-old across the face when he does not come to the table on time. The intensity of the act tempts our observer to conclude that the mother resents her child. However, during a half-hour conversation, the mother indicates her warm feelings for the boy. She hit him because she does not want him to become a "bad boy" and she believes physical punishment is the most effective socialization procedure. Now her behavior seems to be issued in the service of affection rather than hostility. Evaluation of a parent as rejecting or accepting cannot be answered by noting the parent's behavior, for rejection is not a fixed quality of behavior. Like pleasure, pain or beauty, rejection is in the mind of the rejectee. It is a belief held by the child, not an action by a parent.

We must acknowledge an important discontinuity in the meaning of acceptance-rejection for the child prior to 12–18 months, before he symbolically evaluates the actions of others, in contrast to the symbolic child of 3 or 4 years. We require a concept to deal with the child's belief of his value in the eyes of others. The 5-year-old is conceptually mature enough to recognize that certain resources parents possess are difficult for him to obtain. He views these resources as sacrifices and interprets their receipt as signs that the parents value him. The child constructs a tote board of the differential value of parental gifts, be they psychologic or material. The value of the gift depends on its scarcity. A $10 toy from an executive father is not a valued resource; the same toy from a father out of work is prized. The value depends on the child's personal weighting. This position would lead to solipsism were it not for the fact that most parents are narcissistic and do not readily give the child long periods of uninterrupted companionship. Hence, most children place a high premium on this act. Parents are also reluctant to donate unusually expensive gifts, and this prize acquires value for many youngsters. Finally, the American child learns through the public media that physical affection means a positive evaluation, and he is persuaded to assign premium worth to this experience. There is, therefore, some uniformity across children in our culture with respect to the evaluation of parental acts of acceptance or rejection. But the anchor point lies within the child, not with particular parental behaviors. It is suggested, therefore, that different concepts are necessary for the following phenomena:

1. An attitude on the part of the parent.
2. The quality and frequency of acts of parental care and stimulation.
3. Finally, the child's assessment of his value in the eyes of another.

All three categories currently are viewed as of the same cloth.

Fourth, the preschool child needs *models* to whom he feels similar and who he believes possess competence, power and virtue in the group he takes as his primary reference. This phenomenon of vicarious sharing in the strength and positive emotional states of another to whom one feels similar is called identification. A young man recalls his childhood feelings for his father:

"My admiration for him transcended everything. I always wanted to work with my hands on machinery, to drive big trucks, to fix things like he did. I didn't really like spinach, but I never lost the image of his bathtub filled with it, and up until a few years ago I always ate it—it was good for me and would make me strong like him" (Goethals and Klos, 1970, p. 44).

The child's self-concept and values derive, in part, from his pattern of identifications with those models with whom he shares basic psychologic and physical similarities. Although parents are the primary identification figures for most children, each teacher is a potential model, and the teacher's power to sculpt values and self-esteem usually is underestimated.

Since school success is so important in American society, we should not forget that the teacher has the power to persuade the child of the joy, beauty and potential utility of knowledge, even though the typical second-grader initially rejects that idea. The teacher's most potent weapon of persuasion is herself, for if she is seen as kind, competent and just, the child will award to the school tasks she encourages the same reverence he assigns to her.

Finally, the preschool child needs to experience consistency with respect to the standards being socialized. The content of those standards is less critical than the fact of knowing that what is wrong and what is right remains constant from day to day. A child is made uncertain by the dissonance that is produced by being punished for fighting on Monday but jokingly teased for the same violation on Wednesday. It was suggested that during the first 2 years the infant was trying to understand unusual experiences in the world. The primary task during the preschool years is to understand the self, and the child needs information that will help him solve that problem.

THE CATEGORIZATION OF THE OTHER. — Most discussions of experiential influences on the child emphasize the direct practices of parents — their physical affection, their degree of conversation, the consistency of their love, the reliability of their punishment. This emphasis on concrete experiences is due, in part, to the fact that they are indeed influential. But, in addition, these variables are easy to observe and code and, therefore, have an appeal to an empirical scientist. There is an additional set of factors that also are important during the preschool years which involves the child's perception of *others*. Specifically, an important factor controlling individual development rests on the consequences of choosing *another* as the referent to whom one orients and from whom one differentiates. The presence of *another* acts as an incentive for change, independent of concrete, actively imposed experiences. The child holds a set of standards regarding proper behavior and has conceptualized his role in relation to authority, as well as age and sex dimensions. Now let us suppose that *another* enters his life space whom he cannot ignore because the other is a competitor for some of the same resources the child desires. If the *other* is a sibling, the child perceives the *other* to share parental attention. The child now is pushed to differentiate himself from the *other,* toward the values of the parents, in order to retain the favored position. His growth toward the adult role is accelerated so that he can differentiate himself from the *other* and retain his favored position. The only child does not have that incentive and, therefore, is less likely to accelerate his growth toward the adult role. Note that this process is independent of parental treatment of the child. The younger, by contrast, is likely to see the role of the youngest as adaptive and retain it for longer than he needs to. Hence, first-borns with younger siblings are more likely to adopt the values of the parents and to be rigid about adherence to those early standards than younger siblings. The mechanism that accounts for this difference does not rest primarily with the practices of parents and, therefore, is not a function of what is normally meant by direct family experience. Rather, the catalyst of change is simply the introduction of *"another,"* like the introduction of a crystal into a cloud to produce rain. The *other* is the catalyst that creates uncertainty in the child. In response to that uncertainty, the child alters his beliefs, behavior and role.

Consider as another example the growth of sex roles in children. A young child of 3 – 4 years recognizes that boys are stronger and larger than girls and that leads to the inference that boys are psychologically more potent than girls. As a result of that conclusion, held by both boys and girls, the girl diverts her motives for power to other goals, especially affiliative goals, because she does not expect to win in a power struggle with males. The presence of males is the catalyst for a decision and a change in behavior. The girl's behavior was influenced primarily by the presence of boys, not by anything her parents did to her. In the cross-cultural data gathered by the Whitings in 6 different cultures, the raw scores for nurturant and aggressive behavior reveal minimal sex differences when the data for all the cultures are pooled. But within any one culture, girls were more nurturant and less aggressive than boys. This fact implies that it is the conceptualization of one sex by the other that is a major cause of sex differences in behavior (Whiting and Whiting, 1975).

The same logic can be applied to social class. The lower class 6-year-old comes to conclusions about his role after he recognizes the presence of the middle class child. The middle class child, like the first-born, is pushed to differentiate himself from the lower class child once he recognizes the presence of the other category, probably during the early school years.

Thus, although direct practices visited by parents on children obviously are important in shaping the child's behavior, we will not completely understand the child's development unless we also take into account the child's cognitive classification of others.

REFERENCES

Baldwin, A. L., Kalhorn, J., and Breese, F. H.: Patterns of parent behavior, Psychol. Monogr., Vol. 58, Number 268, 1945.

Becker, W. C.: Consequences of Different Kinds of Parental Discipline, in Hoffman, M. L., and Hoffman, L. W. (eds.), *Review of Child Development and Research* (New York: Russell Sage Foundation, 1964), Vol. I, pp. 169–208.

Briggs, J.: *Never in Anger* (Cambridge, Mass., Harvard University Press, 1970).

Edgerton, R. B.: *The Individual in Cultural Adaptation* (Berkeley: University of California Press, 1971).

Goethals, G. W., and Klos, D.: *Experiencing Youth* (Boston: Little, Brown, & Company, 1970).

Kagan, J., and Moss, H. A.: *Birth to Maturity* (New York: John Wiley & Sons, Inc., 1962).

Kagan, J.: *Change and Continuity in Infancy* (New York: John Wiley & Sons, Inc., 1971).

Kagan, J.: Cross-Cultural Perspectives in Early Development. Paper delivered to the American Association for the Advancement of Science, Washington, D. C., December 26, 1972.

Kagan, J., and Klein, R. E.: Cross cultural perspectives on early development, Am. Psychol. 28:947, 1973.

Nakane, C.: *Japanese Society* (Berkeley: University of California Press, 1972).

Schaeffer, E. S.: A circumplex model for maternal behavior, J. Abnorm. Social Psychol. 59:226, 1959.

Schaeffer, E. S., and Bayley, N.: Maternal behavior, child behavior, and their intercorrelations from infancy through adolescence. Monogr. Soc. Res. Child Dev., Vol. 28, no. 87, 1963.

Sears, R. R., Maccoby, E. E., and Levin, H.: *Patterns of Child Rearing* (New York: Rowe Peterson, 1957).

Spitz, R. A., and Wolf, K. M.: Anaclitic Depression: An Inquiry Into the Genesis of Psychiatric Conditions in Early Childhood, II, in Freud, A., *et al.* (eds.), *The Psychoanalytic Study of the Child* (New York: International Universities Press, 1946), Vol. II, pp. 313–342.

Tulkin, S. R.: Mother-Infant Interaction in the First Year of Life. Unpublished doctoral dissertation, Harvard University, 1970.

Tulkin, S. R., and Covitz, F. E.: Mother-Infant Interaction and Intellectual Functioning at Age Six. Paper presented at the meeting of the Society for Research in Child Development, Denver, April, 1975.

Whiting, B. B., and Whiting, J. W. M.: *Children of Six Cultures* (Cambridge, Mass.: Harvard University Press, 1975).

16

Developing Child Caring Skills for a Network of Child Caring Services

Frances Vandivier, M. S.

*Associate Professor of Social
Administration, Temple University,
Philadelphia, Pennsylvania*

In developing recommendations for services for children and families for the 1970s, the Task Force on Mental Health of Children formulated a statement of the Rights of Infants. The statement includes these words: "We believe that if we are to optimize the mental health of our young, and if we are to develop our human resources, every infant must be granted: the right to be wanted . . . to be born healthy . . . to live in a healthy environment . . . to have *continuous* loving care. . . ."[1]

We cannot guarantee rights with recommendations. But children do need, and have the right to, continuous loving and competent care. In this chapter I will present a description of one important way of ensuring that right to an increasing number of children.

In our complex society, parents cannot always provide the continuous loving care needed by their children. Nor, frequently, can the primary institutions that provide services to children and their parents. There are many specialists within those institutions concerned with a child's intellectual development, or his health, or his religious and cultural growth, etc. But the child needs a relationship with a significant adult, a skilled "generalist," who can maintain the integrity of his development as a whole person, be his advocate in the face of the myriad demands that may be made on him by all the specialists. Any child, at some point, may need an adult other than his parent to help him cope with his current realities, should those realities threaten to become overwhelming. Such a person can help connect his past with his present, and look forward to his future.

I would like to introduce you to a person who is making a profession of being just such a "significant adult" for children in need of loving care to supplement

---

[1]Joint Commission on Mental Health of Children, Inc.: *Crisis in Child Mental Health: Challenge for the 1970's* (New York, Harper & Row, Publishers, 1970).

or complement that provided by the parents. He is a colleague of yours—a co-worker who calls himself, generically, a Child Care Worker. I would like to suggest ways he can join you and other professionals in a variety of children's services, to add to the likelihood that continuous, loving care will indeed become a reality for children. Perhaps, if I describe him well enough, you may recognize him as an appropriate candidate for the "parent extender" that Urie Bronfenbrenner is looking for to assist families in caring for their children.

In my description I will use the masculine pronoun for several reasons: (1) to save time, (2) "he" is a human being, so I don't want to use "it" and (3) there's a not-so-hidden agenda, which is that most child care workers, are, in fact, women. With an increasing number of men entering the field, however, I want to present child care as a kind of work that is appropriate for men to do, for which men have as much responsibility as women, and as a rare and exciting occupation in which a person can't possibly, in Mary Howell's words, "Love the work but hate the job!" As a child care worker, you might not be turned on by some of the tasks, but your *job* is a child's growing up. Once you experience the excitement of the relationship, you may become "hooked." I spoke recently with a young man working in a residential facility for retarded children. He was upset and angry because an institution-centered administrator was making the work more difficult than it needed to be. "I could leave the job," he said, "but, how could I possibly leave 10 little boys!"

I am suggesting that other significant adults, along with parents, can help to provide, in varying amounts and in a variety of settings, the caring relationship that allows a child to have his childhood, fully and freely, as a whole person. I am also suggesting that we have an abundant supply of intuitively able caregivers who can become participants in an educational process that increases their skill, competence and confidence. These caregivers can join other professionals in a variety of institutions serving families and children, to amplify the caring component of that service. They can also initiate or facilitate the development of new services to meet more of the needs of families and children that have not been acknowledged or met through existing services.

For your increased understanding, I would like to define child care as a discipline, briefly alluding to knowledge, skills and attitudes necessary to the roles and functions of the child care worker, and to describe the differences between direct child care service and indirect child care service, as well as how the two are interdependent. I will describe one educational program for child care workers, including some statistical and demographic data compiled at the end of the sixth year of operation. Finally, I will show you child care workers in a variety of settings, including several new services they have helped to create.

CHILD CARE WORK DEFINED

What is care—caring for children? Webster's Dictionary says that *care* is "serious attention of mind, heed, solicitude, caution, watchfulness, responsibility for safety, *regard coming from esteem*—the opposite of indifference and apathy." It also says that it can be suffering of mind, grief, sorrow. That's the condition we risk in daring to care! Caring in the verb form is "to feel concern or interest or regard; to watch over, foster, provide."

Skill means "understanding, discernment, judiciousness, practical knowledge, knowledge gained from study, experience or training, the ability to use one's knowledge effectively." The verb form is even more powerful—"to have understanding, to make a difference, to individualize, distinguish, *to set free*."

Child care, as a discipline, consists of both preventive and therapeutic, both developmental and remedial, work with children. It is concerned with the nurturing, management and guidance of any child from birth through adolescence, healthy or handicapped, whose day is determined by child-serving institutions, public or private, day or residential. For some families, child care may extend to the home for after-care, parental support and child protection or supplemental parenting.

The central responsibility of child care is the child's psychosocial development as affected and directed by the reality of daily experiences. The worker's specialty lies in his ability to form healthful relationships and use himself as one of the elements of the environment. He is not a technician. His skills are based on philosophies and values of persons and on interpersonal relationships, not on a philosophy of techniques. For the child care worker, healthy emotional involvement is not a professional liability but a necessity for effectiveness. He must be acquainted with the norms and conditions of healthy human development and with the interferences in that development; he must be secure in coping with behaviors and in building on strengths for stability and well-motivated growth. He must be willing to compensate the child for past deficiencies in his experience. The child care worker accepts the whole child, unclassified, ready to relate no matter how he has been labeled, ready to allow him his childhood.

Role and Functions of Child Care Workers

The functions of the child care worker are difficult to delineate or categorize. Whatever they are depends primarily on the needs of the child, within a specific time and space. The skills must be defined in terms of a generalist's skills—proficiency in the art of caring, that is, in providing the attitudes, philosophy and basic attention that all children require. But where one child differs from another in individual needs, where group membership and dynamics call for special methods, where one agency's services differ from another, there the child care worker adds appropriate knowledge and method to his generalist's skills and becomes a specialist.[2]

Direct and Indirect Service

Child care, itself, divides into two categories of work. The first is direct work with children, from infancy through adolescence. The second category is indirect service in which the child care worker may operate as a member of a planning or executive group concerned with that child and his family, provide assistance to the family, relative to their child (or children), supervise other persons in direct work, administer programs and agencies or teach less-experienced workers and students entering the field.

---

[2]National Conference on Curricula for the Career Ladder in the Child Caring Professions, *Proceedings and Discussion*, Pittsburgh, 1969.

In his direct service role, a major concern of the child care worker is to create an environment in which the child may thrive emotionally and socially, permitting the optimal development of all the facets of his person. Child care functions are determined by whether *preventive* or *therapeutic* work is required. Care of children who are emotionally healthy and functioning socially and effectively within appropriate developmental norms is preventive work. The extent of a child's limitations and of psychologic injury define the remedial work to be done. Unfortunately, much of the caregiver's work often has to be done in the context of defending the child from the institution's dehumanizing system. Most children he will meet already are in need of both developmental and remedial care.

Child care functions are also determined by the specific institution in which the child care workers interact—the goals, philosophy, legal regulations, accountability to funding sources, etc., of that specific institution. Because agencies tend to bring together children having similar overt needs, usually labeled, this practice also defines the duties of the child care worker. For example, where crippled children are served, a worker must undertake a certain amount of physical care. Settings define child care by treatment of the commonly held needs of their population, by the dictates of any peculiarities of their operating principles and by less clearly defined subtleties. The agency's attitude in relation to professional care standards, to the role of the child care worker, to the unique skills of any one worker, can shape the service accordingly.

The range for direct service is from partial-day to 24-hour residential care, with children from 0 to 18 years (measured developmentally, not necessarily chronologically), who may range in function from healthy to severely damaged. A discussion of functions and practices has to be done within the context of all these and many more subtle factors.

Direct service to children usually, and should always, where possible, include supportive services to parents. Special skills are needed to translate the worker's relationship with the child so that it is understood and accepted by the parents. The worker may need to clarify his position thoroughly as a cooperative one, not competitive, and to create a corresponding allegiance in parents for the work being done with their children. Within a wholly consistent interest in the child, skills may be needed to protect him from conflict, if parental and agency concerns are not in accord.

Work with parents clearly defines the thin line between direct service and indirect service to children. Most indirect child care functions, when aggregated to form sets of professional duties, may be defined as organizational and executive; their purpose is to integrate a consistently healthful environment for groups of children, to personalize and oversee the care designed for them in the agency. This may entail coordinating an over-all process engaged in by many persons. Supportive services for parents, coordinating diagnostic and planning services, supervision of line workers, designing and administering developmental and remedial activities programs, in-service training and education of students are all included under indirect services. These services can best be provided by workers who have had extensive experience in direct services.

Functions can best be described as a parallel process, i.e., the caring relationship between worker and supervisor, supervisor and administrator, between teacher and student. Child care has as its central task the integration of all the child's parts, claimed and analyzed by the various disciplines that deal with only that part, into an integrated, living, breathing whole person; just so, the coordination of child care services has as its task the integration of the various fragments of a service, or of services, for the benefit of the child and his family. The most successful delineator of child care functions continues to be the individual child's emotional or social needs being met by an inventive and secure worker. The essence of good child care method is the system represented by the worker, himself, his attitudes toward the child and other persons, the feelings he reveals and owns and the ability to form a relationship.

Body of Knowledge

Child care has a body of knowledge that incorporates theory and experience from many disciplines, tailored to unique skills through sustained, continuous direct application, a knowledge that facilitates interaction with children and within which human values supersede techniques. It affirms the acceptance of an empathy for the condition of the child in contrast to the imposition of specific systems or methods on children to shape them to this or that projected result.

Many professions have contributions to make to any curriculum in child care. For example, psychology and psychiatry offer clinical expertise in understanding abnormalities of development and their symptoms. Researchers contribute not only an important spirit of inquiry but also further insight into children and their lives. From medicine come physiologic and psychosocial explanations of behavior, of organic causes of disorders, of effects of drugs and of medications, etc. Nutritionists supply dietary needs as well as effects of malnutrition. Social workers provide knowledge of community systems as resources for and influences on families and children, plus case work and group work methods. Educators bring programming for cognitive development and methods for facilitating learning. Nurses bring health care, emergency services and rehabilitation procedures. Architects bring insights concerning the arrangement of space. Specialists in all kinds of therapies (art, music, occupational, physical, etc.) broaden child care workers' repertoire of tools and excite their ingenuity.

But with observation of the child's day-to-day experiences as the essence of developmental theory, the teaching of development with emphasis on the affective and psychosocial aspects, the practical application of a developmental point of view, the philosophy and ethics of child care still must come from experienced child care specialists in order to ensure unity of purpose and integration of effort. Differentiation of child care priorities from those of other professionals working with children should help to build the identity of the child care worker.[3]

DEVELOPMENT OF THE TEMPLE UNIVERSITY CHILD CARE TRAINING PROGRAM

Prior to 1968, many Philadelphia child care agencies were employing untrained, poorly screened and often psychologically unfit persons to give direct service to children. There was no preservice training, no continuum of education. In-service training, provided by the agency, often was too little and too

---

[3]*Ibid., Proceedings and Discussion.*

late, so that children suffered the trial-and-error methods of workers in the process of developing new skills, and the high cost of staff turnover was a major budgetary concern. Child care workers, who had the most critical role in the development of the children, had no role as members of the decision-making agency team. For a worker who had achieved a high level of competence and responsibility in one agency there was no reliable method for transferring to a comparable level in another agency, nor any possible way he could transfer to higher education "credits" he had earned in in-service training.

Using a model for generic preservice training of child care workers, which had grown out of a master's-level training curriculum in the Department of Child Psychiatry at the University of Pittsburgh, Temple University began selecting and training potential child care workers in a 2-year, preservice, certificate program (Fig. 16–1). Simultaneously, continuing education courses were offered to employed workers in direct service, including supervisor-trainees, who may have had professional training in a variety of disciplines, such as social work, education, nursing, etc., but who lacked the theoretic base for child care, as well as skills to apply in the training process. Long-range goals were to upgrade the care of children by developing a continuum of education for child care workers, from entry-level to master's-level skills.

Goals of selection process[4]*:*

1. To assess an applicant's potential for achieving a developmental point of view within which he can respect differences in individuals and in groups, as well as find pleasure in his knowledgeable participation in the growth of another person.

2. To communicate the requirements of the training program and of child care as a career choice; to help the applicant assess his potential for meeting those requirements; to support his looking for other career choices if child care comes not to be considered an appropriate choice.

Areas of consideration include:

1. *Style* – warmth, enthusiasm, flexibility, sensitivity, humor.

2. *Attitude* – child-valuing, person-affirming; some feeling for the balance between support, expectation and freedom.

Beginning with the 17 students who enrolled for training in September, 1968, a total of 743 applicants completed the selection process and enrolled as students. Approximately 61% of the students who enroll complete the program. The largest portion (46%) are in the 20–29-year age group; 25% are under 20 and 29% range from 30 to 60 years of age. The racial composition is 58% black or Oriental and 42% white; 47% are parents and 53% are childless. The two largest groups are non-white with children (41%) and white without children (35%). These two groups represent different viewpoints on many levels, reflecting varied educational, cultural and economic backgrounds. They learn much from one another. In fact, the most enthusiastic and committed classes have been those containing the most heterogeneous mixture of students. The non-white mothers (as a group) appear to be beset with many more personal, economic and child-rearing problems than the younger, childless white students, but their degree of success (60.4%) is substantially as high as the 63% success of the young white students. It is even more noteworthy in view of the fact that many of the non-

---

[4]From working paper developed by the Admissions Staff, under the direction of Marion Howell, M.A.

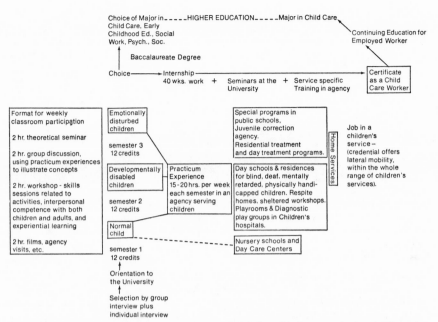

Fig. 16–1.—The curriculum and options for Child Care Workers are depicted. The point of entry to the two-year program is through the selection process described (see text), and indicated at the bottom of the figure. A practicum accompanies three semesters of course work. Students may then choose further academic work leading to a baccalaureate degree or a 40 week internship in an agency, at the end of which time a certificate as a Child Care Worker will be awarded successful candidates. The certified Child Care Worker may later exercise the option for further or continuing education, possibly leading to a degree.

white mothers are middle-aged and have not been in a school atmosphere for many years. Many of them have General Education Diplomas in lieu of high school diplomas.

The program was built, deliberately, without any outside funding sources. The child care courses have been part of the regular tuition-based course offerings of the University; until this year, an average of 41% of the students have received tuition and stipend support from WIN and MDTA sources, because of their eligibility for public assistance. This has made it possible to maintain the heterogeneity of student groups.

Approximately 290 workers with certificates are now working in more than 137 children's services in the Philadelphia metropolitan area (Table 16–1). Another 100 are in the internship phase of their training as full-time employees in these same agencies. Approximately 150 students are doing field placements in many of these agencies—some child care workers act as supervisors.

The entry-level salaries paid to a child care worker in 1968 were in the $2400–$3600 range. Salaries for preservice trained workers in 1975 range from $6500 to $8000. Rates of staff turnover in the agencies that hire preservice trained workers have not been evaluated, but many directors have reported a decline from over 100% per year to 10–20%. Many have felt that despite the higher starting salaries, they actually are saving money as a result of this decline.

Table 16–1
Numbers of Applicants, Students, "Certificates"
(and where they are working)
CCTP, 1968–1975

Total applicants	3000
Total interviewed	1500
Total entered	743
Total certificates (since 1970)	290
Interns completing certification requirements as full-time workers	100
Total working in "Day Care" Infants	
Preschool	40%
School-age	
Total in services for Developmentally Disabled Children	60%
Residential/day treatment centers and schools	
Group health C&Y centers	
Hospitals – Children's Heart and Moss Rehabilitation	
St. Christopher's Hospital for Children – system of services including home training program	
Child guidance clinics	
Residential centers for retarded, multiply handicapped, including group homes	
Residential/day – blind	
MH/MR day care, including infant stimulation, home training for high-risk infants	
Public school classrooms	

Many mature "certificates" have returned to the University, adding Liberal Arts courses to their "introduction to the profession" (the 3-trimester certificate training) to work toward a baccalaureate degree, mainly out of concern for their own developmental process. Younger, less mature trainees often are encouraged to complete a 4-year educational experience before they go for jobs, to compensate for their lack of practical experience or relevant life experience. Currently 65 students are in the baccalaureate program.

Child care students have offered more explicit definitions, not only of caring but also of what is a good child care worker. Caring is:

A human relationship, not a professional relationship; dealing with emotional needs, feelings; talking to kids; comforting with a hug; going after a runaway; putting on Band-Aids; changing diapers; eating with a kid who is messy; playing with kids; being there when they need you, and knowing when to stay away; sometimes reflecting what they're trying to say, and reflecting back how they are – some of the good parts of them they didn't know were there.

A good child care worker is:

A good storyteller; excited about the world; *someone* who listens to a nonverbal kid and understands him; who kisses dirty faces; who doesn't spank; who sets limits; who can hold a cerebral-palsied child in the pool for half an hour; someone who cooks, cleans up and throws out garbage; who gets sopping wet while giving a bath to a child; who takes kids on trips; who isn't afraid to show his feelings; who can make an educational mountain out of a molehill; someone with a sense of humor; a sympathetic ear for parents, supportive of children's rights; *a human being caring about other human beings.*

17

Arbitration between the Child and the Family

Bettye M. Caldwell, Ph.D.[1]

*Director, Center for Early Development and
Education and Professor of Education,
University of Arkansas at Little Rock, Little
Rock, Arkansas*

This volume is indeed very timely, for persons representing many different professions and social backgrounds are raising questions about the viability of the family. They are not only asking "Can it be saved?" but some are daring to question whether it should be saved. Is there a better way to do the things for society that the family has traditionally done?

Some time ago I saw the play "Shenandoah," which is about a man and his love for his family—beautiful, sentimental, and magnificent production. I found it rather interesting that in today's world when somebody writes a novel or puts on a play that shows family life in a positive way, it often seems necessary to kill off one parent or the other. In "Shenandoah" we have only a father. The Waltons are a notable exception, but remember "My Three Sons," the "Doris Day Show" and others. Sometimes it is easier to talk about a happy and sentimental family life if we have just one parent. Otherwise, family shows come to resemble "All in the Family."

But back to my question: Is there a better way to do the things that the family has traditionally done? Most of us would passionately aver that there is not. The one fact about my own personal history of which I am undoubtedly proudest is that I've been married for twenty-seven years to the same man and that we have two children and that within our family most days begin and end with some kind of declaration of love.

I am also very grateful that my own parents, aged 75 and 80, are still alive and reasonably well, and that we still have mutual dependency patterns in operation.

I say all this as something of a disclaimer of my ability to analyze conflict between children and families. That is not to claim, however, that within my own family there have not been from time to time almost unbearable stresses

[1]The author's work is supported in part by grants from the Office of Child Development, the Carnegie Corporation, and the Winthrop Rockefeller Foundation.

and strains, or that there were not many times when the family unit was close to disintegration. And, of course, check with me tomorrow!

My point is that family living is full of stresses, and unfortunately too few of us are adept in finding the humor in the situation in the style of the TV programs. When the things happen to us, it is no laughing matter.

A macabre indication of just how stressful some family situations can be is to note how often mass murders occur—some one member of the family wiping out everybody else; and, it is even more disturbing to note how often these events occur at times of traditional family joy, times like Thanksgiving and Christmas.

An equally macabre reminder is the disturbing frequency with which parents are charged with desertion, with selling or offering to sell a child, or with murder of their children. A typical and heart-rending case is one currently being tried in my state: a young mother, aged 22, is charged with having put her children to bed in a trailer and then having set fire to it. Family life has its stresses.

THE FAMILY

What is a family? What does it do? Presumably—and we can't really go beyond speculation here—families came into existence because of the need to formalize child rearing. Divisions of labor notwithstanding, it was that little creature who clearly belonged to the woman in the den but whose relationship to the hunter was probably less clearly understood, who across the centuries helped establish a pattern of bonding which held people together into family units. We sometimes think of the family as a female invention, but the complicated social patterns of regulating family life which gradually evolved offer in many ways greater protection to men.

Prior to full understanding of the process of procreation, paternity was not easily demonstrated. It had to be established by regulation of the ambience of women and then advertised and preserved by such customs as patronomic designation and a genealogy formalized through the father. Many of the important antecedents of our complicated legal system are rooted in the family, such as the concept of legitimacy, patterns of determining inheritance, etc. All of these bear witness to the fact that family law historically protected the male of the species and enhanced his security just as much as that of the female.

The biological definition of family involves no sentimentality. It describes a classification and nothing more. However, the connotative and social definition of family carries with it a broad array of expectations: "repose, comfort, a place of refuge from the rigors of the wider social environment" (Demos, 1974). That the individual family has perhaps not always provided these highly desirable characteristics is implied in the following sardonic but hopefully tongue-in-cheek definition of a family offered by Sussman (1974): "The family is a group of people somewhat haphazardly assembled (at least initially), related by blood or by marriage, and ruled by its sickest member." In some respects the question of what a family actually is can be as difficult to specify as what a family should be.

PARENTAL RIGHTS AND RESPONSIBILITIES

But now that we have families, what are their rights and what are their responsibilities? Specifically, what are the rights of different members of the family unit? And in particular how do rights of adults differ from or oppose those of children?

The child was not only the point of origin for the whole family unit, but the child has also remained a central figure in decisions about legal or societal regulations of the family unit. Over the centuries the adults in the family have acquired a massive set of rights in reference to children, including the right to legal guardianship and to withhold from children any civil rights until the children reach certain stipulated ages, 18 or 21 most likely. These rights were assigned to parents out of the conviction that children lacked the wisdom to be effective advocates for themselves, the experience to know what it was that they should learn, and the perspicacity to deduce what kinds of traits they should strive to develop during their formative years.

Implicit in this assignment to parents of the right to make decisions for their children—to socialize, care for and nourish them—was the assumption by society that parents accorded these rights would accept fully the responsibilities that accompanied them.

Whether this decision to vest parents with both the rights and the responsibilities for the welfare of children came as a quantum leap in social evolution or evolved slowly cannot be known today. My own guess is that it did not come all at once. I would guess rather that the concept of parental right developed after the perception of obligatory parental responsibilities. Some perceptive parent at some point across the centuries (and I'll guess that it was a father) must have said, "Since I have so much to do for these small creatures, since I have so much responsibility, I must be accorded certain rights to make decisions in their behalf." Thus, the concepts of parental rights and of parental responsibility must have evolved in close relationship to each other.

But just as parents have rights, so perhaps does society have rights with respect to those children for whom parents assume responsibility, the childrens' own civil rights being deferred in the process. To a certain extent these concepts of rights and responsibilities carry an implicit or perhaps inescapable potential conflict, and the settlement of such a conflict may occasionally require outside arbitration. Hence my title for today.

The definition of parental "rights" implies certain territorial guarantees such as that no outsider can intrude and give an order as to what must be done. On the other hand, the concept of parental responsibility implies an obligation to do certain things on behalf of the child. Furthermore, though seldom articulated, there is an implied penalty for failure to carry out certain acts presumed to benefit the child: the unverbalized component of the concept of responsibility says in effect: "If you don't do this or that—." Something else is needed, but we frequently do not finish that sentence. One could finish it with the clause ". . . then you will be held legally liable," or ". . . we will bypass your rights in order to guarantee that you fulfill your responsibilities." Of course, a society might simply say symbolically, "Shame on you," or it could say or do nothing at all.

In any case, the concept of parental responsibility implies that when it is unfulfilled there *must* be some mechanism for its transfer to society in order ultimately to protect the rights of the child.

Our courts represent the forum in which resolutions must ultimately be made of this potential conflict between parental responsibilities and societal responsibilities, and where ultimately children's rights can be considered. Many legal challenges represent attempts to redefine the proper balance between parental rights and children's rights, or between parental rights and inferred children's rights. Let me cite two examples.

The first case illustrates the deep conviction with which the belief in the inviolacy of parental rights has been held, with the invocation of divine authority as justification for that inviolacy. The lawsuit in question occurred in 1842 and stemmed from threats and assaults made by a father on a minister who had baptized the father's son, the son having requested such baptism in a faith other than that espoused by the father. The court's action was to censure the father and require him to post a $500 surety bond for six months. However, the court required the offending minister to pay the court costs.

In a brief prepared for the case the following opinion of a then prominent university president (and clergyman) was quoted as supporting that part of the court's judgment which was against the minister:

"The right of the parent is to command; the duty of the child is to obey. Authority belongs to the one, submission to the other. The relation is established by our Creator. The failure of one party does not annihilate the obligations of the other. If the parents be unreasonable, this does not release the child. He is still bound to honor and reverence his parent . . . . In such matters he (the parent) is the ultimate and the only responsible authority. While he exercises his parental duties, within their prescribed limits, he is, by the law of God, exempt from interference both from individuals and from society. In infancy (under 21) the control of the parent over the child is absolute—that is, it is exercised without any respect whatever to the wishes of the child" (Bremner, 1970).

That opinion is from an 1842 legal case, but it is not out of line with more recent court actions. A case that we should all remember occurred as recently as 1971 in the state of Wisconsin. There a group of Amish fathers had refused to send their teenage children to public high school because of their fear that secular schooling would weaken the commitment of the children to the Amish religious and cultural beliefs. The lower court's conviction of the three Amish fathers, fining them $5 each, was appealed to the United States Supreme Court, which reversed the decision on the grounds that forced attendance of those at a public high school violated the religious freedom of the *fathers*. However, the decision was not rendered without a public expression of the inherent conflict between protection of the rights of the parents and the rights of the children. Mr. Justice Douglas dissented, commenting that the decision hinged on the beliefs and wishes of the parents alone and failed to take into consideration the views and aspirations of the children.

The examples cited dealt with events that occurred a century apart and have referred primarily to the rights and responsibilities of parents to provide, to control and to regulate the religious and secular education of their children. Equally persuasive and possibly conflicted examples could be drawn from the evolution of current social regulations in the fields of child labor, child custody, child placement, adoption, juvenile offenses, child abuse, etc.

These examples help amplify the point that the family is as much a legal institution as it is a biological and a social one. Perhaps in terms of where decision making rests it is more legal than either biological or social. For example, adoptive parents have the same rights and responsibilities as biologic parents, and the rights of inheritance of adopted children are legally defined and protected. Similarly, the state has the power to dissolve families and to decide who shall provide subsequent care for the children of issue in the dissolved marriage.

Perhaps we need to explore ways to make permanent (that is, to endure beyond divorce) the legal relationship between two people who produce a child. As things now stand, the state intrudes just long enough to encourage the entry into this contractual arrangement with profound biological and social consequences, but stands aside modestly when the contract is terminated. Margaret Mead (1970) has said about this:

"Another confusion in our present attitudes toward divorce and remarriage comes from our refusal to treat the conception and production of a child as an unbreakable tie between the parents, regardless of the state of the marriage contract . . . But our present divorce style often denies the tie between the child and one of the parents, and it permits the parents to deny that through their common child they have an irreversible, indissoluble relationship to each other".

After this introduction to the ways in which we have given massive rights to parents to protect their children, along with the assumption that they will assume responsibility for them, we should turn our attention to the rights of children.

THE RIGHTS OF CHILDREN

Where in all this biological/social/legal melée do we find concern for the rights of our children? It is of interest that until the past decade or so—and especially until the past two or three years—we did not encounter much sophisticated concern for the legal rights of children. The 1970 White House Conference on Children included one whole cluster (five or six forums) devoted to the child and the legal structure, including one forum entitled "The Rights of Children" and another entitled "The Child Advocate."

In fact it was the White House Conference that turned my attention to this issue and to the implicit conflicts between achieving children's rights and adults' rights to personal freedom.

The fact that these topics were considered at the White House Conference does not mean that the forum members themselves were without conflict with respect to desirable courses of action. Note the expressions of conflict in the following examples taken from the report of the deliberations of forum members concerned with children's rights. In one paragraph one finds the following quote:

"Although societal services should insure each child his basic physical human needs, family obligation is personal and not governmental."

Yet a few paragraphs down one encounters the following:

"Although parents remain central to the child's guidance and emotional and biological nurturing, they cannot be expected to meet all of a child's needs as he seeks to cope with today's highly complex, mobile, and increasingly stressful world. The state must actively establish and protect those rights which reflect his needs."

And again:

"The family and the society share the responsibility for meeting a child's needs, since these needs are so great that neither the family nor society alone can meet them."

This forum went on to try to specify just what rights a child should have in our society, and came up with the following list.

1. The right to grow in a society which respects the dignity of life and is free of poverty, discrimination and other forms of degradation. (The latter is not defined, but I assume it could have included such things as theft, bodily assault, murder, etc.)

2. The right to be born, to be healthy and to be wanted through childhood.

3. The right to grow up nurtured by affectionate parents.

4. The right to be a child during childhood, to have meaningful choices in the process of maturation and development, and to have a meaningful voice in the community.

5. The right to be educated to the limits of one's capability and through processes designed to elicit one's full potential.

6. The right to have societal mechanisms to enforce the foregoing rights.

This list is very similar to a number of others that have been produced over the years: an International Declaration of Children's Rights by the United Nations, a list published after the original White House Conference in 1930, and a statement by the Joint Commission on the Mental Health of Children and Youth. There seems to be a fair degree of consensus as to what rights children ought to have. However, do we really have any consensus on point 6 above, the right to have societal mechanisms to enforce the foregoing rights? It is in consideration of this presumed right that we deal with the critical question implied in the title of my paper: What do we do when achievement of these basic rights that we wish to guarantee all children means infringing upon the individual personal freedom guaranteed parents as part of their civil rights?

Let us examine one of the above rights, such as the right to be born and to be healthy—and ask how that conflicts with a parent's possible decision to go on a macrobiotic diet, to give birth to that child without benefit of medical care, to be seen by a physician or not as he or she chooses, or to say "This conceptus belongs to me and I have the legal right to make this kind of decision."

Or let us take the right to a meaningful education. What societal mechanisms do we invoke for enforcing this, when we find that a school is not educating 40% of the children, neither to the degree that their parents feel they should be educated nor possibly to the extent that the ones who offer the school have indicated that they would or could?

What do we do about the right to be nurtured by affectionate parents, when we go into homes where there is blatant child abuse, with broken limbs and even death, or into other homes where the degree of neglect is so severe that you identify it as pre-abuse? What can we do besides say, "No child should have to grow up in such circumstances," write our reports, file them, and walk away. How can we guarantee those children who do not have affectionate parents their right to have them?

Please understand that I am presenting issues here for us to think about. You are not even going to know exactly what I think about all these different issues because I do not have any answer with which I am comfortable for the conflict raised in my title. I do think, however, that we have to give a great deal of thought to the last one—the right to societal mechanisms to enforce rights—if we are to go around spewing out the rhetoric of the first five about children's rights. These are rights of children which we want them to have; so presumably we want a society that has some mechanism for insuring that these rights can be guaranteed. At the same time we have a national history and a contemporary value system which say quite strongly that parents have autonomy and that only in the most extreme circumstances does society have the right to intrude if the parents are indeed not ensuring the rights of their children.

I have begun to think a great deal about children's rights to societal mechanisms to defend their rights. It is difficult to arrive at a consensus as to acceptable ways of accomplishing this. I can think of legitimate reasons for opposing almost any recommendation that might be made. Yet, if we are legitimately concerned with children's rights, we must be willing to give some thought to acceptable mechanisms for trying to enforce those rights.

SOCIETAL MECHANISMS FOR ENSURING CHILDREN'S RIGHTS

Let us consider very briefly a few mechanisms that could possibly be utilized.

Suppose we take the putative right of every child to grow up and be nurtured by affectionate parents. Can we mandate pre-parent education? Jerry Kagan referred to the fact that in the Guatemala community to be able to do things well with young children is valued, whereas in our culture value is placed on making good grades. There are other things he could have added, such as being cool, not being square. We require all of our children to take so many years of Math and English, and so on, but we do not require them to take courses in the development of the skills of being a parent. Nor do we do what is necessary to convey to them the importance of this, or to help them realize that this may be the most powerful and significant thing they will ever do in life. We give them plenty of opportunity to make career choices. But we fail to insist that they be trained for parenthood and that society's educational institutions play a role in this. Instead we back off and say that it is the parent's right to teach his or her children what they should do about this problem. But in this pattern, how is the society's responsibility exercised?

Another component of the same statement of rights is that children have a right to be healthy. (Presumably the authors of that statement were not bothered by thoughts of possible genetic dysfunctions.) But in the area of health care, the neediest people do not get to the services. Those who are skilled in the use of the system get all the services, but there are hundreds and thousands of needy children and families that do not get services because the services cannot find them. Many live in little nooks and crannies without even an address over the door, with five or more children in two rooms. The postman doesn't have to know where they are because they don't get any mail. No one knows whether they get immunized because no one knows they are there. We do not know whether they get educated or even get food stamps because they can literally disappear from our society.

One possible mechanism for helping to ensure proper health care is a *national registry*. Although the suggestion makes 1984 come to mind, some such mechanism is apparently necessary to protect the large number of children who fall through the mesh of our present health delivery systems. We are forced by law to register births, but then we have no mechanism for following all children to make certain that they receive the medical care they need during their early years. Specialists in early childhood, in preventive pediatrics, in nursing and in social work consistently proclaim the importance of those first five years; yet we lose track of many children during those years, providing public health services only if they are requested by parents.

The kind of registry I am referring to would require nothing more than the mailing of a change of address card so that a health visitor could at some time during the first three years of a child's life go into the home and check on immunization and nutrition. And if the parent does not show up at clinics with the child someone could call and say, "Your child hasn't had his immunizations or medical exam." Knowing where to find people is necessary if children are to have the right to be-born healthy and to stay healthy through childhood.

In order for children to achieve the "societal mechanisms" right we must have some kind of *monitoring system*. Such a thing scares all of us; yet we need a mechanism for knowing what is happening to the child, how he spends his days, what his living conditions are like, and how or whether his medical needs are being met. Without knowing where our needy children are, without knowing where all our children are, we cannot guarantee them their rights.

It seems to me now that we clearly need *child impact statements* for everything that is done in our society. We have reached the point where we require environmental impact statements on new buildings, on new sewage disposal systems or on zoning requirements within the city. But what might be the impact on children of the destruction of play space, or of tearing down a neighborhood school that children like and want to attend? We need some means for determining in advance whether laws and policies being formulated are inconsistent with or detrimental to the maximal development of children.

Still another mechanism that some groups are now asking us to consider seriously is a *license for parenthood*. This potential mechanism for fulfilling children's rights shocks us perhaps more than any of the others. How seemingly inimical to personal freedom is the thought that you should have to get a license to be a parent! Of course, we do not balk at all at getting a license to get married. That custom has been institutionalized as part of our culture. Maybe the first person who had to get that license objected, but now when we are ready to get married we think of it as merely one of the things we have to do.

The question of considering the acceptability of potential parents for parenthood is a very bold challenge and a frightening thing to think about. On the other hand, we have to get a license to open a child care center, have to be certified to be a teacher, or licensed to practice medicine. But for being parents, the task we pay lip service to as the important one of our lives, the requirements are minimal and do not require any statement of willingness to assume responsibility.

As a way of avoiding some of these more extreme practices, we ought to think about the possibility of using *incentives* to help society create mechanisms which can help ensure fulfillment of children's rights. We have a vast welfare system in this country under essentially constant criticism; everyone wants to see it changed. But no one has come up with a workable formula for change. Out of concern for our children and families we cannot abolish it, but we could use incentives within the system and perhaps reach many more children with important and needed services.

For example, suppose we offered some kind of payment—say $5.00, or free movie tickets, or free rental of a TV set—to persons who see to it that their children are immunized, who enroll and stay with parent education programs, who voluntarily limit the size of their families, who see an obstetrician a prescribed number of times prior to delivery and so on. Quite possibly the use of a simple incentive system would increase the tendency to utilize already available services and, in the long run, save money. Regardless of how abhorrent the thought of "bribing" people to "do what they ought to do in the first place" might seem to us, we should be willing to consider the use of incentives as a means of ensuring that children receive needed services and thereby have their rights protected.

Another mechanism requiring thought is a *statement of legal responsibilities,* laws that specify what is required of parents in order to maintain custody of their children. Again, we seem to have little difficulty with this concept where negative or harmful behavior is concerned. The best example would be in the area of child abuse. What is often forgotten is that most of the statutes pertaining to child abuse also make reference to milder forms or ostensible forms of parental malfeasance such as neglect. However, at this juncture in history few child care professionals have been willing to tackle the complicated legal question of how to define this subtler form of child abuse. And when statements of legal responsibilities are structured in a "thou shalt" rather than a "thou shalt not" vein, definitions become even more vague and sanctions less clearly specified. Yet in some way we need to help parents understand that there are certain positive actions that are required of them as well as certain behaviors that are prohibited.

Although there are many other possible mechanisms for arbitrating between parents and children, I shall conclude my list with one final suggestion for our consideration—*legal accountability of our social institutions.* For example, if welfare institutions have or should have knowledge of a child whose rights are being denied him and cannot give adequate proof that a serious effort has been made to correct the situation, then possibly that institution should be held accountable for such neglect. I have visited homes of children in our school and have come away frustrated and depressed, thinking that I have seen a pre-abuse household and yet feeling impotent and conflicted as to what I should do. In similar situations, most of us are confused as to exactly what kind of action we can take.

I hope I have cited enough examples of possible societal mechanisms for ensuring the rights of children to make you unhappy, or perhaps enough to get you excited about some possibilities and beginning to think of other approaches we might make to our pre-millenium task of occasional arbitration. Some of these possible mechanisms make us recoil in horror at the extent of their implied intrusion into family life; however, each needs to be looked at and thought about, for each is a logical extension of our own fine rhetoric. If we mean what we say about children's rights and what we say about the joint responsibility of the family and society for helping insure these rights, then we must go on and explore such mechanisms for guaranteeing rights of the children even when these mechanisms appear to infringe upon the freedom of the parents. It is not an easy conflict to resolve.

To resolve it, we must develop a social policy that is more accurately attuned to intergenerational realities, a social policy which includes some kind of valid apparatus for making decisions about when and how society should intervene when it is obvious that the needs of the parents or the wishes of the parents and the needs of the child or children are in conflict—that is, when it is obvious that parent/child arbitration is necessary.

SOCIAL POLICY AND INTERGENERATIONAL ARBITRATION

The role played by public policy in this task of intergenerational arbitration may be conceptualized as varying along a continuum from almost complete passivity or laissez-faire to almost complete activity. The likelihood of action – that is, of a society's exertion of its rights in the face of parental failure to assume responsibility – is probably a function of at least two variables. The first of these is the level of concern of the society for the welfare of its children. The second is the political and social philosophy of the society with respect to the priority assigned individual needs over the needs of the society – that is, the level of belief in autonomy, a very sacred belief that Jerome Kagan touched on in an earlier paper (Chap. 15).

These two forces will not always operate in concert. Where concern for children is high and belief in personal or family autonomy is low, as is apparently the situation in China and perhaps in the Soviet Union, you would predict early intervention and aggressive intervention by society on behalf of children. Where concern is low and belief in family autonomy is strong, you would predict almost no intervention short of a life-threatening crisis.

Where you have low concern for children along with low regard for autonomy, or high concern plus high regard for autonomy, there you will find a conflicted society. My own analysis of our situation in America is that we fall into the latter category: much concern for children, but a deeply ingrained belief in personal autonomy.

This conflict between high level of concern and high regard for autonomy is very obvious in America today. We do not feel comfortable about deciding when to intervene and when to refrain from intervention on behalf of the child. Unless the risks appear to be great and the potential gains from non-intervention minimal, we tend to remain passive or at most conflicted.

Although the title of this work may be a cliche, it touches a true problem. The family as a unit is in deep trouble in America today. Part of that trouble is that we are in conflict about this issue of autonomy. We try to make families believe that they must do everything themselves, something that is patently impossible in today's complex world. Furthermore, we make them think they *ought* to do everything themselves. In a stable, non-changing social group wherein the adults accept without challenge the collective values of the group, where religious beliefs and customs are tightly interwoven with family customs and not constantly challenged by rivalrous sets of customs and beliefs, and where the unarticulated goal of socialization is to duplicate the existing adults rather than to create new types of adults who will function in a new society, perhaps the family can manage the socialization process with no outside help. Furthermore, in such a society children should be able to assimilate their expected adult patterns of behavior with a minimum of intrapsychic conflict and with almost no need for interventive services to assist them in their process of humanization.

But do such societies exist today? I think not. My own feeling is that all parents generally do those things that they think are good for their children. Thousands of parents in America and all over the world would talk more to their children (to refer to Jerry Kagan's statement) if they were really convinced that this was important. Thousands more would seek medical care if they were convinced it would make a major difference. Our priorities have been mixed up, however, and we have not given high priority to the task of rearing our children.

We cast a lot of blame for this impasse, incidentally. We blame the social institutions such as the schools, but we really have no right to do that. We should rather blame those policy makers who have insisted that it would violate the rights of families if the schools taught about certain things, such as how to be a good parent, and who have opposed making these things a regular part of the curriculum of our public schools.

It does seem that we can try to develop a policy which communicates to parents that being a parent is not easy, that says in effect "this is a hard job and you need preparation for it; you're going to feel used up sometimes and you're not always going to know what to do. Sometimes you're going to get so mad you'll want to hit your kids and sometimes you will hit them. Sometimes you'll ask two people for help and get two different answers because nobody knows all the answers about children and how they develop. But you aren't the only ones with these feelings and experiences. You live in a society that will help you. We have public health programs, public education programs and public welfare programs. Use all of these resources if you need to, and use them before your problems reach the crisis level."

This is the kind of policy statement I would like to see because it emphasizes the parents' own rights, not the rights they hold in escrow for their children— including the right to have help when help is needed.

Our public policy also needs to emphasize the responsibilities of being a parent, and in our society this is probably more poorly developed than the "rights" side. I've come to use a very old-fashioned word to describe what I think we need: a *covenant*. If children are to be protected as families change and mutate as is happening today, and if their rights are to be given equal weight with the rights of parents, then society needs to demand that parents covenant with their children to provide the basic ingredients for development—including love, availability and the essentials of physical care.

It is interesting that we have marriage ceremonies which involve having two people covenant with one another. Those vows are very easily broken, as we well know, but still they set certain legal limits for behavior of either partner. The covenant I am referring to would also of course, need legal sanctions to back it up.

Apart from baptismal rites I know of no similar covenant required of persons who become parents. If somehow we could encourage a willingness on the part of parents to endorse such a list of rights as those from the White House Conference this might facilitate a generalized consciousness raising about parental responsibilities. When this is done we will not have to worry about arbitrating between parents' rights and children's rights. If opinion influencers and policy makers can encourage parents to covenant with their children, and if the larger society will similarly covenant with the parents, then the needs of children can be met no matter how much or in what ways families change.

COMMENTARY

DR. CAROL GARVEY (Boston): I want to comment in regard to children's rights. I think we are in a confusing time, when children's rights are being advocated to the point where minor children — sometimes with no lower age limit at all — are allowed to seek medical care, often appropriate and needed, but extending to abortion and even possibly to sterilization without parental permission.

I have not heard any recommendations that children under 16 be allowed to decide whether or not they should attend school — which I think is an interesting dichotomy, a kind of schizophrenia in our approach to children's rights.

Some of the legal protections for children are certainly necessary, but I think that in our role as providers of health care or as people who have to process services such as abortion and sterilization, for children and for adults, we have to constantly remind ourselves that these individuals are in fact members of families and that there is the issue of mutual responsibility in addition to the question of individual rights; and that as far as is possible the individual should be treated in the context of the family.

Perhaps one of the very important parts of this is that parents should be given sex education with which they can educate their children. That would probably be more effective than sex education in the schools. I am not saying we should abandon the area of children's rights; but I think we mediate a lot of these rights and we should understand what we're doing in the context of the family.

DR. CALDWELL: I think that's a beautiful comment and I wish I had used that phrase — the schizophrenia in relation to children's rights. I think there really is a schizophrenia, and people are screaming very stridently for some of these things without thinking through their implications.

The White House Conference Forum strongly recommended that children younger than 18 be allowed to seek medical care, including abortion. But the whole question about education is a good one. Most States have laws requiring children to be in school until 16; but, again, one of the recommendations made by that Forum was that children should have the right to influence the curriculum.

I am somewhat reactionary with regard to a lot of this. I don't think kids know all that much. I think they need this period of having their rights held in abeyance. Some of you who know me know that I have given two or three similar talks within the past year, but I have been unwilling to publish them. Point 6 of that White House Conference is so arrogant: "the right to have societal mechanisms to insure these rights."

I have been taking my students one by one and asking "where are the grounds for conflict?" We assume that the family will serve for the child to achieve these rights, but if we know that doesn't happen or frequently will not happen, then we have immediately gotten ourselves into a totally untenable position. And I want us to think about that.

GEORGE ETHRIDGE (Columbus, Ohio): We've been hearing that professionals have created many horrors or mistakes because of their intrusion into the family from a professional point of view. Now you suggest that we should develop more professional service agencies which exercise exacting and possibly intrusive requirements on the child and his family. I am confused as to the exact sequence of activities we should engage in.

192

DR. CALDWELL: I don't think I suggested that, Dr. Ethridge. My point is that if we believe in children's rights we have to face up to the responsibility side, because there will be occasions when the parents who act for children will not see that the children's rights are fulfilled.

Some of the things I was suggesting, the little hypothetical situations, I would not endorse at all. The use of incentives I highly endorse. I am just about ready to endorse a national registry, to come out strongly for it, as a matter of fact. But those are not really intrusions in terms of the individual decision making. Those are things that would make it easier for parents to act to see to it that children's rights are indeed fulfilled.

Things become intrusive when you let problems go too long. As I said, in every State we have a child abuse law that says you can actually take a child from parents if the child has been abused. What we need is to develop pre-crisis services and pre-crisis ways of helping families fulfill the rights of their children. I don't see that as having to be intrusive.

DR. WILLIAM FREEMAN (Seattle, Washington): I am in Family Medicine. Yesterday someone noted that when we study the history of medicine or of child care, we find that many experts who spoke with profound expertise and conviction a hundred years ago are not now considered to be right.

I question some of what is being said in regard to society taking over and establishing laws on these matters, but even more I question the idea that we can be sure that our thinking is correct. In particular, I wonder if some of the rights specified in the White House Conference may not be ethnocentric, in the sense that some things that most of us middle class or educated parents do may not be all that helpful.

For example, skiing is known to be unhealthy for those who ski; yet I don't hear a lot of opposition either to letting adults ski or to letting them have their children ski.

DR. CALDWELL: I don't know if I have anything to add. I agree. The issues are probably time oriented. In relation to this business of the registry I would like all of you to take this as your assignment when you go home: What would be the minimum level and pattern of service that we could offer, with a minimum of intrusion into the autonomy of the family, that would help us insure reasonably good development of children?

That is something I've been trying to crystallize in my own mind. A registry with mandated screening at the ages of 1 and 3 years is really all I've been willing to come up with. And by screening I mean checking on how a child is developing, looking at height and weight and illnesses, and immunization records — hopefully at the same time getting some information about what the home life of the child is like, to see if minimum human standards are met.

Jerry Kagan told us that a hundred years ago the experts were saying "don't let your child interact with other children — he'll learn bad things." We don't say that today, but maybe we should. What is right is temporally and ethnically limited, and culturally limited, too. So we must be careful about what we specify as the minimums or maximums that we want our children to have or achieve.

REBECCA KAUFFMAN (Elementary Guidance Counselor and Educator, East Norwich, N. Y.): I am happy to hear Dr. Caldwell indicate that we do not have all the answers as to what makes the perfect parent. In fact, I don't think there is such a thing as the perfect parent, and in my occupation I find many parents with unnecessary guilt feelings. They are well meaning, but many of these parents have read so many books by conflicting psychologists as to what is the right way to bring up a child that they have gotten to the stage where they no longer have confidence in their own ability to react to their child.

We actually take away from a mother/child relationship or a father/child relationship the feeling: "I am trying to do what is best for the child, and I feel within myself that my child will understand." When we take that away, we see parents going according to a cookbook, taking a warming relationship and making it mechanical.

Dr. Caldwell, I feel basically that the Amish decision was correct. The Supreme Court decision rested not only on religious freedom, but on the feeling that these Amish parents were preparing their children for livelihoods and occupations, that they were in no way really neglecting these children, and that they are giving them a sense of values.

With abuse and neglect of children the abuse situation is clearly defined. With respect to neglect we are in a situation now where 18-year-olds can actually claim their parents are neglecting them, and where the rights of children may become tyrannical. What will happen then?

DR. CALDWELL: Those are excellent comments, exactly the kind of thing I want us all to think about.

MS. KAUFFMAN: May I make another comment? I am a little concerned when the State takes over too many rights. With Plato's Republic, that seemed excellent; but what happened with the Nazi regime?

DR. CALDWELL: I'm not advocating that the State take over any rights—

MS. KAUFFMAN: I don't mean it that way. What I am trying to ask is who is to decide which children are to be born or unborn, or which parents should have children according to whose standards of what constitutes a proper parent?

DR. CALDWELL: I think that if our society would think about that it would be an extremely wholesome thing.

MS. KAUFFMAN: I agree.

DR. CALDWELL: That's all that I'm asking and suggesting.

ARTHUR GREENWALD (Pittsburgh, Pa.): We've talked about a lot of issues today, about nutrition and obstetric and pediatric care and training more competent people to take care of children in different centers. How do we inform the public of these different options so that they can make more intelligent decisions? How can you bring this complex information to the public in a clear and concise manner, so that they will have informed options at hand when they make their own decisions?

DR. CALDWELL: That's an excellent question. Part of our problem is, again, the level of uncertainty of knowledge. Perhaps we have tended to go overboard and overeducate for things before we were really ready.

This is part of the whole concern, the implicit idea that we really know what is good for children. Jerry Kagan's paper makes it obvious that a lot of different things can be good for children; that is, that children can turn out all right after exposure to circumstances that we might have thought of as absolutely devastating.

This is certainly one precaution that we need to keep in mind any time we're seeking children's rights or trying to define parental rights: to be aware that we are always working within a finite and limited field of knowledge, and that we may have a pretty large standard error in what we are encouraging.

DR. KAGAN: Could I be a pastor for thirty seconds? This is just orthogonal, generated by the discussion. I find it very dangerous to consider the use of the law and the courts for what is essentially human endeavor. Society is concerned about a proportion of children who turn out to disturb the fabric. If they did not disturb the fabric we wouldn't be very concerned. This is our responsibility, not the court's. Until this society becomes ready to knock on its neighbor's door and say "let's talk over the fact that your child broke my window," rather than call the policeman, we'll achieve nothing.

Personally, I regard as frightening the discussion of an itinerary that would erect legislation and courts to do something that they cannot do, but that only we as neighbors can do.

DR. ROGER (Baltimore, Md.): I want to speak in behalf of parents who are participants in comprehensive care services, parents who because they have had some contact with health care agencies recognize the fact that their children are in trouble and want to use a preventive method for caring. They want to do something about health problems before they become critical, but they are too often locked into a system of red tape.

How do you get past the red tape of the system that so often turns off a parent who isn't articulate, who doesn't have the coping skills for maneuvering, who has only one dime to make a phone call and has to be referred to some other source when the person who is doing the interviewing can easily transfer the call or in some other way make the task easier?

We talk about supportive care, but it is often rhetoric. How do we make it really available? We need to help many of these mothers and families to get through to the sources of the care that they're searching for and not let them be bogged down in red tape because they do not have the coping skills for getting through. Somehow middle class mothers teach their children to do this.

DR. CALDWELL: Just as Jerry Kagan said, through a feeling of community and mutual concern on the part of people who know one another. But most of us are wary about accepting help and suggestions, and this is why it seems to me we move beyond pre-crisis with things that could be easily handled at an early stage with our resources. We wait until things get out of hand. I would say that just neighborliness, a genuine concern, the feeling that all the community's children are my children—this is part of what it seems is necessary.

Part V

Special Problems in the Child, as They Affect Family Life

18

Chronic Illness in Childhood and Family Functions

Barbara Korsch, M.D.

Professor of Pediatrics, University of
Southern California School of Medicine,
Los Angeles, California

In this chapter I shall try to do three things: give you a small conceptual framework and general introduction on the subject of chronic illness and how it has an impact on the family; show you portions of edited interviews in which I trust that the mothers of some of our patients will make the points that I think are important for you; and, finally, try to relate some of what I have presented to what seem to be the nodal points in this work.

Many find fault in some way with pediatricians and with nurses. This is not hard to do. I think that anyone who works with chronic illness in childhood certainly is tempted to make this kind of criticism, though the faults that we find are not always easy to correct. The way in which the care of chronically ill children is taught and practiced is really one of the glaring paradoxes in medical care. Anyone who has been around a medical center—and a very high percentage of severely chronically ill children are treated in tertiary care centers—realizes that patients are cared for with a gigantic pair of blindfolds. Almost all of the care concentrates on the technologic aspect of the child's health, and usually very little attention is given to the child's personality, the family needs and the over-all concerns of parents, children, families, teachers or others who have to deal with chronically ill children.

Still, when one thinks about it, in day-to-day life or on any particular visit from a chronically ill child, the concerns on the part of the child as well as of the parents tend to be minimal from the technologic standpoint. Once the diagnosis has been established and the child is started on a course of treatment, very often during any given visit some technical aspect needs to be adjusted; but, for the remaining hours of the family's daily life, the concerns lie in other areas. For those areas there are very few resources in most cities.

There has been a lot of discussion this past year at various conferences on chronic illness as to who the right person may be to care for a child and family in the presence of chronic illness. With technologic care as far advanced as it is, many practitioners feel uncomfortable caring for chronically ill children; yet, they might be the ones with the tolerance and patience to deal with the myriad of daily, weekly or monthly problems of everyday life that confront these children. Tertiary care centers in many ways seem less well suited for this, and still, because we all need the technologic support, that is where the child is cared for.

In the training of pediatricians and nurses and other health professionals to care for the main chronic illnesses, what is done seems absolutely upside down. Usually there are short-term exposures to chronically ill children who are hospitalized for some sort of acute episode in their chronic illness. They are cared for by people who didn't know them before and won't know them later.

History-taking is typical of how bizarre the whole thing is. Records are of help in general; but every new intern and every new medical student takes a new history to find out how the baby was fed, what the milestones were and reviews the family history all over again. All of this is put into the record before anybody asks them how they feel or what their concern is or what they're hoping to get from this particular hospitalization. These poor people, who may have been cared for in that same institution for as long as 10–15 years, are put through this archaic drill, which really does not seem very relevant to their acute problem of the moment; and they often feel that somehow somebody in this institution should already know all that, and should be able to take off from there. It has been suggested that we should devise a different format for handling such admissions.

Training seems to be similar in the specialty clinics. Interns, nurses or anyone who wants to learn about the care of children with chronic hematologic disease spends 3 weeks in the hematology clinic. They stand with a group of experts and are shown the cogent features of the disease and told the latest armamentarium of drugs. They don't get to know any one of the patients or families well enough to get a feeling for what it's like to face their problem or what the real needs are for care on a week-to-week and month-to-month basis.

Still, when you suggest to the specialty clinic potentates that perhaps some of those children should be cared for over a period of time by the people who are training for general pediatrics, in a kind of continuity situation by nonspecialists, they get, as you all know, extremely protective and point out that no one except them knows how to care for these patients. They are reluctant to make visits to the general clinic as consultants. They want their patients right there to treat them the way they like.

Most of the exposure on the part of house staff and nurses and other health workers to the problems of chronic illness in hospitals tends to focus exclusively on the technologic aspects and gives them very little experience and training to deal with the problems as they occur.

The concern of my presentation is how chronic illness impacts the family. This is a very difficult thing to discuss because it becomes hard to decide which is the independent and which is the dependent variable; or, how do we decide whether it is chronic illness in the child that influences family life or it is family life, family communication and family function that make tremendous differences in the outcome of chronic illness?

It really *is* a two-way relationship. When you see studies of family breakdown or of the effect on siblings of having a sick child in the family, if you look carefully you find that often the very reason for a particular outcome can be found in pre-existing family conditions. In effect, most of the studies I am aware of show that the kind of family function, or the kind of communication in the family, is a main determinant of how that particular child with his illness will fare and what the over-all outcome for the family will be.

My recent experience with this problem has related mostly to patients with end-stage renal disease who have been treated by means of hemodialysis and/or transplantation. This has been a good model for study, not necessarily because the particular problems posed by the treatment programs to these patients are universal or are in themselves more interesting. I think that whereas in many other fields—like hematology and cystic fibrosis, etc.—we give fairly high-powered technologic treatment to prolong life but don't pay so much attention to the features I alluded to before. There was something that made the medical profession look at its conscience when the sudden onslaught of treatment programs for end-stage kidney disease gave all those patients an alternative or two who previously were sure to die. I guess that we felt keenly aware of what we are doing to these children and families, and that on that account more attention and money have been spent on looking at the quality of life of the survivors and at what the programs do to children.

Partly we feel fiscally responsible because it's a terribly expensive treatment. Partly we feel humanly concerned as to what we are doing to these children and their parents.

When we started doing dialysis and renal transplants in children there were a great many people who questioned their moral and ethical justification. "Are you sure that saving this child's life will not be done at such a cost in terms of money and suffering and family disorganization that it isn't really justified?" We felt that it was necessary to take a close and continuous look at the children and their families, which is what we have done.

In the case of transplant patients, we have follow-up data involving personality tests and family studies on 85 of our survivors with functioning allografts who have had their transplant from 1 to 8 years. They constitute a little population, and some of what I will say is based on their experience.

In general, our findings have been quite like those of other people who have worked in the field of chronic illness, in the sense that it seems not to be the experience with a specific illness that is the main determinant of how everybody is going to fare; rather, the three main factors seem to be: the personality of the sick child, the stage in growth and development at which the illness is experienced and then, most of all, what kind of family situation they have to back them up.

These seem to be the three most important factors in deciding whether you will achieve a satisfactory quality of life, good rehabilitation for child and family and the other desirable outcomes. I'll give you a couple of examples.

As far as personality is concerned, it seems (if you want to be very general about it) that children who come to their experience of illness with fairly intact personalities, especially with good self-esteem and with the feeling that they are in some control of their own fate and are able to master what happens to them, and with other resources, like intellectual strength, etc.—those children will weather the experience better than others, as you might anticipate.

We have found that by personality testing early in the course of management we can identify those children who might need special help and special intervention in order to get through the experience, or those who may not get through it very well at all.

Incidentally, I hasten to say that in our program, as by now in most programs, we do not use this kind of assessment to decide who should have treatment or who should not have treatment. What we are interested in is finding out where the problems are going to lie and how we best can help them. So we attempt to assess the child and the family so as to know as much as possible and give them the best of care.

As far as stage of growth and development is concerned, just to give you an example of how differently different children at certain developmental stages experience the same kind of experience: In the transplant patients, as in some other groups, the female adolescents have been by far the most difficult patients to deal with. Other evidence from Luther Travis and from a study in England involving long-term follow-up on a group of children with chronic illness indicates that any illness that has some cosmetic implications is experienced with special difficulty by adolescent girls.

To document this: We have 26 adolescent girls in our program who have had their transplants more than a year and were transplanted at over 13 years of age. Out of those 26, 13 or 14 have significantly impaired personality on testing and, as a very dramatic manifestation, out of those 26, at some point 11 have failed to take the immunosuppressive medication so necessary for their kidney to survive. And out of those 11, 5 or 6 by now have lost their transplanted kidney, and another 5 or 6 are in some stage of chronic rejection.

When you calculate the investment to treat someone with hemodialysis for 5 or 6 months and then give them a kidney transplant, not just in terms of money, though that can be $40,000–$50,000, but in terms of the emotional investment on the part of patient, family and staff in giving this young woman a kidney, and when you then find that she cannot tolerate the side-effects of the steroids or the kind of life she has to lead, to the point where she stops taking her medication, that is a pretty dramatic indicator that this experience at that point in life must be a pretty devastating one.

And I think this is true to some measure with adolescent girls with diabetes, which you may be more familiar with, or with other diseases. This illustrates the importance of the developmental stage.

Finally, as far as family relations are concerned, we'll be talking about that for the rest of this discussion. We have found, as many other people have, that if there is good communication within the family, if there is one supportive strong adult or even an elder sibling in the family who really is a source of strength to the patient, this is perhaps the single most important predictor of a relatively good outcome for the sick child.

From here I will let the patients speak for me, because they can say it so much better than I.

The issues to be illustrated are the importance of communication among family members in the presence of illness or at any other time; the effect of the chronic illness on the child's siblings; the restrictions in the scope of family life; special problems relating to the nature of the illness; some coping mechanisms; and some of the expectations that these patients have from the health care system.

Here, Dr. Korsch presented from videotape fragments of an interview between a mother and a physician. They discussed the failure of communications that left the mother unable to explain or deal adequately with the child's and her family's questions regarding changes taking place as a result of cortisone therapy.

At one point, the mother expressed her frustration that every question she had asked had seemed to be answered by a returning question. She said that in some ways she felt that what she needed was not so much answers as a hand on the shoulder and a reassuring statement that everything necessary for diagnosis or treatment was going to be done.

The mother described the impact that the uncertainty she felt had had on her marriage, and how difficult it was for her to try to carry information between the medical scene and her husband, who was not able to visit at times convenient to the physicians. Her mediation was not enough to satisfy the father's needs, and their joint frustration threatened their marriage until a point where for the first time they cried almost helplessly together instead of crying one at a time with each trying to comfort the other.

COMMENTARY

PARTICIPANT (Danville, Pa.): Have you made any progress in getting the father more involved and hopefully eliminating some of these potential difficulties?

DR. KORSCH: We're working on it. In this particular case, the mother was very articulate and finally got herself some better help. She alluded to some of the problems. Every time she was in the hospital the father was working. It's very difficult to get members of the health care team to be available for questions at night on the wards, or to create any conference situations in the evening or on weekends. They are all hard-working people. Very often the person parents find, as you well know, is the one who is on duty and not the one who knows their child the best.

On top of that, with the current routines, the regular doctors disappear at 3:30 or 4:00 in the afternoon and the time when the parent has a chance to get at the person they wish to is getting more and more constricted. This is one of the reasons some of us have raised the question as to whether there is a more important place for the private primary physician in the care of chronically ill children. Many of them are fearful of the technology and just refer the whole care of the child to the medical center. Is there anybody else besides the primary physician who can meet some of these needs?

DR. BARRY FARBER (Philadelphia): I'm still dealing with my sadness from the last tape. I don't know that the answer lies within the medical sphere. Somehow I think it's a larger issue than just medical. I think it's more of a societal thing.

DR. KORSCH: I agree with you. I was reminded of it when yesterday Marshall Klaus and some discussants mentioned that doctors have taken death out of the home and put it in the hospital and have taken birth, too, out of the home and put it in the hospital—which I think is a good thing. On the other hand, crucial events in families are being handled in hospitals where there aren't the resources to deal with all the issues. Maybe it is a social issue. I think it also relates to some of the other questions we have heard, such as: Who is caring for the people who care for the kids?

Yesterday Berry Brazelton commented that all of us involved in health care are very fond of children. In his group they love babies. In some other care-taking groups we relate very warmly and readily to the sick child. But for this mother with her problems there is very little in the system. I agree that it is a problem for more than just the health care establishment.

Let me answer my own question, since nobody else has. I do think that in addition to the primary physician and the health care team adapting their schedules a bit more to the patient's needs than to the convenience of the specialist, there are other people who can help with this job. I think that something has to come from the physician in charge. Five minutes spent with the surgeon who is going to do the operation means a great deal more to the patient than 45 minutes with associated health professionals if they have had no direct access to the one who is responsible for them.

I do think physicians giving care are going to have to give a little. I also think we can bring into the act other members of the caring team. We ought to think a little bit more about the roles of referring physicians, or primary physicians, because a large percentage of the patients seen in a regional referral hospital like ours are patients with chronic illness; and patients with chronic illness are very frustrating to take care of. They never get well. They have unending psychosocial problems. They are bottomless pits of whom many caretakers get rather tired.

I have a tape I didn't bring, which would have made Dr. Farber much sadder. A set of parents are complaining because their boy was in and out of the hospital so much that everybody got very sick of seeing him and, as is so often the case, they wondered whether some of his pains were psychosomatic, which in the minds of so many caretakers is equated to malingering. The staff thought he really wanted to be in the hospital all the time.

On the admission the parents were discussing, Michael was greeted with "Hello, Michael, what's going on? It must be pretty tough in school that we see you here again." Every person whom he greeted on arrival met him with the idea "Oh, here is Michael again and what is it this time?" That was 2 weeks before he died. This kind of fatigue in the care of chronically ill patients is seen in most care-taking teams in spite of the best efforts to avoid it, and it may be more pronounced in the people peripherally related to those children on the wards.

Chronic patients are unpopular with nurses and house staff. I think everybody has only so much tolerance and patience and enthusiasm to put into this kind of care. Physicians who care for them as primary doctors may have 3 or 4 or 5 patients in their professional careers who have end-stage kidney disease or diabetes, and they may have a lot to give to these children and their families. In the hospital, where they're all concentrated, it's hard to get or to sustain this kind of caring and support.

Dr. FREEMAN (Seattle, Washington): You are asking who should do the caring. Perhaps a more important question is what should the caring be? I would like to underline the points in the tape where the mother said that she would really like to have the doctor touch her, and where she described herself and her husband for the first time crying together.

It seems to me a major thing, both as a member of a family and as a physician, that we fail to establish human bonds and be human ourselves as professionals. The ideology is not to touch, not to cry, things that if we were not doctors and nurses, we would do in those circumstances and would want to have done to us.

I'm raising the question whether our medical ideology may not sometimes be counterproductive.

Dr. KORSCH: I think it's an important point. As some of you know, I am very interested in the whole business of doctor/patient communication. A phenomenon we find again and again in individual interactions between doctors and patients is that doctors in general shun emotion. I have many recordings of doctors and patients interacting in which it is almost funny that as soon as the patient starts talking about something with feeling—like the fact that they are extremely anxious or afraid they might die or something terrible might happen—the doctor tends to say something like "Was it 5 years ago you moved to Texas?" or "Have you been taking your pills regularly?"

When expressions of emotion enter into the conversation, doctors become uncomfortable and try to shut them off. Still, these are some of the things that need to be attended to and where help is needed. But I think we are not trained to deal with this kind of thing. We're not psychiatrists. Moreover, if you are dealing with a great many seriously ill patients, you can't allow yourself to cry or completely empathize with every one of the really crucial situations you see. So it becomes defensive not to listen to this kind of thing.

At a little more profound level, a lot of wise medical educators have discussed the fact that one reason that some of us go into the health professions is because we are afraid of our own vulnerability and of the possibility of our being sick or disabled or even dying, and that we master these issues by taking care of other people. But if you allow your patient to become too human and yourself to become too aware of these things, then that brings it awfully close to home.

Albert Bandura, in talking about aggression, said that one way to deal with that is to dehumanize the victim. I think dehumanizing the victim also does something for health care professionals, because then the patients are not so much like themselves.

DR. FREEMAN: I would like to respond to that. I can't speak as a person who continually deals with severe chronic illness, so you may be right that it is not possible to feel with patients all the time in that circumstance. But I can say that I feel I am a better physician and a better human being when I let my natural feelings come forth as appropriate. It turns out that in fact I still can't control them. I do not let my emotions interfere with my judgment, and yet I am at that time much more helpful to the family.

Again I want to question, not just for physicians but for the whole health care establishment, the ideology or the understanding that we should not be emotional; that somehow that will interfere with our functions. I am suggesting that in my limited experience both as a member of a family and as a provider that that is not the case.

DR. KORSCH: I think that is a very complex and interesting subject, and we could spend many hours discussing it. I think the problem of allowing yourself to feel but not having it cloud your judgment or make you a less effective physician is a very real one, and you seem to have solved it very well for yourself.

I can tell you of an instance (and this is really speaking on the other side of the argument from where I belong) of a young boy 12 or 13 years old who was cared for in concert by two orthopedic surgeons, while I was the pediatrician. He had a tumor of the leg. I remember a particular visit of his when after having had a mid-calf amputation, he came to us wearing a prosthesis and with a swelling and a painful nodule in the stump. All three of us were sure that this was some sort of keloid and that the prosthesis wasn't fitting right. This attractive, blond, long-haired boy happened to look a lot like the sons of two of the three physicians. We decided it was just a little irritation and sent him home. A couple of weeks later, we measured the lump again and, in retrospect, we all realized that in any other patient we would have thought of metastasis right away. Because the patient looked a lot like someone we were fond of and because of all the feelings one has, it was difficult for us to accept the first indication of spread. The boy ended up with a disarticulated leg on that side. In this case, I don't think it made the difference because there was just a short delay and the prognosis was bad anyway.

What you said is very important in the sense that to allow oneself to feel but also to be aware of one's feelings about a particular patient might make it possible to reach the optimal balance that you allude to, allowing oneself to feel without feelings getting in the way of painful procedures or other appropriate behavior.

DENNIS ROSEN (Pediatrician, Amherst, Mass.): It seems to be my experience with chronically ill children that fathers tend to turn off sooner, and just don't seem to get involved the way mothers do. Do you feel this is purely sociologic or is there something innate about this response? And, more importantly, what can we do to reinvolve these fathers. Should there be formal medical or paramedical support for the parents alone, in a group, in a one-to-one communication? What are the determinants?

DR. KORSCH: It seems to me you've answered a lot of your questions yourself. I think particular attention to the father and sometimes to parents as groups would be helpful. I think some of the things that we've been hearing at this seminar would also be important—like early introduction of the father to the infant, so that it becomes "my son" instead of "her son."

The mother in the first tape made a point that we have to deal with. Often the woman has to be the go-between between the medical establishment and the family, and since often her needs and the family needs aren't being met, she is the one who gets the blame. You remember how she said that her husband asked, "Why didn't you ask the doctor? Why didn't you get the answers?" We hear about this a great deal, and I think there are ways of dealing with that.

One should be aware that that is unfair to the mother, and occasionally getting a father involved might take an evening appointment. For the family already stressed by the illness, if you want the father to take a day off from work, that isn't really very fair.

We see interesting phenomena. We have some data, not yet statistically significant, so that I hesitate to present them, which suggest that these families turn into matriarchies. The mothers assume a new role, often dragging themselves into the clinics day after day with their children for treatments, but more and more making the decisions. Their new assignment in the family is a very hard one, which we should be aware of and help them with, and also diffuse when possible, so that they are not the only ones on the spot.

In the next tape, the mother is one who did get a lot of support from her husband, and he thinks he is her main source of strength. This depends a lot on the pre-existing family structure. Chronic illness doesn't create anything new, but it brings out pre-existing problems in the family. One can predict some of this and try to deal with it.

DR. NAIMAN: I think we all agree that it's easy for the father by virtue of the role that society gives him to stay out of involvement, but that it's much better if he can become involved. At the same time, we have to recognize the fact that there are so many situations where he is not involved for whatever reason, and that his needs are not going to be met. We tend to concentrate on the needs of the mother as she sees them. This is another reason for us to try to help fathers—whether separately if need be or, ideally, together with the mother.

Here, Dr. Korsch presented a second videotape involving an interview with the mother of a boy of 17 years who had had a renal transplantation, following a life of chronic renal disease. The mother discussed the problems she had being fair to both her children: Doug, the patient, and Curt, a healthy boy 16 months older, who was 6 feet 7 inches tall and very mature. The relationship between the boys was touched on.

The mother discussed the impact of Doug's illness on her first marriage. Doug's father had left her on account of Doug's illness. Her second marriage was good and secure. Nonetheless, the mother felt "boxed in" as she discussed the impact of Doug's condition on family life and on her own self-realization. She had held a responsible position in which she had some pride; yet she had wept when she was refused a lesser job that would have made her life easier, having been told she was "overqualified."

The mother was asked whether she had ever wondered why this had all happened to her. She acknowledged such questioning, and said she felt that it was "God's will." The mother closed with a thought expressed as "God has kind of overlooked the whole thing. He must have wanted him to live." Doug had done his part; Dr. Korsch had done her part, or more.

DR. KORSCH: That last line sort of states the plight that we've been dealing with. The first mother said they felt so helpless; and this mother, although she claims to have firm religious faith, does say at the end that God has kind of overlooked the whole thing. She must feel she has been left with this burden and with not as much help as she might have had.

There are some things about her story that I have to fill in. Her present husband, with whom she has excellent communication and a wonderful relationship, has really kept her going through all this. Because she was getting welfare support to help her with the care of this child, which she would have lost if she had married, they waited 8 years longer than they wished before getting married. Otherwise, marriage would have made a financially impossible situation for them.

Also, as you heard, she is a qualified worker and the system doesn't provide for this kind of person. She was willing to do a less-qualified job and she explained why, but there was no awareness of her needs and she couldn't get work and had to go on welfare. She is a very proud woman. She said, "I wouldn't take help from my folks" because she really does feel she can cope with things and doesn't like to be helped.

The sibling business really deserves more attention. We have more and more seen that siblings suffer. Here is this 6' 7'' boy with 14½ shoes who has a car and can drive it, whose mother says that he's not about to leave the home soon because he feels shortchanged, since he has always had to put up with this sick brother who gets all the attention. They're in the same bedroom, which is a big drag to him, and at the same school.

JOAN KNAUER (Pediatric Nurse-Practitioner, Baltimore): My question is around the health team. I think nurses also have something valuable to offer a person or a family with a chronic problem. I know that doctors specializing in certain fields – such as cardiac care or another chronic problem – have referred patients to be followed by nurse-practitioners. We could be used as persons more available to the family, or to receive questions – maybe not always knowing the answer, but able to coordinate or find another person who has the answer.

I have wondered about the rest of the health team. We're not working alone; we're working together, and as we work more and more together and develop more communication, not just between doctors and nurses and nurse-practitioners but with social workers, hospital chaplains and others, I think we have a great deal to offer people with chronic problems.

DR. KORSCH: I think your suggestion is a very good one. We all need to call on all of these resources. Help doesn't have to come only from very highly professionally trained people.

Barry Pless, in Rochester, who has worked so much with chronic illness, did a study in families that needed this kind of care. He put a community worker, who didn't have a very long period of training, with the family to work specifically with the family of a chronically ill child—as a patient advocate, liaison and so on; and he thought he could demonstrate significant improvement in family function after a year. Both the children's personality tests and the family function evaluations were better with someone as an intermediary between the establishment and them.

WILLIAM CAREY (Philadelphia): As a practicing pediatrician, I agree with what you said about chronic illness, but don't you agree that the primary emphasis in pediatric education should be on the comprehensive management of minor illnesses? These are experiences of every family and responsible for a great deal of stress in families today. I think the principal sins of us pediatricians at this point are overdiagnosis and overmanagement of minor illnesses, failures to be attentive to the feelings of children, and not being sufficiently supportive of parents.

DR. KORSCH: I think everything you say is true. The only postscript I would add is that in pediatric training and practice today (and who knows what it will be like in the future?) a good deal of the pediatrician's time and effort is spent with catastrophically ill children. We've had a lot of teaching programs and special programs demonstrating new kinds of child health supervision, HMO's, all kinds of settings where family problems are being attended to, but when there is a major physical illness, that tends to get the whole focus and other things tend to be put aside.

Also, I find that it is easier to get pediatricians motivated and involved around a major catastrophic illness than to get them turned on to the little behavior problems of a well baby. Still, when they see, for instance, that a transplant patient will lose a kidney because she failed to take her medicines because she's so upset, that's pretty strong ammunition to enthuse them into taking interest in things other than technologic care.

DR. CAREY: But all too often there is a failure to apply these principles to minor illnesses.

DR. KORSCH: Right.

CRAIG PRAZER (Baltimore): One of my concerns about tertiary care centers is that too often the house officers don't know the parents of chronically ill children, and neither do the nurses or the social workers. I think house officers, nurses and social workers have intense feelings of frustration in not being able to help the children more than they can, and I think these frustrated feelings often are channeled into anger toward the parents. This really disturbs the house officer/nurse/social worker interface. And these people oftentimes see the parents on a day-to-day basis more than the primary or attending physician.

Who is to help the house officers, nurses or social workers in dealing with those feelings and in becoming more sensitive to the parents?

DR. KORSCH: I think that's a very big question. I feel like recapitulating Urie Bronfenbrenner's remark that we need a social system that cares for those who care for children. And that does not apply only to parents who care for their own children, but to the immediate caretakers of sick children, such as those you have alluded to. We have a long way to go.

19

The Effects of Minor Neurologic Handicaps on the Child, Family and Community*

Eric Denhoff, M.D., and Steven A. Feldman, M.D.

*The Governor Medical Center, Providence,
Rhode Island*

"I will never forget the day I coaxed him into joining a footrace with other kids. He didn't seem to know what to do and stood still while others ran. I felt both embarrassed and angry at myself for pushing him into another situation beyond his ability to learn and my ability to teach."

More than 10 million children in the United States are labeled Minimal Brain Dysfunction (MBD), Hyperkinetic Behavior Syndrome (HBS) and Learning Disabilities (LD) [1]. The terms imply that the effective usage of normal or higher intelligence is hampered by combinations of motor, perceptual, language and behavioral inefficiencies [2, 3].

"Shopping is an ordeal. He handles everything, bumps into people and wanders aimlessly." "In the restaurant and at home, the amount of spilled milk is incredible." "He attracts attention wherever he goes, and we get lots of negative reactions from strangers because we "allow" such behavior as running back and forth, talking in a loud, shrill voice and laughing for no apparent reason."

Short attention span, distractibility, perseveration and hyperactivity coupled with inefficient reading and writing performance, and motor clumsiness, are disabilities that make for such a child the task of living up to normative peer standards and adult expectancies difficult if not impossible to achieve [4]. The behaviors that deter learning combine exaggerated basic temperaments and learned behaviors, which are used as a protective device against societal demands [5].

"Because we feel guilty, we either give in too readily or demand more than he can give." "Our patience often wears thin and minor irritations often become major fiascos because we feel so helpless."

There are many MBD families who can cope with their children's disabilities. Some cannot, and their classic reaction is overreaction, denial and guilt, followed by maternal overprotection, father resentment and sibling jealousy. Some

---

*With the assistance of Mr. and Mrs. John Coggin of Marblehead, Massachusetts.

of these families appear genetically vulnerable to life stresses, as suggested by a high prevalence of neurologic, psychiatric and specific reading disorders in parents and relatives [6]. The incidence is striking even when compared with families with a cerebral palsied child [7]. On the other hand, the rates of emotional problems within the family and of divorce are comparable in both groups (Table 19–1).

"I can feel my child's frustrations, because I was also a hyperactive child. As a young adult, I drank too much to compensate for my failures. After marriage, I underwent psychotherapy for depression and impotence. My father-in-law was also an alcoholic."

The parents of MBD children often have maturity and learning problems of their own. The rates of alcoholism, neurosis and hysteria are high [6, 8] (Table 19–2). Faigel has studied 93 parents between the ages of 35 and 55 years. Twenty-three (24%) never finished high school and likely had perceptual problems [9].

"Knowing about and understanding the problem doesn't prevent irritation and anger."

Family tension compounded by school pressure aggravate intrinsic inadequacies and create secondary emotional and motivational problems that prove more depriving than the basic dysfunction.

"Our parents were hard-working and middle class. Of 19 nephews and nieces, only 1 other is rated as MBD because he can't spell or write well."

Social class can make a difference. Passive, anxious children who verbalize little may come from the higher professional classes, whereas hyperactivity and visual perceptual motor inefficiency (poor handwriting) often are products of the lower middle classes [7]. Children from poverty families may be aggressive, hyperactive and poorly verbal. This may stem from combinations of a higher rate of birth complications, incomplete families and lower family expectations [10].

"We are a high-tension family—yet I'd like to believe that if it weren't for MBD we'd be relaxed and the friction would dissipate."

The MBD child's behavior puts a limit on his family's nurturant capability. Soon after birth the mother feels rejected because the baby does not appear to accept love or be gratified by feeding, fondling or being talked to. Apparently anything that interferes with neuronal nourishment alters normal physiologic and

Table 19–1

Differentiating Familial Factors between Children with Minor Brain
Dysfunctions/Learning Disabilities (MBD/LD) and Major Brain
Dysfunctions/Cerebral Palsies (CP)

Family History	MBD/LD	(N = 48)	CP	(N = 100)
	No.	%	No.	%
Familial neurologic disorders	10	21	10	10*
Specific reading disabilities	7	14	0	0*
Adoptions	3	6	0	0*
Familial emotional disorders	6	12	15	15
Divorce	2	4	5	5

*Sig.

Table 19-2
Incidence of Nervous and Mental Disorders in Families of
Hyperactive-MBD Children

Family History	Hyperactive-MBD	Control Population
Nervous-Mental Disorders	%	%
Armed Forces, parents[1]	45	18
University Hospital, OPD[2]	35	9
Private practice (GMC)[3]	35	10
Alcoholism, parents		
Armed Forces	19	7
University Hospital, OPD[4]	11	5

[1]Cantwell, D. P.: Arch. Gen. Psychiatry 27:1972.
[2]Stevens, J. R.: Am. J. Dis. Child 120:1970.
[3]Denhoff, E.: *Learning Disabilities*, 1971.
[4]Morrison, J. R.: Am. J. Psychiatry 130:1973.

psychologic stress responses, and mothers need very early to be told that the colic and crying isn't their fault.

"Society expects mothers to give and give — and sometimes I feel I'm all 'gived' out."

Mothers soon become fatigued, irritable, defensive and overprotective. Fathers feel unneeded, pushed aside and soon become resentful of the family energy and monies expended to maintain the "maverick" child. Siblings feel ignored, threatened and become resistant because they do not wish to be displaced by a shrieking tyrant.

"His younger brother often acts bewildered because we have established double standards of behavior for our children. He says he can't keep his friends because his MBD brother often acts 'weird' in their company."

The MBD's siblings often are well behaved and excellent students. They may suffer silently or rise in revolt from the poking, shoving and striking out of their "discombobulated" brother. The dual behavior standards in the family create anger, resentment and passive aggression. Peer embarrassment arising from their sibling's unpredictable behavior eventually turns them away from the home — unless great efforts are made to help them understand the fears and frustrations of their parents.

"Doctor, you don't have to examine me, I know what's wrong — 'I do everything good bad' — 'everything bad good.' "

The MBD child himself recognizes his inadequacies and feels that he cannot live up to the standards of the family.

"I can't forget the pediatrician who said our attempt at remediation is a lovely experiment but likely to fail."

"Or the learning specialist who insisted our child was language impaired. Yet, after a year of high expenses with poor success, the language therapist proclaimed, 'I can't go further until I learn the primary cause.'"

"Or the psychiatrist who insisted that drug therapy is an easy way out — conscientious parents will resist it."

"Or the professor who wisely proclaimed the medical model as expensive, wasteful and wouldn't solve the problem."

"Or the teacher who said, 'Why not just admit that he's retarded?' "

"Or the neighbor who called and said, 'I can't believe there's anything wrong; he looks so normal.' "

"Or my mother, who said, 'Why not ship him away to a residential school? Maybe they can teach him to behave.' "

Physicians, teachers, officials and the general community play significant roles in influencing outcome.

Many pediatricians who should know better insist that the problem is not their responsibility and say, "Leave him alone and he'll outgrow it." Some psychiatrists who specialize in labels blame the parents, talk regularly to the child and then call them both inadequate.

The teacher, often an "only one-method technician," cannot conceive that an individualized, low-keyed, direct teaching approach may be better than a host of perceptual motor exercises that may not relate to reading or writing—or that an IQ score often fails to equate with long-term outcome. So she presses and demands and when the child boils over and becomes hyperactive, she complains or gives up.

The school principal who finds excuses not to mix special with normal children is also a provocateur. MBD children often have different lunch periods, different play periods and basement classrooms. This fellow also sees to it that the dedicated teacher never views the available psychoeducational data "lest it make her too subjective."

Together, the professional mix spells poor understanding of the MBD child and the impact he and his afflictions have on the family.

"Our main worry is what will happen to him. In spite of our complaints we love him. He is gentle, kind, perceptive and thoughtful and brought us joy in many ways." "Are we going at it properly?" "Whom do we believe and trust?" "Who will teach us and teach him how to cope with life?"

The long-term outcome of the MBD child depends on the availability and sophistication of a continuum of comprehensive services. A comprehensive program includes good medical and psychoeducational diagnostic services and a variety of management techniques, including medication, behavior modification, family and child counseling or casework and good teaching using individualized remedial techniques.

The earlier the program is started and the more comprehensive the better the outcome. In the Menkes' 25-year follow-up study [11] where psychotherapy was the principal modality, less than half the patients were self-supporting and all of those had been institutionalized previously or had had brushes with the law. Where medication was the main resource, there often was a disappointing outcome [12]. Laufer [13], using a comprehensive approach, reported that 87% of the patients were employed, although 31% had poor temperament.

"Can he survive adolescence?" "Will he outgrow his need for medication?" "Will he be drug dependent or drug addicted?" "Will we be able to handle him?" and again and again and again "What will happen to him?"

As the MBD child approaches adolescence, parents often wonder if they are going out of the frying pan into the fire. Will they be replacing trips to the principal's office with midnight trips to the police station? Will pot replace pills? "Should he drive – will he drink – what will happen to him?"

Studies have shown that the problems of MBD children persist into adulthood, and that our training schools and detention centers are filled with MBD youths. In a survey of 109 adolescent youths who were Rhode Island high school dropouts, 53% fell into the MBD category [14]. Berman [15] studied 45 delinquent males in the Rhode Island juvenile correctional facility and 45 matched controls. Seventy per cent of the delinquent group could be classified as MBD based on over-all impoverishment of adaptive abilities on a series of neuropsychologic tests, whereas normally performing high school students from a low social class population failed to show significant abnormalities. In Rhode Island it costs the taxpayer $26,000 per year for each affected youngster in the training school, for an average cost of $100,000 per youth. Since the return rate of adult prisoners was 85%, the cost to society was not measurable. The common thread in these cases was early school failure, delinquency and a lack of continued supportive services during the troublesome early and later school years.

On the other hand, in a follow-up study of a pediatric-neurologic-psychiatric private group practice model (Governor Medical Center) serving a middle class population where the family related either to the pediatrician or the child psychiatrist, the outcome was excellent with 55% of the youths being problem free and functioning normally, whereas 31% required continuing support. Only 14% can be regarded as failures, and these can be traced to late referral, early dropout and poor continuing educational support in their own community. All diagnostic and remedial services, including a special school, were made available within the model.

Where the forces necessary to provide good patient care could be mobilized effectively, the failure rate was only 6%. This means that a private practitioner who knows the child and his family and in whom the child and family have faith can be a powerful agent in the prevention of significant mental health and adjustment problems.

"We always return to the fear that inadvertently we caused the problem. My diet was poor during pregnancy and I was inefficient and groping as a new mother. My husband tripped and fell with him in his arms, but the baby seemed more frightened than hurt."

The rate of perinatal-neonatal complications is higher in MBD than in a normal population but less than in cerebral palsy. On the other hand, infections and accidents during the infancy-toddler period are much higher in MBD than in each of the other groups (Table 19–3).

Today, intensive neonatal care programs are sending home babies with fewer major disabilities but likely more minor dysfunctions [16]. The querulous behavior of these babies must be dealt with promptly if we are to change the early parental attitudes. In the long run, it is not neurologic aspects that affect outcome but the family's ability to cope effectively with the problems of MBD children. Thus, long-term comprehensive systematic family-centered techniques must be developed to ensure a favorable outcome. We must teach parents how to handle the day-to-day needs of their needy offspring, but we must also teach

Table 19-3
The Incidence of Perinatal-Infancy Complications in Minor and Major
Neurologically Impaired Child Populations

	MBD (N = 48) Per Cent	CP (N = 100) Per Cent	Normal (N = 504) Per Cent
Pregnancy	23	48	5
Delivery	29	37	15
Neonatal	18	50	9
Prematurity	4	30	8
Infancy–Toddler	39	11	6

them to interpret "smoke signals" that say, "Mommy and Daddy, rescue me from myself."

A pilot experience with a low income family group suggests that this is possible. Of 129 infants and toddlers in a Community Health Center program, 21 were considered difficult management problems by their parents. One year after an organized parent-infant enrichment program, 10 of the 21 (58%) were classified as normal [17] (Table 19–4).

Finally, the effects of MBD on the child, family, school and community can be depriving to the child's own self-image and motivation; they can produce anxiety, hostility and guilt in the family; and they can be nonproductive, expensive and wasteful to the school and community. When the family works within a comprehensive medical model and the physician plays an advocacy role, there is a good chance for a successful outcome.

"And by the way, Dr. Denhoff, I had a terrible time in school with math, always hated gym and typed this letter because my handwriting is as bad as my son's."

Table 19-4
Outcome of Babies after a 1-Year Developmental
Enrichment Program

Characteristics of Group
Case load in clinic 129
No. requesting help 21 (16%)
Social class . . . . disadvantaged
Race . . . . Black (11), Caucasian (7), Other (3)
Education . . . . High School/College 6 (28%)
Marital . . . . Married mothers 12 (57%)
Pregnancy complications 17 (75%)
Delivery complications 9 (48%)
Infants, small for date and 2000
  grams or less 4 (25%)
Average age initial examination . . . . 7 months
Results after 1 year
  Normal 10 (58%)
  MBD 3 (17%)
  Unresolved 4 (23%)
  Lost to study 4 (23%)

REFERENCES

1. The American Foundation for Maternal and Child Health, Inc., 30 Beekman Place, New York, N. Y.
2. National Project on Minimal Brain Dysfunction in Children—Terminology and Identification (Phase One of a Three Phase Project); Clements, S. D., Project Director. Monograph Number 3: Public Health Service Publication No. 1415, 1966. Superintendent of Documents, U. S. Government Printing Office, Washington, D. C.
3. Wender, P. H.: *Minimal Brain Dysfunction in Children* (New York: Wiley-Interscience, 1971).
4. Laufer, M. W., and Denhoff, E.: Hyperkinetic behavior syndrome in children, J. Pediatr. 50:463, 1957.
5. Thomas, A., Chess, S., and Birch, H. G.: *Temperament and Behavior Disorders in Children* (New York: New York University Press, 1968).
6. Cantwell, D. P.: Psychiatric illness in the families of hyperactive children, Arch. Gen. Psychiatry 27:414, 1972.
7. Denhoff, E., and Tarnopol, L.: Medical Responsibilities in Learning Disorders, in Tarnopol, L., *Learning Disorders in Children: Diagnosis, Medication, Education* (Boston: Little, Brown & Company, 1971).
8. Morrison, J. R., and Stewart, M. A.: Evidence for polygenetic inheritance in the hyperactive child syndrome, Am. J. Psychiatry 130:791, 1973.
9. Faigel, H. C.: Adults who were perceptually handicapped. Personal communication.
10. Birch, H. G., and Gussow, J. D.: *Disadvantaged Children; Health, Nutrition and School Failure* (New York: Harcourt, Brace & World, Inc. and Grune & Stratton, Inc., 1970).
11. Menkes, M. M., Rowe, J. S., and Menkes, J. H.: A twenty-five year follow-up study on the hyperkinetic child with minimal brain dysfunction, Pediatrics 39:393, 1967.
12. Friedman, R., Dale, E. P., and Wagner, J. H.: A long-term comparison of two treatment regimens for minimal brain dysfunction, Clin. Pediatr. 12:666, 1973.
13. Laufer, M. W.: Long-term management and some follow-up findings on the use of drugs with minimal cerebral syndromes, J. Learn. Disabil. 4:519, 1971.
14. Denhoff, E.: Unpublished data.
15. Berman, A.: Delinquents are disabled: An innovative approach to the prevention and treatment of juvenile delinquency. To be published.
16. Francis-Williams, J., and Davies, P. S.: Very low birth weight and later intelligence, Dev. Med. Child Neurol. 16:709, 1974.
17. Denhoff, E.: Unpublished study.

COMMENTARY

PARTICIPANT: Are you still using your quickie neurological? Can school nurses do it? In trying to pick up the MBD kids prior to school entry may you not influence or prejudice the teacher so that a child at risk is going to become MBD no matter what because the teacher expects it?

DR. DENHOFF: First of all, my "quickie" neurological is good to discriminate the normal youngster from those who are at risk. Those found to be atypical on the "quickie" need more definitive diagnosis. There are dangers to very early diagnosis, even though legislation in Michigan and other states is asking us to identify learning-disabled youngsters at 3 years of age. Some very good studies now demonstrate that maturation in the skills needed for reading, writing and arithmetic probably is not complete until 9 or 11 years of age. Consequently, we are asking for certain skills long before some children are ready. Demands such as these lead to frustration and hyperactivity, among other complaints. Put another way, youngsters who know their right from left, up from down and can copy appreciably at 5 or 6 years likely will not have learning disabilities. But let's not put labels at 5 or 6 on these youngsters who cannot fully display these skills.

Your last question asks if we can discriminate and separate without creating prejudice in teachers that frustrates attempts to help. The answer is "Yes" provided we can change our models of early education. I think we've demonstrated that if we place an at-risk population of youngsters at 5 or 6 in a comprehensive diagnostic classroom for a year, with proper help perhaps only 5% will end up really needing hard-core special education; the many others will need resource help, which many of their parents can give, including life enrichment.

PARTICIPANT: Dr. Denhoff, could you describe the developmental enrichment program you referred to? Who carried it out?

DR. DENHOFF: The program that I referred to is a carryover from the developmental enrichment program that was developed more than 15 years ago with severely handicapped children, especially those with cerebral palsy. Primarily, we have learned that supportive help in feeding coupled with visual/perceptual and gross motor stimulation produces a payoff in later improved social and language skills. Thus, we encourage the parents to learn how to help the baby to suck and swallow—how to touch, cuddle and talk, and how to help the baby to follow developmentally oriented mobiles.

In this special satellite program for disadvantaged families, a district nurse and a nurse-practitioner were taught by a team of therapists how to provide interventions. They, in turn, taught parents, surrogate parents or neighbors how to be the primary programmers.

Half of our families no longer required help after a year. About 16% were incorporated into the Meeting Street School Infant Program because of definitive neurologic disability.

This can be effective elsewhere.

REBECCA KAUFFMAN: I am an elementary guidance counselor; for me, the most important thing about this topic is the identification of the needs of these youngsters, and for teachers to realize that these youngsters have many positive

218

aspects. The fact that they cannot function the same as other children doesn't lessen their rights to having teachers and other professionals meet their needs.

Certainly a youngster who cannot distinguish left from right should not be forced at a particular designated age into a situation where he has to read. Educators must admit that many times instead of helping these youngsters we are putting them into situations of helpless frustration.

I would prefer to see these youngsters have additional help but be kept in the normal school setting. Not only must we cope with the situation of their specific learning disabilities but we must realize that they will be going out into society and working with others. As children, they should not be singled out as so very different. They should certainly be recognized in their particular strengths.

Do you have specific guidelines from your work in Rhode Island? Are your findings available in some educational journal for those who are not here?

DR. DENHOFF: I suppose I could write more; some people believe that I write too much. I find that my best tool for education is to teach teachers through an organized postgraduate course. I would hope that others could also find ways for a more direct educational approach to physicians, parents, educators and others in the child-help professions.

I believe that the greatest current problem in hyperkinesis is a semantic one. Disciplines apply labels according to their own views. Parents may be provocateurs or victims of labeling because of the demands or lack of demands they may make on the child. The British have shown that what is hyperactivity to a teacher is fidgetiness to a psychiatrist and anxiousness to a parent. We will be able to cope better with management, especially medication, when we can develop clear diagnostic principles that we agree with regardless of orientation.

SYBIL BERGER (Philadelphia): Recent studies have indicated that children early identified as having minimal brain dysfunction can be helped if the help is started very early. Here in Philadelphia we identify children hopefully and preferably not beyond the age of 8.

Once they are identified neurologically, medically or in any other way that we can identify them, special schools won't take them for training beyond a certain age. Further, it is believed that if they are identified late, at 11 or 12 years, they cannot be taught to read, and that vocational education is in order, as their only option.

DR. DENHOFF: What you have described is a cop-out that even I have been guilty of. Of course, it is much easier to attack these problems when the child is young and before the secondary emotional problems have affected motivation and feelings. Too often we fail in later years because we concentrate on the emotional aspects without helping the specific learning disability. Too often we fail to provide the adolescent with meaningful, practical learning situations that he can translate into formal academics.

Further difficulties arise when there is a recognition of and an attempt to meet the special requirements of MBD subcategories. For instance, the reasons for the anxiety of the genetically impaired dyslectic may be different from those of the 1500-gram small-for-date infant who cannot at 14 years of age yet write speedily and proficiently.

Thus, we recognize that we can effect positive change in the 10 plus years. We need, however, to change the model that effects change. For instance, it is ridiculous to start vocational training at 16 years of age when, at 10 years, it is possible to develop effective prevocational models. We must insist that some learning-disabled youths be graded by verbal ability and not written performance. We must develop ways to overcome limits imposed by insurance companies so that youngsters can have an opportunity at "work-learn" experiences in the real world of factories, shops and garages.

For success, we need to develop a continuum of services until the youth has found his niche in adulthood.

These glorious youngsters are sending us "smoke signals" for help constantly. If we are unable to translate their signals, the poorer children end up delinquent and the richer become the clients of psychiatrists whereas the struggling middle class youth never attains what he sets out to achieve. All because we still don't listen to the signals of children.

CARRIE SHUSTER (Ohio State University): I have been interested in some of the reactions of parents to the problems they face with children who have disabilities.

One of the stresses I see is the parents' attempt to cope with the disability itself. They have lost the ideal child; now they have to adjust to the real child's special needs, whether owing to minimal brain damage or mental retardation or something else.

A second factor is the parents' emotional reactions. They fear for the future, for what this problem may mean to the child or to their own future. They are angry, too, over the frustrations that they have to face. Another emotion that we often do not recognize and that the parents themselves do not admit is hatred. They hate the child because it creates fear and anger in them. It's normal to hate those things that you fear; and until parents can admit this and begin to cope with it, they will have difficulty in helping their children. On top of those there is also guilt—guilt for their hatred and their anger, and also from the notion that they have created a burden to society.

I think that as health professionals we often perpetuate these reactions. We make the parents feel that they're not accepted, that they're not a part of the team, that they don't know enough, that they can't handle the child. So the professional staff becomes another thing that the parents have to cope with.

I think we have to accept parents as a part of the team and capitalize on the strengths that they have. When we do that, they can begin to accept and cope with their own reactions and will more surely have enough energy left over to cope with the child and help the child cope.

20

The Effects of Fatal Illness in the Child on Family Life

*J. Lawrence Naiman, M.D., Joan Taksa Rolsky, M.S.W., and
Susan B. Sherman, M.S.S.*

*St. Christopher's Hospital for Children,
Philadelphia, Pennsylvania*

I [J.L.N.] am a pediatrician and a hematologist. Many of the children I treat have diseases such as leukemia and cancer. Much progress has been made in the treatment of these diseases in the past 10 years, and increasing numbers of children are being cured; still, most affected children die, after illnesses lasting from a few months to several years. Whether the child dies or lives, the possibility of death is ever present, and this causes fears and stresses within the family. We will discuss some of the effects on families, what kinds of needs are created, with an example of how members of a health care team can respond to such needs. The major goal of our efforts is to help a family remain intact and functioning throughout the course of an illness and after death has occurred.

First we will see a documentary film about a young boy with leukemia, to illustrate how this disease affected the life of one family and how they tried to cope with the problems of living within the context of illness and threat of death. We then will discuss some of the problems that arise in other families to give a broader picture of the impact of such an illness, and then I will describe the Family Support Program that has evolved at St. Christopher's Hospital for Children to help families experiencing such difficulties. Finally, we will have an opportunity to talk with some of the other members of our medical team and the parents of 2 children under our care.

Here, Dr. Naiman showed "I've Had a Life," a film created by Ben Levin while he was a student at Temple University. The film follows a 13-year-old boy and his family through the early, middle and late phases of fatal leukemia, dealing frankly and movingly with the problems encountered at each stage.

The film was awarded First Prize among documentaries by students produced for the Academy of Motion Picture Arts and Sciences in 1974.

The film can be bought or rented through The Eccentric Circle, Cinema Workshop, P. O. Box 4085, Greenwich, CT, 06830.

Comments after the film

DR. NAIMAN: Potentially fatal disease in a child affects everyone in the family—the child (whether he knows his diagnosis or not), the parents, the siblings, grandparents—everyone. The problems that result arise both from within each individual and from the interactions of members of a family unit.

The *sick child* is concerned mainly about the immediate effects of his illness—discomforting symptoms and diagnostic studies, fear of the strange hospital environment and separation from family and home. His needs are simple—to feel better and to go home as soon as possible. With time, however, he may react to the atmosphere of heightened concern around him and, depending on his perception of what is happening, may become confused or frightened. He may regress and become more dependent, creating ambivalence in parents who want to hold on to him but know that they must encourage him to grow up. If his fears cannot be allayed by adequate communication and reassurance, he may withdraw and become depressed or hostile, or resort to immature behavior patterns.

Siblings of the patient sense the same family tensions and, in addition, may resent the fact that they are getting less attention from their parents now. Anger at the sick child and the guilt arising from this are difficult for them to cope with, especially if the parents aren't adequately available to them or are too preoccupied to sense this. They may also fear that they may "catch" or develop the same disease, which adds tensions within the family and may become manifest as various behavior difficulties, adding further to pressures on the parents.

For the *parents,* the otherwise benign difficulties present in most families are heightened under the threat of losing a young child. The past methods of handling stress developed by each parent now become inadequate, creating problems both *within* each parent and *between* the two parents. The *roles* that parents have assumed with each other to cope with life's normal problems often cannot be maintained, creating panic and anger in the marriage. The parents may resent each other's outlets: the father can avoid involvement through the excuse and distraction of his work; the mother may have more contact with friends with whom she can find support and comfort. Overwhelming emotions may lead to increased tension, depression and loss of sexual drive. Issues normally creating some amount of tension in child-rearing become magnified, such as differences in attitudes about discipline, money or working mothers. After their child has died, differences between parents in their ability to work through their grief and reconstruct their lives may create further hardships. With the loss of a child, the parents may unconsciously or otherwise arrange a replacement, either in assigning a new role to an existing child or through a new pregnancy. Children seen as replacements are at risk of parental overprotectiveness, such as heightened concern during minor illnesses and lack of discipline; such children may themselves reflect this in evolving behavior patterns that perpetuate or aggravate a disturbed family relationship.

Families of fatally ill children need help. Ideally, this might come from close friends, from other family members or from the child's physician. Unfortunately, in most circumstances, friends and family, who generally have not experienced the loss of a child, cannot be truly sensitive to the problems faced by such parents. Their efforts usually are directed to "cheering up" the parents, and they thereby unwittingly encourage suppression of the necessary grief response. Physicians, to a certain extent, do the same, perhaps in ways reflecting their own discomfort about facing death. Moreover, the physician can easily and often avoid facing his responsibilities here through the convenient excuse of being medically busy. Who, then, can we look to for help with the family?

A FAMILY SUPPORT PROGRAM

A program has evolved at St. Christopher's Hospital for Children through which physicians have enlisted other members of the health care team, in particular psychiatric social workers, to play intimate roles in the care and support of families of children with leukemia and cancer. Rather than entering the picture at the time of impending death, an almost impossible challenge, such persons are involved in a program of preventive guidance and support from the time of diagnosis until death, and even afterward. Services that are offered in this program include the following.

INDIVIDUAL THERAPY. — Appropriate family members (most often the parents, or the child in the case where he or she has been informed of the diagnosis) are seen regularly during clinic visits or at home visits to enable the family to deal with the ongoing problems they must face throughout the illness of the child.

GROUP THERAPY. — No one understands the emotional difficulties of such families better than do the families of other children with the same disease. For this reason, it often is beneficial for parents of children with leukemia to meet together in a group at regular intervals to share some of their concerns and feelings. These groups are organized by the social workers but the parents are encouraged to give the direction for the discussions. In such groups, parents find that they are not alone in their suffering, but that other parents are going through the same sorts of difficulties, both medical and nonmedical; this often becomes an additional source of comfort and strength to help them cope with their own problems. Currently, we have two groups meeting biweekly for families of children under treatment, and a third group for parents of children who have died.

OTHER FORMS OF SUPPORT. — Our program is designed so that the particular needs of each family are considered, and, when appropriate, other forms of support are offered, such as marital or family therapy. The services of a staff psychiatrist are available, but it has been our experience that psychiatric services are needed only when there is an overt psychosis in a family member. We find that rare, and most likely to occur around the time of diagnosis of the child's illness. Among families with whom we establish a good therapeutic relationship from the beginning, major psychiatric difficulties have not developed.

COMMENTARY

DR. NAIMAN: We have invited some guests to help answer some questions that may arise. Sue Sherman and Joan Rolsky are psychiatric social workers in our Family Support Program at St. Christopher's. Mr. and Mrs. Houpt are the parents of Steven Houpt, a 9-year-old boy who has had leukemia for 5 years now. Mr. and Mrs. Winslade are the parents of Matthew, who died 2 years ago at the age of 7, of cancer of the lymph glands.

Both of these families have been involved in groups. Mr. or Mrs. Houpt, can you tell us what your experience has been and what your involvement with the group has meant to you?

MRS. HOUPT: My son was diagnosed before the support group was founded, so I've seen it both ways: both before we have someone to talk to and now with the group and with someone to call when we're having problems. We go to the parent group meetings. I need the parents. I need to talk to the other parents.

MR. HOUPT: Having people to get information from and having our mutual interdependence was valuable to both of us. Quite frankly, I have not gone to most of the meetings recently because there seems to be a little difference between my wife and myself about how much support and how much help we can get from it, but at one point we did need it quite a bit, and it was a very valuable bridge over a tough period. Possibly the difference between her still going and my not going quite as often is something we could discuss later on. Maybe it shows a difference in her and my needs at this time.

We also get a lot of support from Joan, who is our social worker. She is usually at the hospital when we take Steven for his monthly visits, and she answers questions and also acts as a liaison between us and Dr. Naiman or other staff at St. Christopher's. It's a valuable thing to have more of a friend at the hospital — not in a clinical sense, but just a one-to-one relationship. Although the doctors are really human down there, they are clinical.

MR. WINSLADE: We didn't belong to a group at the time of the original diagnosis, but we did join a group after Matthew died. We found that the common bond better enabled us to communicate our feelings and certain personal problems that we couldn't discuss with the family. We did find that we could get these things off our chest at these meetings. We've been going now for about a year and it has been very helpful in our case.

DR. NAIMAN: Could you tell us some of the things that you found in common with other families that were perhaps helpful to you?

MRS. WINSLADE: I thought I was doing some weird things. I would do something and then think it wasn't right. But when you get together in a group you find that other people are going through this same process. When the group got started, Matthew actually had already been dead a year and I was getting worried about myself — like I was setting an extra plate, and other things that would happen at the cemetery. But almost everybody goes through the same thing and this is what you find out through the group.

MRS. HOUPT: Sometimes when you're down at the hospital you don't think of everything, and then when you get into the group someone might bring up a problem that they've learned to handle and you learn from that. I might suggest

224

that the next time you have a clinic visit you should ask about that. Sometimes I was very ashamed to ask the doctor questions. I didn't want to appear dumb. I would ask a question, and if he would answer and I didn't understand what he said, sometimes I wouldn't ask again. If I did ask again and I still didn't understand what the doctor said, I wouldn't ask him again. But when I went to the group and we would talk together, they would say "you have a right to know and have a right to understand, and even if you have to ask ten times, then ask ten times." And that's what I did. I learned to ask questions and not to be so afraid of "the big doctor."

DR. NAIMAN: Perhaps we now can have questions from anyone in the audience.

PARTICIPANT (Family Practice Resident, Summit, N. J.): Do the social workers talk about the diseases that are involved in the group, and get enough background to answer such questions? Is this an educational thing?

MS. ROLSKY: For the two groups of parents whose children are currently in treatment, all the children have leukemia. The groups serve many purposes; one of them is an educational function. We have had resident physicians as co-leaders of the groups, but parents in both groups voted not to have them come on a regular basis. They felt, first, that the presence of physicians allowed them to get into a position where they only asked medical questions and steered away from feelings. Secondly, they were a little reluctant to bring up problems they might be having with physicians.

On the other hand, when a number of medical questions come up which we feel are beyond our ability to answer, we will invite Dr. Naiman or one of the residents in hematology to come to the group and discuss these questions with the families.

We also have a newsletter. We take the most commonly asked questions of the parents and submit them to Dr. Naiman, who then gives a written answer, which we distribute to all the families when they come to clinic.

JOHN ELLIOTT (Rockford, Illinois): In the case of the children who know the diagnosis, would you give guidelines as to at what ages and in what ways you will tell the child he is dying or may die. In the case of children who are not told they may be dying, perhaps because of the physician's preference, what does the nurse say when the child asks the nurse "Am I going to die?"

DR. NAIMAN: Up until a few years ago, I was among those physicians you alluded to who preferred not to tell the children they had a disease such as leukemia. Paul Hendricks, whom you saw in the film, was the first child I had to face this with—not because I chose to tell him the truth, but because he came to me having already discerned the truth from his own research. It was pretty hard for me.

I realize looking back on it that the reasons I didn't think children should know were my own reasons. I was uncomfortable about letting them know. After the experience with Paul, I found that it wasn't so bad and that perhaps children might be better off knowing and being able to share some of their concerns with their parents, rather than having a wall of evasion created between them.

My experience in the past few years has been that most children from about 8 to 9 years old should know about their disease. I don't mean to say that a child should be told "You're going to die." I've never had to say that, nor do I feel I will have to. Depending on the child's maturity and level of understanding, you can tell him in as simple terms as possible what his disease is about. You can use the word leukemia. I think whenever you use a medical word that a child might look up or hear elsewhere that is associated with death it is important to say that some kids die from leukemia.We're fortunate today that we have treatments that can control leukemia, prolong life and even cure some cases of leukemia; with that, we can inject a fair amount of hope, and we try to stress the hopeful aspects when informing a child of his diagnosis.

I think that before we tell a child his diagnosis we have to have the consent of the family. At first, most parents don't want their children to know. They share the same hangups that most adults do—that children shouldn't know about this because it will depress them. But we have come to realize that the truth is not so depressing as some of the fears that can arise from not knowing the truth.

Another problem that arises in this context is what happens when a child lives to 9 years who was 4 years old when you first discovered leukemia. This is the case with Steven Houpt. Steven was too young to understand and now he is old enough to understand. Living with a partial truth for a long time and then changing it is very difficult. Perhaps Mr. or Mrs. Houpt would like to comment on some of their feelings as they came to the decision to tell Steven, and how it has worked out.

MR. HOUPT: We told Steven 2 weeks ago, after about 5½ years. It was a problem between my wife and me as to when to tell him; we had a difference of opinion about it. It's crossing a bridge that you don't want to even come near. Now that we have told him, it's definitely much better. I think he has known pretty much what he has for some time now, and we confirmed it. He knows now that he has leukemia, but I think he knew all along, at least for the last 2 or 3 years, pretty much the kind of thing he had.

I think that now that he knows, he is much better off. There is nothing that he doesn't know. He knows what all the treatments are.

What precipitated this is that he developed a CNS recurrence, and we were having him back once a week for about 3 weeks. Whenever this happens, it's traumatic for my wife and myself and for Steven. He sees that we're more upset at that point because it is a setback.

In talking to our doctor and to Joan we came to realize that although he was 9 years old, mentally Joan estimates he's about 14, and the doctor says at least 14. I'm really glad we told him and now that he knows, I think it's going to be easier not only for us but for the doctors.

MRS. HOUPT: Last week he was comforting me, telling me not to worry, that he'll be all right. I think it's better too. It's out in the open and I don't have to hide from him when I'm upset.

MR. HOUPT: As to exactly when you should tell him, Dr. Naiman mentioned something about the doctor's decision. Of course, I'm sure he meant that it's the parents' decision in conjunction with the doctor. But you need their help. They're going to help you. Their estimate that he is 14 years old mentally is part of the reason we decided to cross that bridge.

When he's 4 years old and it's diagnosed, you think in terms of how long it's going to be and whether he's going to live. Then all of a sudden he's 9 years old and you think you should wait until he's 13 or 14. I don't think there is an optimum age to tell the child. It depends on the child when he should be told.

PARTICIPANT: I would like to ask Mr. Houpt a question. I believe you were actively involved initially in this program. Was there any difference between, Mr. Houpt, your feelings about involving yourself, and yours, Mrs. Houpt? At this point, Mr. Houpt, what are your feelings about the necessity to remain involved in that group program?

MR. HOUPT: When we first got involved in it there was a lot of clinical interaction and there was a degree of group support. My wife and I are two different kinds of people and to this day I think there is some need for her to go to the meetings. I think I got a lot from them and I go once in a while, more for a specific item. But I'm busy and I have a lot of things to do. I frankly have found that I'd like to spend that night with the kids. We have 4 children. I work just about every evening and I would rather spend that night with the kids as opposed to being with the group.

I got to a certain point where I had to decide what was more valuable for me, but this was after going for about 2 years. I guess it is about 4 or 5 months that I've slowed down and haven't gone regularly.

DR. NAIMAN: Sue, could you say a few words about your experience as one of the leaders of a group of parents who have lost a child?

MS. SHERMAN: This actually is a new project that we started about a year ago. The other kinds of parents groups had been going on for about 3 years before that, and the reason for starting this is that we felt very strongly that the relationship between the families and the hospital shouldn't end at the point of death. We found that the parents felt the same way—that suddenly there was this tremendous vacuum in their lives, that besides having lost their child they also lost all contact with a very important part of their recent life.

We had, as a rule, kept in contact in an individual way; that is, each of the doctors and each of the social workers kept in contact with the specific families that they knew, but we had never brought these people together in a group.

We decided to invite any parents who had lost a child within the past 2 years, just to see what happens. In other words, we did not plan a group and decide what they would talk about, but thought we would see if they wanted a group and what they would want from it. Many of the parents showed up and many of the parents wanted to participate in this way.

It's a different kind of group. There is tremendous homogeneity in the other groups because each family has a child who has leukemia, but in this group the homogeneity is even stronger because everyone is facing the same vacuum of no longer having the child.

We discussed many different kinds of things and we found that despite the homogeneity in their reason for being there, each person had different needs. Lots of the groups are talking about how birthdays and anniversaries are handled—the first birthday after the child dies, the anniversary of the child's death. These are particularly hard times and parents have a lot to say about that. Also, there is discussion about how parents are changing their lives and filling the gaps that they now have. Many of the parents have become involved in fund-raising activities for the hospital and in supporting other parents going through the same thing.

PARTICIPANT: Mrs. Houpt, you have 4 children. I wonder about the effects on the other children. How old are they and what have you learned?

MRS. HOUPT: I have a boy 16 and a girl 15; Steven is 9, and I have a 5-year-old. From the very beginning, we shared everything with the two older ones. We talked openly. When Steven was diagnosed, Camille was 9. I've always talked in front of them. You don't really know what they're thinking about or if they're upset. I think they treat him normally. They fight with him. They play rough with him. Because it has been out in the open, I don't think that they've really had questions that they're afraid to ask.

We have our ups and downs. When he is fine and he looks healthy, you would never know anything was wrong with him, so you don't think about it. But when he had the increased cells 3 weeks ago we were sad, and I think they feel that, too, and they're upset. They try to comfort me. They don't really talk about how they feel. I've always said to them that if they have anything to ask they can. They know that they can talk to me.

PARTICIPANT: How about the little one?

MRS. HOUPT: I don't know how much she understands. She has gone to the clinic and has watched the treatment. We don't let her see spinal taps, but she sees him getting the intravenous injection. I was afraid of what would happen when she had to get a needle, but a couple of weeks ago she had to get a booster shot and she was brave. She wasn't afraid and she didn't cry.

MR. HOUPT: The baby doesn't realize the gravity of it. She doesn't understand quite what's going on. The older two grew up with this. In fact, when we first told them, we tried to impress on them that nothing should be changed, that they should be the same. We have attempted to keep everything on an even keel. It's hard. I'm not saying it's easy, but you don't want to change the family life. You try to keep everything standardized. We've tried to impress on the older two to treat Steven as a normal child—which, frankly, he is. There is no real difference at all except for the treatments. Fortunately, it hasn't been a real problem for us as far as the other children, though it can be.

Sometimes when he comes out of one of the drugs, after certain treatments, he's touchy. You think it's a direct result of the drug and you kind of shrug it off. We tell the older two and they lay off a little bit. As I said, they've actually grown up with it and they don't get too involved one way or the other. We've brought both of the older kids down to the clinic from time to time with us, and they've seen what he goes through. We wanted them to try to appreciate what he goes through, and that is a good idea.

PARTICIPANT (Pittsburgh, Pa.): You said that Matthew died 2 years ago and that the group started about a year ago. Do you find any difference in your need to go to the group now than you did maybe a few months after you started it?

MRS. WINSLADE: I think now we really feel more that we're helping others than getting help ourselves. Of course, it's still a help to us. But I feel when I go down now that somebody might need me there.

Part VI

Special Problems Primarily Involving Parents

21

Marriage: Changing Structure and Functions of the Family

Albert J. Solnit, M.D.

Yale Child Study Center, New Haven, Connecticut

The place of the nuclear family as a desirable, continuing institution has been challenged. In several new societies there has been an effort for the past 50 years or more to change the setting of the child's socializing experiences, with the assumption that the modern family alone cannot or does not have sufficient resources and knowledge to be trusted with the rearing of the future adults. This line of concern and questioning has been associated particularly with the industrialization and urbanization of our communities and is most clearly reflected by the conditions of life in any one of the large cities of this country. It is also associated with an increased awareness of scientific knowledge about child development and with the assumption that the "ordinary devoted" mother and father, using the resources of the conventional marriage, do not, owing to the changing conditions of life, have the education or preparation to carry out competently and knowledgeably the rearing of today's or tomorrow's healthy children. These are the children who will or should become those adults who will live and function more effectively, more constructively, more peacefully and with more human decency and dignity than in preceding generations. Many of us assume that the family will survive, but that for it to flourish, parents will need and should have increasing assistance and support.

A recent article is entitled Families Can be Unhealthy for Children and Other Living Things [1]. We are concerned that human survival depends on our children being able to be more humane and more socially viable in a technologic world than has been demonstrated by our past and present records in family affairs of life and death. The triumph of science and technology has carried us from an uncertain world in which nature was fate and we were impotent and fearful to the point where we see nature submitting to man's techniques and technologic knowledge. On the other hand, we seem unable to control human nature, ourselves, and to regulate our communities and societal structures.

The family, too, has fallen prey to this process of historical evolution. In a recent essay [2], John Silber, the President of Boston University, has clarified this perspective by pointing out, "Our society's pattern of two-generation families – and this for only a few years – is typical of the instant culture. Children are denied the important discoveries that are to be made about human existence by observing old age and death. The very old are denied the sense of renewal implicit in birth and childhood. Children are deprived of wisdom and grandparents of hope. Persons are bereft of the sense of enduring family ties: they spend most of their lives in isolation from those who care most about them." And later he adds, "The pollution of time is most obvious in our loss of a sense of history, in a loss of the recognition of the past as our own, in the loss of the awareness of any past, in the loss of the past in general."

Phillipe Aries [3] points out that in the medieval society in Europe, the family consisted of parents and children under the age of 7 or 8 years, since older children were placed out to work. Children became part of a work force at that early age, usually living away from the family as a part of the adult society. Childhood and the family as we know them are modern concepts, reflecting a dramatic transformation in the physical, intellectual and emotional meaning of life experiences, and reflecting also the steep decline in child mortality and morbidity that has been brought about by modern nutrition and medicine. And yet we are embarked on a challenge to the family as a basic nurturing, culture-transmitting societal form, the lowest common denominator of our social institutions.

In the family in medieval times, which contained the parents and those children under the ages of 7 or 8, as soon as the child could control his sphincters, feed himself, dress and undress himself and avoid obvious dangers, he became a *working* member of the household. As a worker, he was placed in the fields or in the shops, where he worked along with others and where his teacher was the boss or the master artisan to whom he was apprenticed. In those days there usually were many children born of a marriage, a large percentage of whom died from infection or pestilence. Those who survived left the immediate family at a young age to work elsewhere. As Rousseau said in *Émile,* "The less one has lived the less one may expect to live. Of all the children, not more than one-half will reach youth."

The concepts of adolescence within the family or of normative conflicts between the generations did not then exist in their present form.

As the industrial revolution took place and as the concept of parenthood changed, children stayed with their families beyond the ages of 6 – 8. There was an intuitive effort to accommodate to these continuities in family living with development of new institutions and traditions that reflected the impact of these changes on the community. Churches had youth groups, the concept of Sunday School arose and there were organized places away from home in which children learned, socialized and developed a sense of self and of their group identity. The historical roots of the Scout movement, the YMCA and YWCA, of the public schools and other institutional expressions of these social groups can shed an important illumination on these changes in family and community structure and functions. Thus, parents became responsible for and involved in their children's lives for longer periods of time following the advent of the industrial revolution. And, further, the parents' own development as adults reflected this change in family function. They came to respond to the changes in adolescents' development and behavior with conflict and frustration and with a greater wish for fulfillment and continuity.

Another change also had a complex and enduring influence on the family. As we were able to improve our nutrition, prevent infectious disease and cure or overcome infections and certain surgical diseases, the infant mortality sharply decreased. The expectation of longevity for each human being has more than doubled over the past several hundred years.

Accordingly, the meaning of family changed, inasmuch as children once born could be expected to survive and to live in the family longer. Adults lived to a riper age, increasing the continuity of generations. At the same time, other conditions tended to lengthen the time space between generations. For example, several hundred years ago marriages occurred at an earlier age and it was not unusual for the adult who survived to become a grandparent in his mid to late thirties.

As each child's survival and development to adulthood within the family became more common, as the industrial revolution introduced our technologic age and as democratic values prevailed in this country, there came an increased need for and urge toward more education for all our children. And, as parents attached themselves emotionally to their children as intimate members of their household for 16 to 18 years rather than 7 or 8 years, the meaning of parenthood changed and the sense of family changed. Each parent now could invest more in each child as a carrier of his hopes, values and aspirations for the future. Children have come to represent our replacements and our wishes for immortality. These representations are powerful and ambivalent, having a potential that ranges from the most intense love for children to the most fearful resentment of them. It is this understanding of parenthood that has illuminated one of the most vexing and painful questions of our day.

Why are we so unsuccessful in assuring children of a high priority in terms of our resources, values and limited altruism? Adults have deeply ingrained, irrational reservations about the primacy of children's needs because they expect to be replaced by them. Similarly, adults have a deep love and concern for children because parents hope their children's lives will fulfill their own values and aspirations. Unwittingly, in this way, parents express their wishes for immortality and reduce their fear of death. Thus, parents universally experience children as representatives of their mortality as well as their immortality. In each culture, certain ethnic, political and social patterns of a given historical period will be in resonance with the family structure and functions of that setting in that epoch. On the other hand, the helplessness of the newborn and our patterns of socializing and living together in population concentrations of more or less density are crucial, elemental forces that evoke the family as a basic social unit.

As society develops, there are changes in the mosaics that we call family and community. These changing mosaics reflect an unfolding of human expression and hopefully of human improvement. One can see such expressions in efforts to equalize the opportunities of men and women, of minority groups and of the economically and socially deprived.

The velocity of historical change has been accelerated by our technologic advances unilaterally, without regard to the tempo of the developing child and the richly woven tapestry that is created gradually, not instantly, by the healthy family. We do well to heed the words of Rousseau [4] in his classic *Émile*, "Nature wants children to be children before they are men. If we deliberately pervert this order, we shall get premature fruits which are neither ripe nor well-flavored, and which soon decay. . . ." "Childhood has ways of seeing, thinking and feeling peculiar to itself; nothing can be more foolish than to substitute our ways for them." ". . . they are always looking for the man in the child, without considering what he is before he becomes a man."

One other radical change in this country, and more recently in Europe and in some of the developing countries, is the development of a universal educational system for children from prekindergarten through high school, or its equivalent. Children now remain home longer and more dependently, as essential members of the family, while growing up physically more rapidly and more exuberantly. Meanwhile, the human resources and services made available by society to parents and to families have not kept pace with the needs of these families. Our increased knowledge and changing conditions of life require more if we wish our children to be healthy and our families to remain the most important bastion of our democratic, humanistic values and hopes. The family as a societal form requires a continuity of the generations and a sense of how the past and present can give meaning and validity to living in the future. For the family is not only a nourishing, protective and guiding unit; it also is a meaningful bridge from the past to the future. If we were to decide that the family unit is antiquated or that it has outlived its usefulness, following our best knowledge of human development, we would have to create a form of social environment for children and their closest adult relatives that would have many or most of the features of the family as we know it today and have known it for the past hundred years. Accordingly, it is imperative that we avoid the unnecessary rediscovery of what we know or can predict, and that we find what societal resources can be mobilized to support the family today and as it will evolve in the future. Meanwhile, man must come to grips with new methods for regulating the conflicts that threaten to destroy the human world.

The quality of family life is affected by positive and negative factors in our technologic age. At the same time, while we can enjoy unprecedented excellence of nutrition and prevention of infectious and parasitic diseases, we cannot quarantine the pockets of good health in the world from contact with those threatening areas where the promises have not been made nor from those areas where they have been made but have not been kept. Recent statistics indicate some of the weak seams in the web of our family-centered society, in particular with respect to the instability of modern marriage.

Marriage has two main functions from the point of view of a psychoanalyst as a student of human development. The first function, sanctioned by marriage as an institutionalized form of human life, is to provide an opportunity for parents and children to regain at the adult level the intimacy and continuity of closeness, of affection and of shared experience that had in infancy and early childhood been the basis for survival and of future development. The second function of marriage is to provide a major patterned environment in which children can be begotten and raised in an orderly and civilized way.

It is noteworthy that marriage is not necessary for what many persons consider adequate sexual relationships and experiences; nor is it the only patterned human setting in which to rear children; nor a guarantee of intimacy and of the continuity of affectionate relationships. Moreover, marriage has not, especially in recent years, been the bastion of stability and continuity. The rising divorce rate and the prevalence of unstable and strife-torn marriages characterize an important part of our current societal pattern.

What I am emphasizing is that marriage, de facto or de jure (and in this chapter I do not examine the significant psychologic differences between these two states of marriage), provides an agreement for two people who find sexual and social satisfaction together to utilize the past as a guide to their future. The past stems from the social addiction that babies develop for the physical care (later translated into psychologic-emotional care) at the hands of the adult or adults who keep them fed, warm and feeling cheerful for the next hour, day, week and other future times. This addiction, rooted in the infant's biologic helplessness, becomes transformed into the urgent need for company, approval, affection and a sense of continuity, as biologic helplessness yields to maturation and development.

Throughout childhood, this addiction is gradually modified and the capacity to want and to accept substitute gratifications is heightened with the support of the parents and siblings. As adolescence is traversed and the child defines himself or herself against the parents, there is the emergence of the young man or young woman who achieves increasing independence and uniqueness as an adult. What then?

The young adult has a deeply ingrained longing for closeness, outside the family, a longing that will enable him or her to resume, at the adult level, the closeness, affection and continuity that had been established in a patterned way in earliest childhood as derivative of biologic helplessness. Paradoxically, such an engagement, or such closeness to a nonfamily member, often is associated with the resumption of closeness with parents as adults with adults.

Some of this feeling is captured in the words of a contemporary ballad from *West Side Story:*

> "When you're a Jet,
> you're a Jet all the way.
> From your first cigarette
> to your last dying day.
> When you're a Jet
> If the spit hits the fan
> You've got brothers around
> You're a family man
> You're never alone
> You're never disconnected
> You're home with your own
> When company's expected.
> You're well protected!"

Of course, as the following statistics indicate, the increasing numbers of single-parent families and the changing expectations of women will have their own influences on marriage. In fact, we now define family as at least 1 adult and 1 child, acknowledging the separation of marriage from childbearing. As the evolution of equal rights for women continues, the concept and pattern called marriage will not only reflect the changing functions of the family but will in turn be one of the vital influences for change in the functions and the structure of the family.

Let us look at some of the trends. The *New Haven Register* of March 19, 1975 reported that according to the National Center for Health Statistics there were 393,000 divorces in the United States in 1960, at the rate of 2.2 per 1000 population, and that there had been a steady increase without plateau such that in 1974 there were 970,000 divorces, at the rate of 4.6 per 1000 population. In Connecticut, the rate had risen from 2 divorces for every 1000 persons to 5.2 per 1000 in 1973, and the number of divorces had risen from 2597 in 1960 to 10,748 in 1974.

A few more indicators of family life in the United States will be instructive, and should be understood in terms of their effect on the quality of the child's life when he is a child.

In a recent speech (First Annual Delegate Assembly, Human Services Institute, Rosslyn, Virginia, October 3, 1974), Senator Walter Mondale explained, "One of my wise colleagues once told me, 'You're spending too much time on children; remember, they can't vote.' " Of course, Senator Mondale refuted the value preference expressed by his cynical colleague, knowing that we can also say that children aren't as dangerous or as demanding as adults. He refuted this preference, because in a society with our professed values there are two major reasons to support the rights of children as coming before that of adults. First, in a hard-headed way it is a good investment because it is the most logical, economical way of protecting their future capacities to work and to avoid institutionalization and pathologic dependency. We cannot document this by longitudinal studies, but we can estimate the impact of maintaining school-age children's progression into and through adolescence in such a way that they are able to enter the labor market with a developed capacity for earning and socializing.

Second, from a practical point of view, it should not be too difficult to understand that the quality of life we want for ourselves cannot be any better than the quality of life we try to ensure for our children; and *now*—not 10 years from now.

In the same address, Senator Mondale outlined some well-known statistics, in back of which are live, warm, changing human beings. Some of these "facts" are:

"One out of seven American children—about eight and a half million in all—is now living in a single-parent family.

"Most single-parent families are headed by women, and the number of families headed by women has increased by more than one million in the last three years alone, as much as it increased in the preceding ten years, to a total of 6.6 million families.

"Female-headed families are now growing at a rate twice as fast as husband-wife families, and female-headed families with children under 18 are growing even faster."

Then he added, "There is a common tendency to think of single-parent families as poor families and welfare recipients. It is true that many single-parent families have severe economic problems. They do have considerably lower median incomes than two-parent families, and there are higher concentrations of single-parent families among the poor than among other groups.

"But most single-parent families are not poor, and they are not on welfare. Only 35 percent of them are receiving AFDC. Female-headed families with children are increasing faster among the non-poor and the middle class than they are among the poor.

"There also seems to be a tendency on the part of some to think of single-parent families as minority group families, but the facts indicate that sixty-seven percent of female-headed families with children are white.

"Finally, some people seem to assume that all or most female-headed families are headed by unwed mothers. Nothing could be further from the truth. Of all these families in 1973, 37 percent were widowed, 26 percent were divorced, 25 percent were separated, and only 13 percent were in the unmarried category. I think the point of all this is quite simple. Single-parent family problems cannot be dismissed either as a minority problem or as a problem of poverty, or as some sort of abnormal, maladjusted phenomenon that will quickly disappear."

In a recent review (*New York Times* Book Review, April 27, 1975, p. 4), in referring to marriage from the woman's point of view, there is reference to the ". . . human bondage-in-marriage status," and the reviewer, Doris Grumbach, in commenting on the novel *Crucial Conversations* by May Sarton, states, "She knows, as so many other women have learned in our time, that she cannot live creatively on the edge of her wifely and motherly existence."

In a recent comic strip* there is a conversation between two children playing in a sandbox. The girl asks the boy, "Howie, are you ever going to get married?" He answers, while building a sand castle, "I sure am, Sally! I'm planning on being very successful when I grow up. And you gotta have a wife if you're gonna be successful!"

Sally asks, "How come?" Howie answers, "So that when you're out making a name for yourself, you'll have someone to clean the house, do the cooking and raise the kids!"

Sally asks, "A wife will do all that stuff?" Howie answers, "Uh-huh, for free, too!" Sally exclaims, "Really!" Howie continues, "Sure! A wife's a pretty good deal – I can't wait for mine!"

Sally says, "Gee, maybe I should get one, too!" Howie answers, "Well try to get a pretty one, they never get traffic tickets!"

So, who will take care of the children?

The family is an intuitive social group, with all of its variations reflecting simultaneously the needs of children for continuous affectionate relationships and the needs of adults to find some hope and assurance that their lives have not been in vain and will have an influence on the future. Man's need to be concerned with the future is ethical, humanistic and at bedrock, a way of coping with his own mortality. The transmission to children of the values and aspirations of adults, a concept viewed as immortality by some groups, reflects the hopes and ethically the most constructive side of man.

I am indebted to Dr. Joan Costello for calling my attention to two examples of what she terms "The Child's Inheritance."

"Never call a man happy until he is dead; his true epitaph is written in his children" (Ecclesiastes: 11, 30).

---

*"Doonesbury" by Garry Trudeau, *New Haven Register,* April 27, 1975.

A bird once set out to cross a windy sea with his three fledglings. The sea was so wide and the wind so strong, the father bird was forced to carry his young, one by one, in his strong claws. When he was halfway across with the first fledgling, the wind turned to a gale, and he said, "My child, look how I am struggling and risking my life in your behalf. When you are grown up, will you do as much for me and provide for my old age?" The fledgling replied, "Only bring me to safety, and when you are old I shall do everything you ask of me." Whereat the father bird dropped his child into the sea, and it drowned, and he said, "So shall it be done to such a liar as you." Then the father bird returned to shore, set forth with his second fledgling, asked the same question and, receiving the same answer, drowned the second child with the cry, "You, too, are a liar." Finally, he set out with the third fledgling, and when he asked the same question, the third and last fledgling replied, "My dear father, it is true you are struggling mightily and risking your life in my behalf, and I shall be wrong not to repay you when you are old, but I cannot bind myself. This though I can promise: when I am grown up and have children of my own, I shall do as much for them as you have done for me." Whereupon the father bird said, "Well spoken, my child, and wisely; your life I will spare and I will carry you to shore in safety" [7].

If regrets about the limitations of one man's or woman's life are transmitted as a dignifying rather than a degrading legacy, the family can be viable, essential and reflective of the most crucial needs of the child, born into life as a helpless infant, for whom human care becomes the basis for biologic and social elaboration, enrichment and survival.

If our understanding can be balanced by our creativity, the concept of survival can become a positive and humanizing influence. In the same sense, the need for the closeness and exclusiveness of family ties matches the need of children and adults to find strength, meaning and boundaries in their life's experiences. Variations of family structure and function and new forms are to be expected; and they can be viewed as efforts to humanize and enhance our development and survival, so long as the continuity of affectionate bonds and exclusive intimacies are keystones to these new forms. On the other hand, those communes or new social structures that blur the uniqueness of each individual and decrease human intimacy through a diffusion of feelings in groups larger or less stable than family groups will run counter to what facilitates the full unfolding of each child's or adult's capacity for tenderness and versatility in searching for a better world for the next generation.

REFERENCES

1. Skolnick, A.: Families can be unhealthy for children and other living things, Psychol. Today, August, 1971, p. 18.
2. Silber, J. R.: The pollution of time, The Center Magazine, September/October, 1971, pp. 2–10.
3. Aries, P.: *Centuries of Childhood* (New York: Alfred A. Knopf, 1962).
4. Rousseau, J. J.: *Émile*, in Coveney, P., *Poor Monkey—The Child in Literature* (London: Rockliff, 1957).
5. Senator Walter Mondale: Speech given to Delegate Assembly, Human Services Institute, Rosslyn, Virginia, October 3, 1974.
6. Ecclesiastes: 11, 30.
7. *Memoirs of Glukel of Hameln, from Early 18th Century*. Translated by Marion Lowenthal (New York: Harper & Bros., 1932).

22

The Young Parent Family

Marion Howard

Former Director of Consortium on Early
Childbearing and Childrearing, Washington, D. C.

At one time in our history, people began family life at an earlier age than is now seen as appropriate. Currently, young people are not needed in jobs, and unskilled, untrained labor is not rewarded by our society. Thus, economic means for supporting families are not readily available to the young. Schools have basically replaced work institutions for young people. Indeed, currently close to 75% of the United States student population graduate from high school. Almost half of these go on for some form of higher education.

The family as a social and economic unit has greatly changed too. A son-in-law, daughter-in-law or additional children are not needed for help in the house, on the farm, in the family business. Family units are kept small in size. Nuclear families often live far from other family members. Contact among relatives may be minimal. Thus, the nurturance, protection and support that may have come from a close-knit or large family structure has to a great degree been lost to young parent families.

Laws designed to protect young people also inhibit their participation as adults in society. Young people cannot on their own consent to services such as their own medical care or engage in legal contracts such as apartment rental or marriage.

Institutions that touch on the lives of young people are not prepared to treat them as adults. Even institutions that support older parent family life are at best neglectful and most often punitive and hostile toward young parent families.

Schools, until the past decade, almost without exception expelled pregnant girls—married or unmarried—and discouraged their re-entry. Young parents were prohibited from participation in extracurricular school activities.

Health care systems traditionally have denied youth easy access to birth control, pregnancy tests, prenatal care. Parental consent has most often been required. As late as the 1960s, a survey of physicians [1] indicated that even *with* parental consent, three-quarters did not provide contraceptive advice for younger adolescents and over half did not provide it for high school students.

Pregnant girls choosing to keep their babies have been less likely to receive social services than those placing their babies in adoption. Welfare systems have refused to grant aid directly to young mothers living in the home of a parent receiving Aid to Families with Dependent Children. Mothers as young as 15 have at times been urged to move out on their own to be eligible for more money. Unpleasant legal action against even those fathers too young to contribute realistically to the needs of the mother and child often has been a requirement for financial assistance.

For these and other reasons, when young people take on family life, they experience a handicapping by society. This makes it difficult for them to carry out the necessary functions of family life and threatens the success of their undertaking.

Recently, the birth rate for every group except that of very young teen-agers has been stable or declining. The birth rate of young teen-agers has been rising. The results are startling. Currently, 1 of every 10 girls in the United States will give birth to a baby while still of school age; that is, before reaching the age of 18. Although the majority of the girls will be married by the time the baby is born (approximately 60%), evidence is that a high proportion of the in-wedlock births actually were conceived out of wedlock (marriage having resulted from conception rather than conception having resulted from marriage).

Sixty per cent of young mothers are white, 40% are members of minority groups. Of those under age 16 and therefore at greatest risk socially, educationally and medically, 40% are white and 60% are members of minority groups. Therefore, those in greatest need of services are the least likely to have access to care [2].

What perhaps is most important to note about school-age mothers, however, is that most live in their own homes during pregnancy and close to 85% keep the baby and attempt to mother the child, thus beginning young parent families.

FAMILIES-AT-RISK

That these are families-at-risk is all too evident. Young parent families are overrepresented in negative national statistics—rates of infant mortality, attempted suicide, school dropouts, unemployment, underemployment, welfare dependency, family instability, divorce rates, single parenthood.

The risks begin with the establishment of young parent family life. Young people often do not have enough factual information about how pregnancy occurs to prevent it. Even if knowledge is present, they may not have access to appropriate methods of birth control or support for birth control use. Certainly the risk of not being able to do anything about an early termination of pregnancy through abortion is still a very real one for young people despite liberalization of abortion laws. Often young people are not aware of the pregnancy or are afraid to involve others until it is too late.

Adolescent pregnancy means health risks during pregnancy for the young mother and the fetus. Infants of young mothers are less likely to be well born.

In the establishment of young parent family life, young parents experience the risk of becoming married—often inappropriately. Yet, beginning family life as a single parent is an unhappy alternative.

There are risks in the continuance or maintenance of early family life. Young married parents may face unusual stress as they try to adjust to living with each other, complete their own growth and development and meet the needs of an infant all at the same time. School-age married couples often experience a demoralizing social isolation. The single parent may face social ostracism, lack of support and punitive policies and practices.

Both in and out of wedlock, young parents are likely to have too many children too soon. One 10-year community-wide fertility study indicated that 60% of the girls who have their first baby under the age of 16 are likely to have another baby while still of school age [3].

Young parents may drop out of school because of lack of day care or pressures to work. Certainly many young parent families fall victim to unemployment, underemployment or welfare dependency. Young parents may face definite risks of not completing life goals. Many, within a few years, find themselves locked into an unsatisfactory life pattern and begin a frustrated wishing for a life that "could have been."

Infants of adolescent parents may experience the care of a generally immature person – with some chance of neglect or potential abuse.

Finally, there are the risks of dissolution of young parent family life. More than 1 out of 2 of those who marry at school age will divorce within the first 5 years of married life. For the young people involved, this separation often comes after bearing additional children. Infants of young parents are likely to be reared in homes in which there is unusual stress – at times, total disintegration. For the single parent, the child often proves to be an increasing burden. Many young parents find that the crisis period comes when their child begins to walk and talk and make demands. Some abdicate responsibility. The child then may be reared by the grandparents in a sibling relationship to the parent.

Although stability of family life is to be sought after, in a group this young, reality is that many young families will have to break up and re-form in different ways before stability can be achieved. Better ways of dissolving such families with less injury to parents and children therefore are needed.

THE NEED FOR CHANGE

However, without meaningful intervention – both the removal of punitive policies and practices (a part of societal handicapping) and the development of programs and services to meet special needs – young parent families are not likely to thrive in either new or old forms of family life. How can needed changes be brought about?

Herman Kahn, in his book *Things to Come*, speaks of educated incapacity [4]. He defines this as an "acquired or learned inability to understand and see a problem much less a solution. Increasingly, the more expert or, at least, the more educated a person is the more likely he is to be affected by this. Education necessarily involves selection, indoctrination, a special intellectual environment, the development of a framework of accepted givens. . . ." We are encouraged to think about a subject in a required way.

When a problem or the solution to a problem lies outside the accepted framework, a professional often is less likely to understand the situation or see the solution than an amateur. The more educated, the more involved in our own discipline we become, the less we are able to actually have a degree of reality testing about what we do.

Certainly with respect to young parent families we have exercised an unusual degree of educated incapacity. For example, fetal deaths and infant mortality have long been of concern to health professionals. Yet, requiring young girls to have parental consent for birth control, pregnancy testing, abortion and prenatal care frustrates identification of sexually active adolescents and early enrollment for prenatal care.

Educators for some time have expressed concern about school dropouts. And pregnancy is the major known cause of dropouts among young women. In reality, however, most such young women have been pushouts, not dropouts. In many communities, policies outlaw school attendance by pregnant girls. Indeed, an amateur could have suggested a solution — that pregnant girls be allowed to continue in school during pregnancy and encouraged to return following the birth of the baby.

Thus, the removal of punitive policies and practices may in part involve overcoming our educated incapacity with respect to young parent families. Along with this, however, service efforts do have to be made to deal with the special risks of young parent family life.

The approach must be to see the total person and his/her total needs — not to separate out a part of the individual's needs a particular agency is set up to serve; not to expect the young parent to meet various agencies' criteria for service. As such, a variety of community institutions must be involved — the school system, the health institutions, the social service agencies, among others.

Currently in the United States there are close to 300 community-based multiservice programs geared to meeting the needs of young families. One organization generally takes responsibility for the coordination of the efforts made by other institutions participating in such programs. This coordinating and integrating function may be filled by any agency. The focus is on providing comprehensive services, *not* "coordinated fragmented services."

NEEDS OF YOUNG PARENT FAMILIES

The needs high-risk young parent families present are varied.

First of all, support needs to be given in the community for prevention of early family life. There are few people who today would argue that the establishment of family life at an early age is beneficial to either parent or child. Yet, reality is that by age 19, 63% of female youth are sexually active.

For a variety of reasons, old methods of pregnancy prevention, ignorance, limitation of opportunity, fear of societal disapproval, exhortation to be good or do right, threat of punishment — no longer are adequate to meet today's needs. The community needs to make new assessments about what makes young individuals decide to prevent pregnancy, what makes society want to help them prevent pregnancy and what is the most useful way to deliver services to help individuals carry out their decisions.

Unfortunately, opponents of sex education believe that providing young people with sex education is merely filling empty bowls. Even those who support sex education are not sure which youth should have it, how to give it to them or who should give it. Nevertheless, one recent study indicated that when asked what time of the month women were most likely to become pregnant, only 2% of the teen-age girls interviewed said they didn't know. Ninety-eight per cent said they did know. However, 50% gave the wrong answer. Certainly, therefore, sex education is not merely filling empty bowls but dealing with facts and fantasies and correcting misinformation that already exists.

Yet, telling young people how they become pregnant and how to prevent it surely is not enough. Perhaps more important, we should be telling them something about family life – about what it means to be a parent. Without that understanding, we are expecting young people to control behavior on the basis of a very limited perspective.

Services and support should be given for use of birth control. It is ineffectual to hand a young girl a packet of pills and say "Come back in 3 months." Especially if her parents disapprove, or her boyfriend disapproves. We must think of ways to support individuals who want to prevent pregnancy and increase the motivation of others to want to do so as well. One way may be to say it is just as OK *not* to have sex as to have it. This is particularly important for young people to hear when they are experiencing peer group pressure. In many instances it may be helpful to have the girl and boy attend rap sessions with other youth about their concerns. That opportunity can be used to provide support for birth control use.

Among those young people who fail to prevent pregnancy are many who do not want to become pregnant. The beginning of family life for these youth may be full of indecision and unhappiness.

For a number of young mothers, the pregnancy was planned. When asked why they become pregnant, common answers were: "I wanted something to love," "I wanted something of my own." These mothers almost never mention love of children. Often they have a baby as a means to achieving something else. Although adults do not always have better motivations, the likelihood of adolescents realizing their goals may be less. The girl who becomes pregnant to escape a deteriorated home situation often finds herself in a few years in an unhappy home situation of her own.

In particular, we must begin to ask ourselves what would make a 14-year-old want a baby – see that as a solution to her problem? What is the quality of that young person's life?

One recent study showed that as self-esteem went up, so did age at first intercourse [6]. Therefore, major efforts should be made to assess the problems of young people, and help should be given toward resolving them in ways that improve self-esteem. In many cases, the life expectations of young people must be upgraded.

Free and confidential pregnancy tests must be available to young women. For those who become pregnant, the option of abortion should be introduced. Particularly for young people, careful counseling prior to any abortion coupled with follow-through services are needed. This must be done in order to prevent later regret, substitute pregnancy or repeated abortions.

For young people who choose to go through with the pregnancy, prenatal care must be offered with age-appropriate methods. Nutritional information, prepara-

Table 22–1
Patterns of Adolescent Pregnancy

PLANNED PREGNANCY	Purposeful Group	Some adolescents consciously choose pregnancy. Others plan the pregnancy in less obvious but still purposeful ways. (Examples: "I had a baby because I wanted something to love." "I wanted to get back at them." "My mother always said I would get pregnant and, see, I did."
	Indifferent Group	"Sure I knew there was such a thing as birth control." "I guess I just didn't care enough to take precautions." "If I use birth control, I'm a bad girl—If I don't and get pregnant, I'm a good girl who got caught."
UNPLANNED PREGNANCY	Invincible Group	This risk-taking is similar to hanging onto the back of a bus. "I didn't think it could happen to me." "After this baby, I'm off boys. I don't need birth control because I'm not going to have sex again."
	Ignorant Group	Adolescents do not know as much as we assume. "I didn't know it could happen at my age." "I thought you had to be married." "I'm not sure how I got pregnant."
	External Failure Group	Since adolescents prefer their sex to be spontaneous and little support is offered for use of birth control, failures are higher than would be expected. This group can also include "contraceptive" failures such as trying to use Saran Wrap as a condom and Coke as a douche, etc.
	Helpless Group	A small group whose pregnancy is the result of rape, incest or other aggression.

tion for labor and childbirth, postpartum care and interconceptional care with emphasis on secondary prevention are vital.

Young parents, both mothers and fathers, should be encouraged to continue their education.

During the past decade, a number of school districts have established separate educational programs for pregnant students. These programs, however, do not begin to reach the numbers of students who become pregnant. Moreover, such programs often are criticized because they isolate pregnant students from their peers. Currently there is a trend toward allowing pregnant students to remain in their regular school classes. One disadvantage is that the school system may not then provide an appropriate alternative educational program for the student who cannot or does not want to remain in regular school. Further, separate education classes in many communities have been the basis for coordinating comprehensive health and social services for young parents. When the special educational services are discontinued, the comprehensive aspect of care usually is lost. Consequently, if school systems are going to continue to move toward regular school education, new ways to ensure that pregnant girls and young parents receive needed additional services must be found.

With increasing numbers of young parents returning to or remaining in school, education must be made more relevant to their needs. To support young parent family life, curricula must embody the kind of information important to young people involved in a different life phase than many of their peers. For example, young mothers do not readily absorb information about child care during the pregnancy period. For many, the baby is not a reality until it is born. The main thrust then must come following the birth of the baby. Child development curricula offered in schools must be changed to offer the kind of day-to-day practical information young mothers need. Use of models, such as observation of and interaction with caregivers in a day care center, should be employed. Parenting education should continue as the baby grows and the mother matures. Consumer education is an example of another subject of immediate concern and assistance to young parents.

Continuity of care is especially important for the young parent. Introduction to the pediatrician or other pediatric staff members long before the baby is born can help ensure this. Use of the same counseling staff during pregnancy and following can be useful. Also, obstetric staff members can be present in the well-baby clinic at times specifically set up for young parents, to enhance the sense of continuity.

Young parent families must have access to counseling. Young parents are likely to range all along the developmental continuum from childhood to adulthood. Physical, intellectual and psychosocial development in any one individual may be unequal at this time. Pregnancy is likely to interrupt normal adolescent growth and development. In legal terms, young parents are minors, regardless of their pregnancy or parenthood—that is, individuals who, not having reached the age of majority, are unable to give consent to their own care and actions and, in some instances, actions and care affecting their child. Young people are most often financially dependent. Educationally and vocationally, they are not yet fully capable. If young people do find jobs, they are low paying.

Counseling, therefore, should be available from the beginning as young people decide whether to have sex or not, use birth control or not, carry a baby to term or not, keep or not keep the baby. Young parents must work out relationships with each other—marriage, shared unmarried parenting, single parenthood. Relationships with the infant must be developed. Child care plans, if the young parent is to be absent for any period of time, must be made. Relationships with peers, systems, society must be dealt with. And, very important, relationships with parents and other family members must be worked out.

Families are still jumping-off places—oases for young people. Moreover, most young parents will continue to live at home. As such, the families of young parents cannot be ignored. They can be a crucial source of emotional support for young mothers and fathers. Yet, many of these older families are multi-problem families. Mother-daughter relationships often are poor. Counseling services to assist in solving the problems of both families may be needed.

In trying to meet the needs of young parents, it is important to recognize that they are not a homogeneous group, and differences among them create differences in the kinds of services required. For example, young mothers (those under 16) are less likely to finish school, more likely to have rapid repeated pregnancies both in and out of wedlock, less likely to marry or, if they do marry, to have a stable marriage. Therefore, they need different kinds of services and services given over a longer period of time than do many of their older peers [7].

Counseling goes on all the time by a high proportion of those people youthful parents come in contact with. Nurses, doctors, teachers all do counseling. Since young people are naturally suspicious of adults and don't form relationships easily, a young parent may turn to an unexpected person for counseling. This may be to other than a professional trained in or assigned to the counseling area. Further, the person may not be knowledgeable about areas of concern raised by the young person. The social service role in such cases may be that of outreach: supporting, helping the young person and the individual she or he has chosen to maintain and benefit from continuing their critical relationship.

YOUNG FATHERS

In the past, the young father has too often been seen only as some sort of adjunct to the mother. Services are set up for her, not for him. Those who sought access to him generally have done so for reasons related to mother and baby, primarily financial.

In our society, one of the main ways to become a man is to take a wife, father children and support them – the "wed, bed, finance-till-dead" syndrome. For the very young father it is precisely this contribution that is not feasible for him. If he, too, is in school, he does not have the economic capability on his own to care for the needs of the young family. Part-time jobs after school can be only a contribution. If he does drop out of school, he is likely to be able to find only a low-paying job with little potential.

Another traditional view of the young father is that he is the aggressor, the male seducer. As often as not, the situation is more that of two young people who feel some affection for each other, neither of whom is very experienced in love or life. The girl may be equally or more the aggressor. The pregnancy may occur just at a time when the young father is beginning to feel confident that he can be an individual on his own in society. The added responsibility of a family may thrust him back into dependence and interfere with his growth and development.

In Philadelphia, a 14-year-old boy walked his pregnant girl friend back and forth to a special school program for pregnant girls each day. When the baby was born, he ran away from home for 2 weeks. Obviously, inside the school, assistance was being given to the girl but no one had reached out to meet his needs. Young fathers have many of the same concerns that young mothers have and the same need for information and services.

If we are to strengthen family life, we must first see the father as an individual just as we have traditionally tried to see the mother. We must ask him the same questions we ask of her: Who are You? What are your concerns? How can we help you?

Jobs and future economic potential are a major concern of young fathers. Some may already be supporting other members of their families. Young fathers may have problems with drugs, staying in school – a myriad of other things. Until we relate to their primary concerns and help them in those areas, we may not be able to help them in relation to the start of family life. Often I am asked about trying to work with fathers when the girl wishes the relationship terminated.

Even if the father does not intend to be a father to the child, he will be a father to some child someday. This may be an ideal time to add to his understanding about fathering and the father role. Certainly if we are to think of prevention of other inappropriate pregnancies, we must think about working with the young father.

To date, the most successful programs for young fathers generally have involved male workers and outreach activities—that is, going where the fathers are (Y's, pool halls, the street corners) and relating to them as individuals with genuine needs and concerns. Serious attempts to help them—such as opening up job opportunities for them in the community—then must be made.

INFANTS OF SCHOOL-AGE PARENTS

Churchill once said a crisis is a dangerous opportunity. If pregnancy in adolescence can be defined as the crisis, what we do with the infant may well be the dangerous opportunity.

Although we know little about the strengths and deficiencies of adolescent parents, we do know that infants of young parents are less likely to be well born than infants of almost all other age groups. Certainly caring for a handicapped child is difficult enough for any parent; for young parents, it may be devastating.

Most commonly, children grow in the security of their parents' love. Without reinforcement, kindness and security, a child will not be able to explore and learn about his world. Adolescence is a time of mood shifts, changing ideas. Parenting demands large amounts of consistency and patience—qualities that adolescents may not be well suited to give. Lack of confidence as well as knowledge may also affect the ability of young parents to carry out parenting tasks.

One study of adolescent parents showed that they had very unrealistic expectations for the child and little knowledge of child growth and development. They believed that the infant should be toilet trained at 24 weeks and should walk about 40 weeks of age [8]. Other observations have shown that young parents expect the baby to know right from wrong at a very early age. Young parents may slap their baby for assumed misbehavior that is really an expression of curiosity. Young parents are known to be less likely to talk to their infants than are older parents. Crying particularly seems to bother young parents. Some at first treat the infant as a doll.

Infants of young parents are likely to be separated from their parents for substantial periods of the day while one or both parents try to complete school and/or work. This may affect the young parents' attachment to their infant and their view of parenting responsibility. Since the pattern set in caring for the first child is likely to be carried out in subsequent parenting, the first such experience of young parents is most important.

Infants of young parents may be exposed to caregiving by a variety of others. Since so many young families live with the girl's parents, the maternal grandmother often assumes the major part of the supplemental care responsibility. In fact, this is so common that there is a tendency to forget that it is a supplemental care arrangement and that supportive services may be needed.

Conflicts in the home can result from different attitudes, knowledge about and experiences with child-rearing. If information is conveyed to the home by the girl, through literature, by a home visitor program or by inviting the grandmother to participate in learning sessions outside the home, interference with the young mother's caretaking can be lessened. If conflicts with the grandmother are not diminished, the child can become a battleground. Resulting inconsistency in behavior—one gives a pacifier, the other takes it away, for example—can be harmful. The child will not learn in an environment that is strange, hostile or uncaring. For the girl, one way of coping with frustrating conflicts may be to abdicate responsibility for the care of the infant. Another may be to leave home with her infant before other circumstances merit it.

However, this is not to say that all young girls are poor mothers or all home situations are negative. There are some very mature mothering 14-year-olds. Moreover, grandparents often make many adjustments in their lives to enable the young parent to continue in school or work. They become a vital center of support for the young family and carry the burden of helping rear a small child long after that phase of their own life was considered complete.

Numbers of young parents do not have relatives able to assist with child care. They may need help with finding, selecting and paying for substitute care arrangements. They also need to understand that the quality of care being given the infant is their responsibility even if the child is left with another person. The caregiver should be someone able and willing to respect the judgment of a younger person.

In some cities, group infant day care centers have been opened in connection with special school programs for pregnant girls and young mothers. In a few cases they have been developed in connection with regular schools. Such day care centers are seen at times as laboratory training for child development classes in schools. The infant's need for a primary caregiver and continuity of caregiving must not be overlooked in this process. The other point to be aware of is that schools, in some sense, have become holding or storage tanks for the young. The basic skills needed for survival in the world are not being passed on to young parents in many of them. Adding their children to such nonmeaningful situations may be at best a short-sighted solution for young parent families.

Time must be structured for the young parent to be a person in addition to being a parent. Substitute care occasionally should go beyond just the hours in school, so that the adolescent parent can develop the social skills needed for successful living. Group activities for young parents, both with and without their infants, can foster communication about parenting and provide support for young family life.

Above all, as professionals working with young parents, we must keep in mind that we cannot fulfill all our rescue fantasies in relation to the infants. The children are the responsibility of the young parents. Therefore, our job is to support these mothers and fathers as they grow in their parenting tasks. Young parents do have many strengths. They have boundless energy, enthusiasm and the ability to still learn from adults and occurrences around them.

A NEW VIEW OF YOUNG PARENT FAMILIES

To continue to ignore the needs of young parent families will have a profound effect on our lives. The children of today's young parents will be in the school system within 5 short years—with our children, or our grandchildren.

What then must be done? We must change our view of young parents. We must change our ways of relating to them. We must increase our understanding of options and alternatives for serving them. We must think of what we want to be the consequences of our actions.

We cannot continue to see young parents as a problem — a negative element in society — not useful, not welcome, tolerated, handled, dealt with. As young people experience early parenting, we must encourage them. We must also give them freedom to deal with the changes in family life that are occurring, give them the liberty to experiment, make mistakes, try again without guilt.

A pregnant girl from Indianapolis, Indiana, wrote a poem which I included in my recent book, *Only Human: Teenage Pregnancy and Parenthood* [9]. She says so well something that is all too easy for those of us who serve to forget:

No Better Than Me

I am only as human
As nature allows,
Governed by virtues
And morals and vows,
Doomed to be judged
By persons I see,
All in God's eyes
No better than me.

Followed by snickers
And comments and stares,
I try to pretend that
I really don't care,
Carrying a child
That's destined to be
Doomed in their eyes
No better than me.

My mind has matured
As my judgment has grown
I know now I never
Have *once* stood alone
God has opened my eyes
And now I can see
That those who will judge
Are no better than me.

TONIA WELLS

INSTITUTIONAL CHANGE

Really caring means more than just providing quality professional care. It means trying to bring about needed change. This means attitudinal change on the part of the professional community, lay public and, yes, the parents themselves. This means dropping of artificial barriers that produce societally induced handicapping. It means development or utilization of needed services delivered comprehensively. To do this, we must educate and involve the lay community and obtain the commitment and cooperation of the professional community.

So much can be done. But if you who know best the meaning and importance of sound, stable family life, don't do it, who else will? I ask you: Who else will?

REFERENCES

1. Survey of physicians, Ortho Panel, January, 1969.
2. Howard, M.: Comprehensive community programs for the pregnant teenager, Clin. Obstet. Gynecol., Vol. 14, No. 2, June, 1971.
3. Keeve, J. P., *et al.*: Fertility experience of juvenile girls: A community-wide ten-year study, Graduate School of Public Health, University of Pittsburgh, Pittsburgh, Pennsylvania, 1968.
4. Kahn, H., and Briggs, B. B.: *Things to Come* (New York: The Macmillan Company, 1972).
5. Zelnik, M., and Kantner, J. F.: Sexuality, contraception and pregnancy among young unwed females in the United States. Commission on Population Growth and the American Future. News release, May 10, 1972.
6. Fischman, P. H.: Factors affecting the decision of unwed adolescents. Speech before Symposium on the Pregnant Teenager, Chicago, Illinois, 1975.
7. Howard, M.: The Webster School: A District of Columbia Program for Pregnant Girls. Children's Bureau Research Reports #2, U. S. Department of Health, Education, and Welfare, 1968.
8. De Lissovoy, V.: Child care by adolescent parents, Children Today, July-August, 1973.
9. Howard, M.: *Only Human: Teenage Pregnancy and Parenthood* (New York: Seabury Press, 1975).

COMMENTARY

JACK FUENTE (Guidance Counselor in Public High School, Rockville, Md.): In counseling the so-called problem child, with a little research into the child's background I invariably find some kind of family problem, and in as many as 3 out of 4 cases the parents of the problem child have been teen-age parents themselves.

I also find that when girls or boys are planning on early marriage—at 15, 16 or 17—the family picture almost invariably is intolerable, as though "this is a way out for me right now."

Ms. Howard, you were describing for us situations in which we already have teen-age parents, and we have to help them help themselves to be good parents. But what should we do in cases where teen-age marriage is still only a prospect? Can they be just as good parents as anybody else, or is there something we should do besides accept the situation? Should we perhaps discourage what may lead to real problems for future children?

Ms. HOWARD: I do not advocate teen-age or early parenthood. I think that it can be carried off successfully in some cases. Seventy-five per cent of our children graduate from high school. The ultimate competition for jobs and status is just too stiff. Most youngsters would do best to get further education and then do lots of other things before beginning parenting.

There is very little in our society now that prevents teen-age parenthood, because the old forces just don't work any more, such as the exhortation to do right or to be good or fear disapproval (what will so-and-so think?). No longer do we imply "You can't get pregnant after 10 o'clock because you have to be in at 10." Our school systems used to think that if they kicked the girls out of school that would help solve the problem, through not rewarding sin. It never diminished the number of pregnancies.

What we have never openly done is to try to prevent pregnancy by the means available to us. Take sex education for example. We don't really know who is to do it, where they're to do it or what they're to say.

In a national survey just reported from Johns Hopkins (Kantner), teen-age girls were asked what the most likely time of the menstrual cycle might be for becoming pregnant. Ninety-eight per cent said they knew; only 2% said they didn't know. But 50% gave the wrong answer.

The people who are against sex education imagine that they are filling empty bowls, that children don't know anything, and that if you give them information they're going to find out something. On the contrary, what we are really trying to do in sex education is to correct the misinformation that most children have accumulated since the age of 5 or 6. We have never tried to give children the basic facts about how you become pregnant. And we certainly have not given them birth control information in the same environment and with the same support that we have given it to adults.

Young people today do not have emotional support for birth control. One girl put it very well when she said that she wasn't going to use birth control because "If I use birth control, I'm a bad girl." She is acknowledging that she is going to have sex, and knows that society doesn't want her to do that, "but if I don't use it and get pregnant, I'm a good girl who got caught."

251

These are the messages that we're sending to our children. We don't give them appropriate information, nor the tools that we give adults.

I have found that what these kids sometimes need as much as anything is for somebody to say to them that it's just as OK not to have sex as to have it. They respond to peer group pressure in many cases, and they need support for resisting it.

And then we must give them some understanding of what it means to be a parent. In many cases they are trying to escape a terrible home situation and think of pregnancy as a way out, not as a way of fulfilling a love of children.

I think that if we could put these things all together, we would see a diminution of early marriage and parenthood. But we just haven't tried it; until we try, I don't see how we can know whether it's going to work or not.

JOE HOPKINS (Rochester, N. Y.): Ms. Howard, you spoke of the teen-age mother who ends up isolated in an apartment of her own, with no help from her family, and later of the competition that can develop between a teen-age mother and her own mother over babies when she tries to remain in her mother's home and in some ways continue with her life in school, and so on. What do you feel the best place for the teen-age mother is?

Ms. HOWARD: I think there is no one answer. I don't feel very happy about any 15-year-old being out on her own. I'm not even so sure I feel comfortable about 16-, 17- or even 18-year-olds. In some places in this country there has been an attempt to establish group living arrangements for young mothers who have such deteriorated home environments that they must get out. It may be apartment living where duties are shared among the girls. Or there may be house parents provided who can care for the babies when the girls go to work or to school. I think that that kind of peer support system with some adult input is much preferable to a girl living on her own.

What you find in the apartments of some of these young mothers living alone is potato chips and Coke being fed to a 1-year-old. Often the baby eats just when the mother is hungry. There is just nobody there to give support or to encourage them, to help such mothers take delight in or see the joy in their children.

I would much prefer, if possible, that these young persons remain with their own families. Parents and family life are still the most basic supports for young people in our society. Home is an oasis, a jumping-off place. These young girls are going to have some form of relationship with their parents for the rest of their lives, and parents can be supportive. If we can reach out to each home and help with some of the problems, we will do more for mother and baby than if we take her out of the home.

It is not always possible. A grandmother said to me, "My young ones are skipping school and my older ones are taking dope, but she is just pregnant – she doesn't have any problems." Some parents don't see this as the serious problem it is. I think that we must get inputs into such homes.

CAROL GRANT (Public Health Nurse, Baltimore, Md.): Dr. Solnit, could you explore for us again in a different way the future of the nuclear family? What options are there?

DR. SOLNIT: We already know some of the options; for example, the single-parent family. Some single-parent families are a deliberate choice; some result from divorce or from death in the family. I think that the definition of a family as at least 1 parent and 1 or more children is important for us to accept and to support.

Whether it's a nuclear family of 2 parents and a small group of children or 1 parent and children, the problem is in the ways in which families live now, in the ways in which our communities present opportunities for experience. We have to mobilize and make available options for assistance, not only to make up deficits in preparation for parenthood but also to supplement what parents can provide in the care of children. After all, the reason that we are so concerned, whether it's a teen-ager who is pregnant or a single-parent family, is that it's the children who are at risk. It seems to me that we often can provide for fulfillment on the part of the adult or the teen-ager if we can ensure a society that has options for caretaking adults that will help them to take care of their own children without diluting the intensity of their relationships.

It has been some time now since many families could really expect to be completely comprehensive and self-sufficient in raising their children. It is even required in our society that children go to school and that families use school and other kinds of resources within the community to help them raise children who have balance and health.

I would say that the alternative is not really whether you have 1 parent or 2 parents, but whether or not or how we will supplement the responsible adults who wish to take good care of their children. The answers to that will have more to do with shaping and influencing the function of the family unit than anything else. As an affluent society, we have not been very successful in being systematic, thoughtful, imaginative or bold in overcoming some of what Silver calls the pollution of time.

MICHAEL FOX (Baltimore, Md.): My question is addressed to any member of the panel. Assuming that one of the ways in which the community and we as a society can influence this problem is through involving the schools directly, could anybody comment on the advantages and disadvantages of keeping pregnant teen-age children in the mainstream of the school rather than separating them into special schools?

Ms. HOWARD: That is one of the things being debated throughout the United States right now. The original educational programs for pregnant girls pulled them out of their regular classes and into special classes. This was partly because you couldn't get funds to do special things for girls left in regular school.

As school systems became more aware that pregnancy was not contagious and that the girls came back to regular school within a short time anyway, a number of school systems decided to drop their special programs. A number of states even passed laws saying that it was OK for a girl to remain in her regular school classes.

I think the critical thing here is that the girl should have options. I don't think that she should *have* to go one way or another. It's very appropriate for some girls to remain in their regular schools. As a matter of fact, if they're taking special courses, such as advanced calculus, it's terribly difficult to put such special things into a special school program. For other girls, it's very inappropriate that they remain in their regular schools. They may just have too many problems. Some may have to have an irregular schedule because they need to work while they're pregnant; or the conditions surrounding their pregnancies may be such that they need additional support, particularly if they are very young. I am not really very excited about leaving pregnant girls in grade school, nor in junior high school either. They need a lot of support.

An interesting study we have done has begun to show that younger girls are very different from older ones. Recent data supporting this come from Baltimore. As the index of self-esteem in young girls rises, the age at first intercourse also rises. The girl who becomes pregnant under the age of 16, for instance, is less likely to have a meaningful relationship with a boy, is more likely to come from a deteriorated home situation, is more likely to be having problems in school. If you leave such a girl in a regular school, I think there is very little hope of her finishing and very little hope of her solving the problems that are going to contribute to her lack of parenting skills.

ARTHUR GREENWALD (New Haven, Conn.): When young families start out raising children, especially when both parents are professionals or both are working, and when they have increasing demands on their time, what strategies would you recommend for sharing the responsibilities of raising the children, especially when the children are very young?

What about day care at a very early age in a situation where both parents are very busy?

DR. SOLNIT: In terms of the best interest of the child, supposing that economic factors do not require both parents to work simultaneously, there is not much evidence that it's advantageous for a child to be going to day care under the age of 2½ or 3 years. Ideally, in a modern marriage in which both partners have careers, one would like to see the kind of flexibility in which the mother and father would arrange for a schedule that would guarantee that at least one of them is not working full time during the first 2–3 years of the child's life and that the other would have a flexible schedule so that the career choice of the one working part time would be protected.

We have used with some success the kind of day care programs in the home that Pacific Oaks College has used, but we've used them in a clustered situation in New Haven. The young child is left only 3 or 4 hours a day while the mother or the father, whichever is on the part-time basis (and usually it's the mother), is enabled to continue on a part-time basis with teaching or research or graduate student activity.

One of the things that a young child needs is that our institutions bend and not penalize young women for being part time, either as professionals or as students. There are many men, though I think they are a minority, who enjoy taking care of young children and are well prepared for it; in those instances, they ought to be able to take on part-time activity, or to alternate years of full-time activity with the wife, so long as those two have a satisfying agreement and are able to work out some kind of alternation that puts the interests of the young child before those of their own careers or of their own needs. I think we can all agree that it is the child who is particularly vulnerable and at risk when this kind of effort is made to explore such more imaginative and flexible family arrangements as may allow everyone to have what is important for him or her.

As for advice: one, stay away from big day care centers; two, try to keep the very young child at home; three, use home day care centers a few hours a day, with small groups of children, such as 2 or 3, in instances where one parent is employed part time and the other parent is flexible. That would be the best our present knowledge can tell us about what would be in the best interest of the child.

23

The Role of the Parent: Problems and Prospects

Sarane Spence Boocock, Ph.D.

Sociologist, Russell Sage Foundation, New York, New York, and Visiting Associate Professor of Sociology, Yale University, New Haven, Connecticut

It is not news to any parent that raising children is hard work, although the unending flow of advice from experts on child-rearing often seems to overlook this basic fact. A review of historical research suggests that parents have, throughout history, gotten out of as much work as possible (see, for example, Aries [1] and de Mause [7]). The care and education of children has also been problematic to societies as a whole. This is partly because the work is difficult and partly because of the low status generally accorded to those who work with children compared to those who work with money, power and/or ideas.

However, each time and place has its own unique problems with respect to the care and socialization of the young. This chapter will discuss the combination of social trends, unique to modern industrialized societies, that seem to be making it especially difficult to be a parent.

One of the major problems in this country is that the costs of raising children have gone up steeply. In the early years of this country, each additional child born into a family represented an additional hand with the harvest or additional insurance of future support for a parent. By contrast, a child is now a large cost both to his parents and to the community. A study commissioned by the U. S. Commission on Population Growth and the American Future estimated that the cost of raising 1 child in the United States to age 18 is $34,464. This figure goes up to $98,361 if one adds a college education and an estimate of the wages the mother "lost" by taking care of a child instead of holding a paying job. The study concludes: "Having a child will not only mean giving up one life style for another, but also potentially giving up one standard of living for another" (Reed and McIntosh [21], p. 342).

The status and treatment of children have also been affected by changes in

NOTE: The research reported here has been supported by grants from the U. S. Office of Child Development and from the Russell Sage Foundation.

adult sex roles, changes in the structure and functioning of the family and changes in the pattern of life course or life cycle transitions and in the pattern of relationships between the young and old.

CHANGES IN SEX ROLES THAT DOWNGRADE PARENTHOOD AND CHILD-REARING

It is difficult to construct an image of the "traditional" role of the parent unbiased by analysts' opinions about what family life *should* be like. Historical analysis suggests that the American parent role has been characterized by, on one hand, virtually total responsibility for the care and supervision of children and, on the other hand, relatively limited authority. "Only when a child reached age six did society at large take a major hand by insisting that he attend school and by providing schools at the taxpayers' expense. What happens to the child the rest of the time is his parents' business. Society intervenes only if he is severely abused or neglected or runs afoul of the law" (Schultze *et al.* [24], p. 253). At the same time, the dynamic, individualistic nature of American society gave family life a relatively temporary quality that limited the authority of parents. European visitors to America in the eighteenth and nineteenth centuries noted not only that American children were indulged and had a position of relative equality and a say in family affairs that would have been unthinkable in Europe, but that American parents "give very little advice to their children and let them learn for themselves" (from Rousiers, *La Vie Americaine,* quoted in Sorel [25], p. 89).

Until recently, however, Americans have at least given lip service to the cliché that the presence of children strengthens the family. Now that central assumption seems to be in question. Data gathered during the past two decades show rather consistently that the presence of children has a negative rather than a positive effect on the husband-wife relationship. Members of childless marriages report greater marital satisfaction than those with children; among marriages with children, the greater the number of children the lower the satisfaction reported by the parents; and, on a variety of marital satisfaction indices, satisfaction drops sharply with the birth of the first child, sinks even lower during the school years and goes up markedly only after the exit of the last child (Campbell, Converse and Rodgers [5]).

One explanation for the current discontinuities in the parent role is that life in most areas of our society does not allow young people to experience the expectations and tasks of parenthood before they actually take on the role. (It should also be noted that parenthood is one of the few adult roles that can be taken on without presenting any kind of "credentials.") Our small nuclear families and increasingly age-segregated residential communities do not allow potential parents opportunities to observe young children or to communicate regularly with older persons with extensive parenting experience. By contrast with a society like Sweden, where boys and girls, from elementary school years, have classes in sex education, home maintenance, child care and the dynamics of family life (Linner [19]), American schools offer little in the way of practical education in subjects relevant to family life. What preparation for parenthood exists during pregnancy is dependent on the initiative of the parents-to-be and is largely confined to reading and informal consultation with friends. As Rossi [22] points out, the most concrete action most parents-to-be take is to prepare the baby's room. The birth of the child thus constitutes an abrupt transition rather than a gradual taking on of the responsibilities of a new role. There is a flood of advice from "experts" on every aspect of child development and care, but the very existence of so much expertise may discourage rather than reassure the new parent, since it sets such a high level of expectations for their role performance. A recent review of a number of child care books (Bane [2]) concludes that most assume "enormous amounts of good will and understanding" on the part of parents, and perhaps demand "more time and energy than most people have, and thus unwittingly contribute to parental anxiety and guilt."

Another explanation is that the responsibilities and skills involved in caring for young children are increasingly in conflict with other things adults value, both within and outside marriage. Among the findings of the Detroit Area Study is that proportionately more women in the 1970s than in the 1950s said that companionship with husband was the most valuable part of marriage (60% in 1971 compared to 48% in 1955); fewer said that their prime motive in marriage was the chance to have children (26% in 1955 to 13% in 1971, Duncan *et al.* [9], p. 8). This seems to reflect a separation of the love-companionship aspects of marriage from the child-rearing aspects, with the presence of children having a negative rather than a positive effect on the former. Certainly the self-development that is an important component of an individualistic society is at variance with the constant attention and the frequent selflessness required in the nurturance of babies and young children. Likewise, the youthfulness and glamour that are so valued for both sexes in America are inconsistent with child-rearing.

Finally, parenthood may bring to the surface unresolved, and even unrecognized, conflicts about the appropriate roles of men and women. However much in principle the couple may value sexual equalitarianism, the arrival of a child means that someone must be available 24 hours a day to care for it. It seems unlikely that current difficulties in the relationships between men and women in our society will be resolved until questions concerning both the value of children and the locus of responsibility for their routine care and supervision are acknowledged and resolved.

In addition to the problems peculiar to the parent role in general, the mother and father roles have unique problems related to changes in sex roles in our society. Probably the most significant change in the pattern of women's lives is the ever-growing propensity of women with children to work outside the home (now a majority of American women with school-age children and about a third of mothers of preschoolers).

Although the percentages of women in the labor force at various phases of the life cycle vary from one country to another, what seems to be generally true is that working mothers do have double work loads—they do their paid work *in addition to* carrying the major burdens of housework and child care. In a survey of working mothers in 4 Communist and 6 non-Communist countries conducted in 1972 and 1973 by Alice Cook, it was found that neither employers nor husbands were doing much to ease this double load. In every country:

"working mothers responded to the question, 'what kind of help do you most need?' almost without exception by asking first for more and improved child care and then for opportunities to work part-time. It was quickly clear in most interviews that they were not thinking only of the pre-school child and of so-called child care centers. They were asking for before- and after-school care, for care of sick children, and for some coverage for school vacations and holidays that cannot be meshed with work schedules (Cook [6], p. 30).

A second important kind of change in women's lives is in their orientation toward motherhood itself. Theorists of all branches of the women's movement have argued that the primary reason for women's second-class status is their responsibility for children, and as women come to think more highly of themselves, it is predictable that they will be less willing to perform the tasks in the society that carry less weight and prestige, including the more tedious aspects of child care.

The effect on children of their mother's employment has been heatedly debated, the claims more often based on the writer's personal biases than on any substantial body of empirical evidence. There are some Swedish studies showing no substantial or consistent differences in either school achievement or social adjustment between children whose mothers work outside the home and those who do not, although there are more problems if the mother has to work for economic reasons than if she is working for "professional enthusiasm" (Leijon [16], p. 98). The most thorough analyses of the available American research (Hoffman and Nye [11]; Lein [17]) conclude that there is no unequivocal evidence that outside employment of mothers affects children favorably or unfavorably. "So many other factors enter into the picture—social class, full-time versus part-time employment, age and sex of the child, and the mother's attitude toward the employment—that the impact of employment per se is lost in the shuffle" (Bernard [4], p. 78).

The role of the father has received relatively little attention in the sociologic literature. The most recent full-length sociologic analysis (Benson [3]) notes that the father role links the family with the larger society, and has been the embodiment within the family of the social control function. Until recently he has not had much to do with the housekeeping and child-rearing functions. Benson also points out the distinction between biologic and social fatherhood, and notes that these two functions have not always been filled by the same man. The latter was a social invention that has taken a variety of forms in different societies. Children have been raised in the home of their mother's relatives, and have been provided for by their uncles, stepfathers and older brothers as well as by their biologic fathers. Benson concluded that: "The biological father, the progenitor, is not as important as the social or nurturant father precisely because the latter has a family role to play after conception" (Benson [3], p. 44).

One of the problems in the United States and other industrialized societies is that the social father role is not being filled in many families by the biologic father or any other male. In 1970, about 10% of all children under age 14 were being raised in families in which the father was absent (White House Conference on Children, 1970, pp. 22 and 141), and this figure now is over 15%. Although some of these children undoubtedly have meaningful relationships with other men other than their biologic fathers, studies of lower class "streetcorner" men, such as Liebow's *Talley's Corner* [18] and Hannerz's *Soulside* [10] show how peripheral these men are to the lives of children. One explanation for the streetcorner man's lack of welcome in the homes where their children are raised is that they have failed to achieve occupational status and security. Unlike the mother's, the father's position in the family is strongly related to his position in systems outside the family. Komarovsky's study of unemployed blue collar workers [14] showed how the loss of a man's job led to the decline of his position vis-à-vis his wife and children.

Although there have been some recent pleas for a "return to fatherhood" in this country, it is not possible, with the currently available research, to conclude whether fatherhood was a more fully developed role in the past. It is true that households and communities in which a man's work was typically in or near his home allowed a father to be in contact with his children more often during the normal course of a workday than in our present metropolitan areas, where the place of work usually is at a distance from home (and the time added to the workday by commuting often cancels out any time advantages won by the trend toward shorter hours of work). However, the distance imposed by the more authoritarian character of the father role in the past may have outweighed the advantages gained by mere physical proximity. It should also be noted that the call for greater activation of the father role can be differently interpreted. Male writers calling for a "return to fatherhood" usually are expressing nostalgia for the undisputed authority of the male head of the household attributed to the traditional families of the past. Women, on the other hand, usually are asking not for a return to a form of family life perceived by them as oppressive for both women and children but rather (a) for men to show more interest in and affection for young children and (b) for a more equitable distribution of the more onerous duties involved in caring for them.

Rhetoric to the contrary, there is little evidence of a strong trend toward male caretakers of young children. The few well-publicized cases of "paternity leave," where fathers have won the right to spend more time at home caring for their children without the loss of their job or its fringe benefits, have so far been limited to a few occupations, such as teaching, that allow relatively flexible working schedules. Mirra Komarovsky's studies of American college men indicate that although many give lip service to the general principle of equality and liberation for women, most assume that *their* future wife will stay home with the children during their preschool years and arrange her working schedule around their school hours if she later goes to work. "Though they are willing to aid their wives in varying degrees, they frequently excluded specific tasks; for instance, 'not the laundry,' 'not the cleaning,' 'not the diapers,' and so on" (Komarovsky [13], p. 879).

The most extensive changes have occurred in Scandinavian countries. For example, Swedish corporations and agencies allow men to work less than full time in order to share domestic responsibilities with their wives, and it now is Swedish policy to recruit men into day care center positions by such means as favoring male applicants for day care training programs. These policies are so new that their results cannot yet be documented. In interviews conducted with Swedish government officials and social scientists by the author in 1973, it was reported that few men had taken advantage of the "opportunity" to share household responsibilities, and visits to about 24 day care centers revealed few male employees, never more than 1 to a center, and most of these were conscientious objectors or older men who were for some reason unemployed (Boocock [4a]).

In sum, the ideology concerning the role of the father does seem to be changing in modern societies, but there still is a large gap between the rhetoric of a more active, equalitarian role and the actual behavior of men in the role. Nor do we have the institutional arrangements that would allow—and motivate—men to change their role behavior. Women, on the other hand, no longer feel that they should be solely responsible for the day-to-day care of young children, work that in the past has always been done by the persons with relatively low status in the society. Thus, whether or not one views the relationships between men and women as "political," there is a clear conflict of interest between the sexes with regard to the allocation of child care responsibilities.

CHANGES IN THE STRUCTURE AND FUNCTIONING OF THE FAMILY

Social historians such as Peter Laslett and John Demos have in recent years been reconstructing the size and structure of households in the past, and their findings contradict some of our romantic notions about the way families "used to be." Large extended families have always been rare. Laslett's research on the pre-industrial family in England [15] shows an average family size of about 5 for over 3 centuries, with few households larger than a dozen. It is true, though, that households used to contain apprentices, servants and other persons not related by blood. They were also more likely to contain children of a greater range of ages and the male head of the household, since his work often was in or near the home.

As economists have pointed out, the care of young children, an activity that requires full-time availability but not full-time attention and action, is most "efficiently" carried out in a setting in which other activities are also being carried out. The American home during the colonial and frontier periods was such a setting. "As long as other activities are going on in the household—cleaning, cooking, or specialized activity for sale on the market, like working on the family farm—the extra time cost of having children around is less than it would be for an organization specializing in child care. Besides time, the space needed for child care often is costless in the home where it is needed anyway (for sleeping, cooking, etc.)" (Nelson and Krashinsky [20], p. 3).

In sum, although there is no evidence that homes in the past were consciously organized for the care of children—in fact, children were less likely to be considered full human beings worthy of love and care than they are now (Aries [1]; de Mause [7])—the economic and other functions of the home necessitated an organization that, at the same time, ensured that a number of persons were available to share in looking after children. Most of these functions have been lost to the family and, at the same time, the close of the frontier, the decrease in the proportion of the population engaged in farming and the enactment of compulsory education and child labor laws have removed many arrangements outside the home that relieved parents of some of the burdens of child-rearing.

Intensive case studies of American families (e.g., the interviews of middle income Boston-area families conducted by Lein [17]) reveal that many families are experiencing a great deal of stress in trying to coordinate their work and child care activities and express considerable anxiety about the kind of job they are doing as parents. Although the 2-parent nuclear family still is considered the norm in this country, there is, in fact, a good deal of variation in family structure, some of it a response to difficulties in fulfilling the responsibilities of parenthood. Over 15% of the children in the United States are in 1-parent households (this percentage is much higher in cities and among certain racial-ethnic subgroups) and at least another 5% are in households with several adults. The latter includes everything from communes and other pseudofamilial arrangements to extended families, both of which young parents often join in the hopes of getting help with the care of children. The 5% figure probably is an underestimate, but such households are hard to enumerate accurately, since people in such situations often are vague or evasive to interviewers (Benjamin Zablocki, personal communications).

CHANGES IN LIFE CYCLE PATTERNS AND TRANSITIONS

Sociologists studying age and life cycle patterns are particularly interested in life cycle *transitions* — i.e., important turning points when the individual moves from one stage or stratum to another. All such transitions produce some problems, but there probably are none in our society today as stressful as the transition to motherhood. In simpler societies, there generally are rituals surrounding the transition to motherhood plus the assumption of a new status, which often means greater prestige and freedom from some tedious housekeeping tasks. Among middle class Americans, by contrast, the transition to motherhood is most often problematic because of a conflict in norms held by the mother and because of a conflict between life expectations and possibilities for fulfillment of these within the role of motherhood. In pre-industrial times and in many agricultural societies today where the extended family still is prevalent, full development of women's personalities through active participation in adult social, economic and family life is the norm. However, for more than a century, the woman's role in Western society has been limited primarily to the family function. Experiences during World War II showed that women could indeed still perform both familial and extrafamilial functions well. Thus, in the past few decades, there has been a dramatic change in the social reality and opportunity for women. This entrance of women into important sectors of the social scene, however, has complicated the transition to motherhood by introducing many new norms to govern women's varied new roles, which vie for pre-eminence with the norm of motherhood as the normal, natural and joyful lot of women. Fulfillment through others (i.e., children and husbands) no longer is the only means of fulfillment for women.

Women's liberation, even in its most rudimentary form, results in an acute dilemma for many young women. Contemporary woman is socialized to expect equality of opportunity. Having been educated and usually having worked for several years, she has become accustomed to financial and social independence. On reaching the childbearing stage, however, she usually must make a choice between her career and her maternal role. If she chooses not to become a mother, she subjects herself to criticism, since motherhood has great normative value in our society.

On the other hand, if she chooses to become a mother, the transition is a particularly difficult one, for, in all likelihood, her most recent social role as a member of the work force has inculcated in her norms in direct conflict with those governing maternity. The norm of independence will compete with the reality of a very dependent infant. The mother may lose her status as an equal within the marriage, since the actual chores of motherhood are classed with housework and are held in very low esteem. Since she is out of the labor force and has entered a state of relative social isolation, she will be reliant on others for her social identity and fulfillment. This social fact of motherhood, however, is becoming increasingly less normative for society in general as women's roles change rapidly. The transition to motherhood is difficult for those women who have desired, planned for and properly timed their new role. It may be insupportable for someone for whom the timing is inappropriate. Thus, in the past few years, there has been a wide-scale recognition of the potential social problems involved in the transition to motherhood, and there has been a tremendous demand for a means of controlling the timing of maternity, through both contraception and abortion (Kertzer [12], pp. 6–8).

The age stratification system in our society produced further difficulties. Persons of different ages have unequal opportunities and responsibilities. The youngest and oldest age strata have comparatively little power and responsibility, comparatively great amounts of leisure and are increasingly segregated in age-homogeneous institutions and other settings. Parenthood, however, comes during the middle years of the life cycle, when responsibilities in many areas are the heaviest and leisure most scarce. Unlike the pre-industrial family, which typically contained persons from a cross section of the stages of the life cycle, the model nuclear family is now limited to husband and wife (when both are present), usually near each other in age, and a couple of children, also near each other in age and separated from their parents by a generation gap! Ironically, this miniature two-generation unit places a heavy burden on the parents, especially the mother, since there is no one to share in such tasks as looking after young children.

SUMMARY

In sum, there seems to be a good deal of ambivalence and conflict surrounding the parent role. We are just beginning to examine, and question, people's motives for becoming parents, and many of them are not conducive to the welfare of children. Marion Howard's work with teen-age mothers suggests that many of these girls see having a baby as a "way out" or a way of filling an otherwise impoverished life. Suzanne Keller, a sociologist at Princeton University, has said that the most common reason for having children is a need to conform. As a society, we still pretty much insist that everyone become a parent—or be prepared to defend themselves if they don't—though we do less than any other industrialized society to share the burdens of child-rearing.

Finally, it seems that many of our well-meaning attempts to create social policy and programs to help the family are hindered by our tendency to attack the problems of one age stratum with too little consideration of the implications for other strata. For example, many of the statements made by government officials and child care professionals about what we "must" do for children imply that making life better for children will automatically improve things for adults, or at least not be costly to them. Research reported in this chapter indicates that, on the contrary, the ever-rising level of expectations for the care and education of children, not to mention the well-documented rise in the costs of bearing and rearing children, is in conflict with the interests of increasing numbers of adults. Women in particular are displaying greater interest in self-development and in modes of life that are not consistent with even greater investment of time and energy in childbearing and childrearing. Moreover, there are studies (e.g., Ruderman [23]) showing that different sectors of our society (parents, day care professionals, labor leaders, businessmen, clergymen, etc.) hold widely differing views about the locus of responsibility for children and what constitutes adequate care. The general point is that policy issues in this area cannot even be formulated accurately, let alone resolved, unless one is willing to consider how a given child care program or arrangement will affect men, women and children, the childless as well as those engaged in childrearing.

REFERENCES

1. Aries, P.: *Centuries of Childhood* (New York: Alfred A. Knopf, Inc., 1962).
2. Bane, M. J.: A review of child care books, Harvard Educational Review 43:667, 1973.
3. Benson, L.: *Fatherhood: A Sociological Perspective* (New York: Random House, Inc., 1968).
4. Bernard, J.: *The Future of Marriage* (New York: World Publishing Company, 1972).
4a. Boocock, S. S.: A Crosscultural Analysis of the Child Care System. Final Report to the U. S. Department of Health, Education, and Welfare, Office of Child Development.
5. Campbell, A., Converse, P., and Rodgers, W.: *The Perceived Quality of Life* (New York: Russell Sage Foundation, 1975).
6. Cook, A. H.: *The Working Mother: A Survey of Problems and Programs in Nine Countries* (New York: New York State School of Industrial and Labor Relations, Cornell University, 1975).
7. de Mause, L.: *The History of Childhood* (New York: Psychohistory Press, 1974).
8. de Shalit, N.: Children in War, in Jarus, A., *et al.* (eds.), *Children and Families in Israel* (New York: Gordon and Breach, Science Publishers, Inc., 1970), pp. 151–182.
9. Duncan, O. D., *et al.: Social Change in a Metropolitan Community* (New York: Russell Sage Foundation, 1973).
10. Hannerz, U.: *Soulside: Inquiries into Ghetto Culture and Community* (New York: Columbia University Press, 1969).
11. Hoffman, L. W., and Nye, F. I.: *Working Mothers* (San Francisco: Jossey-Bass, Inc., Publishers, 1974).
12. Kertzer, S.: The Transition to Motherhood. Department of Sociology and Anthropology, Bowdoin College. Unpublished paper, 1975.
13. Komarovsky, M.: Cultural contradictions and sex roles: The masculine case, Am. J. Sociol. 78:873, 1973.
14. Komarovsky, M.: *Unemployed Man and His Family* (New York: Octagon Books, 1971).
15. Laslett, P.: *The World We Have Lost* (2d ed.; New York: Charles Scribner's Sons, 1971).
16. Leijon, A.-G.: *Swedish Women—Swedish Men* (Stockholm: Swedish Institute for Cultural Relations, 1968).
17. Lein, L.: *Families, Institutions and Child Development* (Cambridge, Mass.: Center for the Study of Public Policy, 1974).
18. Liebow, E.: *Tally's Corner* (Boston: Little, Brown & Company, 1966).
19. Linner, B.: *Sex and Society in Sweden* (New York: Pantheon Books, Inc., 1967).
20. Nelson, R. R., and Krashinsky, M.: Public Control and the Economic Organization of Day Care for Young Children. Yale University, Institute for Social and Policy Studies. Mimeographed paper, 1972.

21. Reed, R. H., and McIntosh, S.: Costs of Children, in Morss, E. R., and Reed, R. H. (eds.), *Economic Aspects of Population Change,* Volume 2 of the Commission of Population Growth and the American Future Research (Washington, D.C.: U.S. Government Printing Office, 1972). pp. 333–350.
22. Rossi, A.: Transition to parenthood, J. Marriage and the Family 30:26, 1968.
23. Ruderman, F. A.: *Child Care and Working Mothers* (New York: Child Welfare League of America, 1968).
24. Schultze, C., *et al: Setting National Priorities: The 1973 Budget* (Washington, D.C.: The Brookings Institution, 1972).
25. Sorel, G.: *Reflections on Violence* (London: Collier-Macmillan, Ltd., 1950).

Part VII

Special Problems of Adolescence: Parents, Children and Institutions

24

Cognitive Frames and Family Interactions

David Elkind, Ph.D.

*Professor of Psychology, University of
Rochester, Rochester, New York*

In contemporary sociology, the concept of a "frame" is used in several different senses. As employed by Basil Bernstein [1], "frame" and "framing" have to do with the structuring of the environment. For example, the office of a clinician practicing behavior modification would be differently framed from that of a clinician who employs psychoanalysis. One might expect the office of the behavior modifier to be relatively plain and the office of the psychoanalyst to be relatively rich in terms of furniture, paintings, plants and the like. In this sense, framing helps set the tone for the kind of interpersonal interaction that will take place in the particular environment. Although Bernstein's concept of framing is of relevance to clinical work, it is not the sense in which frame will be employed in this chapter.

Rather, the term frame will be employed as Erving Goffman [2] uses it in his book, *Frame Analysis*. For Goffman, the frame is not a surface structure, as it is for Bernstein, but rather a deep structure. It is the set of rules, expectancies and understandings that regulate human behavior in repetitive social situations that Goffman calls social encounters. For Goffman, much of human behavior is situationally determined, but this does not mean that it is casual or accidental. Rather, Goffman's point is that even momentary social situations are highly structured and that these structures play a very important part in human behavior.

Although Goffman's concept of frame is more general than Bernstein's, it remains relatively ahistorical. It is, to use a favorite phrase of Jean Piaget, "a structuralism without a genesis" [3]. In this chapter I will try to add some genetic considerations to the concept of frame. That is to say, assuming that frames operate in the way Goffman says they do, how are they constructed or reconstructed by children in the course of their development? And, more important from a clinical point of view, what part does children's understanding of frames, or their lack of it, play in their everyday behavior, particularly in their family interactions? These are the questions for which this chapter will attempt to supply some early, tentative answers. But first we will have to look at the nature of frames in a little more detail.

THE NATURE OF FRAMES

In the everyday life of the child there are many repetitive social encounters, some with adults, some with children and some with children and adults. Each of these encounters has its own sets of rules, expectancies and understandings that serve to make the encounter successful, or those involved to attain their respective ends. Each social encounter involves a social equilibrium that all members seek to maintain. Disruptions of the equilibrium usually are not catastrophic, but they often are socially uncomfortable. Frames, then, are basic units of social interactions, and the understanding of frames is an important part of every child's socialization.

To make the concept of frame concrete, consider the adult-child frame of "bedtime." When a parent suggests that it is time to go to bed, this elicits characteristic frame behavior. Parents expect children to resist their edict, but are prepared to permit some token resistance so long as the command is obeyed eventually. Children, too, know that it is all right to protest, to argue, but only up to a certain point. Sometimes, of course, the frame rules may be broken. The parent may be in no mood for fun and games and demand immediate obedience. Or the child may go to bed without protest (and baffle his parents)or put up a violent, uncompromising fight.

Violations of frame rules are important because they make the implicit frame rules manifest and because they illustrate, as Goffman suggests, that each frame has its own emotional rhythm. When a frame rule is broken, so too is the emotional rhythm, and some "remedial work" has to be done to complete the emotional cycle of the frame. For example, suppose a child goes to bed without protest. This "spoils" the rhythm for the parent who is prepared to deal with a little bit of rebellion. In its absence, the parent is almost forced to provoke it and may say, "You mean you are not going to give me a hard time? I can't believe it." In effect, the "going to bed" frame provides the parent an opportunity for verbal banter; when the child's resistance does not provide the occasion for the banter, his nonresistance becomes the occasion. Without the "banter," the ritual is "spoiled" for the parent and for the child.

Children, and adults, can be put into frames by different sorts of cues. Sometimes a setting is sufficient to cue a frame. A public library is a case in point. The setting cues a "keep quiet" frame that involves talking in whispers, walking quietly and elaborate efforts not to disturb others who are in the setting. If anyone should violate these frame rules, the looks of recrimination and the librarian's reprimands usually suffice to punish the offender and to restore the frame's equilibrium.

Frames can also be cued by particular activities. The "going to bed" frame described earlier is but one of many activity frames. "Lunchtime" at school is an interesting frame because many of the rules about talking and moving around are more relaxed than in the classroom. In addition, of course, the lunchroom "setting" adds to the cuing of this frame behavior. And, in general, frame cues usually are multiple rather than singular and, as in the case of the "lunchroom" frame, reinforce one another as signals for particular behavior patterns.

Some frames are cued by certain people. Just about everyone has a favorite person who exudes happiness and enjoyment of life. When such a person enters the room, a new frame comes into play wherein the other participants can be more free, more open in their expressions and language. Such individuals often bring out the latent wit, good humor and human concern of otherwise dour people. In the presence of such vital personalities, other individuals feel permitted to be more alive themselves. The same is true for children who recognize, in the presence of a favorite uncle or aunt, that they can behave in ways not usually permitted or condoned by their parents. The reverse is also true, however, and some puritan personalities signal a "best behavior" frame.

Finally, frames can be cued by emotional moods and attitudes. Children learn to read these cues very early in their careers as offspring. Take, for example, the "asking for things" frame. Children learn early that to initiate the "asking for things" frame when the parent is angry or upset may not be worth the gamble. On the other hand, when the parent is in a good mood, initiating an "asking" frame carries little risk. Even if the parent refuses the request, it is likely to be done with good humor. Of course, a child may initiate an "asking" frame when the parent is in a bad humor, just to get the parent's goat. A child's understanding of frame cues thus has offensive as well as defensive possibilities.

The foregoing description of frames and frame behavior is far from being an exhaustive one. It may convey the general concept of frames and their pervasiveness in the child's everyday life. In any case, an important part of socialization is the construction or reconstruction of frames on the part of the child. It is to this issue of how children come to comprehend frames that we now turn.

THE DEVELOPMENT OF FRAME BEHAVIOR

From a developmental point of view, the child's understanding of frames is dependent both on the child's level of cognitive development and on the social circumstances to which he is exposed. A young child of 3 or 4 may, for example, not comprehend a "gift-taking" frame because he cannot construct the "equivalence rules" that would allow him to identify new "gift-taking frames " as such. A young child's failure to learn to say "thank you" in gift-taking frames does not speak to his perverseness so much as it does to the difficulty inherent in learning frame rules and frame cues.

The same holds true for the frames learned in childhood and adolescence. It is my thesis that at least some of the behavior typically ascribed to adolescent "rebellion" and "*Sturm und Drang*" may, in part at least, reflect the difficulty the young adolescent has in dealing with the many new frames and frame rules he is expected to abide by. And, perhaps more important, the adolescent is expected to respond in new ways to old frames and to give up some old frames entirely. Not surprisingly, frame cues in these situations are very ambiguous. Hence, the young adolescent, no less than the preschool child, may "misbehave" not out of perverseness, but rather because of the ambiguity of the frame rules that are in play.

But an individual's life circumstances also determine his understanding of frame rules. There are, for example, many frames associated with travel, such as with eating in restaurants, that are learned by children of well-to-do parents but not by those who cannot afford to travel or to eat out. Social class differences in the understanding of frames go far beyond matters of sophistication in eating and travel. There are very real differences in the kinds of frames and frame rules to which children in different social classes are exposed. At least some of the difficulties that middle class teachers encounter in dealing with the children from low income families come from the different frames within which they are operating.

Quite aside from social class differences, the social world of all young people expands as they grow older, and the more social circumstances they encounter the more new frames they must learn. The elementary school child, for example, has to learn all the frames associated with public school, sitting in class, eating in the cafeteria, etc. The adolescent has to learn frames associated with dating, jobs, clubs and social occasions such as dances and parties.

How are these frames acquired or reconstructed? My guess is that, for the most part, they are acquired in a very practical way, through participation in frames and through the processes of social correction that operate in frames themselves. This practical learning, it needs to be said, involves a complex system of cognitive operations that nonetheless remains unconscious. The extent of this "intellective unconscious" was demonstrated by Piaget [4]. In his book, he showed that children could, for example, construct a house of cards long before they could understand, at the conceptual level, the complex physical principles required in building such edifices. At the level of practice, the child "understood" the difficult principles, although he could not verbalize them until much later. The situation is really not different from the excellent therapist who has trouble articulating what it is he or she does. What the therapist does clearly involves many intricate, intercoordinated skills, but the therapist may not be aware of all or even part of the process he or she employs with a patient. Children, I believe, learn to behave in frames in much the same way, through practical experience. After this long prologue, it is time to look at what "frame analysis" can tell us about the interactions of adolescents and their families.

FRAME ANALYSIS OF ADOLESCENTS AND THEIR FAMILIES

At the outset, it is important to distinguish between frames and social roles. A frame is dictated by the social situation, by the nature of the interaction. In a given frame, all individuals operate according to the same rules. A role, in contrast, is dictated by certain functions to be performed or carried out and the behaviors usually associated with those functions. In general, roles are ascribed to persons whereas frames are ascribed to places and events.

In the discussion regarding the construction of frames it was suggested that the period of adolescence constitutes a difficult period with respect to frame behavior. For one thing, adolescents must give up participation in some familiar and pleasant child-adult frames. For another, he or she must learn new rules for familiar frames. In addition to these difficulties, frame behavior is made more difficult because of the adolescent's new cognitive abilities—what Piaget calls formal operations. Thanks to formal operations, adolescents become aware of frame rules and begin to use them for their own purpose. In addition, their new awareness of frame rules makes them supersensitive to violations, particularly on the part of their parents. Some examples of these various difficulties of frame behavior in adolescence can be given.

It is simply a fact that some frames must be given up as children mature. Trick-or-treating on Halloween is a frame in point. In the trick-or-treat frame, as everyone recalls, the child wears a costume, rings the bell and politely says "trick-or-treat." Within moments, the adult puts a sweet in the bag, the child says "thank you" and the frame is terminated. But the frame holds only for children and adults, not adolescents and adults. The gangling adolescent who puts on a sheet and goes ringing doorbells may get gentle – or not so gentle – reprimands. It is only when he is an adult (or older adolescent) that the young person can enter the trick-or-treat frame from the other end.

Some frames undergo a subtle transformation as young people mature. The "going to bed" frame, for example, is progressively transformed into a "don't stay out late" frame. The emphasis no longer is on being in bed but rather on being in the house at a certain time. Again, parents expect a little resistance and young people often stay out just a little longer than the time limit. The ritual is spoiled if the parent becomes too adamant about the young person being home "on the dot" or by the young person who arrives in the early hours of the morning without a "salable" story.

In addition to these changes in familiar frames, adolescents also begin to think about other people's thinking, about motivations and about the rules of social interaction. Much like Piaget's children, who could build a house of cards as children but understand what they are doing only as adolescents, so children behave according to frames but become conscious of frame behavior only as adolescents. This makes possible a whole new level of frame behavior that Goffman refers to as "strategic interactions." In strategic interactions, young people deliberately exploit frame rules to attain their own ends.

Consider the adolescent who comes to appreciate his English teacher's "embarrassment" frame. She likes to choose young people who have not done the required reading in order to embarrass them before the class. This adolescent makes it a point to raise his hand on occasion and always to know the answer when he does. After these frame rules are established, he can raise his hand and be assured that the teacher will not call on him because she is sure that he knows the answer. Used on occasion, this procedure of raising the hand can protect him when in fact he does *not* know the answer.

In family interactions, similar strategic games are played every day. The adolescent girl who wants to go to a dance that her parents might question, arranges a date for a friend whom her parents respect because she knows that they will say, "Well, if Ellen is going, I am sure it is all right." Young people who have chores to do, such as cleaning their rooms or doing the dishes, keep some homework in abeyance so that when parents ask them to do the chores, there is homework to be done and no time for chores. "You don't want me to fail, do you?" reflects the adolescent's keen awareness of parents' frame priorities.

A somewhat different method of strategically employing frames involves what Goffman calls "the management of expressive control." Young people are particularly good at this, in contradiction to children who have trouble keeping a straight face when they are deliberately telling a tall story. But, adolescents can lie with great conviction and can put on an amazing performance. As a young clinician, I saw an adolescent delinquent for over a year. Although the young man occasionally described some questionable behavior, he never really told the truth about his activities, which came to light only after a year in therapy. Skill at management of impressions can aid adolescents in undermining adult "honesty" frame expectations.

Of course the young adolescent's awareness of frames can work to his or her detriment as well. In social situations, such as asking for a date, talking to someone in the lunchroom and so on, the adolescent may say something not appropriate to the frame, then realize it and castigate himself or herself unmercifully. Thus, the new awareness of frames that comes about thanks to Piaget's formal operations can give rise to new forms of guilt and embarrassment quite unknown to elementary school children.

Part of frame behavior is giving to others a certain impression of self; and young people, and adults as well, often torture themselves when their behavior inadvertently gives the impression opposite to the one that they wish to convey. Examples of such spoiled frames are familiar enough. The young man who trips while bringing refreshments to his date spoils the impression of male cool and control necessary to the "romantic" frame that was in play. The young lady who inadvertently gets a very visible run in her hose when wearing a short skirt finds that her attempts at a well-dressed appearance have been undermined by bad luck. The frames within which young people interact often involve giving certain impressions, and the frames are spoiled when the impressions are not effective.

In family interactions, the adolescent's sensitivity to frames is turned toward parents. Recognizing that surface appearance is an important part of frame behavior, the adolescent becomes hypercritical of parents, of their dress, their manner of speech, their eating, smoking and drinking habits. Young people feel that what they regard as their parents' inappropriate frame behavior (particularly in interaction with their own friends) embarrasses them and lessens their standing in the esteem of their peers.

It is important to recognize that whether or not parents actually break frame rules is less important than the adolescent's sensitivity to them. This sensitivity exaggerates even minor infractions and reflects as much on the young person's concern with frame behavior as it does on the parents' actual violations of frame rules. The contention of this chapter is that much of the day-to-day antagonism between parents and adolescents may have to do with disputes about appropriate frame behavior. This is not to deny that emotional conflicts are present as well; it is only to say that these conflicts often can be consciously expressed in conflicts over frame behavior.

SUMMARY AND CONCLUSIONS

In this chapter, the concept of frame, as it is used in sociology, was looked at from a developmental perspective, particularly with relation to its part in adolescent behavior. Frames are the rules, expectancies and understandings that underlie repetitive social situations. Learning frames is an important part of a child's socialization and much of this learning is spontaneous and unconscious. Frame learning is conditioned by social class as well as by age. In adolescence, young people must give up some frames and come to understand old ones in new ways. Particularly significant is the fact that the adolescent becomes conscious of frame behavior and capable of manipulating frames to suit his own ends. In addition, he becomes supersensitive to violations of frame behavior on the part of himself and of his parents. Accordingly, much of adolescent behavior that formerly was attributed directly to emotional conflicts probably is mediated by the adolescent's awareness of and sensitivity to cognitive frames.

REFERENCES

1. Bernstein, B. B.: *Class, Codes and Control* (London: Routledge & Kegan Paul, Ltd., 1971).
2. Goffman, E.: *Frame Analysis* (Cambridge, Mass.: Harvard University Press, 1974).
3. Piaget, J.: *Six Psychological Studies* (New York: Random House, 1967).
4. Piaget, J.: *Reussir et Comprendre* (Paris: Presses Universitaires de France, 1974).

COMMENTARY

DR. HETZNECKER: Thank you, Dr. Elkind, for a refreshing and provocative view of family interaction. I realize now that when my 8-year-old besieges me with a lot of questions at the wrong time, I have been deframed.

DR. VICTOR VAUGHAN: I wonder if David Elkind will tell us how he has used the concept of frame analysis to deal with problems in his school, where a group of children who had come with a set of expectancies with regard to the control of behavior are faced with an alien setting.

DR. ELKIND: We have a school for children from 7 to 9 years with learning disabilities, most of whom are inner-city children. What we have done is simply not move toward any academic work in the beginning. We spent weeks getting to really know the children, doing a lot of things like taking walks, taking trips and the like, getting to know one another and getting to know where we were, rather than trying to become academic immediately. I think that that sort of "getting to know you" helped us to learn what their frame rules were and them to learn ours. We deliberately verbalized what the rules were in each situation, and what could or could not be permitted.

For example, if one of the children picks up a chair and wants to throw it across the room, a teacher holds him and says, "You can't do that here." That is a frame rule. The kids began to accept that these are things you cannot do.

I once broke up a fight, and one of the involved little boys was very angry and ready to spit at me. The next day I said, "Jimmy, I have some really good news for you." I said, "I am going to the dentist today."

Without looking up, he said, "I hope you have 100 cavities." My statement and amused reaction were meant to convey the frame rule that anger can be dealt with verbally.

Our pupils are permitted to deal with their hostility in that way; they know they can verbalize it. They don't hit it out. They can talk about it and they can be allowed to get angry. In this way, I think we set down the frame rules, taking time to do it, weeks and sometimes months.

I think that many teachers would be well advised to spend a lot of time just doing that, not worrying about teaching or about the curriculum for a while until those basic issues get sorted out.

DR. MATTLEMAN: What worries me very much is disparity among the participants in a group, such as when teachers hold one expectation and children hold another. I couldn't help think about the culture shock facing teachers from middle class backgrounds who are confronted with kids from inner-city schools, who are poor, who have migrated from place to place and who really haven't had time to internalize and build that classroom frame.

As a very extreme example, I was visiting a first-grade classroom of children who had not attended kindergarten. A little boy asked to go to the bathroom. I don't remember how he asked, but it was not offensive to me with my middle-class background. The teacher said to him, "I beg your pardon?" Of course, he didn't know what "I beg your pardon" meant. He asked again. She said "I beg your pardon" again. He wet the floor and then she yelled at him.

That doesn't happen often, I hope. But that is the kind of thing, you know, that can happen. I confronted the teacher afterward, rather blatantly, and she answered, "He'll have to learn the right way to say it."

But what is the right way to say it? I think that the answers to these kinds of things, which come way before academics, are terribly important. There is not just the culture shock that comes from visiting other cultures, but this kind of thing right within our own cities.

JUDGE LISA RICHETTE: What do you do, Dr. Elkind, when there is a spurious frame set up? For example, in the juvenile justice system, some of the trappings of a courtroom have been removed and the judge doesn't necessarily wear robes. But the power is there, and it is extremely difficult for a young person to verbalize in that setting. There is, it seems to me, an enormously confusing manipulation of frames; the child comes in and is told "We're here to help you, et cetera, et cetera." And then he gets zapped.

DR. ELKIND: I worked with the Juvenile Court for 10 years; in some ways it depends on the court. I have worked in situations where I felt that in the context of laws that had been passed we could do a lot of screening beforehand, and where we could keep a lot of these kids from being filed upon. You can't do that now. Every child's case has to enter the files and the child has to go through this whole business.

I worked with a judge and a probation officer who used to play this game: the judge would be the very stern guy and the probation officer would be the soft guy. It wasn't really done in a bad way. The child could talk to the probation officer in a way, and the probation officer would present the case to the judge. That would work very well. You split off the bad guy and the good guy and they could deal with it. The judge is in a position of strength and it is sort of informal and you don't have the usual hearing.

We don't protect the rights of juveniles, though we're doing it more than we have before. It's like getting programs for early childhood into the public schools. When you get them in, it's great for some reasons. But there immediately develops a bureaucracy. The same is true with juveniles and the courts. As soon as the juvenile court is made more like an adult court, we lose a lot of freedom we used to have.

I used to counsel juveniles in trouble before a case ever got filed, and I could do a lot of preventive work. But now I can't see or talk to a kid until a charge is filed. By that time he's already branded. The law says we're recognizing his rights, but in some ways I think the recognition of rights can sometimes work to the child's detriment. I don't know how to deal with that. I really don't.

WILLIAM BREM (Seattle): You seem to imply that frames are without value. That is, you don't make a value judgment about the goodness or badness of a particular frame. For example, you spoke of a bantering frame. In some families, bantering is a way of keeping people apart, where the rules are "don't give a positive statement like 'I like you' or 'I'm proud of what you're doing' or 'I need you as a parent.'" Instead, there is sarcastic bantering all the time. Would you comment on that?

DR. ELKIND: The question has to do with values and frames. I think I'm using frame in a descriptive sense, simply as a concept. At this stage of psychological science, I think that we really need basic concepts to organize our experience.

One can go deeper into frames and look at good frames and bad frames. As

I'm presenting the concept, it's an analytic tool that one can use in a variety of ways. I believe that in psychology we're still at a point where we need to know what the nature of our data is. The concept of frame may simply be a way of looking at what's going on, and describing it, and perhaps getting some handle on interactions and perhaps some ways of dealing with them. Frames may be good or bad, but I don't know exactly what makes such decisions.

DR. BRAZELTON: I think that we really haven't come to enough closure in some of our conceptual thinking. Your frame idea applies very aptly to our approach to people in medical settings. Patients come to us for one sort of thing and get looked at for lots of other things. Take the poor mother, for instance, who brings a child in for otitis media and gets the whole social service work-up. If we outlined what the original frame consisted of, and if we announced it when we switched from that frame to another, it might make things a lot easier and clearer for them and for us. I think this notion is extremely applicable and clarifying for a lot of the things we do in medicine, often unconsciously. Our frame is to cover the waterfront and hand it all up on a silver platter.

DR. ELKIND: I feel that one of the appealing things about the frame is that it is much more specific and concrete than the "social role." Social role is already a very useful concept in social psychology. But, as in most sciences, one moves from broader concepts to more specific. And frame is much more concrete and specific. I think social role is a very valuable concept but already quite a level of abstraction beyond frames.

A further written question asks about frames in terms of the adjustment to adoption of older children, and how parents, workers and social systems can help. "Frame" is still relatively new to me. I am still trying to get a handle on it. I have no preconceived notions about the frames in terms of adoption. We have to deal, I suppose, with how old the child is, where the child came from and the parents' own frames with respect to the child, which would embrace the whole relationship, their own feelings about the child and so on, and the extent to which those interacted with feelings and dealings with the child. The question is fairly general, and an answer would depend, I guess, on the specifics. With questions like this, like a physician, I don't want to prescribe over the telephone.

In general, as I tried to indicate, frames are an analytic tool. They are a way of looking at a lot of different situations and stating what the rules are that operate in each situation, and asking whether the people in each situation understand the rules, or whether we are creating special problems, particularly for children, as they move through a variety of changing frames. Can we help by making the frame rules more explicit or more exact? The frame is a tool of analysis that we can perhaps learn to use. But in any particular case it would have to be applied to the games that were in play. We'd have to look at what people are actually doing in adoption situations.

25

How Courts and Welfare Relate to Family Needs

Hon. Lisa A. Richette

Judge of Court of Common Pleas,
Philadelphia, Pennsylvania

It is very good of you to have invited a foot soldier from the human trenches known as the justice system to contribute to this work. I come bespattered, but not dazed, with a sense of urgency and mission to give you a very brief communiqué on the ongoing battle for humanism and due process that continues, believe it or not, to engage the energies of large numbers of legal, paralegal and social workers in America's courts and welfare agencies.

I first want to give a brief field report on the latest adolescent casualty, which was reported recently in the local Sunday supplement pages. A 16-year-old boy died in a correctional institution right here in Pennsylvania. He was white, middle class and from the most affluent suburb of this Commonwealth, an area just a few miles to the north of this rather elegant meeting place. The crime for which he had been sent to Camp Hill, which is our maximum security institution for adolescent men, was a very common and uniquely adolescent state offense called incorrigibility: a very quaint, meaningless, Victorian value judgment that is a part of the law's archaic way of categorizing or labeling those who are too young or too powerless to fight back.

It seems that until a year or so before his court appearance this boy had been a very superior student, a conforming youngster who really gave no concern to his family, to his teachers, to his community. Then something occurred that is an adolescent phenomenon. It's known as transmogrification. And all of us who are parents of adolescents have experienced it. This charming, delightful, warm, outgoing youngster suddenly became a stranger to his family. He began to miss school. He began to use drugs, including a well-stocked parental wine cellar, and to mingle with what his parents thought were undesirable peers.

His parents looked down the prosperous and tree-lined streets of their community for assistance and found none—no one who could simultaneously cope with their monstrous son and with their own frustrations, anger and all the other feelings that we all understand only too well. The only channel that seemed open to his family was the juvenile court process, and into it they plunged with their manacled teen-age son in tow.

279

A judge heard their complaint and hopefully spent at least a few moments listening to the young man, although, as I indicated in my question to David Elkind, that justice system in which we operate is not a very conducive frame for communication.

When the parents refused to have their young disruptive son come home with them, the judge sent him to Camp Hill. There he lived through months of utter terror, constantly under the threat of homosexual rape. He begged to return in letter after letter. But under the prevailing legal machinery, he could not, although perhaps a more activist judge could have ordered a rehearing and a review of his sentence.

Finally, just a few weeks ago, he died, under circumstances that are yet to be fully explained. His father and mother say now that they did not understand what Camp Hill truly was, even though they had pleaded with the judge to send him to Camp Hill.

A few months ago I was in San Diego at a juvenile justice conference and, as a part of my busman's holiday, I went to the Juvenile Court and sat through an afternoon of proceedings. A Chicano mother came in with her 16-year-old son. She, too, could no longer cope. She could not give this boy what he wanted. She could not buy him the fancy boots, the tight-fitting jeans that were part of his quest for identity as an adolescent part of his macho response. And she told the judge that she was certain that he was going to begin stealing and finding illicit ways to obtain this money, and would he please do something for that boy.

She explained that her husband had deserted this family a year earlier, that, having 6 children, she found it extremely difficult to secure employment that would pay her enough to provide adequate at-home child care services for her family while she was working and that she felt constantly beleaguered and harassed by the insistence of the welfare workers that she place her children, for they could not see beyond the somewhat untidy and littered plastic-covered furniture and the very large color TV set to the organic reality of the relationships that were going on in the family.

And so she came to court. And as her boy was led out of the room, she stood up and began to shout, "I hate that welfare. I hate that welfare. If it is the last thing I do, I'm going to get off welfare." And she left, announcing to all assembled that she would indeed place every one of her 6 children, that she would go out and find an occupation that would give her enough money so that she could reunite her family.

I looked at her and I recognized that this was a woman with an extremely limited background, whose only work experience had been as a migratory farm worker, that her dreams and her hopes along with her children were being deposited at that courtroom and welfare agency door.

What is the meaning of these frozen bits of human horror in the larger issues that we are addressing, today, the relevance of courts and welfare agencies to the needs of adolescents and of their families? I think that these are both pathologic enlargements of the counterproductive system traps that are too often our only available resources for dealing with the problems of rebellion in adolescents, alienation in their families and very real social and economic crises that beset people. All too often these forces place them into legal frames that they cannot control, frames that lead to nonhuman results that are destructive to adults as well as to children. These are not isolated stories. America is littered with these human mine fields, which occasionally do blow up in our faces, though they may perhaps lie dormant for 5,10 or 20 years.

I would like to suggest that the family and the justice and welfare structures are essentially power systems, power systems in which individual members establish rules and have the power to enforce them. Both the family and the justice and welfare systems have a very deceptive cosmetic camouflage of protectiveness. Everything is done for the good of the young person, and the errors that are permitted usually are excused and rationalized by society through looking at the good motivation of those who perpetrate these indignities on people.

The law and the welfare system do reflect, I think, most clearly the confusion and the social ambivalence toward adolescents. It is interesting that if one wishes to find current court decisions and current discussions of the legal rights of children and adolescents, one must look in the various Key Digest Systems under the heading of "Infants." Infants! And I suggest that that is not merely a coincidence. For Anglo-American law has always used processes of infantilization as a means of social control. This is particularly true when we look at the legal structure that governed the relationship of the black slave to his white master or, and this may be a shocking kind of example, the situation of women in the legal structure until fairly recently. The total denial of rights and the total closing up of options to children, blacks and women stem from a desire to nurture and protect them, but it also resulted in the complete inability of any member of these groups to assert effectively any of the basic rights that ordinarily attach to American citizenship.

Another way of thinking about this infantilization process is to perceive very clearly that our law still regards children as the property either of their parents (that is, the chattel of their parents) or, if the parents are not present, of the State. And a phrase that Justice Fortas called "rooted in the murky and dubious history of English Chancery Courts" has been used to describe this relationship: *parens patriae*, which is basically a totalitarian concept. What it means is that the State is the parent, and that the State may do at will what the State wishes to.

These attitudes, this infantilization, this rendering of young people as property, these are reflected very clearly in the social ambivalence that we see toward adolescents. I would like to suggest that courts and social agencies do not operate in vacuums, that the courts, particularly, are extremely susceptible to political pressures. That is to say, to the community's desire for certain results. And at the moment, in American society, there is a feeling that the adolescent symbolizes all that is wrong and all that is out of kilter in our society. There is an extreme hostility and paranoia toward young people.

My adolescent son reports, for example, that it is impossible for him and his friends to browse peacefully in center-city shops or even in suburban shopping centers without being followed and even confronted with accusations of shoplifting and dishonest behavior. It is clear that we have fallen into the trap of categorizing and stereotyping all adolescents as potential, if not actual, deviants.

In juvenile justice systems, what we see is an enormous pressure on the part of the public, the police and agencies, which cannot cope with the kinds of patient working out of processes that David Elkind was describing as recreating new frames. These children are literally dumped in large numbers onto the juvenile courts, and the juvenile courts must in some way "process them" and provide for them the one experience that society seems to feel will solve the issue of the adjustment of the adolescent to society's framework. And that experience is the incapacitation process, taking the adolescent out of that community and putting that boy or that girl on ice by locking up that youngster in one of our institutions.

I would like to suggest, for example, that as racism and as our own hostility toward the poor are reflected so amply in our justice system in what we do with the black and poor, so, too, in the justice system we see very clearly the kinds of sexist attitudes that bear down more heavily on young women who run afoul of parental and social expectations. Over 85% of the young women who are committed nationwide to training schools and to institutions for adolescent girls are there not because they have committed a crime or the kind of offense for which boys are routinely committed, but they are there because of sexual promiscuity, incorrigibility or truancy, but always with this sexual overlay.

The law is excessively concerned with the sexual morality of young women. Routinely, when they are brought into detention centers, they are subjected to pelvic examinations, no matter what the technical legal charge against them may be, and they are periodically confined for longer periods than the boys. And this is, of course, because of the law's unconscious and sometimes very conscious acting out of this demand placed on it to incapacitate young people.

I would like to deal for a moment with some changes that are going on in the justice and welfare systems. I began with those rather jolting narratives deliberately, but I want to move on to a more composed analysis of ways in which some of us in the justice and welfare systems are seeking more compassionate and more humane and original approaches. We are doing this very often without any support from other systems and under fire from our colleagues in other disciplines who find us to be antipathetic and think that our disciplines are just per se antihuman and irrational.

For a long time the justice system was perceived, and, I believe wrongly, by the entire professional community as a therapeutic agency. This is a Lewis Carroll kind of misconception, because the court is not a social agency. The court is essentially a power structure in a society that is operating under a very fixed system of legal principles to achieve a certain result, which is not rehabilitation necessarily but is much more the goal of incapacitation, of removing the child from community structures to which he has made negative adaptive responses without ever substituting viable alternatives.

Starting in the 1960s a massive legal assault was waged on this system, for it had resulted in severe injustices and in the kind of grotesqueries that I outlined in the two stories that I opened with. And, instead, a new purpose was conceived for the juvenile court. And that was that it would be very much a court of last resort. It would be a place to which children would be brought for whom all other alternatives had failed, or for those children whose behavior was so serious and so disruptive that it could no longer be tolerated or managed within a nonlegal setting. And this, I submit to you, is an enormously mature and healthy growth process for this system. We are no longer in the business of child saving. We are very realistic and very modest in our aims. But what this means is that the other therapeutic disciplines, the true therapeutic disciplines, the places where there is skill, where there is research, where there is room and time for experimentation, have had thrust on them today a new responsibility for which I see no evidence at all of acceptance.

To cite an example, when the laws in Pennsylvania were rewritten in 1972 as an aftermath of all those legal assaults and when the new Juvenile Code excluded truancy as a basis for filing a juvenile delinquency petition, what happened, in essence, was that nobody did anything about truants, which has led now to a growing movement on the part of educators and juvenile justice personnel to amend the Statute to put truancy back, on the grounds that this is the only way that these children will get any effective service.

It seems to me that this kind of buck displacement and dumping is a result of a reluctance on the part of large numbers of professional people to confront the ugliness and the difficulties of really dealing effectively, not with nice, supine middle-class children who are accustomed to our frames but with children who have come from enormously different worlds, who challenge our values, who see our fraudulence and who see that we are masters in the art of applying Band-Aids but that we really understand very little about basic organic kinds of helping interventions.

I know that it is fashionable and faddish to think that the justice and the welfare superstructures in America really are terminal cases. But I don't concur in this prognosis. I think that in a violent, in a transitional, and particularly in an economically unstable social system, the justice and the welfare systems will be increasingly called on to exert more energetic intrusions into an increasing number of American families. We started to see this in the 1960s, when, for the first time, middle-class children began to fill the courts with charges of drug abuse and runaways and general rebellion. The parents could think of nothing more to do to control the child gone wild or hippie or turned into a flower child than to invoke the legal structure of a community.

As unemployment figures rise, there will be more and more adolescents who will be forced back into the family drama: young people who will not be able to move out, who will not be economically independent, but will instead experience more forced and extended periods of dependence. And families will be cut adrift from the conventional consumerist safe harbors.

Of course, I just wanted to tell you that poor adolescents have always been there. This current reality is exactly what they have always experienced: lack of job opportunities, lack of educational skills and families hoping to make ends meet. We talk about the people trading down. Well, many of these families have never even had the experience of trading at all, but live from welfare check to welfare check.

Somehow the needs of these poor children for self-actualization, for acceptance, for rebellion and to have something to which they can be faithful, to use Erikson's terms, and their total human condition has been left by society to overburdened probation and correctional officers and to welfare workers.

I know that Marciene Mattleman is going to address herself to educational questions. Her can of worms is almost as big as mine, and I'm going to listen with anticipation to her views on how our mass educational system can really impinge on the lives of teen-agers and their parents.

I would just like to suggest to you that instead of wringing our hands in Cassandra-like fashion we acknowledge that it's a great testament to the vitality of the human spirit that so many of the poor adolescents who have been pushed through these welfare and justice systems have survived. I think the survival rate is really rather remarkable. So I want to say that we are struggling, and hopefully we are growing. Since the Gaultt, Windship and all the other decisions by the Supreme Court and the Federal Courts have effectively forced us to drop these inappropriate and grotesque roles, I think that lawyers, judges and welfare workers have begun now to see themselves, perhaps, as effective change agents for the systems rather than as change agents for the children, which is what we were trying to be. I think our best role is to see to what extent our own systems can be changed and how we can mesh with other structures.

We have a great awareness now, I think, of the inherent role limitation and our own modest skills in conciliating, judging and programming therapies for adolescents. Conference after conference that I attend focuses on the very issue that was just discussed in our last discussion period; that is, to what extent can we keep young people out of this system, to what extent can we make those children who come either through the police or through schools or through welfare to the attention of the court, to what extent can we offer these young people alternative services that do not involve this branding, this categorizing, the dehumanization that goes on once a person is on this kind of a treadmill. "Diversion" is a very important concept today in the juvenile justice system, just diverting people out of this process. On the other hand, the Law Enforcement Assistance Administration, which is funding walkie-talkies, mace arsenals for police and all the rest, has at this time devoted less than 30% of its funding for juvenile justice programs.

Nevertheless, the programs that LEAA is interested in are precisely these diversionary programs in which we are looking for alternatives to the nonexistent family for the adolescent period. There are, of course, the very familiar concepts of group homes, of community-based residential treatment centers, extended family arrangements such as the so-called therapeutic community, which I'm not going to discuss with an audience like this since I do not believe in carrying coals to Newcastle. But we are doing this increasingly.

We are also involved in some interesting approaches that are an alternative to the dismal foster home situation. All of you know that it is extremely difficult, as difficult as it was for Diogenes to find an honest man in Athens, for us to find a foster home for an acting-out adolescent youngster over the age of 14. And so, because there are no foster homes, welfare departments petition courts to find these children to be incorrigibles. This is an expanding, omnibus term. All of us could not have become adult without having at some point in our lives been incorrigible adolescents. These children get pushed into this category and placed in institutions because there are no alternatives.

Father Paul Engle has established a new kind of concept, a spinoff from the European concept of affiliation, which is halfway between adoption and foster home placement. This concept is one of an extended family in which parents take on the responsibility and establish an actual family role with adolescents, with State subsidy, but with no State intervention. The social worker, the case worker, becomes an almost invisible part of the background, and the primary focus is on the family and the youngster in that relationship; that is where the attention goes.

I've had experiences, as I'm sure many who have worked with young people have had, of encountering children at the age of 15 who have been in as many as 15 foster homes, and who have had half as many social workers. The only real thing that ever happened in their lives was that each year they knew there would be a new social worker on the scene. The turnover in welfare departments is just astounding!

We need to think how these kinds of problems can be cut down. There are magnificent experimental alternative programs set up throughout the country to deal with the problems of runaway youngsters. Here in Philadelphia we have a program called Voyage House, which is a kind of model. And like most of these models in child welfare and in alternatives to the juvenile justice system, it is constantly in danger of closing down. We live from week to week and from month to month because the funding is so tenuous and so difficult.

So I say that I am reassured that we are no longer so obsessed with Clockwork Orange approaches. With all due respect to this audience, I don't hear so many presentations at juvenile justice conferences of the spectacular results that have been obtained in a training school by the injection of a new program. I think we are beginning, all of us, to give up our collective fantasy that we can save children in a vacuum, without doing something about the society in which they live. I think that what I'm really saying here is that we are not sure how to help adolescents and families, but neither are you. How much will it cost and who is to pay?

For example, take the meager appropriation for the Juvenile Delinquency and Control Act of 1974, which will do a lot of things we are talking about here today. That meager appropriation has been impounded for months by President Ford. Yet he and his advisors blithely propose billions of dollars for intervention, humanitarian and otherwise, in Southeast Asia.

It is impossible, then, to divorce these questions from political issues. For if we wish, in fact, to alter the reality of the lives of these children and their families, we are, in fact, engaging in what Orwell called political behavior, which is behavior that seeks to change reality and to push society in a certain direction.

Many of us who are down in those trenches do dream of the leisure to speculate on new schemes, even to quantify our experience into some meaningful patterns. It is a luxury we cannot afford. I submit that you as well cannot. I think at the moment we must try to make a political structure more responsive to the needs of these children and their families. We must do this by helping communities to understand our situation and come to our aid. America really can no longer ignore its Throwaway Adolescents and their families, for they will become the hollow men and women tomorrow on whom a totalitarian order can very easily build its support.

We who struggle with the constitutional and legal rights of young persons as well as with their social needs don't want to meddle, and we certainly don't want anyone's good wishes. What we need more than anything else is the active involvement of those who have knowledge and who have skill, devotion and power in this society to help us light some flares along those darkening trenches.

COMMENTARY

PHIL SWARTZ (New Jersey): We've had some excellent papers on needs of and services for families and children, and on how we strengthen our institutional set-up. I want to get some reactions regarding another area where we may possibly have a role, and that is in strengthening our fields through setting higher standards and commitments within our professions. How do we police and control incompetent and insincere physicians? How do we get substance instead of empty form in course work in some of our poorer graduate schools? How do we keep the incompetents and fast-buck people from becoming teachers, social workers or psychologists? How do we exert control on poorly prepared research and on proliferation of worthless articles in various professional fields? How can we strengthen our image and credibility among the people that we try to serve?

DR. MATTLEMAN: I'd like to talk to that. It is one of the things I care about very much. You know that it is harder to become a plumber than to become a teacher. The plumbers control the entrance into their profession, and I think that that is important. Competency-based programs for teachers are now mandated in 21 states. We don't even know what teacher competency is, and yet we're writing those programs because we want the states to be certifying agents. I think the *professions themselves* should stand up and control that very admission.

One of the things Judge Richette talked about, and I will certainly talk about, is how to organize. We have been sitting back, most of us, for too long, waiting for things to happen.

SANDY ELLIOTT (Rockford, Illinois): We are now in Rockford experiencing what I think is a common phenomenon as our population growth gets closer to zero. Many of our committed young teachers are out of work, women as well as men. We have a population now which is not eager to have new children. Perhaps numbers of them, educated as they are in the raising or education of children, could be further trained to make inroads on our legal and welfare and educational systems, or could help in the rehabilitation of youngsters who have gotten punched by the system.

DR. MATTLEMAN: I think we need *more* teachers. Everybody says we don't need so many, but we need *more*. We're putting our money in the wrong places. School budgets are topheavy with administrative costs. There is audio-visual equipment in every closet in the Philadelphia school system, locked away and not used. Who needs it? We *do* need *teachers*. We have to look at school budgets and make sure that we use those people you mention. We still have a lot of kids who can't read.

LESLIE EVANS (Philadelphia): I am a Voyage crasher. We've been crashing kids for about 4 years now, ever since you people started. These are some of the most limited children I have ever seen. I am wondering that the whole focus of this conference has been in terms of human interaction and how we develop ways of reacting with people. I wonder if somehow we couldn't begin to use what we've learned in order to teach children not to be switched off by their environment.

We have been talking about frames and ways of reacting. Maybe what our schools need to begin to do is to teach people and children to see how they can change the way they react to people. So that when you become an adolescent and you rebel against the system that you've always known, you have some way of treating yourself or of creating your own environment, rather than being so switched off by what you're living with that all you can do is run away or simply act out in protest.

JUDGE RICHETTE: Leslie is absolutely correct. She is from Voyage House, the facility that I mentioned in my talk. We have learned not only from Voyage but from another organization I helped to found here in Philadelphia. which is called the New Horizons Center, a place for adolescent mothers. We started the New Horizons Center in 1960, when these children, these young women, were being routinely pushed out of schools simply because they were pregnant, and we had discovered that only 20% of these 1000 girls every year in Philadelphia were ever going to go back to school.

We set up a different kind of frame, a different school, to which they could come with their babies. Samuel Bullock, who was our consultant psychiatrist, talked constantly on what Leslie has said, that a growing sense of mastery is so necessary for growth, that children need to feel they can really master some part of their environment, some part of their total setting. So many of the children that I'm talking about and that Marciene Mattleman will be talking about are programmed to failure and to defeat. Nowhere are they helped to get these skills toward mastery that are so important. This is what alternative programs like Voyage House are trying to do.

As to the other question about alternatives to education, I know that we are all very committed to the bureaucratic legally based system of public education for the masses. But I think that both the crises in Philadelphia and San Francisco and other large cities and the general economic period in which we now live and in which we are going to stay for at least a decade or two are going to compel us to think of alternatives to our present educational structure. Maybe we can develop frames outside public mass education where some of these skills can be developed.

DR. ELKIND: I'm attempting to go in a lot of different directions. One of the things we have learned from working with children with learning disabilities is that between the ages of 7 and 9 some children don't learn to read by themselves. Learning to read is a very difficult process, complex and hard. The reason children learn, I think, is because adults reward them and model and reinforce their behavior. The importance of attachment has become very clear to me. Basic attachment in infancy doesn't stop there; it goes on. Children at pre-elementary school levels learn not because it's the spontaneous nature of the child. I don't think there is a "nature of the child." Children learn from adults whom they love and about whose rewards they care.

I think that what we have in *our* school is caring adults, and that children make tremendous progress there because there are caring adults. I think the same is true for adolescents. Once a kid has gotten so far out that he gets in trouble, the only way we can bring him back is through a long-term relationship with an individual. And the longer a person is involved, the more that individual relationship is important.

You know, I think it works at all levels, whether children are disturbed or not. The attachment is very crucial. We see many children who get into all sorts of trouble to please their parents, because their parents need troubled children. It works in many different domains. There are a lot of people in our community who can work with young people and would appreciate doing that. But it has to be a long-range commitment, and it has to be supervised.

I think that once young people get into trouble, you can't restore them by programs. It has to be people dealing with people.

RICHARD EMERSON (Miami): I'm a child psychiatrist and family therapist. It seems to me that many of the problems will still be before us at the end of this conference that we started with. John Franklin identifies institutional barriers to the normal and successful function of the family. Judge Richette points out that institutions in fact demolish families. Berry Brazelton points out that some child-loving, child-caring groups in fact elbow the family aside and take over, because they feel they can do it better, once again interfering with whatever success they might have.

The real task isn't any easier than it was before the meeting. Our problem will still be to foster the normal and successful coping capabilities of the family as an organic unit without intruding ourselves into their lives in such a way that once again we'll find ourselves destroying ourselves.

26

Parents and Schooling; What, How and When

Marciene S. Mattleman, Ed.D.

Professor of Curriculum and Instruction,
Temple University, Philadelphia,
Pennsylvania

As a complement to other points of view presented, I will tell you something about inner city schools in the hope that we can come up with some ideas that will be helpful for poor children growing up in those settings.

To gain some perspective on the situation in the schools now, we have to step back a decade, to the year 1965. That was the year of massive Title I funding, which went to schools as an instructional allotment: but I think it was basically a political decision. Those were the years of slogans and along with the War on Poverty we had the Right to Read. Those slogans were calls to action, and the 1960s brought forth many solutions. "Innovate" was the word: it was a time of change, a time of conscience.

It's interesting and ironic, I think, that at a time when young people were re-belling against too much government in their lives, educators were courting Washington to get more money. They were pushed in turn by publishers, who, like other Americans, really believed that huge amounts of money would make a difference. Many people thought that, both in Vietnam and in education. Now all of that spending is coming under justifiable scrutiny.

Now, 10 years later, I'd like to talk about where we may possibly be in 1975. Schooling begins earlier now, and although gains of early intervention programs are not easily attained and may not be gauged immediately, many aspects of pre-school education have already been shown to be successful. Martin Deutsch was able to show that gains in achievement for children in kindergarten showed in performance at the 5th-grade level. (The term "preschooling" is amusing in itself! How do you use preschool for kids who are in school?)

Much of the effort has been like research on cancer. Different people do things in different places and the hope goes out to everybody that there is going to be some kind of cure and that everyone will be helped at once. We know that that isn't so in medicine and certainly it isn't so in education either.

As the public and politicians became more concerned with schooling, the word "accountability" came into use; it was considered a scare word that came from industry, speaking of efficiency. But people don't talk about efficiency in education. If you are a salesman and you don't sell, you lose your job, whereas if you are a teacher and your students don't achieve, then your door remains closed and nobody does much about it. To me, that seems unfair; I think we have to hold people accountable.

Let me tell you my definition of accountability. Accountability, whether it applies to industry, to teaching or to all of us, is to know why something happened or why something didn't happen. I know we cannot necessarily expect to have a child grow 9 months in a reading achievement test in 9 months in school; but the teacher should be able to tell me either why a child didn't grow or why he did grow. To me, that is accountability. Teachers have to be accountable to parents, parents to kids, kids to principals and principals to teachers. I don't buy the notion just that teachers have to be accountable for the achievement of children; accountability goes all the way around.

Entrained in this discussion of accountability is the new decision about school records. Students and parents are now permitted to see what those records say. In my view, this legislation is very good and it will foster more honesty; a responsible school faculty has an obligation to let parents know what all that jargon on the records means. Education is full of hyphenated words. Don't let the parents that you work with be cut off or taken in because they don't understand. It's important for parents to understand that a *standardized* test is a norm-referenced test. It compares populations. A *mastery* test just deals with the individual child, where he is and where he was before. Today, there is less "IQ" testing than 10 years ago; but where IQ tests are done, parents have to know that "intelligence" is what a particular IQ test measures. And schools have the responsibility for informing parents as to what all of this means.

I find it difficult to talk about parents and schooling to a group like this because of its diversity. This audience looks very different from a Philadelphia group, as a matter of fact. We have many more minority group people in our helping professions in Philadelphia. So I must assume that you are not the usual Philadelphia audience, but that when we talk about schools, we are talking about a variety of different situations. Philadelphia has 280,000 children in its schools; New York has over a million. I have a friend who feels he works very, very hard in a district near here that has 15,000 school children. And everyone does work hard, whatever the population.

With that caveat, what I'd like to do is share some ideas with you as to how you can help the parents you work with to cope with the situation in the schools. I tell my students that if they can positively affect one child in the class, they've done a good job. Maybe some one thing that I will say can work for you.

Research shows that *reading to children* has a very positive effect. Teachers who read to kids in addition to giving reading instruction help them to better reading achievement. Studies show that at young ages children who have been read good books as a supplement to regular instruction have learned to read better. It's amazing to find out that many children entering school don't know that pages are numbered, that pictures have anything to do with print, that print is sequential or that print goes from left to right. If children of the poor don't have books at home, they have not discovered this. So it's important to get parents to read to young children.

With older children it's important to have a *newspaper in the house*. Many of the teachers I work with plan activities around the newspaper, because they know that newspapers represent literacy. They don't realize that homes of the poor don't get newspapers. They don't get subscriptions; they move around too much. This is a shocking discovery to beginning teachers who plan all these wonderful activities. So, encourage parents to buy a newspaper and share some of it with the children. We know that that is a potent way to help kids learn to read. More than that, it enunciates a value: print is important.

Many skills are gleaned from a newspaper. You learn about categorization when you look at the want ads; you learn about consumerism, of course, through advertisements, and about fact versus opinion through editorials. Weather is charted in graphs and in maps. In a print culture, children have to know how to read, and it's important for that value to come from the home.

Another thing that might sound simplistic, but I think is not, is *talking to children* and giving them your opinions. We meet many opinionated children with whom we really disagree, wondering where they got all those ideas. Well, it's better that they have ideas from home than to have no ideas that they can defend.

Dinner time is important in the middle-class home. It's very easy to have a family reunion at dinner time when parents have jobs that terminate at 5 o'clock. But the poor may not have those kinds of jobs, and people wander in at all different times. We know that children who have been exposed to more discussion and to more ideas through language do better in school. It is important to bring this to the attention of parents.

With regard to what we call dinner time, the literature is fascinating that shows how much more important time is to middle-class people because of the way they work. Doctors, social workers, nurses or teachers work regular hours. Less skilled people don't and their children don't know how to tell time. Their lives don't run by the clock.

I heard a wonderful speaker some years ago describe the built-in time clock of the middle-class child. You know, one afternoon is the piano lesson, another going to the orthodontist and another going to religion school. For these children, the weeks are punctuated. They learn to internalize time whereas poor children do not.

Getting back to talking, William Labov, a linguist who teaches at the University of Pennsylvania, has a wonderful audio-tape recording of two situations in which a child asks a mother who opens her refrigerator, "What's that?" The mother, who is tired and has just gotten home from work, says, "That's applesauce." Another mother, who has not been working, has a lot of time and doesn't feel pressured with dinner, answers the child's question "What's that?" with "Oh, that's applesauce! First, you get apples from a tree. And then you boil them and then you take the skins off," and so on, including cinnamon, sugar, etc. Look at all of the language that comes into that answer! That is what talking with kids can do. I think it's all-important to bring to the attention of parents that talking means exposure and learning.

Telling is only one part of communication; another is *asking questions*. Research shows that if you vary the level of discourse in a classroom (and again I'm going to generalize this to parents), you encourage different kinds of thinking. A study has revealed that, on the average, a hundred questions a day were asked in an elementary classroom, 96% of which were factual. Two-thirds of them were asked by the teachers. That gives you a picture of what school may be like.

Now, if parents could only be asking questions at home, and hopefully other than factual questions! But what are parents most likely to do if they're busy? They ask "How was school?" Look at the difference if the question is worded "How was your day?" It's much broader and leads to a different kind of response. It is not just your intent but your effect that matters. Compare the effect of a question that elicits a short factual answer and the effect of a more divergent question.

Another thing I'd like to talk about are *real experiences,* as opposed to vicarious ones. A lot of our children watch television a tremendous amount during the week. When they come to read about concepts and ideas in books, they really can't relate to them because they don't have the same quasi-reality as television. The importance of real experiences is indicated by an interesting experience I had working with a group of children here in Philadelphia, half of whom were Puerto Rican. The word "seacoast" came up in a story. Now, think about the word "seacoast." There are two letters in the word that don't make a sound. You could really spell it s-e-c-o-s-t if both vowels were long, because the two "a's" don't make sounds. It's a hard word to remember. But every one of the Puerto Rican kids knew what a seacoast is. To a child from the inner city who has never seen a seacoast, it is a line on a map, and even that doesn't mean much; so he doesn't remember it. Real experiences go a very long way.

I often tell parents of young children how important it is to go on a picnic. And very often a parent will respond, "Well, we have a barbecue every Sunday in the back yard." But barbecuing in a back yard isn't going on a picnic. A picnic has a lot of other ingredients. They are real only if you experience them. Think of the word "democracy." A democracy has to be experienced, too. Children need to live in homes that are democratic. Again, what is most meanful is that which we experience.

Some of you work with children with learning disabilities. And in those cases it's fascinating to observe how a child's experience corresponds to what he or she remembers. I worked once with a child from a very fortunate home who had traveled a great deal with her parents; she had difficulty with a lot of book learning, but what she had seen she related to in those books.

Another thing of importance is *school attendance.* Children who attend school and stay in their classes do better in school, but it's not enough just to say this is so. When performance contracting was popular a few years ago, the people making contracts with school districts demanded that the kids attend school a certain amount of time. We couldn't teach them if they weren't there. We found that when you say "help kids get to school," you have to look at the kinds of programs that attract and hold them. There are alternative programs almost everywhere now and even where there aren't alternative programs, children don't necessarily have to go to a neighborhood school. Some school districts have voucher systems and even without such formalized systems there usually is no law (and I've done a lot of reading on this) that says you have to go to a particular school. It's simply expected. Parents are afraid to go to authorities and say, "I want to move my child." So we have to help children attend school, but we must also get them to places where attendance is educational and rewarding.

That brings me to my next point, about *parents getting involved in schools.* For both parents and professional people I would urge the same thing. I don't think that people other than professionals in education should be making curriculum decisions or banning books; so I don't want either you people or parents involved in this unless you know something about it. But there are many administrative decisions that we might question; we could find out more about them and not accept the jargon in the pat answers. Parents can certainly influence the sizes of schools. Mammoth organizations with 1500 children in an elementary school and 5000 in high school really don't make sense. How can relationships develop among so many transient people? Changing the size of schools is something that parents might lobby for. The maintenance of school buildings is another. If more people from the communities complained about all those broken windows, something might be done.

The mobility of families is very high in cities. I think we should encourage parents who move around a lot to be sure to maintain contact with their schools. Parents and schools have to do this together.

One of the Philadelphia schools receives its entire student body of 500 children from within the distance of one city block. Much of that school's population is in and out as often as three and four times a year as families move back and forth just one to three or four blocks away. The area schools work, meanwhile, as autonomous organizations. We have to bring pressure on school districts to identify clusters of schools and programs in such a way that the instructional programs are consonant with one another, and so that the children don't lose in the curricular dislocations that accompany moving.

There are other areas in which I think we can be effective. I think that no matter how difficult or threatening it is to do, we have to try to get onto school boards, and to *use the power of groups.* In Philadelphia at this moment, the Welfare Rights Organization is holding up delivery of 29 million dollars to the Philadelphia schools because it feels that federal guidelines have not been adequately followed. Now, that is pretty potent action. I'm not encouraging just exactly that, but I am encouraging you to see whether or not regulations are being carried out and whether or not the children in our schools are getting a good education.

There is a candidate now for Philadelphia City Council who has an educational background. It's important that such people serve on City Council. And we should all of us write to legislators, and get parents to write to legislators. Legislators are not well enough informed of issues in the schools. I think informed parents can make effective stands where their concerns are at stake.

It's very popular now to have homogeneous grouping in classrooms, where children of supposedly the same ability (and ability generally means school achievement) are grouped together in the same classes. It's much easier to teach with homogeneous groupings, but not necessarily easier to learn. (Don't ever assume that because somebody is teaching somebody is learning.) We don't know that children do better in homogeneous groups, and we have some evidence that slower children who are not stimulated by their peers do not tend to do as well. There really is a case for heterogeneous groupings, and I think that that is one of the things that parents can investigate, even if they have to go to school boards with their own experts!

Bilingual education has been terribly ignored in many areas of the country. For our large Hispanic populations, many models of bilingual programs could be employed if pressure were used. Children should not be made to feel "second class" because of their differences. Helping minority children to achieve must be a cooperative effort.

Getting the universities involved is another must if we are to solve our mass problems of illiteracy. At Temple University, I go out with my students and conduct all of my classes in public school settings. When my students tutor, I tutor. I think it's a great thing for them to see me work with a group of kids who can't sit in their seats. And it's important to be out there, because if they're not part of the solution, then university people are part of the problem. The universities have trained the teachers. Now, we and parents and other groups have to push the universities to get more involved and more accountable.

Parents can also push for more realistic approaches. Again, I don't mean that parents select the books, but that where there are low-achieving high school students who can't read, sometimes parents will have to take some initiative. Good programs have been developed for functional literacy in some cities. Philadelphia is one example. The immediate goal may be teaching kids how to fill out applications. Although the reading of Shakespeare is an important part of our heritage and I wish everybody could read Shakespeare, with an 11th grader who can't read I'm willing to forfeit the traditional English class and teach him how to read with a very pragmatic approach.

The very best educational experience that I have ever had was in teaching a group of 14-year-old boys how to read; I used the hoagie shop menu from across the street. Every one of those boys could order a hamburger, but they couldn't read the word "hamburger." At the end of 3 months it was great to hear those kids casually say to the waitress "I'll have number 7," knowing they could read number 7. The right material is important.

I'd like to urge parents to *use television more wisely*. We know that many children watch 40–60 hours a week. Some television, of course, is very good. Research shows that younger kids who have watched Electric Company or Sesame Street are able to discriminate among letters much better than those not exposed to these shows. They come to school knowing the alphabet, which is the code; and you'd better know it if you want to get into print.

There are other values to television. Terry Bortin has developed a program accompanying some television shows that has the viewer involved in talking about some of the concepts. For example, where the television show talks about a mountain, the audio part of Bortin's program would ask, "Well, is a hill different from a mountain? A hill is much smaller. You must know that." Another program in Philadelphia uses reruns of television shows for teaching reading. The scripts from such shows as Mod Squad have been procured, which permits kids to read the script as they watch the show. They can in this way use television effectively. Television has a vast potential curriculum that we're not tapping.

I want also to mention expectations. I think we have to *have high expecta-*

tions and encourage parents to do the same. During my own doctoral study, I found an inner city child with an IQ of 149, whose teacher said that it must have been a mistake. It wasn't a mistake, of course. There are some such kids everywhere. I shudder when teachers say, "These kids can't learn," and I'm afraid that both parents and people in the helping professions are picking up such attitudes. When we work with low-achieving kids all day, it's difficult; but we do have to maintain high expectations, sometimes through very simple, specific things. Parents have to ask kids about homework, for example. Very often I ask audiences how many have ever received a dollar for an "A" on a report card. The hands go up very slowly. If I make it a quarter, there are more hands. Many people are very negative about expecting good grades and rewarding children for them. But you are rewarding desired behavior. We know that learning should be its own reward, but when we are dealing with low-achieving kids who feel stigmatized, perhaps we must rethink our strategies. David Elkind's discussion of frames is important here. We have to look at what we're faced with, and seek and adopt some solutions that perhaps we haven't earlier appreciated.

Along with expectations, kids need *a place to study*. I used to say that such a place had to be quiet and secluded. I don't subscribe to that now, because research shows that kids come from very stimulating environments, and that we all operate in busy environments. Some of you are listening, adjusting tape recorders and knitting all at once. We can do it and so can kids; I don't, therefore, say any more that a child needs a quiet place, but he does need a place of his own where he has his things together. Many kids are not coming through with their work in school because they live in such crowded environments that they have no place of their own. We must help parents to see that.

Our job, then, is to educate parents, and in other ways to play our roles as professionals. It has to be well timed, like helping with a phonics rule. A teacher doesn't tell a child every minute that when an "E" comes at the end of a word, it's usually silent and the preceding vowel is long. But the teacher must have that rule in the back of the head to bring out at the right moment. There comes a time when we have to be able to tell certain parents the difference between poor vision and poor visual discrimination. With poor visual discrimination, for example, a child may have difficulty with likenesses and differences, e.g., in differentiating b and d. This problem is not corrected by glasses but by training. We have to be able to explain these things to parents, so they can better understand their children and get them the correct kind of help.

The area of learning disabilities has become a major one in education today and I've been bothered because it's very easy to blame everything on some functional disability and to overlook other things. Even in very large cities, where there are specialists, the problems are poorly diagnosed. It's important to have more specialists in urban settings and to get them to the schools. Here, again, parent groups can be very potent.

With current problems of illiteracy, a lot of people are tearing down the educational institution. I hope I haven't sounded that way. But we do have a lot of low-achieving children and those of us close to the schools become frustrated. Problems are more apparent today, partly because children stay in school longer whereas failures used to drop out. Our task is to look for positive ways that schools and professionals and parents can act together. We are really supposed to have the same community of interests. I like to feel that we are not working in adversary relationships, though sometimes it looks that way.

Dickens wrote a long time ago, at the time when our country was young, that it was the best of times and it was the worst of times. Perhaps it is now, too.

COMMENTARY

DON SAWCHUK (Summit, New Jersey): I've been sitting here for the last 3½ days trying to assimilate everything. The question comes up constantly: What can we do? It breaks down into three discrete but inseparable quantities: first, our impact as professionals on the people whom we try to help and our effects on government; second, our impact as citizens, as voters in our local communities, for school boards and things of that type; and third, our impact as people, with our own personal commitments and our own characters, as we attempt to help people (but not to mold them toward what *we* think they should be).

In all of this there are trial and error. Once we do something, we must step back and see the effect, and see maybe if we should have done it some other or better way.

MEMBER OF THE AUDIENCE: Judge Richette, a question to you has been stimulated by an article in the *Philadelphia Inquirer* this morning on Bettye Caldwell's comments on the monitoring of parenting and on having registries and a system of accountability for parents. Along with a lot of people in the audience, I think that the *Inquirer* reported her remarks as if they were a rather totalitarian approach to parents and their responsibilities to children. Would you comment?

JUDGE RICHETTE: My information comes also from the newspaper article. I was not here to hear Bettye Caldwell. Long experince has taught me that one ought not to rely on recorded reality as reflected in the press. I feel that I would be doing Bettye Caldwell and her presentation a great disservice if I spoke to what was reported.

I do want to say that there is a very strong movement in our country on the part of poor people and on the part of parent groups to resist any kind of further legislative intrusion into intimate family relationships. There is a right of privacy that has been recognized and respected by the United States Supreme Court, Mr. Justice Rehnquist to the contrary notwithstanding. I think that is an important democratic value. I think that to go the route of further legislative intrusion (I'm not sure that this is the route that was described) is to return to the wonderful kind of Victorian idealism that inspired the juvenile court, through which the juvenile court was going to be a kind of monitoring agency in a community and be all things to all families.

As Santayana said, if we don't learn the lessons of history, we'll be condemned to repeat them. I'm always very fearful of these legislative solutions. I think they give a lot of people a false sense of security, and they serve as effective masks for the retention and preservation of the same social forces that brought about the problem. If there is one thing that I would like to see us think about more clearly, it is how social forces produce these patterns in families. I feel very strongly that we have to keep a balance always between society and the individual.

GREG KRASER (Baltimore): It is said that children who frequently play hooky from school have parents who have education as a very low priority. I think I found that to be so in some cases. How do you change the priorities of parents to make education more important for their children?

DR. MATTLEMAN: I think that many of those parents subconsciously proba-

297

bly do value education, in that they blame the system that didn't give them an education for what happened to them. It's kind of a negative thing. I think the way to change this is to find the programs that would attract these children to school. The alternative programs in Philadelphia have been very successful that way. I'm pleased, too, that a lot of the larger units in Philadelphia are being broken up into smaller ones where kids can relate to people.

STEPHEN GALLAGHER (Elementary School Counselor): My basic premise is that the schools are just failing miserably, and that you can substantiate this with research data on just about any area. We are not providing what we think we are for our children — not the values, the reading scores or whatever. This conference indicated that the school should be more responsible to the family. If the child needs a place to study, and if maybe 60% of your students come from 1-parent families, then I think the school has to do more toward providing that need.

A lot of specialization has hurt. For instance, the child in the first grade with a reading problem goes from the teacher to the counselor to the reading specialist, who, in turn, if the child needs help, will go to the school psychologist and the Home and School Visitor to arrange a talk with the family, after a visit to the nurse. Other institutions do the same thing. The poor person who has problems probably has to work with 6 or 8 different helping people.

I think the school system, as one of our larger organizations, has somehow to begin to adjust this. There has to be something that the school can do for parents who, I feel, basically care. With all their problems, they care about their offspring, and they want to do something about the situation. But I think it's going to have to be big changes, rather than new funding this year for one thing and the next year for the Right to Read and the following year you get 2 Title I teachers instead of 1, and you get half a Title I counselor. Whatever there is must be responsible to families.

DR. MATTLEMAN: I agree with a lot of what you said. Parents feel so out of things in schools that very often they don't complain about those very situations. One of the most successful moves I know took place at the Durham School in Philadelphia. Aside from their educational programs, a very positive thing is their room for parents. When neighborhood parents come in, this is their room. They don't have to wait on the office bench; they have become part of the school, and they can hold other kinds of meetings in that space. I think it's a marvelous use of a classroom.

Someone talked with me a few minutes ago about a second-grade child who had had 4 different teachers. I think we have to fight that kind of thing. The one teacher in a classroom can see all facets of a child and hopefully build on some of those. But parents have to be engaged in the process.

I think we can keep our schools open longer into the evenings. They can be community centers, and ought to work with churches and other organizations.

GEORGE NAMUTH (Summit, New Jersey): I want to offer an area that hasn't been touched on as a source of help in prison reform, justice reform, school reform and even reform in medical and health care, and that is religious organizations. Many church organizations have regular discussion periods on a weekly basis and are just thriving. They are looking for topics of concern, and have many different people in their congregations from all walks of life, interested in reform and interested in areas they can work at.

DR. ELKIND: I want to return to an earlier question. As a school principal now, I have to say that I think that parents' involvement is very important, but I feel that as a professional I know what my school should be doing. I don't feel that the parents should dictate to me how my school should be run or with what kind of curriculum. There is a danger in getting parents too much into decision-making in education. Our big problem in education is that our teachers have not been given sufficient freedom to be the kinds of people that other professionals are. We don't tell social workers what to do. We don't tell doctors what to do. But we do tell teachers what to do. They are the lowest people on the professional totem pole.

The schools can't do everything. The schools can teach and teachers can teach. And having worked with school people around the country, I'm impressed with how many good schools, good teachers and good dedicated people we have. I see many good teachers working very hard, and very good principals working very hard to do things against insuperable odds, everybody telling them what to do and what they are supposed to be doing, rather than letting them do what they do best, which is teaching and working with kids.

I hope we can get parents involved. But let's get parents involved with professionals who know what they are doing, and let the teacher say, "Let's work this way," rather than parents and everybody else dictating to them. We are never going to get education if we can't do that.

JUDGE RICHETTE: There is a very interesting sociology to this undervaluation of the teaching profession in this country. For a very long time the teaching profession was largely dominated by women, mainly single women, whose lives were ruthlessly regulated by school boards. They represent a very good example of how our society tends to undervalue what women do. In keeping with some of the things that have been discussed at this conference, if we can get men back into the whole learning, child-rearing, nurturing process, that is fine. But I think you should be aware that your government in the Department of Labor dictionary of occupations classifies nursery school and elementary teachers in categories along with parking lot attendants and massage parlor attendants. This is absolutely true! This is an official government document. And the only people who have been working very hard to get this dictionary of occupations changed have been women's groups.

I would like to see the teaching profession come right back in and say, "We are professionals; stop rating us this way, and stop judging people on the complexity of the paper operations that they have to do." Engineers are rated very high in an industrial-oriented capitalist society. They deal with worker products and sales and all the rest. This is just part of the whole undervaluation of people and of humanity and skills dealing with human growth.

I think that what Marciene Mattleman is talking about is not that the parents at the Durham School are dictating curriculum or anything like that, but that they are seeing that this school becomes a resource in their own struggle for recognition and for dignity. The schools have not been aligned with goals of human dignity for large numbers of people. I think they should be.

DR. ELKIND: There is a danger if parents feel they can run and control the schools.

JUDGE RICHETTE: You may get a group of paranoid parents who take over school board meetings. Like everything else in life, you just have to cope with it. You can't push parents away because you have a few crackpots or people with power drives. A lot of people have come forward in the political process just by disrupting and taking over school boards, including a nice lady in Boston. You have to deal with that. But you just can't think of the stereotype of the hysterical, unreasonable parent as being all parents.

DR. MATTLEMAN: I hope I didn't provoke that picture. I began by saying I didn't want parents dictating curriculum. Parents have to be included, however, because we do have the same goals.

JOHNNIE ADAMS (Bloomington, Illinois, a Nurse): I want to make a few comments about this symposium. At the very beginning. I was delighted, infatuated with the whole process that we were dealing with. But I'm slowly going toward disillusionment. We've alluded to blacks, to strengths, to the society that we are dealing with, to "the family; can it be saved?" As we've gone through this process in 3½ days, I'm wondering what family can be saved. I feel that blacks have been shelved, that we've alluded to their problems, and that many of the participants have more concerns about where they are in dealing with black families, but that blacks as a whole have not been discussed.

I feel that we're dealing with the white family, and "can the white family be saved?" I'd like to offer a suggestion for the next symposium that you have some black participants who can possibly testify and express themselves on many of the subjects discussed here. I have felt isolated during the conference.

JOAN LARGE (Philadelphia, a Nurse): I think the previous speaker is actually in support of what I was about to say. I'm not really concerned with pronouncements like Bettye Caldwell's regarding a National Registry or a Parent Registry, nor am I concerned with pronouncements like Marciene Mattleman's that children should have a place alone and a place to study, because I think that parents and families create the checks and balances to our onerous pronouncements as experts. Further, large organizations such as the PTAs and the Parent Medical Groups and some more vocal people involved in feminist movements, civil rights and all these kinds of things are here; and we should listen to them. They, too, provide checks and balances.

But these checks and balances are always tested by other realities. I once made the pronouncement to a patient in regard to her cardiac status during pregnancy that she should have more rest, take naps and put her feet up several times during the day, only to be told with a great deal of anger, "How do you do that with 10 children during an 11th pregnancy, living in two rooms and with no other adult in the house? If you can tell me how to do that, I'll follow your orders."

27

Recapitulation and Unfinished Business

Robert A. Aldrich, M.D.

Vice President, Health Affairs and Professor
of Pediatrics and Preventive Medicine,
University of Colorado Medical Center,
Denver, Colorado

The task of summing up is a bit of a challenge. I've had a chance to talk to a great many of the contributors and I've been particularly impressed, almost uniquely impressed, by the apparent agreement in very broad principles that everyone seems to have. There is a feeling of willingness to listen to others coming from completely different disciplines but who are recognized as important because of what they can contribute in some dimension to the family or to the rearing of children.

I would like to mention a few of the many highlights that have caused me to make a particular synthesis that I will come to shortly. What I've done is organize these remarks into four categories. One category is what is wrong, what the severe problems of the family are and what they are likely to lead to. The second category is things that were either overlooked or unmentioned—certain points of view. A third category and one that, I think, is exceedingly important is the identification of some major areas for new research or new interpretation based on findings through new research. And last, and the most important, what are the things that we can do, each of us can do, that will help to prosper the family.

I can't shake off the impact of Urie Bronfenbrenner's chapter. Some of you who have had to deal with members of the Congress and their committees, the Senate Appropriations Committee or the House Appropriations Committee know from hard experience that you don't try to fool them. It just doesn't work. For many years, I'm afraid that a great many of us have not done our homework sufficiently well that what we were advising these congressional leaders to do was based on very hard verifiable evidence. That is why I think that Urie Bronfenbrenner's chapter is so important.

It is not an emotional outburst of opinion. Far from it. It is the best documented chapter that I have ever seen on the subject, and I think that it disposes of any question that the American family is indeed undergoing very substantial change, or that some of this change is a bit frightening. Some of it probably is for the good. But there is something significant happening, and the Congress and other people had better jolly well listen and see what they can do to help.

He also documented quite well in his chapter the growing evidence of failure of our social institutions to deal with the needs of the American family. Not only with the traditional needs that have been there a long time, some of them going all the way back, I guess, to Adam and Eve, but with some of the new needs that have developed because of the changes in the American family. At the end of his chapter he makes a powerful plea for the development of some important support systems that would be for the purpose of helping families, both the traditional and the ones that are emerging as new kinds of families.

Under the heading of "What is wrong?" there is some very impressive material on the specifics of violence. We can read about the impact of television, both good and bad; how to use it, how not to use it. We can learn about the isolation of various age groups in society, and I was particularly entranced to be reminded of what I have always called social parthenogenesis, which is the absence of fathers. The father, it seems, may be coming back into this whole picture before too long.

We learned about administrative barriers. Many of us don't like to talk about administration, because "they" are the bad guys. But, believe me, as long as we keep that point of view we are never going to get anywhere with broken families. Our institutions have got to have good administrators, and they need help, too. So I think that John Franklin's presentation of what he has been able to attain is very significant, and we all should pay a lot of attention to just exactly how he went about doing this.

These stresses on the American family are really very severe. There is no doubt that we just have to conclude at this point that many of our social institutions buttressing the family are in part failing. One other aspect of the what's wrong business that intrigues me is, what each of us can do as individuals.

Now, Berry Brazelton discussed just a little bit about some omissions, and I'll be very brief here. It struck me, too, that there was really no discussion of black families. Where I come from, in Colorado, we would have heard vociferously not only from blacks but from Chicanos, who, in Colorado, outnumber the black population almost 2 to 1, and we would have heard also from the American Indians, or the native Americans, as they call themselves.

I was sorry, too, that there weren't nurses on the program, because I think we would have delved into the concept of teamwork a lot more than we did. There was an omission here that should be corrected in future efforts.

One oversight was the absence of children. You may think that is an odd thing to say, but I will take just a moment to fill you in on a most remarkable project that the Canadians did. About 1969, and turning into 1970, they had a national project called "Milieu '70." Its purpose was to define what they should do in their country through their institutions and government to prosper their families and to prosper child-rearing. I was involved in the western section of Canada at their first major conference. Half of those at the conference were young people from the ages of about 10 or 11 up to maybe about 18 or 19, and then a variety of adults—bankers, school board members, blue-collar workers, every kind of person you can think of. The communications were covered live by the Canadian Broadcasting Company.

The main point I want to make is that young people presented the research papers. I'll give you two examples. A group of 3 or 4 who, I think, were about 14 years old and gave a magnificent paper on why teenagers run away from their homes in small towns. Basically, there wasn't much for young teenagers to do! Absolutely beautiful when stated by them. Another group from Vancouver gave a paper on why their high school was vandalized so often.

The papers not only presented well-documented facts with film clips and slides, but indicated a good job of investigation and had some very specific suggestions. The deputy chairman of the Vancouver School Board, who is a prominent architect, promised the group who told about the vandalizing of the high school, "I'll make a commitment to you right now. We'll turn over this whole business to you, to a student committee," and he did. And they don't have vandalism in that school anymore, either.

But in terms of direct interaction among the mixture of generations, it was very impressive.

Let me go on now to some of the new fields for research. Many of them could be a full symposium or maybe a series of full symposia. Marshall Klaus's very stimulating, exciting work on early socialization is the kind of thing that captures public interest in the subject of early child development. It is so human, so real and so new to many people that we should be sharing this information publicly. We should be displaying it any way we can, and we should be supporting much more activity in this field of research.

Another subject was just barely scratched by Oscar Newman, who wrote about the impact of the man-built environment, like housing, on the growth and development of children as well as its effects on families. I have spent several summers participating with an international group of engineers and architects, planners and social scientists on this same subject. Whereas only 10 years ago there was a very limited body of knowledge about what the design of buildings or the design of a city does to human growth and development or to the family, there now is a large body of knowledge available. A lot of the best data have come out of countries other than the United States. There are only a handful of people in this country who have linked themselves together to begin to do serious quantitative studies of this phenomenon. What Oscar Newman wrote opens up what could stimulate us substantially with this subject of growing significance. It is an important area for the training of anybody going into child development. One needs to know the anatomy and physiology of cities, and you need to know how this impacts on the family and on the children.

I'll just mention in passing Victor Vaughan's revealing some of the lessons from ethology. We need to become acquainted with them, because they have a lot to teach us. The interplay would be very fascinating between people interested in family and child development and the ethologists. We need this very badly.

Sarane Boocock stressed that when you start making changes for one age group or start setting up social systems or support systems that affect one age group, it is going to affect all of the other age groups; and you'd better have the whole life cycle in focus when you start going about making these changes, or you may make some things much worse than they were before. I have often thought there ought to be a field in medicine that comes in between pediatrics and geriatrics. Let's call it "Mediatrics."

Pediatricians particularly, and others working with children, have got to learn about other stages of life and what, for example, are the pediatric antecedents of aging, how they are identified, what meaning they have in guidance to a family or in guidance to the career of a young man or woman.

I would like to spend the remainder of this chapter on what each of us can do. It's my belief that the support systems that families need have got to be a part of the fabric of what we call human settlements. The human settlements can be any size from a crossroads to a metropolitan community like Philadelphia.They are made up of building blocks, with the basic unit the family; and families in groups become a neighborhood. Then, if one looks at a much larger community or human settlement, he will find that an aggregation of neighborhoods flowed together and became a metropolitan community. Those of us who have been through the discipline of microscopic anatomy in our professional training will remember looking through a microscope at a liver preparation under low power. The organization of the liver is surprisingly similar in appearance to one of those huge maps of a metropolitan area, used by city planners, particularly the color-coded ones showing the roads and residential blocks.

My point is that there are identifiable building blocks, the family being the most important in the formation of the neighborhoods, and the neighborhoods flowing together as larger human settlements. These human settlements show enormous differences. They usually are different in their cultures. This will reflect the ethnic origins of the populace, their color and customs, all modified by geography, climate, economics, etc. Some neighborhoods have their own unique flavor, such as shopping, residential, business, etc.

The uniqueness of a human settlement with its many neighborhoods leaves a stamp on all who grow up there. We are so accustomed to meeting somebody we never met before and saying, "Well, he's a typical Bostonian, and she's obviously lived in Dallas all her life," and, just like that, you make an identification. And you are right most of the time.

A friend of mine was raised in Russia as a young boy, and he kept up his fluency in Russian. He was asked a few years ago to go to Russia and teach for a year in their school system. He told me that one of the fascinating things to him was that many people he met in the Soviet Union not only could tell that he had been born in Russia but could identify what town he came from, which I thought was an example of this kind of imprint that the human settlement puts on you. How this happens is a promising field of research.

So, in my view, human settlements are the support systems that human beings have built for themselves since ancient times. They contain the support systems that really are reflections of the biologic and social needs of the people who live in them. They are a biologic and social reflection of man.

Human beings are both the research director and the guinea pig on the Spaceship Earth. Here we are together trying our best to live successfully.

It is important that we grasp this idea conceptually and begin to learn how to use the explosion of knowledge about ourselves at all ages so that the family can succeed.

People who are frightened about the knowledge explosion are likely to feel much better if they are provided opportunities to introduce their knowledge into the system and thereby advise and influence the various "research directors" who are defining our destiny.

How do we plan and build a city or a human settlement that is an effective support system for human development? How do we build a house for a child? If you ask architects and engineers, they will be very responsive. They will also have many doubts, because much of what is done in building a house doesn't have a very solid basis from the behavioral standpoint or even from a biologic standpoint. So these are legitimate questions to ask.

Most of us are so inhibited that we don't ask them at the coffee klatch or social gatherings elsewhere.

Building a city for the development of human beings is a legitimate goal, and I think it's the kind of goal that any age can participate in and benefit from. So I would suggest that each of us should, through our own circle of contacts, through our own root system that hooks into various things—the neighborhood or the city or on a broader scale—each of us should ask questions: how is this going to help families?; or how is this going to improve child development in this neighborhood or in this town? Ask these questions and always be prepared to know where to look up the evidence that things aren't going well, as Urie Bronfenbrenner did. His chapter would be a good source. You can also get local data that are good. You can be very effective. The other thing you always have to have in your hip pocket or your purse is a proposal of a positive nature, so that you're always casting a positive image.

Many times when we do raise questions within the neighborhood, the city or even at a national level, we are looked on as being hypercritical. Sometimes we don't ask questions because we are just plain bashful. However, if one has no more than two or three things one would like to see accomplished, do your homework, know the facts and then have a constructive, positive proposal to make. You will soon see yourself emerging as a leader.

Here are a few examples of support systems that are built into the human settlement, particularly metropolitan ones. There are parks. There is a fire department and a police department. There are all kinds of communications, particularly telephone systems, roads, housing, waste disposal, electricity, heat, water, schools, medical services, stores, sidewalks, banks and so on. You can go on and on. On a nice day take a long walk through your neighborhood and try to make a list of the kinds of things that you see there that are services. We take them for granted, as the goldfish takes the water he swims around in in his bowl. He probably isn't aware of the fact that he is in water and of what else is in that environment. It's part of his assumed environment. We are a little like that in our own neighborhoods. So let's each try to pick out a few things that we are well informed about and that we can use for leverage in our own circles to improve support systems for the family.

The groundswell that has to develop before we see major changes will take time. Look how long it took to get out of Vietnam and what it cost in human effort and misery. It is just enormous. Well, we are faced with something of at least this large magnitude in trying to prosper our families and prosper child development.

I would like also to make a specific suggestion to those who have contacts at different governmental levels in the city, the state government or the federal government. There must be some follow-through, so that the hard evidence and its implications can be talked over thoroughly, and worked through into a pattern. A few points that are very well documented and cohesive could be molded into a program that would be acceptable to people who have to make public decisions and place priorities. There must be someone working at these levels. The reason this is so important is that if one goes just to the Congress, or to the President, or to higher levels of state government, it is too limited an approach. They will want to know what people think at the grass roots. Thus, the grass roots, the neighborhoods, must be cultivated, so that those same questions are on everyone's mind. If you have both approaches going at the same time, what I call a "push-me pull-you" technic, you may start things happening much more rapidly than anyone had a right to believe.

When the history of this century is written, we are going to have to recognize that the most prominent phenomenon was urbanization, and that we have an obligation to understand this phenomenon and to turn it to the advantage of families so that the next generations are benefited.

In answer to the question "Can the family be saved?" my answer would be undoubtedly, yes, if we have the courage and the drive to tackle the complex organizations that we live in and make them work for us.

EPILOGUE

The Symposium ended with the thoughtful summary of Robert Aldrich. On the whole, we feel that the Symposium had conspicuous success in attainment of the modest goals set forth in the Preface. We feel that it created a substantial base of shared information and concern about the family and our society, upon which more discussion and perhaps further conferences or symposia can be planned. We hope that this further discussion will be enriched by the experience shared here.

For all its apparent success, the Symposium had a substantial flaw of such importance that knowledge of it must be shared, especially with those who may wish to plan similar affairs in the future. The flaw was that minority representation was inadequate. We had intended at the outset to have racism addressed directly, on the first day, as an issue and a symptom of malaise. We failed to land the first two speakers invited, and ultimately constraints of time and program were accepted as warranting modification of this intent.

We should not have compromised our original commitment. The Symposium discussed black families and their special problems, and we needed the input of persons who could speak to their conditions and needs. This is not just a matter of giving some kind of token visibility to a minority, but a deeper issue. This deeper issue is that no studies, no data, however statistically reliable, nor any prescriptions, however insightful or wise they may be, can fail to be suspect until they have been examined and validated by those who have lived within the minority experience. We urge those who will take off from this Symposium into a variety of action programs in their regional or local level to consider that when they begin to deal with problems of minorities, they must involve the groups under consideration in the planning, implementation, and evaluation of whatever programs of social action they may deem appropriate.

We hope that our experience and the experience of this Symposium may be helpful.

V.C.V., III
T.B.B.

Index

309